Modeling Methods for Business Information Systems Analysis and Design

Selin Erben
Beykent University, Turkey

A volume in the Advances in Business Information Systems and Analytics (ABISA) Book Series

IGI Global
DISSEMINATOR OF KNOWLEDGE

Published in the United States of America by
IGI Global
Business Science Reference (an imprint of IGI Global)
701 E. Chocolate Avenue
Hershey PA, USA 17033
Tel: 717-533-8845
Fax: 717-533-8661
E-mail: cust@igi-global.com
Web site: http://www.igi-global.com

Library of Congress Cataloging-in-Publication Data

Names: Erben, Selin, 1978- editor.
Title: Modeling methods for business information systems analysis and design / Selin Erben, editor.
Description: Hershey : Business Science Reference, [2018]
Identifiers: LCCN 2017045865| ISBN 9781522555223 (hardcover) | ISBN 9781522555230 (ebook)
Subjects: LCSH: Management information systems--Design and construction.
Classification: LCC HD30.213 .M634 2018 | DDC 658.4/038011--dc23 LC record available at https://lccn.loc.gov/2017045865

This book is published in the IGI Global book series Advances in Business Information Systems and Analytics (ABISA) (ISSN: 2327-3275; eISSN: 2327-3283)

British Cataloguing in Publication Data
A Cataloguing in Publication record for this book is available from the British Library.

Advances in Business Information Systems and Analytics (ABISA) Book Series

ISSN:2327-3275
EISSN:2327-3283

Editor-in-Chief: Madjid Tavana, La Salle University, USA

MISSION

The successful development and management of information systems and business analytics is crucial to the success of an organization. New technological developments and methods for data analysis have allowed organizations to not only improve their processes and allow for greater productivity, but have also provided businesses with a venue through which to cut costs, plan for the future, and maintain competitive advantage in the information age.

The **Advances in Business Information Systems and Analytics (ABISA) Book Series** aims to present diverse and timely research in the development, deployment, and management of business information systems and business analytics for continued organizational development and improved business value.

COVERAGE

- Strategic Information Systems
- Legal information systems
- Business Intelligence
- Management Information Systems
- Business Process Management
- Business Decision Making
- Decision Support Systems
- Data Analytics
- Business Information Security
- Performance Metrics

IGI Global is currently accepting manuscripts for publication within this series. To submit a proposal for a volume in this series, please contact our Acquisition Editors at Acquisitions@igi-global.com or visit: http://www.igi-global.com/publish/.

The Advances in Business Information Systems and Analytics (ABISA) Book Series (ISSN 2327-3275) is published by IGI Global, 701 E. Chocolate Avenue, Hershey, PA 17033-1240, USA, www.igi-global.com. This series is composed of titles available for purchase individually; each title is edited to be contextually exclusive from any other title within the series. For pricing and ordering information please visit http://www.igi-global.com/book-series/advances-business-information-systems-analytics/37155. Postmaster: Send all address changes to above address.

Titles in this Series

For a list of additional titles in this series, please visit:
https://www.igi-global.com/book-series/advances-business-information-systems-analytics/37155

Sentiment Analysis and Knowledge Discovery in Contemporary Business
Dharmendra Singh Rajput (VIT University, India) Ramjeevan Singh Thakur (Maulana Azad National Institute of Technology, India) and S. Muzamil Basha (VIT University, India)
Business Science Reference • ©2019 • 333pp • H/C (ISBN: 9781522549994) • US $215.00

Law, Ethics, and Integrity in the Sports Industry
Konstantinos Margaritis (University of Crete, Greece)
Business Science Reference • ©2019 • 307pp • H/C (ISBN: 9781522553878) • US $195.00

Institutional and Organizational Transformations in the Robotic Era Emerging Research...
Albena Antonova (Sofia University, Bulgaria)
Business Science Reference • ©2019 • 178pp • H/C (ISBN: 9781522562702) • US $155.00

Utilizing Big Data Paradigms for Business Intelligence
Jérôme Darmont (Université Lumière Lyon 2, France) and Sabine Loudcher (Université Lumière Lyon 2, France)
Business Science Reference • ©2019 • 313pp • H/C (ISBN: 9781522549635) • US $210.00

Handbook of Research on Expanding Business Opportunities With Information Systems...
George Leal Jamil (Informações em Rede Consultoria e Treinamento Ltda, Brazil)
Business Science Reference • ©2019 • 455pp • H/C (ISBN: 9781522562252) • US $245.00

Qualitative Techniques for Workplace Data Analysis
Manish Gupta (IFHE University, India) Musarrat Shaheen (IFHE University, India) and K. Prathap Reddy (IFHE University, India)
Business Science Reference • ©2019 • 317pp • H/C (ISBN: 9781522553663) • US $215.00

Machine Learning Techniques for Improved Business Analytics
Dileep Kumar G. (Adama Science and Technology University, Ethiopia)
Business Science Reference • ©2019 • 286pp • H/C (ISBN: 9781522535348) • US $195.00

For an entire list of titles in this series, please visit:
https://www.igi-global.com/book-series/advances-business-information-systems-analytics/37155

IGI Global
DISSEMINATOR OF KNOWLEDGE

701 East Chocolate Avenue, Hershey, PA 17033, USA
Tel: 717-533-8845 x100 • Fax: 717-533-8661
E-Mail: cust@igi-global.com • www.igi-global.com

Table of Contents

Detailed Table of Contents

Many applications in wireless sensor networks perform localization of nodes over an extended period of time. Optimal selection algorithm poses new challenges to the overall transmission power levels for target detection, and thus, localized energy optimized sensor management strategies are necessary for improving the accuracy of target tracking. In this chapter, a proposal plan to develop a Bayesian localized energy optimized sensor distribution scheme for efficient target tracking in wireless sensor network is designed. The sensor node localization is done with Bayesian average, which estimates the sensor node's energy optimality. Then the sensor nodes are localized and distributed based on the Bayesian energy estimate for efficient target tracking. The sensor node distributional strategy improves the accuracy of identifying the targets to be tracked quickly. The performance is evaluated with parameters such as accuracy of target tracking, energy consumption rate, localized node density, and time for target tracking.

In today's business environment, business competition has increased due to market needs and advancement in technologies. This forces organizational managers and consultants to identify techniques that enable organizations to cope with an ever-changing business environment. In their efforts, many organizational performance improving techniques have been discovered. Among the techniques discovered, business process re-engineering is the technique reported to improve business processes for enhanced organizational performance. Therefore, this chapter explains what business process re-engineering is and presents modeling methods for business process re-engineering.

R has grown tremendously over the years in terms of number of users and capability with the development of hundreds of packages. In this chapter, the authors investigate the usage of R in finance and banking areas. They begin with a comparative analysis of R with other computing software like SAS and Python. Then they discuss the reasons for the growth of R's usage in financial sector. They end with a comparative evaluation of Python and R's strengths and weaknesses in a classroom. R is software designed to run statistical analyses and output graphics by user-input code. It can run on virtually any operating system and is open source. This makes the software highly appealing, as it is able to keep up with the demands of a growing number of varied business structures. Standard software has been SAS and Python; however, a growing number of jobs are posted looking for experience using R in the data analytics field.

The ratio of benefiting from company's own memory is one of the most important factors for a company's success. However, firms are not aware of their memory capacity or failure to protect. Therefore, the success of the company is delayed and or affected negatively. Because of organizations' natural tendency to forget, memory loss is evaluated as an inevitable consequence. Memory loss or organizational amnesia at the organizations is defined as restricting the ability to develop organizational learning or failure to create a value by using owned information of the company. Organizational amnesia in organizations shows itself in various forms such as repetitive losses of competencies and previously learned information because effectiveness decrease leads to repetition of the same mistakes. In this context, the aim of this chapter is to create an organization memory database known as a knowledge repository in order to minimize memory loss in the organization and to determine the information types which is being recorded in the database.

In the software development cycle, the requirement traceability link is one of the important factors. Information retrieval techniques typically produce links with low precision and/or recall because, due to their very nature, they depend on the textual similarity between requirements and source code. The developers may not evolve requirements in synchronization with source code. But, they frequently update other sources of information including CVS/SVN repositories, bug-tracking systems, mailing lists, forums, and blogs. These sources of information will be used to build improved requirement traceability-recovery approaches. After the source code was developed, the developer compiles the source code and commits the source code into versions. Then admin needs to compare the templates and versions based on similarity measurement. Based on textual comparison, the similarity is calculated. The admin can do the same process for the forum requirements.

The transformation of requirements specification into an architectural design has been a crucial endeavor for the information systems analysis and design community, with ever-new challenges to tackle. Despite the wide and diverse existing proposals, the lack of a common structure and use of different strategies makes it close to impossible to analyze or compare these approaches. Therefore, the use of model-based methods benefits from a detailed specification in order to support their analysis and evolution, also in comparison to other approaches. Following work on the derivation of a logical architecture from business-process use-cases requirements in a service-oriented approach, the authors propose a detailed specification, within a SPEM approach, of a transformation method, which they further analyze and refurbish in order to meet current and future challenges.

The innovative and effective solutions for the strategic and operational planning management of organizations are discussed. The author reviews current and past challenges of the strategic and operational planning and describes two novel solutions with practical implementation for improving these processes. The first one is a numerical indicator V-index that represents the level of accomplishment of operational plans of the entire organization, its units, and members of staff. The V-index serves operational plans with hierarchical and non-hierarchical structures. The second solution is a novel context-free grammar operational planning language for a formal definition of the planning process. All examples and case-study presentation are based on fragments of the faculty/departments/programs of some fictional educational institution (university).

Enterprise models are created to analyze, document, and communicate the state of an enterprise under multiple perspectives. In addition to being large and complex, the construction of these models presents several difficulties: firstly, they require information provided by sources that might be inaccurate, incomplete, or even obsolete; secondly, although they should be structured, it is not possible to completely define their metamodel a priori. To support this construction process, the usage of enterprise model drafts is proposed, which should have the capacity to conform to changing metamodels and should also support incomplete or imperfect information. Unfortunately, current frameworks and tools have limitations for supporting these two features. Therefore, a set of strategies for the construction of modeling environments that make it possible to properly handle drafts is also proposed. These strategies include the support of metamodel flexibility during the modeling process and an approach to model imperfect information.

Preface

In today's world, business organizations and startups have to adapt to new circumstances and have to set new rules for surviving. Such as core management, operations, or even managing company data. This is the where business information systems steps in. Business Information Systems (BIS) comprises the analysis and organization of business information through the application of technology.

Information is the key concept in BIS. It is easy to store information and yet the cost is very low. Moreover, it is easy to transfer and the most important one is it advances throughout technology. On the other hand, information is the most fragile concept and it is hard to replace when it is lost. In the past, companies used to store information with printed documents which made it difficult to search and find. Also it cost a lot when it needs to be transferred.

After the invention of computers and computing devices, information systems were born. Information system is an integrated set of components for collecting, storing, and processing data and for providing information, knowledge, and digital products. Even the small sized organizations rely on information systems to manage and control their operations, interact with their customers and collect feedback from them and control also collect information from market itself. Not only companies but also governments deploy information systems to provide services cost-effectively to citizens. Today, with the help of the software and information systems, citizens can interact with services easily. Some areas cannot be thought without information systems such as banking and shopping. In banking sector, information and value is everything and it needs to be protected well. Banks are good example to understand the difference between data - information and knowledge. Data is the smallest and the less meaningful part of the information. It can be represented with bytes. One thousand (1000) can be data. In order to understand something from the data, it needs to be converted to information. So when currency is put near the data it can be meaningful which is $1000. Now it can be understood that, it is money. But it is not enough to determine the full picture. Whose money is this? The answer of this question converts information to the knowledge. Information systems works with knowledge and information and with the right set of rules it can create new information from existing one.

Studying information systems involves, among other things, learning how to design, build and evaluate these systems. To do this, it must be developed an intricate understanding of the information needs of the organization, the business processes that generate and consume information, the roles of people and working groups in these processes and the efficiency of these processes. In order to achieve that component, information systems needs to be understood. The main components of information systems are computer hardware and software, telecommunications, databases and data warehouses, human resources, and procedures. The hardware, software, and telecommunications constitute information technology (IT), which is now ingrained in the operations and management of organizations.

These days, even the smallest firms have computer systems; in the bigger firms those systems can create a link between departments. Tables-smartphones and other wearable devices can help to compute in bigger scale. Large organizations typically employ distributed computer systems with parallel computing power. Those servers can allow to access data from any location in or out of the firm by securely. But the most important part is computing power and with the computing power companies can forecast situations or even sales numbers. This power is directly related with the power of the microprocessors. According to Moore's law: the power of the microprocessors at the heart of computing devices has been doubling approximately every 18 to 24 months. Which allow developers to develop more useful software with complex algorithms.

Hardware is not enough for computing power. It can be divided into two parts. First one is operating system the other one is application software. Operating system is the principal system that operates the hardware. In business information systems application software is mainly designed for the problem. Databases, Word processors, mathematical problems or even presentations are created in those applications and helps companies to solve problems in their lifecycle. Many information systems applications are primarily delivery vehicles for data stored in databases. Companies store any information in their databases and use that information to calculate their knowledge. With the progress of the World Wide Web, those software and databases can be used online and that helps companies to access their data and information anywhere.

In the previous description of data-information-knowledge and hardware systems now business information systems can be defined. Planning, forecasting, control, coordination, decision making, operational activities are the examples of problems that Business Information Systems (BIS) try to solve. In most organization Business Information Systems (BIS) has high flexibility due to their ability to be programmed. However one of the biggest disadvantages of BIS is the lack of creativity. They can calculate decisions and outcome but then human process needs to be involved in the decision making process.

Business Intelligence Systems (BIS) are needed due to the vast amounts of data and methods in organizational information systems and the need extract useful information from this in the form of patterns, trends and present this in a understandable way to decision makers (Elizabeth Hardcastle, BIS). Software and hardware are primary ingredients for BIS but also modeling method needs to be defined in order to create BIS and convert data to information and extract knowledge from them. Modeling methods are plans and set of rules that helps defining and developing Business Intelligence Systems.

Over the years, a wide range of analytics, also known as mathematical models, have been successfully applied to business planning problems to assist managers in making intelligent decisions. These models use concepts and methods from statistics, econometrics, data mining, applied probability theory, queuing theory, decision analysis, mathematical programming, heuristics and other disciplines of applied mathematics. Modeling systems employ model generators based on these methods that are linked to software for accessing data inputs and writing reports. The vast majority of applications have used ad hoc approaches unconnected with BI systems for these data input/output functions.

This book is organized in nine chapters. A brief description of each chapter follows;

Chapter 1 proposes a plan to develop a Bayesian localized energy optimized sensor distribution scheme for efficient target tracking in wireless sensor network is designed. The chapter underlines the importance of developing and using localized energy optimized sensor management strategies which is crucial for improving the accuracy of target tracking.

Chapter 2 explains what Business Process Re-engineering is and presents modeling methods for Business Process Re-engineering. Business Process Re-engineering is a technique which helps organizations to cope with the challenges of ever changing business environments.

Chapter 3 investigated the usage of R in Finance and Banking sectors. Chapter also discusses the reasons of the increase in the usage of R in finance sector. Moreover, chapter makes a comparative evaluation of Python and R's strengths and weaknesses in a classroom setting.

Chapter 4 underlines the importance of Information Technology on preventing a vital problem names as Organizational amnesia. The main purpose of the chapter is to create an organization memory database as known as knowledge repository; in order to minimize memory loss in the organization and to determine the information types which is being recorded in the database.

Chapter 5 discusses the importance of the requirement of the traceability link in the software development cycle. Chapter also explains the sources of information that will be used to build improved traceability-recovery approaches.

Chapter 6 proposes a detailed specification, within a SPEM approach, of our transformation method, which is further analyzed and refurbished in order to meet current and future challenges.

Chapter 7 reviews the current and past challenges of the strategic and operational planning and describes two novel solutions with practical implementation for improving of these processes. In the chapter, all examples and case-study presentation are based on fragments of the faculty/departments/ programs of some fictional educational institution (university).

Chapter 8 explains the importance of the usage of enterprise model drafts. Enterprise model drafts have the capacity to conform to changing metamodels and should also support incomplete or imperfect information.

Selin Erben
Beykent University, Turkey

Chapter 1
Bayesian Localized Energy Optimized Sensor Distribution for Efficient Target Tracking

Alonshia S. Elayaraja
Bharathidasan University, India

ABSTRACT

Many applications in wireless sensor networks perform localization of nodes over an extended period of time. Optimal selection algorithm poses new challenges to the overall transmission power levels for target detection, and thus, localized energy optimized sensor management strategies are necessary for improving the accuracy of target tracking. In this chapter, a proposal plan to develop a Bayesian localized energy optimized sensor distribution scheme for efficient target tracking in wireless sensor network is designed. The sensor node localization is done with Bayesian average, which estimates the sensor node's energy optimality. Then the sensor nodes are localized and distributed based on the Bayesian energy estimate for efficient target tracking. The sensor node distributional strategy improves the accuracy of identifying the targets to be tracked quickly. The performance is evaluated with parameters such as accuracy of target tracking, energy consumption rate, localized node density, and time for target tracking.

DOI: 10.4018/978-1-5225-5522-3.ch001

INTRODUCTION

One of the important characteristics of the mobile device lies in its efficiency to analyze its current location. In increasingly many applications, the information regarding the current location is alone not sufficient but energy efficient analysis of location is essential. Although there exist many type of energy efficient target tracking methods for wireless sensor networks, we are more interested in implementing a method that improves the accuracy of the target being tracked at an early stage.

However, different from traditional WSN model, a new tracking framework called Detecting Movements using Face Tracking (DM-FT) (Wang et al, 2014) predicted the target location employing a spatial region. DM-FT used edge detection algorithm helped in detecting the target in a timely manner. Continuous target tracking for varied polygon size rapidly increase the energy rate. To mitigate this issue, Target Tracking and Mobile Sensor Navigation (TT-MSV) (Xu et al, 2013) was proposed to improve the energy consumption by applying min-max approximation approach. The intuition behind this approach was to improve the tracking performance at the cost of energy consumption. Optimizing energy consumption alone is not sufficient for enhancing the tracking performance, but also localization of sensor nodes is also considered to be an essential model. Localization through sensor node distribution by adopting distribution-free approach was investigated in (Penga et al, 2011). This in turn resulted in the improvement of the network lifetime.

Unfortunately, providing guarantees for tracking accuracy and consequently also for network lifetime, is difficult as the tracking accuracy depends, among others, on the sensing-based model, range-based approach (Liu et al, 2011; Zhao et al, 2013). Instead of endeavoring to bestow a comprehensive assurance on tracking accuracy, the target tracking system should ensure an individual application's needs, not only in terms of accuracy, but also in terms of location-based routing, spatiotemporal properties (Wang et al, 2013; Stoleru et al, 2012). Location-based routing optimized the distance travelled by the location update to minimize the overall energy cost. On the other hand, node localization in WSN based on spatiotemporal properties reduced the localization error by applying Event Distribution Function. Most schemes presented above localize the sensor nodes by exploiting routing information based on the distance. These schemes eliminate the need for sensor node localization at the cost of energy optimality. However, the sensor nodes energy usage varies over time, the time for target tracking increases with the increase in localized node density.

This paper proposes BLEOSD, a localization and target tracking scheme that efficiently tracks the target quickly. Using a Bayesian Sensor Node Localization architecture, BLEOSD offers a localized and energy optimized sensor distribution to obtain results tailored to requirements. Any number of sensors may be localized within a covered area, making BLEOSD scheme suitable for large-scale deployments.

The rest of the paper is organized as follows. In Section 2, we introduce the existing works on localization of sensor node and target tracking problem. In Section 3, we introduce the Bayesian Localized Energy Optimized Sensor Distribution (BLEOSD) scheme for efficient target tracking in wireless sensor network. Section 4 gives a comprehensive experimental evaluation of BLEOSD scheme. Our numerical results are shown in Section 5. Concluding remarks are included in Section 6.

RELATED WORKS

Existing systems for sensor node localization such as location anonymization algorithm (Chow et al, 2011), typically focus on aggregating k-anonymous locations with the aim of providing high quality location monitoring system. As an example, Trajectory-based data forwarding (Jeong et al, 2011) using link delay model develop a data forwarding scheme for light traffic vehicular ad hoc networks. A passive vehicular traffic measurement to increase sensor time synchronization error was designed in (Jeong et al, 2011) with the aid of autonomous passive localization algorithm.

WSNs are increasingly being envisioned for efficient data collection, from a geographical region of interest. In several surveillance applications of WSNs, target tracking is one of the main objectives once the sensor nodes are localized. At the same time energy, efficient target tracking has been extensively studied in the literature. In (Lai et al, 2011), Channel Adaptive Multiple Input Multiple Output mechanism was designed to reduce the complexity while detecting objects were designed. An experimental effort based on Redundant Radix-based Approach (Sinha et al, 2011) was designed for extending the network lifetime. In (Chin et al, 2010), intelligent mobile target in a mobile sensor network was explored by presenting optimal movement strategy.

One of the most significant applications of WSN is target tracking which has been extensively researched from many angles. First, tracking was studied for minimization of sensor installation cost (Amaldi et al, 2012). Second target tracking was considered as an anomaly detection problem (Chin et al, 2010) by applying sequential testing. Third in certain cases, target tracking was considered as an optimal decision rule problem (Zhao et al, 2010) using Bayesian formulation. Fourth few efforts were conducted based on distributed target tracking (Wang et al, 2010) under ideal binary sensor model. Finally, a few target tracking used adaptive node selection for reducing the energy cost and computational complexity as well as ensuring the tracking accuracy. A voronoi-based distributed sensor handover protocol was designed using localized algorithm with the objective of target tracked ratio, i.e., the quality of target tracking service. A quantized measurement fusion framework was investigated in using probabilistic quantization scheme to reduce the average communication energy saving.

In contrast to previous work, this paper emphasizes accuracy of target tracking, energy consumption rate with localized node density and proposes BLEOSD scheme, a system for robust and efficient target tracking. The proposed system provides competitive tradeoffs between energy-efficiency, tracking accuracy, and time for target tracking.

DESIGN OVERVIEW

Target tracking is one the most important applications in wireless sensor network. A target prediction scheme is based on kinematics rules and theory of probability which enhances the energy efficiency. However, energy-efficiency alone is not sufficient for tracking applications. In this section, we first describe the problem specification and how these are addressed in the BLEOSD scheme. Section 3.2 discusses the energy-efficient sensor node localization model employed in BLEOSD scheme. Section 3.3 focuses on node distribution based on Bayesian energy estimate for efficient target tracking.

Problem Definition

Given a rectangle sensing area '$M * N$', a grid deployment scheme partitions the sensing area into '$M * N$'grid points where sensor nodes are placed on wireless sensor network. Each grid point 'G_i' is associated with a coordinate '$G_i\left(x\right), G_i\left(y\right)$', where '$G_i\left(x\right), G_i\left(y\right)$' represents the '$x - axis\, and\, y - axis$' coordinates of '$G_i$' respectively, and also '$0 < G_i\left(x\right) < M\, and\, 0 < G_i\left(y\right) < N$'. One of the challenging issues when dealing with sensor nodes in wireless sensor network is the localization of the sensor nodes. With the decrease in the energy of sensor network, the performance of sensor network also gets deteriorated. As one of the most fundamental issues in WSN is energy consumption, the problem considered in this work is to minimize the consumption of energy with the goal of efficient target tracking in WSN using localized energy optimized model.

Design of BLEOSD Scheme

We first define how the Bayesian energy can be localized in Bayesian Localized Energy Optimized Sensor Distribution (BLEOSD) scheme for efficient target tracking in wireless sensor network. Then, we present our Bayesian Sensor Node Localization algorithm. At last, we introduce our optimal Single Hop Sensor Node Distributional algorithm and its features. In order to describe the problem of detecting the target as a sensor node localization problem through Bayesian average energy estimate the detailed explanation of BLEOSD scheme is explained in the forthcoming sections.

Bayesian-Based Sensor Node Localization

In our sensor node localization model, we assume that each sensor energy acts independently and the energy update is based on the number of hop counts from sender sensor node to receiver node at a particular time. Based on the Bayesian network model, let us consider three sensor nodes ‘ SN_1, SN_2, SN_3 ’ with three subordinate nodes ‘ N_1, N_3, N_6 ’ to communicate with each other. The sensor node localization is done with Bayesian average, which estimates the sensor node’s energy optimality. Let us consider energy ‘ E ’ for a sensor node ‘ SN_i ’, then the average energy of the sensor network is as shown below.

$$sAvg(E) = \sum_{i=1}^{n} E\left(\frac{SN_i(M * N)}{n}\right) \tag{1}$$

where ‘ $M * N$ ’ symbolizes the network size. The Bayesian average energy level of the sensor network is compared with the energy of each sensor node and is formalized as given below.

$$if\left(Avg(E)\right) < E(SN_i) \tag{2}$$

Node localization is performed based on the sensor nodes in the network that satisfies the above condition, aiming at reducing the energy consumption rate. Node localization is carried out using the Bayesian network model. The Bayesian network model with three sensor nodes ‘ SN_1, SN_2, SN_3 ’ the sensor node ‘ SN_1 ’ is connected with ‘ N_1 and N_2 ’ (i.e. sub ordinate nodes), the sensor node ‘ SN_2 ’ is connected with ‘ N_3, N_4 and N_5 ’ and the sensor node ‘ SN_3 ’ is connected with ‘ N_6, N_7 and N_8 ’ respectively. The conditional probabilities of above Bayesian network is factorized and is as shown below.

$$P\left(SN_i, N_i, N_j, N_k\right) = P\left(SN_i\right) P\left(N_i\right) P\left(N_j \mid SN_i\right) \tag{3}$$

$$= P\left(SN_i \mid N_j\right) P\left(N_k \mid N_i N_j\right) \tag{4}$$

The information from (3) and (4) constrains the possible locations of a sensor node. The energy for each sensor node is measured. Corresponding to the energy measurement and Bayesian formulation, each sensor node constructs a constraint on its location estimate and is formalized as given below.

$$LE\left(i,j,k\right) = P\left(SN_i \mid N_j\right) P\left(N_k \mid N_i N_j\right) \forall\, Avg\left(E\right) < E\left(SN_i\right) \tag{5}$$

where '$P\left(SN_i \mid N_j\right) P\left(N_k \mid N_i N_j\right)$' is the conditional probability of Bayesian network of the average energy level of sensor network, corresponding to sensor nodes 'N_i, N_j, N_k', and '$Avg\left(E\right)$' symbolizes the average energy of the sensor network. Figure 3 shows the algorithmic description of Bayesian Sensor Node Localization. The algorithm, sensor node localization is performed with the aid of Bayesian average. Followed by this, the sensor node energy optimality for the entire sensing area is measured. Consequently, the Bayesian average energy of the sensing area is compared with the energy of each sensor node. Finally, the sensor nodes are localized.

Single Hop Sensor Node Distributional Strategy

Once the sensor nodes are localized, sensor node distribution is performed for efficient target tracking. The objective of applying sensor node distributional strategy is to improve the accuracy of identifying the targets to be tracked and also at a quicker rate. Once the location estimate constraint is computed, each sensor node applies the Bayesian inference to evaluate its New Bayesian Energy Estimate (NBEE) from its Old Bayesian Energy Estimate ($Avg\left(E\right)$) and the location estimate constraint (LE).

$$NBEE\left(i,j\right) = \frac{Avg\left(E\right) * LE\left(i,j\right)}{\sum_{i,j=1}^{n} \left[Avg\left(E\right) * LE\left(i,j\right)\right]} \tag{6}$$

In this Single Hop Sensor Node Distributional Strategy, a centralized sink node is at the center of network where all other sensor nodes are assumed to be one-hop distance away from the sink for target detection. Whenever the sensed value of physical attribute exceeds a threshold 'τ' in any node, the sensor node transmits this value to the sink node. The packets include the node identity 'SN_i' along with its location '$Loc(SN_i)$' and also the timestamps '$Timestamp(SN_i)$' of detection of the target and is formalized as given below.

$$Packet = SN_i, Loc(SN_i), Timestamp(SN_i) \tag{7}$$

Let 'n' be the number of sensor nodes sensing the target 's above the set threshold 'τ' and that all the that all the 'n'sensors report the sensed value within a time period '$Timestamp$'. In single hop distributional strategy, the positional values of '$X - coordinate - Pos(X)$' and '$Y - coordinate - Pos(Y)$' of the target is measured as given below.

$$Pos(X) = \frac{\sum_{i=1}^{n} SN_{ix}}{n} \tag{8}$$

$$Pos(Y) = \frac{\sum_{i=1}^{n} SN_{iy}}{n} \tag{9}$$

where 'SN_{ix}' and 'SN_{iy}' denotes the '$X - coordinate$' and '$Y - coordinate$' of the 'ith' sensor. The velocity for target tracking is obtained as given below.

$$Vel(X) = \frac{Pos(X)(t) - Pos(X)(t-1)}{Pos(X)(T)} \tag{10}$$

$$Vel(Y) = \frac{Pos(Y)(t) - Pos(Y)(t-1)}{Pos(Y)(T)} \tag{11}$$

where '$Vel(X)$' and '$Vel(Y)$' symbolizes the velocities for '$X - coordinate$' and '$Y - coordinate$' along 'X' and 'Y' directions respectively. From the position and velocity information, sensor node distributional strategy improves the accuracy of identifying the targets to be tracked. Therefore, target tracking at different instances is as given below.

$$Target(X) = Pos(X), Pos(Y), Vecl(X), Vel(Y) \tag{12}$$

From (12), the target being tracked for sensor node '' at time instant '' is obtained. This in turn improves the accuracy of targets being tracked. From the Single Hop Sensor Node Distribution algorithm given above, the target tracking accuracy of the sensor nodes s improved by applying the positional and velocity updates to the updated Bayesian energy estimate values.

EXPERIMENTAL SETTINGS

Bayesian Localized Energy Optimized Sensor Distribution (BLEOSD) scheme for efficient target tracking uses the NS-2 simulator with the network range of 1400*1400 m size. The number of sensor nodes selected for experimental purpose is 70 nodes and uses Random Way Point (RWM) model for BLEOSD scheme. The BLEOSD scheme uses Destination Sequence Based Distance Vector (DSDV) as routing protocol to perform the experimental work.

The BLEOSD scheme's moving speed in the network is about 10 m/s for each source node with a simulation rate of 50 milliseconds to perform target tracking. The values of each parameter for performing experiments are shown in Table 1. Experiment is conducted on the factors such as energy consumption, target tracking accuracy, localized node density, time for target tracking. The results of the metrics of BLEOSD scheme is compared against the existing methods such as Detecting Movements using Face Tracking (DM-FT) [1] and Target Tracking and Mobile Sensor Navigation (TT-MSV) [2] in WSN.

Table 1. Simulation setup

PARAMETER	VALUE
Protocols	DSDV
Network range	1400 m * 1400 m
Simulation time	50 ms
Mobility model	Random Way Point
Localized node density	10, 20, 30, 40, 50, 60, 70
Network simulator	NS 2.34
Mobility speed	10 m/s
Pause time	10 s

DISCUSSION

The performance of Bayesian Localized Energy Optimized Sensor Distribution (BLEOSD) scheme is compared with the existing Detecting Movements using Face Tracking (DM-FT) [1] and Target Tracking and Mobile Sensor Navigation (TT-MSV) [2] in WSN. The performance is evaluated according to the following metrics.

Scenario 1: Impact of Energy Consumption Rate

In wireless sensor networks, all sensor nodes are said to be energy constrained. In such scenarios, it becomes highly essential to reduce the energy consumption rate. We incorporate Bayesian Sensor Node Localization algorithm to further reduce the energy consumption. The energy consumption for target tracking ‘ EC_{TT} ’ from any source sensor node is written as given below.

$$EC_{TT} = Energy_{SN} * Total_{SN} \tag{13}$$

From (13), the energy consumption ‘ EC_{TT} ’ for target tracking is obtained by the product of the energy for single node ‘ $Energy_{SN}$ ’ and total sensor nodes ‘ $Total_{SN}$ ’ in the network. It is measured in terms of Joules (J). Experiments are conducted in NS2 to validate the Bayesian Localized Energy Optimized Sensor Distribution (BLEOSD) scheme, Detecting Movements using Face Tracking (DM-FT) [1] and Target Tracking and Mobile Sensor Navigation (TT-MSV) [2] in WSN.

The Table 2 represents the energy consumption rate obtained using NS2 simulation and comparison is made with two other methods, namely DM-FT [1] and TT-MSV. To conduct experiments, localized node density in the range of 10 to 70 sensor nodes are considered. The average energy consumption for target tracking versus number of localized node density in the network. As shown in the figure, the energy consumption rate is proportional to the localized node density. With the increase in the simulation time, as the localized node density increases there result in an increase in the energy being consumed. The BLEOSD scheme consumes less energy compared to DM-FT and TT-MSV. Moreover, the energy consumption rate observed in the graph is not linear and differs due to the change in the node position. From results, we observed that as the localized node density increases, though energy consumption increases, comparatively the performance of BLEOSD scheme is better than that of DM-FT by 7.65% and TT-MSV by 18.42%. Here the BLEOSD scheme consumes less energy as we are performing Bayesian-based Sensor Node Localization that performs the localization of sensor nodes using Bayesian energy estimate based on node energy

Table 2. Tabulation for energy consumption rate

Localized node density	Energy consumption rate (J)		
	BLEOSD	DM-FT	TT-MSV
10	58	63	68
20	75	78	86
30	89	93	99
40	70	78	96-
50	85	95	101
60	92	99	108
70	88	93	99

optimality. As a result, it consumes less energy for target tracking in an efficient manner (Wang et al, 2014; Xu et al, 2013).

Scenario 1: Impact of Target Tracking Accuracy

In order to study the impact of target tracking accuracy, the localized node density and the objects (i.e. sensor nodes) being tracked are considered. The target tracking accuracy is then formulated using these two factors and is as given below.

$$A = \sum_{i=1}^{n} \frac{Targets\,being\,tracked}{SN_i} * 100 \tag{14}$$

From (14), the target tracking accuracy 'A' is measured with respect to the localized node density 'SN_i'. Higher the target tracking accuracy more efficient the method is said to be and is measured in terms of percentage (%).

In order to increase the target tracking accuracy with respect to different number of sensor nodes, the target tracking accuracy rate using the BLEOSD scheme and two methods, DM-FT and TT-MSV are presented with visual comparison is presented in Table 3. The results for 70 different sensor nodes. The target tracking accuracy rate while using our scheme BLEOSD scheme offer comparable values than the state-of-the-art methods. The results utilizing BLEOSD scheme shows that using Single Hop Sensor Node Distribution algorithm has resulted in better tracking accuracy rate compared to (Wang et al, 2014; Xu et al, 2013). While DM-FT and TT-MSV improves the target tracking accuracy rate, but at the cost of energy consumption, whereas by applying Hop Sensor Node Distribution algorithm not only the target tracking accuracy rate is improved but also at minimum energy consumption. On the

Table 3. Tabulation for target tracking accuracy

Localized node density	Target tracking accuracy (%)		
	BLEOSD	DM-FT	TT-MSV
10	68.35	62.45	58.14
20	73.87	67.82	63.72
30	75.83	69.78	65.68
40	79.21	73.15	69.05
50	81.36	75.31	71.21
60	84.19	78.14	74.04
70	89.32	83.27	79.17

other hand, Single Hop Sensor Node Distributional Strategy applied in BLEOSD scheme further measures the position and velocity before tracking the targets with the aid of New Bayesian Energy Estimate. In figure 6, the BLEOSD scheme achieves an increase of about 7.69% and 12.96% in target tracking accuracy ratio.

Scenario 3: Impact of Time for Target Tracking

To study the impact of time for target tracking, the localized node density and the time for target tracking for each sensor node is measured and is as given below.

$$Time_{TT} = SN_i * Time\,for\,target\,tracking \quad (15)$$

From (15), the time for target tracking '$Time_{TT}$' is measured with respect to the node density 'SN_i' and is measured in terms of milliseconds (ms).

The comparison of time for target tracking is presented in Table 4 with respect to different sensor nodes in the range of 10 to 70 is presented. With increase in the node density, the time for target tracking also gets increased. The quantitative results to compare the target tracking time performance of the three methods. To investigate the impact of target tracking time, we ran a simulation varying the number of sensor nodes in the network. Specifically, we fix the maximum speed of mobile node to 50 m/s and vary the number of sensor nodes from 10 to 70. Figure shows that the target tracking time with varying sensor nodes increases as the number of sensor nodes increases by applying all the methods. However, by applying BLEOSD scheme, the target tracking time is comparatively less. This is because of the Single Hop Sensor Node Distributional Strategy that tracks the target based on the node's position and velocity, leading to minimum utilization of time for target tracking.

Table 4. Tabulation for time for target tracking

Localized node density	Time for target tracking (ms)		
	BLEOSD	DM-FT	TT-MSV
10	0.09	0.14	0.17s3
20	0.14	0.22	0.28
30	0.19	0.27	0.33
40	0.25	0.33	0.39
50	0.36	0.44	0.50
60	0.49	0.57	0.63
70	0.55	0.63	0.69

Moreover, by applying sensor node distribution Bayesian distribution strategy, the time for tracking is reducing in BLEOSD scheme by 34.27% compared to DM-FT and 58.78% compared to TT-MSV.

CONCLUSION

In this paper, a Bayesian Sensor Node Localization algorithm is proposed based on the concept of Bayesian average energy level to satisfy the two different requirements, high accuracy of target tracking and low energy consumption rate, over the same WSN simultaneously. The Bayesian Sensor Node Localization algorithm is proved stable using the sensor node energy optimality. Moreover, the experiment results on a small testbed and the simulation results on BLEOSD scheme demonstrate that by applying Bayesian Sensor Node Localization algorithm can significantly improve the target tracking accuracy and decrease the energy consumption rate by comparing average energy with the energy of each sensor node. BLEOSD scheme also ensuring tracking accuracy at less time interval because only single hop sensor node distribution strategy is applied, which simplifies the implementation.

REFERENCES

Amaldi, E., Capone, A., Cesana, M., & Filippini, I. (2012). On the design of wireless sensor networks for mobile target detection. *IEEE/ACM Transactions on Networking*, *20*(3), 784–797. doi:10.1109/TNET.2011.2175746

Chin, J.-C., Dong, Y., Hon, W.-K., Ma, C. Y.-T., & Yau, D. K. Y. (2010). Detection of Intelligent Mobile Target in a Mobile Sensor Network. *IEEE/ACM Transactions on Networking*, *18*(1), 41–52. doi:10.1109/TNET.2009.2024309

Chow, C.-Y., Mokbel, M. F., & He, T. (2011). A Privacy-Preserving Location Monitoring System for Wireless Sensor Networks. *IEEE Transactions on Mobile Computing*, *10*(1), 94–107. doi:10.1109/TMC.2010.145

Cohen, K., & Zhao, Q. (2015). Asymptotically Optimal Anomaly Detection via Sequential Testing. *IEEE Transactions on Signal Processing*, *63*(11), 2929–2941. doi:10.1109/TSP.2015.2416674

Jaehoon Jeong, Shuo Guo, Tian He, & Du, D. H. C. (2011). Autonomous Passive Localization Algorithm for Road Sensor Networks. *IEEE Transactions on Computers*, *60*(11), 1622–1637. doi:10.1109/TC.2010.260

Jeong, J., Guo, S., Gu, Y., He, T., & Du, D. H. C. (2011). Trajectory-Based Data Forwarding for Light-Traffic Vehicular Ad Hoc Networks. *IEEE Transactions on Parallel and Distributed Systems*, *22*(5), 743–757. doi:10.1109/TPDS.2010.103

Lai, I.-W., Ascheid, G., Meyr, H., & Chiueh, T.-D. (2011). Efficient Channel-Adaptive MIMO Detection Using Just-Acceptable Error Rate. *IEEE Transactions on Wireless Communications*, *10*(1), 73–83. doi:10.1109/TWC.2010.101810.091129

Liu, L., Zhang, X., & Ma, H. (2011). Localization-Oriented Coverage in Wireless Camera Sensor Networks. *IEEE Transactions on Wireless Communications*, *10*(2), 484–494. doi:10.1109/TWC.2010.01.080956

Miao, P., Chenb, H., Xiao, Y., Ozdemir, S., Vasilakos, A. V., & Wue, J. (2011). Impacts of sensor node distributions on coverage in sensor networks. *Journal of Parallel and Distributed Computing*, *71*(12), 1578–1591. doi:10.1016/j.jpdc.2011.04.011

Sinha, K., Sinha, B. P., & Datta, D. (2011). An Energy-Efficient Communication Scheme for Wireless Networks: A Redundant Radix-Based Approach. *IEEE Transactions on Wireless Communications*, *10*(2), 550–559. doi:10.1109/TWC.2010.120610.100244

Stoleru, R., He, T., Mathiharan, S. S., George, S. M., & Stankovic, J. A. (2012). Asymmetric Event-Driven Node Localization in Wireless Sensor Networks. *IEEE Transactions on Parallel and Distributed Systems*, *23*(4), 634–642. doi:10.1109/TPDS.2011.227

Wang, G., Md, Z. A. B., Cao, J., & Wu, J. (2014). Detecting Movements of a Target Using Face Tracking in Wireless Sensor Networks. *IEEE Transactions on Parallel and Distributed Systems*, *25*(4), 939–949. doi:10.1109/TPDS.2013.91

Wang, Z., Bulut, E., & Szymanski, B. K. (2010). Distributed Energy-Efficient Target Tracking with Binary Sensor Networks. *ACM Transactions on Sensor Networks*, *6*(4), 1–32. doi:10.1145/1777406.1777411

Wang, Z., Bulut, E., & Szymanski, B. K. (2013). Energy-efficient location services for mobile ad hoc networks. *Elsevier, Ad Hoc Networks*, *11*(1), 273–287. doi:10.1016/j.adhoc.2012.05.012

Xu, E., Ding, Z., & Dasgupta, S. (2013). Target Tracking and Mobile Sensor Navigation in Wireless Sensor Networks. *IEEE Transactions on Mobile Computing*, *12*(1), 177–186. doi:10.1109/TMC.2011.262

Zhao, J., Xi, W., He, Y., Liu, Y., Li, X.-Y., Mo, L., & Yang, Z. (2013). Localization of Wireless Sensor Networks in the Wild: Pursuit of Ranging Quality. *IEEE/ACM Transactions on Networking*, *2*(1), 311–323. doi:10.1109/TNET.2012.2200906

Zhao, Q., & Ye, J. (2010). Quickest Detection in Multiple ON–OFF Processes. *IEEE Transactions on Signal Processing*, *58*(12), 5994–6006. doi:10.1109/TSP.2010.2071869

Chapter 2 Business Process Re-Engineering

Joseph Sungau
Mzumbe University, Tanzania

ABSTRACT

In today's business environment, business competition has increased due to market needs and advancement in technologies. This forces organizational managers and consultants to identify techniques that enable organizations to cope with an ever-changing business environment. In their efforts, many organizational performance improving techniques have been discovered. Among the techniques discovered, business process re-engineering is the technique reported to improve business processes for enhanced organizational performance. Therefore, this chapter explains what business process re-engineering is and presents modeling methods for business process re-engineering.

INTRODUCTION

Business systems are characterized by three elements: inputs (materials, information and customers, labour, facilities), processes (logical arranged business activities) and output (service/good). The system forms an input-transformation process-output model. In the model, there are two types of inputs, transformed inputs and transforming inputs. Transformed inputs are inputs which change their shapes and/or properties once passes through the transformation process. On the other hand, the transforming inputs are inputs which remain unchanged at the end of transformation process, they neither change their shapes nor properties.

DOI: 10.4018/978-1-5225-5522-3.ch002

The transformation process is a set of interrelated activities with a clear sequential relationship which are done with the aim of delivering an organizational offering. In that understanding, organizations have several activities which are arranged in different sections depending on their functioning, meaning that activities which perform similar functions are put under one section. Once the activities in a process are done, they results to an output. The outputs can be categorized in two types; good or service depending on the type of organization. Goods are tangible output of a business process produced from manufacturing organizations while service are intangible output of business process offered by service organization. Business processes in an organization can be presented in Input-transformation-output model as presented in Figure 1 (Heizer & Render, 2011; Slack et al., 2007).

In many organizations, a problematic part is a business process that delivers what is required by customers. A business process is a set of logically arranged activities that takes in inputs and transform them to their desired outputs. During the process of transformation, the transforming inputs act on transformed inputs. In so doing, business process creates values to inputs stage to stage up to their desired final output. In this regard, business processes are very important part of business system, they need to be perfected for delivering organizational offering. Therefore, organizations need to improve business processes for delivering what is required by customers (Slack et al., 2007). On that view, the perfection of business processes facilitate organizations to deliver goods and/or services of required quality, within reasonable time and costs. However, organizations have been adopting many techniques, but their problems remain unsolved. Therefore, this chapter presents BPR techniques as a technique that perfects business processes for enhanced organizational offerings (Housel & Bell, 2001; Attaran, 2004). The chapter aims to create understanding of

Figure 1. Input-transformation process-output model

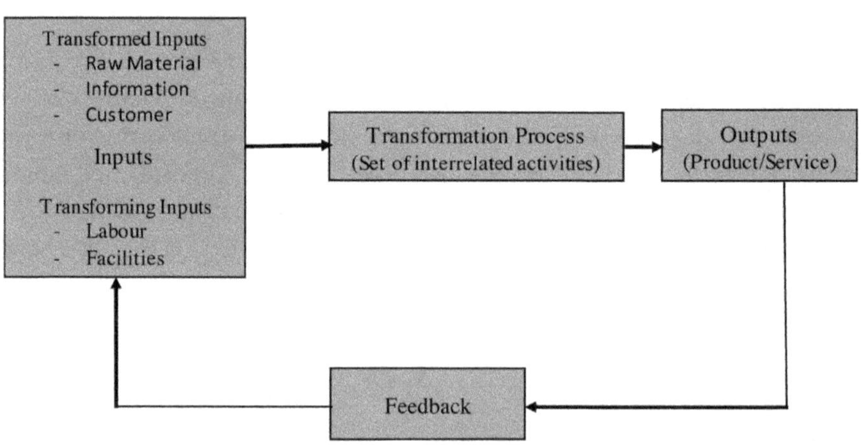

the techniques BPR and finally presents the modeling methods that can be used to implement BPR for effective business process improvement.

Historical Perspective of Business Process Re-Engineering

In the first time, Business Process Re-engineering technique emerged in America in 1980s and early 1990s, first in private sector and later in public sector (Parys & Thijs, 2003). The emergence of BPR in America is often explained by the need of organizations to radically improve business processes for dramatic improved organizational performance in order to compete with Japanese companies. Furthermore, the emergence of BPR followed the failure of division of labour concept to improve organizational performance (Hammer & Champy, 1993). Later on, BPR techniques was adopted by many countries.

The emergency of BPR challenged many techniques that were used to improve organizational performance for some past centuries. The challenges imposed by BPR technique includes; rejection of reductionism idea which focused in fragmenting and breaking down of organizations' works into simple tasks which were assigned to specific departments or sections. The other challenge was the need to transform mechanically operated business process to either semi-automated or full automated business processes. Furthermore, the need to exploit the advantage of emerging new technology was also a challenge that forced organizations to abandon other performance improving techniques in favour of BPR. The last challenge was a need of many organizations to exploit developed education and capabilities of staff rather than sticking on past experiences of organizations (Beckford, 1998). Following these challenges, BPR was inevitable as it enabled organizations to organize work around processes rather than activities, restructure processes prior to structuring institutions and hierarchies, and structure processes in different ways than before (Hammer & Champy, 1993).

UNDERSTANDING OF BUSINESS PROCESS RE-ENGINEERING

Business Process

Several authors have defined the concept business process, although the key concept of the definitions remains the same. For instance, Davenport and Short (1990) defines business process as a set of logically related tasks performed to achieve a defined business outcome. In the definition of Davenport and Short (1990), the main concept that can be deduced is that, a business process is made up of tasks. The tasks are arranged in groups of sensibly interrelated tasks. In each group of tasks, the tasks are sequentially linked for effective and efficiency execution of organizational tasks to achieve the predefined organizational outcome.

In the year 1993, Davenport defined business process as a specific ordering of work activities across time and space, with a beginning, an end, and clearly identified inputs and outputs: as structure for action. In this definition, it can be deduced that, business process is a detailed sequencing of work activities that will be performed over a given time. The sequenced activities need a clear starting and ending points. All in all, according to Davenport, business process is an arrangement of deeds that convert defined input to output.

Talwar (1993) defined business process as any sequence of pre-defined activities that are executed to achieve a pre-specified type or range of outcome. In this definition, it can be deduced that, business process is a series of activities which have been pre-defined. Once the pre-defined activities are executed they produce pre-specified outputs.

ISO 9001 define a process as a "set of interrelated or interacting activities, which transforms inputs into outputs. From the definition, it can be deduced that business process is composed of activities which interact to each other to convert the inputs to their required outputs. This definition does not state categorically the inputs and output although it states the elements of input-transformation-output model.

Hammer and Champy (1993) defines a business process as a collection of activities that takes one or more kinds of input and creates an output that is of value to the customer. From the definition, it can be deduced that, a business process is made up of activities that take in one or more inputs to produce an output that have value to customers. This definition involves all three elements of the input-transformation process-output model; input, collection of activities and output.

Stoddard and Jarvenpea (1995) defined business process as a set of activities that transform a set of inputs into outputs (goods and services) for another person or process using people and equipment. From the definition, it can be deduced that a business process is made up of activities that take in one or more inputs to produce an output that have value to customers. This definition involves all three elements of the input-system-output model; input, system and output. The definition further specifies the types of input to be either transforming input (people and equipment) or transformed input (raw materials, information and customers). Not only that, but also, the definition went further by pinpointing the two major types of output; good and service, that can be obtained after taking the input into the system.

Based on the presented definitions by different authors, it can be deduced that, business process has three aspects; system (set of interrelated activities), inputs (transforming and transformed resources) and desired outputs (good and/or services). The system is a set/package of logical arranged activities in such a way that it generates goods/delivers services after the transforming resources act on transformed resources (Slack et al., 2007; Heizer & Render, 2011). In this case, Business Process is a series of related activities that are aimed at transforming the input (such as raw material, information, customers etc) to predefined output (goods or services) through application of appropriate transforming resources (facility and/or labour)

On the other hand, engineering is a branch of science and technology which is concerned with the application of scientific, economic, social and practical knowledge in order to design, build, and maintain structures, machines, devices, systems and processes. In business processes, engineering is concerned with designing or structuring of business processes.

Re-engineering is restructuring of an organization or part of organization by removing non value adding processes or adding value adding processes through renovation, automation and networking. Re-engineering business process is restructuring part of an organization. In re-engineering business process, an organization needs to identify business processes that are less effective for perfection.

According to Chen (2001), there is no commonly agreed definition of BPR. Several authors have defined the concept BPR in different ways. According to Hammer and Champy (1993), BPR is the fundamental rethinking and radical redesign of business processes to achieve dramatic improvements in critical contemporary measures of performance, such as cost, quality, service, and speed. From the definition of Hammer and Champy, the main concepts of BPR which can be deduced are fundamental rethinking, radical redesign, process and dramatic improvement as explained in the following paragraphs.

- **Fundamental Rethinking:** When an organization is undertaking re-engineering, it has to consider some basic questions about herself and the way it operates, such as, why do we do what we do?, and why do we do the way we do?. These are fundamental questions that force people look at the unstated and assumptions that underlie the way their business is conducted. Often these ways of conducting business turn to be outdated, obsolete, wrong or not applicable. In this case, the fundamental changes need to be done to improve business processes for improved organizational performance.
- **Radical Redesign:** An organization or an enterprise should throw away the old ways and inventing the new way to make a better performance. This term might be called as "clean-slate". Re-engineering looks at business reinvention, not only that it looks for improvement, enhancement or modifications of existing business structures or procedures.
- **Dramatic Improvement:** Re-engineering is not about making marginal or small improvement, but about the achievement of big or quantum leaps in performance which is in accordance with risks that are involved with BPR.

The accomplishment of BPR is expected to bring jumping result, not as an improvement or incremental results.

- **Processes:** Collection of activities that takes one or more kinds of input and creates output(s) that is of value to a customer by using people and equipment. Processes should be re-engineered to better processes by sequencing tasks. The re-engineering of processes results in reduced coordination costs. Meaning that, an organization can achieve a better performance in both financial and non-financial terms.

According to Manganelli and Klein (1994), BPR is defined as the rapid and radical redesign of strategic, value-added business processes and the systems, policies and organizational structures that support them – to optimize the work flows and productivity in an organization. From the definition of Manganelli and Klein (1994), it can be deduced that a process is an interrelated series of activities that converts inputs into outputs. In these processes, three main activities can be identified: Value adding, hand-off and control activities. Furthermore, in this definition, it has been identified that BPR is concerned with change in processes that are both strategic and value-adding to products and services. Also, from this definition, it can be deduced that BPR looks at all of the systems, policies and organizational structures that, support these business processes. In this case, it can be figured out that a business process cannot be changed unless all the supporting elements are changed as well.

Additionally, Davenport and Short (1990) define BPR to be the analysis and design of workflows and processes within and between organizations; Teng and Kettinger (1995) define BPR as the critical analysis and radical redesign of existing business processes to achieve breakthrough improvements in performance measures and Al-Mashara, Iran and Zairi (2001) define BPR as a continuum of change initiatives with varying degrees of radicalness supported by IT means, at the heart of which is to deliver superior performance standards through establishing process sustainable capacity.

Based on these definitions, BPR is a studying of business processes to identify weaknesses and take quick and appropriate corrective actions to improve them for improved organizational performance through the application of information and communication technology. Many people misunderstand the BPR concept. It should be understood that, BPR is not downsizing (it eliminates works but not job or people), restructuring (it is concerned with how work is done) and automating (It enables new business processes design, rather than providing mechanisms to old business processes) of existing business processes. Those who label any organizational change as re-engineering have victimized it. Following of failure to understand the technique, it has resulted to failure of appreciating the promise of BPR (Housel & Bell, 2001).

It should be understood that BPR is revolution of a business processes (Changing from old business processes to new business processes). It is concerned with business process design, process management, and process innovation. Furthermore, BPR involves revising and re-configuration of work to serve customers better. All in all, BPR forces organizations to challenge the way they run and redesign the business processes around the desired outcomes (Attaran, 2004).

In order to avoid the misunderstanding of the technique, it should be further understood that BPR involves; discovering how business processes currently operates, redesigning business processes to eliminate the wasted or redundant effort and improving efficiency in order to gain competitiveness advantage (Chen, 2001). Also, according to Sherwood-Smith (1994) as quoted by Chen (2001), BPR is seeking to devise new ways of organizing tasks, people and redesigning IT systems so that processes support the organization to realise its goals.

In general, BPR is focusing to get customers oriented business processes. In that regard, the technique is aiming at eliminating customer complains (customer focus), minimizing time it takes to complete a task (speed) and reducing operational cost (compression). Other aims of BPR techniques are enabling organizations to; change with conditions (flexibility), be obsession with the superior service and value to customers as the level of the quality is always controlled and monitored by the processes, innovate the business processes and to improve productivity of an organization (Zygiaris, 2000; Attaran, 2004). Therefore, BPR is a technique that aims at improving business processes for enhanced quality, operational cost, delivering speed and productivity of organizations (Kock, McQueen & Baker, 1996).

In theory, BPR provides a missing link between a layer of strategy and that of information system design. Moreover, BPR recommends a holistic perspective which encourages the bringing of objectives, human resources, organization, IT and culture into a coherent perspective (Lenk, 1997; Covert, 1997). In so doing, BPR brings about the following changes to an organization as presented in Table 1.

In contrast with other techniques, BPR is about dramatic improvement of business processes through fundamental rethinking how the organizations' work should be done. This thinking distinguishes BPR from other business process improving techniques; which focus on functional or incremental improvement (Hammer & Champy, 1993). Although BPR differs from other business process improving techniques, but they share some common themes (Beckford, 1998). For instance, both they start with needs of customer and work backwards. The techniques that share some common themes include systems engineering, benchmarking and activity based costing (ABC). Other techniques includes scientific management, customer satisfaction measurement, cross functional team building, business process improvement (BPI) and total quality management (TQM) to mention few (Beckford, 1998).

Table 1. Changes which occurs in an organization as a result of re-engineering from conventional process

Changes in the world of work	
From conventional	**To Re-engineering**
Functional departments	Process teams
Simple task (Division of labour)	Empowered employees
Controlled people (by management)	Multidimensional work
Training of employees	Education of employees
Compensation for skill and time spent	Compensation for results
Pay raises based on promotions and seniority	Low pay plus high performance-related bonuses
Advancement based on ability	Advancement based on performance
Protective organizational culture	Productive organizational structure
Managers supervise and control	Managers coach and advise
Hierarchical organizational structure	Horizontal (flat) structure
Executive as scorekeepers	Executive as leaders
Separation of duties and functions	Cross-functional teams
Linear and sequential processes	Parallel process
Mass production	Mass customization

Source: Hammer and Champy, 1993

Difference Between Business Process Re-Engineering With Other Techniques

BPR cannot stand on its own. It needs to be supported by Information Technology. In this argument, the application of Information Technology in BPR is one of characteristics which distinguishes BPR from other business process improving techniques. The other differences between BPR and other techniques are summarized in Table 2.

Business Process Re-Engineering and Information Technology

A key stimulus for BPR is the continuing development and deployment of sophisticated information system and networks. This can be evidenced by leading organizations which have been dominant in using technology to support innovative business processes, rather than refining old ways of doing work (Dodaro & Crowley, 1997). Following the use of new technology, IT has been identified to be an enabler of BPR project in organizations (Sungau & Msanjila, 2012). For instance, by implementing BPR, organizations explored opportunities provided by IT systems and tools to automate business activities for improved services to satisfy customers (Laudon & Laudon, 2006). Not only that, but also, IT provides potential roles by creating more flexible, team-oriented, coordinative and communication-based work capability in organizations (Whitman, 1996).

Table 2. The comparison of Business Process improving techniques

Attribute	Technique			
	Six Sigma	Lean	TQM	BPR
The cause for introduction of the technique	The quality evaluation in Japan and Motorola	The quality evaluation in Japan and Toyota production system	The quality evolution in Japan	The quality evolution in Japan
Underlying theory	Reduce variation/no defects	-Remove waste/non-value added in the process -Customers value driven	Focus on customer	-Business transformationm -Discontinuous thinking -Radically redesigning the end-to-end business process to add value to customers
Focus	-Problem focused -To solve problems in operations processes in response to customers' requirements	Flow focused, aiming to eliminate waste in the process for driving the perfection to customers	Customer-focused	End-to-end business process (cross functional)
Improvement approach/principles	-The main improvement approach follows the DMAIC methods consisting of five phases: Define measure, analyse, improve and control -Design for Six Sigma including; Define, Measure, analyse, design and verify	-identify customer value -Value stream analysis -Flow -Pull -Perfection	-The improvement approach is based on Deming or PDCA cycle (Plan-Do,Check-Act)	-Rethink business process in cross-functional manner -Radically rethinking and redesigning the process -have those who use the output of the process -Put the decision point where the work is performed, build control to the process
Tools/techniques	-Statistical process control -process map -Measurement system -FMEA -DOE -Root cause analysis -ANOVA Cause and effect diagram -Parato analysis -Histogram -Benchmarking -Brainstorming	-Kanban -Pull scheduling -Kaizen -5S -Value-stream mapping -Time-value diagram -single piece flow process -TPM -SMED	-Analytical and statistic tools -seven quality control tools -seven management tool -Statistical process control tools -Quality function deployment (QFD)	-Process mapping/ flow charting -benchmarking -Just-in-Time -Activity Based costing (ABC) -Supporting IT -Simulation modelling

Source: Nave, 2002; Anderson *et al*, 2006 and Dahlgaard-Park, 2006 as cited in Buavaraporn (2010)

Hammer (1990) considers IT as the key factor in BPR for organization that wants to witness a "radical change" in its operations. Not only that, but also, Hammer (1990), Aremu and Saka (2006) argued that, IT is a strategic resource that facilitates major changes in competitive behaviours, marketing and customer service environment in achieving competitive advantages over others. Furthermore, Davenport and Short (1990) posted that, IT should be viewed as more than an automating or mechanizing force to fundamentally reshape the way business is done. It should be noted that IT and BPR have recursive relationship. Meaning that, IT capabilities should support the re-engineered business processes while BPR should provide a conducive environment for IT to work on. In this case, IT helps organizations to facilitate changes promoted by re-engineering for improved OP (Shin & Jemella, 2002; Davenport & Short, 1990; Hammer, 1990). According to Davenport and Short (1990), the roles of IT in BPR can be summarized in Table 3.

Table 3. The role of IT in BPR

Role of IT	***Organizational impact***
Transactional	IT can transform unstructured business process into standardized transactions
Geographical	IT can transfer information with rapidity and ease across large distances, making business process independent of locations
Automation	IT can reduce human labour in certain process by replacing manual works
Informational	IT can bring vast volumes of detailed information into a business process
Analytical	IT can bring complex analytical methods to bear on a process
Sequential	IT enables changes in the sequence of tasks in the process, often allowing multiple tasks to be worked on simultaneously
Knowledge management	IT allows the capture and dissemination of knowledge and expertise to improve the process
Tracking	IT allows detailed tracking of status, inputs and outputs
Reduction of intermediaries/networking	IT can be used to connect two parties within a process that would otherwise communicate through intermediaries

Source: Davenport and Short (1990)

Circumstances That Influences Organizations Adopt Business Process Re-Engineering

Theoretically, there are circumstances that trigger organizations to adopt BPR. The circumstances can be categorized into three main groups depending on a situation an organization is experiencing or will experience. The situations which can be experienced are crisis management, anticipatory management and market leadership. The organizations which fall in any of the three groups of situation may undertake re-engineering project as follows (Hammer & Champy, 1993).

- **Crisis Managemen Situationt:** The group of organizations which fall in this situation, they have no choice rather than improving business processes. They re-engineer so that they move out of the crisis;
- **Anticipatory Management Situation:** The group involves organizations that foresee a crisis is approaching. Therefore, organizations which are in this situation re-engineer the business processes so that the coming crisis won't affect their business, and;
- **Market Leadership Situation:** The group involves organizations that want to continue to be market leaders. The re-engineering projects enable them to achieve their dreams by providing a better services than the current ones.

Principles of Business Process Re-Engineering

The BPR project needs to be done as one-time event. Not only that, but also, BPR needs to be treated as a project which is critical to the future of the organization (Hammer & Champy, 1993; Cross, Feather & Lynch, 1994; Covert, 1997). Like any other project, BPR has an analysis phase, a design phase and implementation phase. Cross, Feather and Lynch summarize BPR phases in Figure 2.

The analysis phase is concerned with the understanding of markets, customer requirements and how organizational works are done. The understanding is done by benchmarking with best practices in the industry. In this stage, the identification of processes for re-engineering is done before specification of designing needs. According to Cross et al. (1994), design specification are the initial blueprint for re-engineering project which are developed from the customer requirement and existing business process analyses.

In the design phase, the process of rethinking and designing the best way to serve the customer is developed. Cross et al. (1994) suggested six key design principles for successful re-engineering. The six design principles includes:-

Figure 2. Implementation of BPR in an organization
Source: Cross, Feather and Lynch, 1994

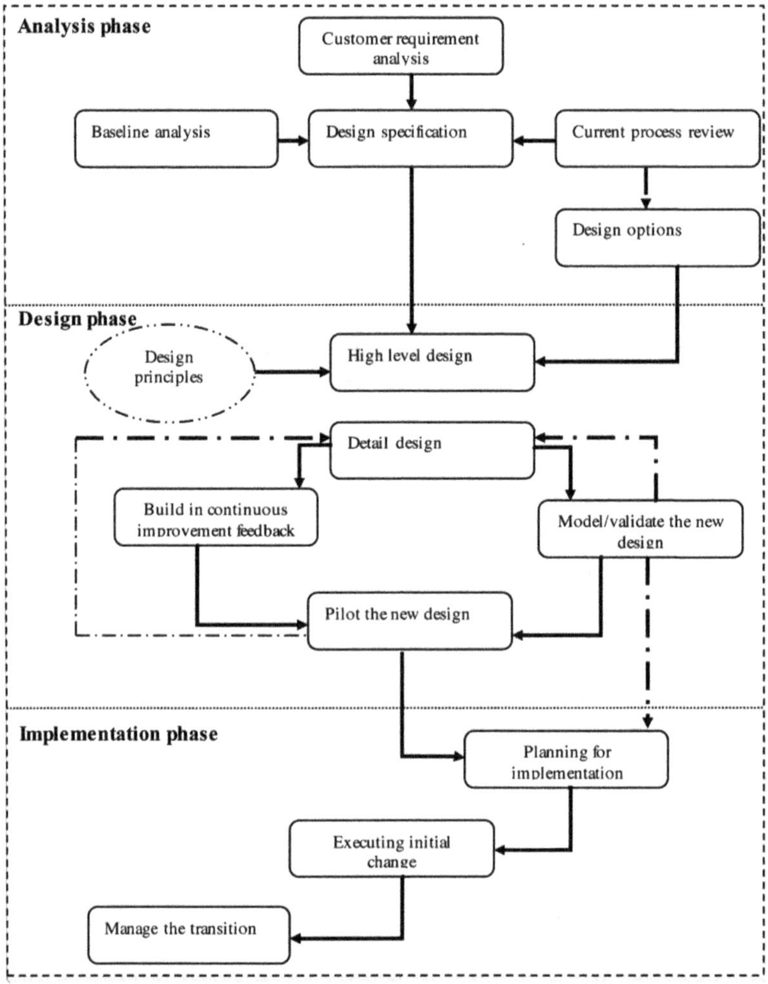

- *Service quality* principle which provides guidance regarding the design of process as they relate to customer contacts;
- *Workflow* principle which relates to the basic nature of managing the flow of work through a series of steps;
- *Workspace* principle which addresses the ergonomic factors and layout options;
- *Continuous improvement* principle which helps to ensure that a process can be self-sustaining by implementing continuous improvement and learning;

- *Workforce* principle which is based on the premise that any workflow requires manpower as an integral part of it, and;
- *Information Technology* principle which provides guidelines for ensuring that technology is viewed as an enabling option to improve the value added workflow.

Based on specifications and options developed in the analysis phase, an outline for process to be re-engineered is developed at design phase. Detail business maps, procedures and operating policies and the design supporting infrastructure are developed too. The design is validated through business modeling and interviews. Also, key performance measures are determined during the design phase. The design phase is concluded with testing the new process with a pilot before implementation phase.

At BPR implementation, the entire organization applies and institutionalizes the new design into its daily operations. The implementation phase has two components:

- Planning and executing logistics of converting on a large scale to the new mode of operation and;
- Managing the transition of the project.

Once the re-engineering plan is in place, the organization has to pull all the stops and execute it. The organization cannot live in the limbo between what it used to do and what it is going to be done. Otherwise dramatic improvements are sacrificed, people lose focus and re-engineering slips into process improvement. The re-engineering project does not end with initial change; the change has to be institutionalized into the daily operations of the organization. The transitional period is more crucial and the organizational inertial may cause the company to slip back into the old state.

The implementation of re-engineering needs people who have different roles in the re-engineering horizon. The roles played by people in re-engineering includes:-

- **Leader:** A senior executive who authorize and motivate the overall re-engineering effort;
- **Process Owner:** A manger with responsibility of the process that is re-engineered. It is his process that is re-engineered;
- **Re-Engineering Team:** A group of individuals who are dedicated to re-engineering of the particular process;
- **Steering Committee:** A strategy team made up of senior managers who will make the strategy for re-engineering in the company and monitors the re-engineering effort and;

- **Re-engineering Czar:** An individual responsible for developing re-engineering techniques and tools within the company and achieving synergy across various re-engineering effort that are taking place at an organization. Czar has two important functions; Enabling and supporting the process owners and re-engineering teams, and coordinating all the ongoing re-engineering activities in an organization.

Modeling Methods for Business Process Re-Engineering

Business process modelling is a representation of organizational information with an idea of abstraction through use of tools such as a conceptual framework. An organization need to model a business process for easy studying of a problem that lead to inefficient and ineffective business process. At this juncture, identifying a modeling methods is inevitable. In this regard, modeling methods are used to study and identify a business process with a problem, identify causatives of such problem and suggest a solution to a problem. There are many modeling methods for BPR technique, however, in this chapter only three modeling method has be presented. The methods presented are flow charts, real business process modeling and cause-effect diagram.

Flow Charts for Business Process Re-Engineering

This method was introduced by Frank and Lillian Gilbreth in 1920. It uses flow charts. Flow Charts show the relationships between the activities in a process. It documents, studies, plans, improves and communicates business processes. To represent a process, flow charts use several symbols. The symbols includes, but not limited to, ovals (for start/end), circle (for linking another page/flow chart), rectangle (for a process), diamond (for decision making), parallelogram (for input/output), arrow (for connecting), and cylinder (for storing data) (Heizer & Render, 2011; Slack et al., 2007). In order to study and re-engineer a business process, there are procedures to be followed, as outlined thereafter: -

1. Decide on the process to be studied. In this particular stage, identify the business process that need re-engineering.
2. Establish the boundaries and details of the process to be studied. Indicate the limit of the business process to be studied such that, what is the start and end points? At this stage, details of each activities to be re-engineered need to be presented.

3. Brainstorm and write the activities the process to be studied. By using a group of experts and experienced people identify all the activities involved in the process to be studied, however at this stage, sequential relationships among the activities is not important.
4. Arrange the process activities in appropriate sequence. By using participants, observation and documentations, establish the sequential relationships of the activities of the business process.
5. Draw the process flow chart once you reach in an agreement on the activities and sequence of the process. Use appropriate symbols, to either sketch or draw the process draw chart.
6. Review the process flow chart drawn with all stakeholders who are involved in that process to seek for their comments and consents.

Real Business Process Modeling for Business Process Re-Engineering

Business process modeling (BPM) is an activity of representing business processes for analysis, improvement and automation. Organizations have objectives to achieve, such as to improve quality, to increase delivering speed, to reduce operational costs. Business process modeling enables an organization to document information for improving business process (Heizer & Render, 2011).

Business process modeling was used at the first time by S. Williams in his 1967. The concern behind the idea was to understand better a business process for improvement. Despite that initiation, the technique gained popularity in 1990s when organizations were emphasized to think for processes and not the functions. For studying a business process, the process need to be modelled, where circles (for start/end), oval (for activities to be done), diamond (for decision making) and arrow (for connecting) are symbols used to model a business process for re-engineering and later on the following steps are used.

1. Identify a business process to be re-engineered and document it
2. Review, simulate and analyses the current business process to identify the process bottlenecks
3. Design the new business process for improved business output
4. Implement the new business process
5. Monitor the implemented business process and improve it when necessary.

Cause-Effect Diagram for Business Process Re-Engineering

When an organization is in a problem, it is better to explore all causes of the problems. The tool that can be used to explore all the causes of a problem is cause-effect diagram. Cause-effect diagram was introduced by Ishikawa in 1960s. Again, the technique was published in 1990 by him. The tool was developed for improving quality of organizational offering, however the method can be used to discuss other problems in a business process and improve it. Been the case, cause-effect diagram can be used as method for business process re-engineering (Heizer & Render, 2011; Slack et al., 2007). In order to re-engineering the process, the method has the following steps.

1. **Identify the Problem:** At the first time, an organization need to write down the problem it faces. In additional, identify who is involved, what the problem is, when and where the problem occurs.
2. **Identify the Main Factors Involved:** In this step, the organization need to identify the main causes of the problem in hand. The causes of the problem may be a system, equipment, materials, external factors, or labour.
3. **Identify the Possible Causes of the Problem:** Taking consideration of all factors presented in step 2, scrutinize all possible causes of a problem as a results of identified factors. The causes of a problem will be presented by shorter lines from the fish born of the diagram of cause-effect. If the cause is relative large or complex, it is better to break down it down into small and easy to model sub-causes.
4. **Analyse the Presented Diagram:** At this stage, one has a diagram which shows all possible causes of a problem. Therefore, one can further study and identify the causes of a problem. The process will enable one to identify the causes that actually contribute to a problem.

CONCLUSION

The chapter aimed at explaining Business Process Re-engineering and the modeling methods that can be used to implement the technique. From the chapter, it can be deduced that Business Process Re-engineering is technique that enables organizations to study a business processes to identify weaknesses and thereafter take quick and appropriate corrective actions for improved business processes and enhanced organizational performance. However, it has been deduced that Business Process Re-engineering differs with other business process improving techniques. The main difference is that Business Process Re-engineering uses information technology in effecting the business process improvement process.

Furthermore, in this chapter, it is deduced that there are several situations that lead organizations adopt Business Process Re-engineering. The situations are crisis management, anticipation management and market leadership situations. An organization need to identify a situation which is in and adopt Business Process Re-engineering for appropriate action. In this regard, Organizations which find themselves in these situations adopt Business Process Re-engineering as their salvation.

Finally, in order to effectively adopt the Business Process Re-engineering, there are modeling methods that an organization need to apply. Among the methods to be used, flow charts, real business process modeling and cause-effect diagram are modeling's to be used to effectively apply Business Process Re-engineering technique for improved business process and enhanced organizational performance.

REFERENCES

Adeyemi, S., & Aremu, M. A. (2008). Impact assessment of business Process re-engineering on organizational performance. *European Journal of Soil Science*, *7*(1), 115–125.

Al-Mashara, M., Iran, Z., & Zairi, M. (2001). Business process re-engineering: A survey of international experience. *Business Process Management Journal*, *7*(5), 437–455. doi:10.1108/14637150110406812

Aremu, M. A., & Saka, S. T. (2006). The impact of information technology on library, Management: A Marketing Perspective. Advances in Management, 5(1), 141 – 150.

Attaran, M. (2004). Exploring the relationship between information technology and business process re-engineering. *Information & Management*, *41*(5), 585–596. doi:10.1016/S0378-7206(03)00098-3

Beckford, J. (1998). *Quality, a critical introduction*. London: Routledge.

Buavaraporn, N. (2010). *Business process improvement methodology adoption for improving service quality: Case study of financial institutions in Thailand* (PhD thesis). University of Nottingham, Nottingham, UK.

Chen, Y. (2001). *Empirical Modelling for Participative Business Process Re-engineering* (Thesis). University of Warwick, Warwick, UK.

Covert, M. (1997). *Successfully Performing Business Process Re-engineering*. Visible Systems Corporation.

Cross, F. K., Feather, J. J., & Lynch, L. R. (1994). Corporate renaissance, the art of re-engineering. Cambridge, MA: Blackwell Publisher.

Davenport, T. H., & Short, J. E. (1990). The new industrial engineering: Information technology and business process redesign. *Slogan Management Review,* 11 – 27.

Dodaro, G. L. and Crwley, B. P. (1997). *Business process re-engineering assessment guide.* United States General Accounting Office-Accounting and Information management Division, 3rd Version.

Hammer, M. (1990). Re-engineering Work: Don't Automate, Obliterate. *Harvard Business Review,* 104–112.

Hammer, M., & Champy, J. (1993). *Re-engineering the Corporation: A Manifesto for Business Revolution.* New York: Harper Business.

Heizer, J., & Render, B. (2011). *Operations Management* (10th ed.). Prentice Hall.

Housel, T., & Bell, A. (2001). Surges and sediments: Shaping the reception of re-engineering. *Information & Management, 38*(4), 239–251. doi:10.1016/S0378-7206(00)00069-0

ISO 9001. (2008). Introduction and Support Package: Guidance on the Concept and Use of the Process Approach for management systems. ISO/TC 176/SC 2/N 544R3.

Laudon, K. C., & Laudon, J. P. (2006). *Management information system: Managing the digital firm* (10th ed.). Upper Saddle River, NJ: Prentice Hall.

Lenk, K. (1997). Business process re-engineering in public sector. In Beyond BPR in public administration. Amsterdam: IOS Press.

Manganelli, R. L., & Klein, M. M. (1994). *The re-engineering Handbook: A step-by-step guide to business transformation.* New York: American Management Association.

Nakatani, K. (1999). *An Extended Object-Oriented Modeling Method for Business Process Re-engineering* (Thesis). Texas Tech University

Shin, N., & Jemella, D. (2002). Business process re-engineering and performance improvement: The Case of Chase Manhattan Bank. *Business Process Management Journal, 8*(4), 351–363. doi:10.1108/14637150210435008

Slack, N., Chambers, S., & Johnston, R. (2007). *Operation Management* (5th ed.). London: Prentice Hall.

Stoddard, D. B., & Jarvenpea, S. L. (1995). Business process redesign tactics for managing radical change. *Journal of Management Information Systems, 12*(1), 61–107. doi:10.1080/07421222.1995.11518071

Sungau, J., & Msanjila, S. S. (2012). On IT enabling of business process re-engineering in organizations. *Advanced Materials Research*, *404-408*, 5177–5181.

Talwar, R. (1993). Business re-engineering-a strategy-driven approach. *Long Range Planning*, *26*(6), 22–40. doi:10.1016/0024-6301(93)90204-S

Teng, J. T., & Kettinger, W. J. (1995). Business process redesign and information architecture: Exploring the relationship. *ACM SIGMIS*, *26*(1), 30–42. doi:10.1145/206476.206481

Whitman, M. E. (1996). IT divergence in re-engineering support: Performance expectations vs perceptions. *Information & Management*, *30*(5), 239–250. doi:10.1016/S0378-7206(96)01046-4

Xiaoli, L. (2011). Correlation between business Process re-engineering and operation performance of National Commercial Banks. *Journal of Innovation and Management*, *7*, 981–985.

Chapter 3
The Usage of R Programming in Finance and Banking Research

Ceyhun Ozgur
Valparaiso University, USA

Sanjeev Jha
Valparaiso University, USA

Bennie B. Myer-Tyson
Valparaiso University, USA

David Booth
Kent State University, USA

ABSTRACT

R has grown tremendously over the years in terms of number of users and capability with the development of hundreds of packages. In this chapter, the authors investigate the usage of R in finance and banking areas. They begin with a comparative analysis of R with other computing software like SAS and Python. Then they discuss the reasons for the growth of R's usage in financial sector. They end with a comparative evaluation of Python and R's strengths and weaknesses in a classroom. R is software designed to run statistical analyses and output graphics by user-input code. It can run on virtually any operating system and is open source. This makes the software highly appealing, as it is able to keep up with the demands of a growing number of varied business structures. Standard software has been SAS and Python; however, a growing number of jobs are posted looking for experience using R in the data analytics field.

DOI: 10.4018/978-1-5225-5522-3.ch003

INTRODUCTION

R is software designed to run statistical analyses and output graphics by user-input code. It can run on virtually any operating system, and is open source. (Ooi, 2011, The R Foundation, 2017). This makes the software highly appealing, as it is able to keep up with the demands of a growing number of varied business structures. Standard software has been SAS and Python; however, a growing number of jobs are posted looking for experience using R in the data analytics field (Muenchen, 2017). This shifting interest paradigm has consequences not only for those who have graduated and are seeking employment, but also for those who are currently in statistics or analytics programs. The changing field preferences should be reflected in the way data science is taught so as to give students the best possible education and preparation for working in the field. One of the core benefits of teaching R to students is that it is a highly standardized programming language (Economist 662f, 2014). This means that students need not worry about highly variable language structures or deep understanding of the different languages with which one can code. Rather, they are free to focus on the analytics side of R and understand the applications of the program in a real-world setting.

LITERATURE REVIEW

R's Growth and Comparison to Other Software

R's growth in the data analytics field has come to the point where it is beginning to surpass the field standard software such as SAS, SPSS, Stata, and MatLab (Muenchen, 2017). This surge in the number of R users has led to an increase in job postings asking that applicants understand and can use R. The field paradigm changes are well marked by Muenchen (2017) who shows the overall trend in Figures 1, 2, and 3. These figures clearly show the spike in R's popularity, especially over the last 5 years.

As is evidenced by the figures, R is beginning to overtake the big names in the field. While it is more popular than SAS, it has not yet reached the same level of triumph over Python. However, Muenchen (2017) notes that this could be due to the fact that Python jobs are much more diverse in nature than R jobs are, by virtue of the way the two different programs are set up. Python is just as code-heavy as R, but R is restricted in its application just to data and information science applications. Therefore, one must be careful when attempting to draw conclusions from the general trend and must look closer at the data science landscape specifically.

As you can see the Figure 4, popularity of Python is increasing the most in this 10 year period. However, R is stable also showing slight growth in usage.

Figure 1. Number of data science jobs posted on a job search website with over 250 job hits

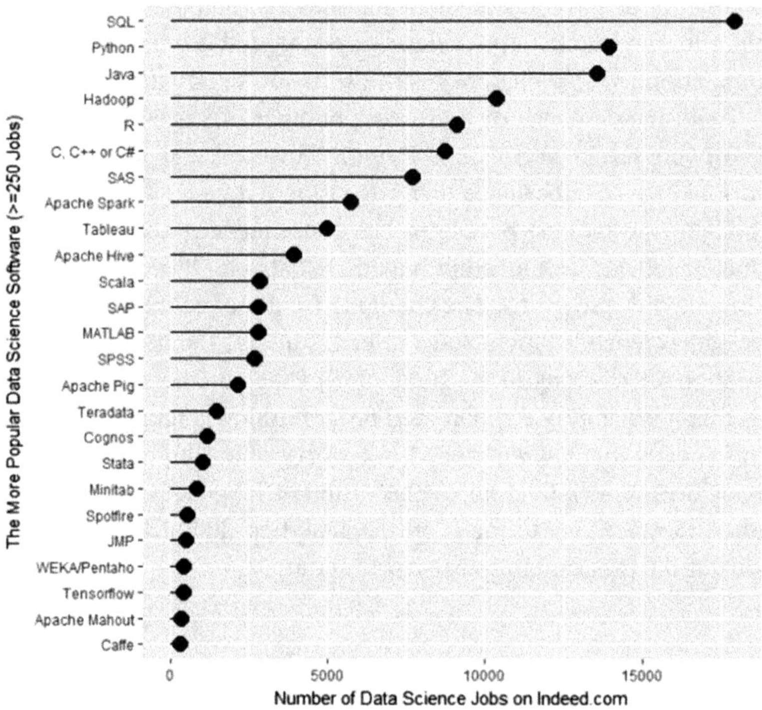

Figure 2. The job posting trends for SAS (orange) and R (blue)

Figure 3. The job posting trends for Python (orange) and R (blue)

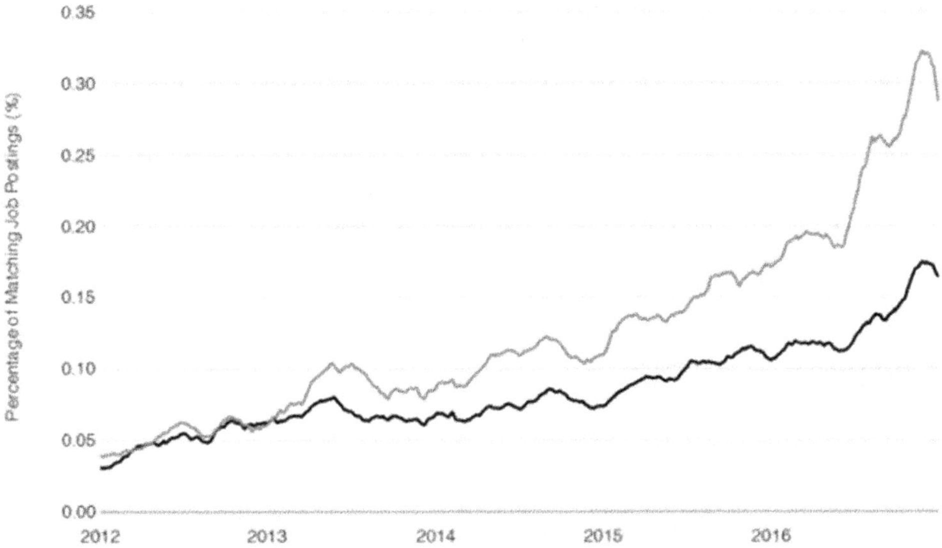

Figure 4. Comparison of primary of programing languages

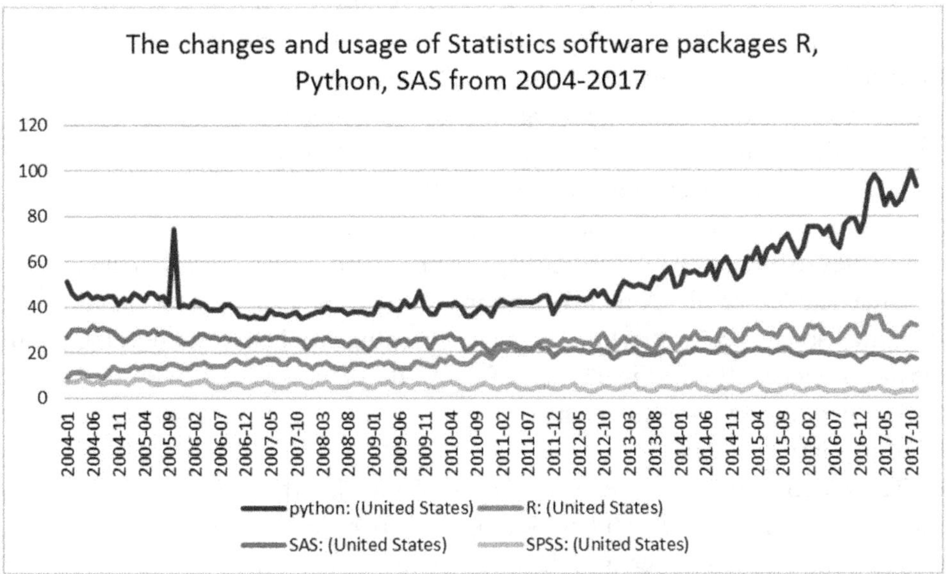

The popularity of R in the field is reflected by the amount of resources available with which to learn R. There are several books written devoted to the software overall and to general packages (Varma, 2016, Springer 2014) which can complement the various websites, blogs, video tutorials, and conference papers available to new and veteran users (Rickert, 2014, Mejia, 2013). This plethora of available information also makes teaching the software easier, as students are able to access information about specific packages or the debugging process with a quick web search. The packages themselves are easy to use and install; they are available from R's CRAN depository (R Core Development Team, 2016) and need only be installed once (Arriata, 2016).

DISCUSSION OF R

R in Finance

R's flexibility as a software means that it is fully able to perform the necessary tasks for any branch of data analytics. One of the main subsets of analytics where R shines is the financial applications. There have been several programs written to facilitate the usage of R in such a setting; one of the most popular is jrvFinance (Trajanov, 2017). This package, alongside the standard tools of R and the bundle package Rmetrics (Trajanov, 2017), allows users to perform the necessary standard financial computations in the software. The largest advantage of this program is that it is set up to mimic the Excel format with which students and new users are likely very familiar. This decreases the time spent trying to decipher a readout or table produced from the R code and as well facilitates learning by analogy. As Varma (2016) notes in his overview of the jrvFinance package, there are several specific commands to ensure that the correct operations are being performed. In addition to this, the detailed breakdown of the options of the commands also can aid new and learning users in acquiring skillsets that will continue to help them develop within the data science field. JrvFinance specifically allows for the Internal Rate of Return (IRR) operations within R, which are arguably indispensable and should be taught to all incoming students.

These applications of R extend outside of the classroom and job settings. As Moore (2014) notes, one could use R to manage one's own finances. This handling of personal data on a personal level has twofold benefits. First and foremost, consumers are able to better understand the practices around data analytics (and may therefore be more willing to participate in data collection on the whole, which facilitates greater analytical power in future tests) because they can manipulate their own data and understand the security measures upon examining the files received from their banks. Secondly, this careful tracking of one's own finances could be considered good practice or even as a simple introductory exercise to learning R. This could reduce the user or student push back against learning a new method, as they can immediately see and apply the benefits to their own lives. In addition, there are several packages available to help students analyze financial data from large companies if they would rather work with truly anonymous data (Rickert, 2014).

Teaching With R

As noted earlier, R is becoming more and more commonplace when looking at the data analytics landscape. This means that those wishing to go into a career in big data analytics should be looking to learn this software. However, there has been some pushback against it from the academic community.

As Mohamed (2017) notes, there are different optimal uses for different software packages. This means that users may feel they are wasting their time in learning new software if they can manipulate the data in another. However, learning the new program can give one a competitive edge and make tasks which are possible in other software much less cumbersome when run in R.

The argument against learning R as a code is that it is typically difficult to handle, since it has its own syntax (Markham, 2015). However, this ignores the plethora of material available to help one learn the course, which has been previously addressed. The other main concern is that code-heavy software is not as user-friendly in the initial stages. While this may be true, R lends itself to a greater understanding of the data by those running the software. The plotting packages (especially ggplot2) can make the data readable to the layperson (Arratia, 2016, Markham, 2015, Meija, 2013, Nau, 2016). The main concern for those teaching others to use software should be whether or not the student understands the program's logic and method of operation. There is a multitude of ways to make data friendly to the average consumer later; the primary focus for education should be on mastery of software operation.

Returning to the financial application mentioned earlier, a simple overview program of teaching R for IRR could look as follows: the user would download FinCal or jrvFinance (or any similar package) and load its syntax. The next step would be to load the package in the current R session (as packages are not stored from session to session). In FinCal specifically, the IRR function is computed by providing cash flow (the first of which is the initial outlay). The syntax would be written as: *irr(cf)* where cf is the cash flow. To extend the example, the syntax *irr(cf=c(-10, 3, 4, 5, 6))* would compute an IRR of 0.2488813for the cash flow specified in the function. The FinCal package can be further extended into computations such as future or present value, however that is beyond the scope of this argument. The presented example is a fairly simple string of code to learn, and should not be considered difficult for experienced undergraduate students. Even those without coding experience could find this to be a simple exercise, as this is not drastically different from applying a function in hand-calculation of a value (Markham, 2015).

As students learn the basics of R and become accustomed to using the software, they can understand the bidirectional effect it has on the job and data analytics market currently (Rickert, 2014). The software grew in popularity in response to the increasing overall demands on big data analytics and the need for programs which could handle massive data files. As R grew in popularity by filling this need, it also changed how computational finance was done; the availability of a new and versatile tool is apt to reframe at least a portion of the discussions around calculation and application. This in turn affects the way people think about the standard equations and affects the solution to current, ongoing problems. All of these factors are highly relevant for those entering the field, and thus point to a necessity to teach this software.

While it may seem overwhelming at first to attempt to use R for financial applications, this is certainly not the case. Rickert (2014) notes that there were at least 70 separate finance packages available in 2014. This may seem daunting to instructors attempting to select the easiest packages to learn for first-time students, but there are several features and sources available to help one make the decision. The R and CRAN websites both showcase prominent packages (R Core Development Team, 2016, The R Foundation, 2017) and the packages themselves are often hosted on the authors' webpages which have further breakdowns and instructions (Rickert, 2014). There are also multiple blog or article comparisons of the package as well as video tutorials available to those who wish to examine packages in greater detail.

CONCLUSION

Concerns of Teaching R

R is not without its drawbacks, however topical it may be (Ooi, 2011). There could be conflict between the main package and a supplemental one. This could especially be the case for older packages which may not necessarily be compatible with the latest version of R. While the development team does attempt to mitigate this problem by having strict submission guidelines (R Core Development Team, 2016), it is possible that a once-favored package could stop being updated and, in turn, break down other packages which were relying upon it. This could be compounded by the fact that open source software does not necessarily have a dedicated IT team (Ooi, 2011), which could lead to headaches for both instructors and students.

A further complicating factor of using R is that there could be issues ensuring version standardization across different machines (Ooi, 2011). This is an especially relevant concern if students are using their own personal computers or laptops to do homework. The versions available to them and written for their Operating Systems may have a different setup to what the classroom computers hold or what the instructor is familiar with. A majority of these problems, however, can be remedied by working through third-party software (Ooi, 2011). This software can help refocus R and the packages associated with it to fix buggy installations or known user errors. The major downside to using third-party software, however, comes in the form of cost (Ooi, 2011). Students may find themselves paying for additional software to fix one package that the instructor is familiar with when they could instead be using a separate package at no additional cost to them. This may mean ensuring that staff are all making the most optimal choices for their students both in terms of learning and cost, which can take up more instructor time (particularly when taking compatibility issues into account).

As you can see Table 1, Python is the most preferred primary language followed by R, SAS, and SPSS.

It is possible that the outside materials students could use to aid their understanding are outdated or perhaps incorrect for a particular application of the program (Economist 662f, 2014). This could lead to students having difficulty as they attempt to piece together separate methods of learning or perhaps incorrectly integrate classroom and outside information. R itself is also inconsistent once one gets into the user-created packages. The different authors all have a unique way of writing their code, and

Table 1. Comparison of Primary programing language based on more than 1000 developers

Primary Programing Language	Total sample size	Preferred as primary language
Python	7955	6073
R	7955	4708
SQL	7955	4261
Java	7955	1453
Hadoop/Hive/Pig	7955	1378
SAS Base	7955	738
IBM SPSS Statistics	7955	472
Amazon Machine Learning	7955	425
Minitab	7955	150

this lack of standardization could cause headaches for students and instructors. The easiest solution may be to spend time developing a course-standard language and package set, however this also adds to the time burden on the instructor.

The focus of R itself may not expand well outside of the classroom. R as a program is concerned with how interpretable a model is (Markham, 2015), which comes at the cost of forecasting integrity. While this is useful for a purely statistical course, this does not lend itself well to the finance world in particular. Forecasting is a large part of the field and cannot be ignored if one is to get a full understanding of how data interacts. This is especially true in analytics, where forecasts are often used to make business decisions and should therefore be as accurate as possible.

Data input into R can be difficult at first. This is because of the necessary steps to transform raw data into something meaningful (Markham, 2015). The more time a user has to spend inputting data, the more likely they are to get frustrated with the process. This is especially true when having to ensure that there are no format incompatibilities or inconsistencies with the software being used. R is also not the best tool on the market to explore data (another key component of real-world finance applications). There are packages out there but more elegant solutions can be found by abandoning the software altogether.

Benefits of Teaching R

While R, like any software package, does have its drawbacks, there are also massive benefits to using R. The first is the plethora of webpages with a comprehensive list of packages with brief description of each package on a variety of data analysis subjects. For example, Dirk Eddelbuettel (2017) maintains a webpage with a list of packages in the domain of Empirical Finance. The webpage is grouped by topics such as standard regression models, time series, finance, risk management, books using R for Financial analysis, data and date management, and a list of R packages. Similarly, others have maintained webpages on topics like time series, econometrics, multivariate analysis, and optimization. We truly believe this consolidated list of packages and methods would help instructors and researchers in keeping up with the latest development. This thorough documentation means that instructors who are concerned about getting the best value out of the packages used are able to examine each one in a good amount of detail. This can cut down on time commitments from the instructors, as they are able to research what has already been written rather than attempting to put together a course from scratch. Rickert (2014) also notes that there is a wide variety of resources out there to aid in the decision of which packages with which to begin.

The interdependent relationship mentioned earlier is also a benefit of teaching R. Software that has, as Rickert (2014) notes, changed the way a field looks at a problem is not likely to fall by the wayside. Additionally, keeping up with such innovative software gives students a competitive edge in the job market as well as a real-time understanding and application of the software. This allows for current-issue exploration and earlier research starting points, which can further bolster a student's career or opportunities.

The field of interest is highly relevant to the decision to teach or not teach R. While R may not be the best decision for finance based solely on the focus towards interpretability over forecasting, this is not to say it is not applicable (Markham, 2015). Certainly, there are those who would be more concerned with understanding models, especially in an introductory course to R. Better forecasts tend to come with higher understanding of a program or method and the underlying assumptions it contains. This understanding can only be garnered by first starting with highly interpretable models; from there, one could expand to forecasting-specific R packages (to shift focus) or to another language or software in order to double-check the computational output. While this may initially seem like more of a drawback than a benefit, the experience of double-checking models is very handy when considering outliers or unique market events (both of which are highly applicable in the real world).

If one starts in R, one is likely to have an easier time setting up the process. One need only read data into the frame, use a standard model in the simple formula language, and then review the output. This process can be much more challenging in Python or other languages (Markham, 2015), as there are a greater number of choices to be made regarding how one analyzes data or constructs the model to run the analyses. Therefore, the software with fewer initial choices, R, is better for those who are just beginning to work with statistical software. As one develops model complexity a shift to other languages or software may be more comfortable, but the basics should be presented in a bare-bones environment to allow for a simple breakdown and higher student understanding of the underlying processes. Even the installation of R is made simple; R Studio (the "de facto IDE" for R) and CRAN are both easily installed atop the basic package. Even the packages from the GitHub website is simple thanks to the devtools package that comes in CRAN (Markham, 2015). This means that students will spend less time on installation and more time working with the program directly and interpreting output, which facilitates faster learning. Additionally, the process of reusing installed packages (booting only the ones needed in a particular session) can save on CPU and RAM, which also speed the learning process and decrease frustration by reducing or eliminating time spent fixing errors or waiting for lag to subside.

R is also superior in data visualization. The best data visualization is done through R's ggplot2 package (Arratia, 2016, Markham, 2015, Meija, 2013). Once the core principles (and the "grammar" of graphics) are understood by students, ggplot2 becomes a natural extension onto plot building and produces sophisticated and attractive plots. This means that students are able to work more with complex and realistic plots as they advance in the course and their understanding of the software overall (Meija, 2013). Ggplot2, when compared to other packages or software, tends to outperform. While there is some argument for working directly with the basic R capabilities (Nau, 2016), the overwhelming argument is that more complex plots are better created in ggplot2. This package has a higher caliber default setting than the barebones R installation and necessarily makes it easier to work with multiple levels of a variable in one plot rather than examining them side-by-side. This also means that users are able to begin presenting their findings in a method that is accessible to the layperson. This coding- and user-friendly graphic creation can therefore increase the time spent on interpretation and application rather than presentation aid creation. Multivariate plots are made more understandable by adding in a faceting command. This means that each value of a variable receives its own plot in its own color. This color scheme can carry over to continuous variables instead of just working well for categorical variables, and it can contribute to the multi-layered plots (Meija, 2013). This further increases the readability of graphs as the color distinctions make separate categories or treatments more apparent. Meija (2013) does note, however, that ggplot2 could be a poor choice if one is dealing with a large variety of fancy graphics, and to that end Nau (2016) agrees; the best solution for each course or student should be determined individually in order to ensure the highest quality outcome for effort input.

The package fidelity concerns have been greatly addressed by R's Core Development Team (2016). Their site submission guidelines for package acceptance are quite strict. Every submission must go through a form and must then be confirmed by the author of the package. Uploads must adhere to strict formatting guidelines and should be thoroughly debugged by the author before being submitted. There should not be any errors that arise when working with the package (or, if there are errors, they must be ignorable and clearly not interfering with the analyses). Furthermore, updates are expected to be the responsibility of the package owner. Therefore, continued use of a package is left up to the author, and special treatments of the package need to be noted upon submission (such as a lack of backward compatibility). R's Core Development Team (2016) expects that the authors are proactively involved in the maintenance and status of their submissions, and they also expect that patches should be few and far between. To that end, they require that packages submitted to them be tested in Windows (especially if the author is not working from a Windows machine), which could reduce compatibility headaches for instructors so long as one is able to secure a computer lab with working recent updates. They also require that any packages which may be affected by a software update are diligently reported to them and that those who rely on the packages are given ample time to make the necessary changes to their systems. This also means that the author is to be proactive in the application of their package and that they are expected to keep up with the community feedback around its usage. They need to stay informed with what's going on, and to that end, this prevents a large number of poor packages from being submitted.

Personal Experience

One of the authors has personal experience with learning separate statistical analysis software. It should be noted that this experience was in the context of statistical applications rather than strictly business or finance, but it is nonetheless a student's perspective on the possible outline of a course in order to ensure students are receiving the maximum amount of exposure to different software. This author believes that Excel, as common software, works as a jumping-off point for a program. To that end, SPSS should be the next logical step. The setup is virtually identical except that SPSS contains built in statistical functions which are not available in the standard installation of Excel. This primes new users to understand the basics of statistics by computer computation in a format highly analogous to one they have seen before. As familiarity with SPSS increases, users are free to work outside of the spreadsheet window in order to directly code the statistical commands. The commands for SPSS are highly forgiving and very straightforward, meaning that little to no prior programming experience is not a hindrance. Moving forward into higher-level software, this author presents the possible path of SPSS to Python to Stata to SAS to R. Stata has more stringent coding than SPSS but is still fairly lenient compared to languages set up to mimic computer coding. This makes Stata the perfect software to transition from a menu-based approach to a code-based one. Once a user has achieved Stata mastery, moving on to SAS is simple. While the formatting of SAS code is much stricter than Stata, the logic is fairly consistent. Plus, upon mastering SAS coding, one can easily shift to coding in R as the programs are quite similar. This experience could be gathered over three or four undergraduate courses, which are certainly manageable for students and instructors.

Overall Conclusion

While R may be comparatively new in the data analytics field, this does not mean it should be discounted for undergraduate business students. In spite of its newness, there are several preset packages which solve a large portion of the current finance and data analytics problems. These packages will continue to remain relevant, especially as user-generated data continues to grow. Thus, giving students an understanding of the software in their undergraduate programs primes them both for more advanced courses (either in undergraduate or graduate programs) as well as for the real-world applications and problems that come with using software. There are drawbacks to R, just like there are to any specific program, but these do not outweigh the benefits. R is clearly making a mark on the analytics field, with finance in particular, and should therefore be considered when updating collegiate programs to reflect the modern concerns and approaches to problem solving.

REFERENCES

Arratia, A. (2016, October 7). *Getting started with R*. Retrieved from: http://computationalfinance.lsi.upc.edu/?page_id=87

Economist 662f. (2014). R v. Stata v. others. [Web log comment]. Retrieved from: https://www.econjobrumors.com/topic/r-v-stata-v-others

Eddelbuettel, D. (2017, April 25). *CRAN Task View: Empirical Science*. Retrieved from: https://cran.r-project.org/web/views/Finance.html

Google. Trends. (2004-2017). Retrieved from https://trends.google.com/trends/explore?date=all&q=python,%2Fm%2F0212jm,SAS

Krill, P. (2016). *Businesses stick with Java, Python, and C*. Retrieved from https://search.proquest.com/docview/1808338164?pq-origsite=summon

Lambert, K. (2013). *Fundamentals of Python: Data Structures*. Retrieved from https://ebookcentral.proquest.com/lib/valpo-ebooks/reader.action?docID=3136674

Markham, K. (2015, February 2). *Should you teach Python or R for data science?* Retrieved from: http://www.dataschool.io/python-or-r-for-data-science/

Mohamed, O. (2017 February 27). R software for statistical computing: useful in finance? [Web log comment]. Retrieved from: https://www.researchgate.net/post/R_software_for_statistical_computing_useful_in_finance#view=58bd86c196b7e4950c77810e

Moore, B. (2014, January 4). *Analyse Your Bank Statements Using R*. Retrieved from: https://www.r-bloggers.com/analyse-your-bank-statements-using-r/

Muenchen, B. (2017, March 1). *Data Science Job Report 2017: R Passes SAS, But Python Leaves them Both Behind*. Retrieved from: https://www.r-bloggers.com/data-science-job-report-2017-r-passes-sas-but-python-leaves-them-both-behind/?utm_source=feedburner&utm_medium=email&utm_campaign=Feed%3A+RBloggers+%28R+bloggers%29

Ooi, H. (2011, December 15). *R and SAS in Banking*. Retrieved from: http://files.meetup.com/1685538/R%20and%20SAS%20in%20Banking.pdf

R Core Development Team. (2016, November 18). *Submission*. CRAN Repository Policy. Retrieved from: https://cran.r-project.org/web/packages/policies.html#Submission

Rickert, J. (2014, May 8). *R and Finance*. Retrieved from: http://blog.revolutionanalytics.com/2014/05/r-and-finance.html

The R Foundation. (2017). *The R Project for Statistical Computing*. Retrieved from: https://www.r-project.org/

The R User Conference. (2013 July 12). *Book of Contributed Abstracts*. Retrieved from: https://www.r-project.org/conferences/useR-2013/docs/useR2013_abstract_booklet.pdf

Trajanov, D. (2017, February 27). R software for statistical computing: useful in finance? [Web log comment]. Retrieved from: https://www.researchgate.net/post/R_software_for_statistical_computing_useful_in_finance#view=58bd86c196b7e4950c77810e

Varma, J. (2016 August 29). *Package 'jrvFinance'*. Retrieved from: https://mran.microsoft.com/web/packages/jrvFinance/jrvFinance.pdf

Chapter 4 The Importance of IT on Preventing Organizational Amnesia: An Empirical Study on Preventin Organizational Amnesia

Gül Selin Erben
Beykent University, Turkey

ABSTRACT

The ratio of benefiting from company's own memory is one of the most important factors for a company's success. However, firms are not aware of their memory capacity or failure to protect. Therefore, the success of the company is delayed and or affected negatively. Because of organizations' natural tendency to forget, memory loss is evaluated as an inevitable consequence. Memory loss or organizational amnesia at the organizations is defined as restricting the ability to develop organizational learning or failure to create a value by using owned information of the company. Organizational amnesia in organizations shows itself in various forms such as repetitive losses of competencies and previously learned information because effectiveness decrease leads to repetition of the same mistakes. In this context, the aim of this chapter is to create an organization memory database known as a knowledge repository in order to minimize memory loss in the organization and to determine the information types which is being recorded in the database.

DOI: 10.4018/978-1-5225-5522-3.ch004

TYPES OF KNOWLEDGE

Knowledge is a familiarity, awareness or understanding of someone or something, such as facts, information, descriptions, or skills, which is acquired through experience or education by perceiving, discovering, or learning.

Organizations should determine its strategies in order to produce information. Moreover, that strategy determination can be completed after giving the decision who is the information creators. Level of individuals? Whole team? Or entire department? To reach that information, potential information creators should be detected in the company before starting to operate. When the organization cannot create information, it can not even mention the existence of information sharing and information usage. Individuals, teams or departments are the creators of information in the company because company by itself can never create information.

"The key players, departments and their interaction among each other, have an essential role during information creation." (Nonaka, and Takeuchi, 1995; 14). Created information can be in two different form. Which are; "Explicit Knowledge" and "Tacit Knowledge" .

Explicit Knowledge is a knowledge that can be expressed clearly by words, symbols, pictures, photographs or diagrams. These explicit forms can be easily shared via presentations or verbal interactions. (Collins,2001;71) In explicit knowledge, academic or technical data can be expressed in formal language and can be stored in the company's knowledge store. Explicit knowledge is stored in hierarchical structure. This type of knowledge can be very helpful for the potential problems which company will face in the future. Therefore, it is very important to save and store this kind of information in company's knowledge store or database and re-access them when its needed. (Smith, 2001; 315). Tacit Knowledge is the collective information. Individual's past experiences and the knowledge that is developed based on the beliefs and attitudes in their minds are the examples of tacit knowledge. There are two dimensions which are technical and cognitive. "Tacit knowledge's technical aspect is the information" (Barbiero, 2003;22). "Cognitive side consists of beliefs, ideals, ideas, opinions, stereotypes and mental models. (Barbiero, 2003;22)." These models are divided into two models. The first item is named as 'Human Information Processing' which means how human beings process the information in their mind by them. The second item is known as 'Social Information Processing'. In other words, people with a social presence by using their own social circles emphasize how information is handled. (Ocasio, 2001; 39-60).

Orgnizational Learning

Since 1980's it has been understoof that the most valuable and important source of the organizations are its human resources. Therefore, to ensure organizational learning, companies need to focus on individual learning firstly. Individual learning does not guarantee organizational learning, but without presence of individual learning, organizational learning cannot be done (Senge, Personel Mastery,2004;132). One of the most important things in organization level is sharing information with each other in the organization. As a part of organizational culture, employee roles and principles play an effective and active role on the way of becoming a learning organization (Marquardt, 2002;12-14). Basic elements of creating a learning organization can be seen in figüre 1.

These five elements dynamically affect each other and they also complement each other on the way of being a learning organization. If one of these elements is weak or missing, all the rest are in danger or in risky situation. Learning process is the core of learning organizations.

Increased productivity in organizational level shows continuous and consistent development. Ray Stata (1998) explained the difference between organizational learning and, individual learning from the perspective of two different axes. Firstly; he specified that the ideas regarding organizational learning can be created via

Figure 1. Basic Elements of Learning Organization
Source: Marquardt, 2002

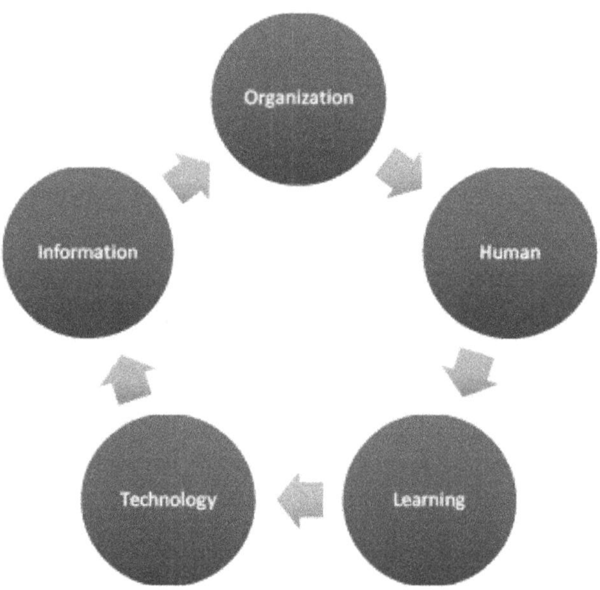

information and individual's intellectual models in the company. Secondly Marquardt noted that organizational learning can be created via organization's past experiences and information (Marquardt, 2002; 43).

LearningTypes

Taking lessons from past means to learn process after analyzing the things that has been done in the past. This style can be applied for the learning process in a specific level (individual, team or organization). The mistakes that have been done in the past are being maintained to avoid having the same mistakes all over again. This will lead to change or take a precaution for future actions or mistakes.

Anticipatory Learning based on prediction, it is an ideal learning style to provide the mistakes that can happen earlier. It requires more creativity. It needs knowledge and skills to understand future possibilities and the ability to collaborate in creating a preferred future. Anticipatory learning has four dimensions: **foresight, identity, direction setting and innovation**. The foresight dimension analyzes what we need to know about alternative futures. The future is not predetermined. It is shaped by countless events, conditions, and choices. The methodologies of foresight make learners aware of what the future will require of them. These methodologies include orienting in time, exploring future images, environmental scanning, forecasting, brainstorming wild cards, and scenario development.The identity dimension examines what we believe about the world and ourselves. We cannot understand future possibilities or collaborate in creating preferred futures until we grasp how much of what we see today and expect tomorrow comes from inside us. Our mental models shape our thinking and evolution as individuals, organizations or societies. What we learn and do is bounded by our values, beliefs, emotions and intelligences. If our identity is bound in a set of beliefs that is no longer useful, we need to adapt to new ways of thinking about ourselves and our world. The methodologies of identity include using metaphors, values, alternative cultures, multiple intelligences, learning style and personality preferences, and emotional intelligence.The direction setting dimension forges the learning of foresight and identity into decisions about what we want to create in the future and how we will do it. We use personal reflection and strategic conversations to define our vision for the future. Then we choose goals and actions that will organize our efforts into making this preferred future happen. Collaboration gives us the capacity to take on difficult challenges at any level from individual to global.

The innovation dimension explores the solutions we can create together. What innovations are required to achieve our preferred future? Improvements and breakthroughs emerge from processes of creative, cross-disciplinary learning. Innovation practices and techniques that increase the quantity and quality of ideas are like calisthenics for the mind and spirit. The methodologies of innovation are unlearning, brainstorming, multidisciplinary learning, simulations, experiencing the context and evaluation.

Peter Senge's 5 Discipline and Learning Organizations

In Early 1990's "Fifth Discipline" book of Peter Senge has been chosen as "the book opens new horizons" administrative book of last 75 years by Harvard Business Review. Peter Senge's "The Fifth Discipline" is being understood by many companies and public corporations as a brand new concept in other words they started to learn concept of organization and to become learning organization. (Smith, 2001).

5 disciplines of Peter Sange which he found in order to create a learning organization in the companies are: *personal mastery, mental models, building shared vision, team learning and system thinking.* Although these five components have been developed separately, they are very critical and vital values to ensure the success of organization and way to create a learning organization (Senge Fifth Discipline, 1994,:10). Personal mastery is a discipline of continually clarifying and deepening our personal vision, of focusing our energies, of developing patience, and of seeing reality objectively. (Senge Fifth Discipline, 1994; 56-57):

Organizational learning begins with individual learning. Individual's learning should not mean organization learning. For the personal mastery subject Peter Senge said "People that have personal mastery always live like students. For them, learning never ends. Therefore, personal mastery is not a skill or competency it is a process. Personal masters are aware of their strengths and weaknesses. Thus, they have self-confidence."Shared vision means to ask this question: "What do we want to create?" For creating shared vision individuals needs to focus on common picture.An organization can promote its own vision in the organizations hand book with formal language.

Learning as a team in organizations, needs team working rather than personal success. The collection of important information in single individual can have negative consequences that could turn into disaster for organization. On the other hand, problems which organizations face today can not be solved by a single person. Teams should consist of individuals who undertake different tasks in accordance with same objective. When team members act in common purpose, they will exchange information with each other. This will create healthy mechanism in the team.In the means of organizational learning, the importance of individual learning and the group learning is different. Individuals can learn but it doesn't necessarily be reflected to the organizational learning. Group learning is the building block of the organizational learning hence reflecting this action to the organizational scale could be achieved by group learning.Team achievements would be the basic format to the organizational success (Senge, 1994, p.219). Point of views and assumptions of individuals effects relations and actions. Mental model affects how people perceive the world and how they behave. According to our experiences and perception mechanisms, individuals have different mental models. In different conditions the responses of different individuals prove that there are different mental model.

System thinking helps to see the bigger picture and think together. It is not possible to evaluate events individually and see the connections in between. Everything in the world is in a systematic order. In order to understand how it rains, one should think in a systematic scale. Thus, it is also be thought and considered that organizations are systems. Every unit in the system is a system which is consists of smaller systems. (Senge, 1994;10). The reason that the system thinking is the fifth discipline, is its role as unifier.

Organizational Memory and Knowledge Loss in the Organizations

Individuals' problem solving and decision making abilities effect the organizations oreflect to the organizations. Every employee's (individual) problem solving abilities, strategies or techniques are different from each other. These skills can be reproducing by transferring one employee to another. In each transfer different techniques and strategies are created. The thread of coherence that characterizes organizational interpretations is made possible by sharing of interpretations. Thus, thorough this process of sharing the organizational interpretations system in part transcends in the individual level. This is why an organization may preserve knowledge when the key organization members leave. (Walsh James P. (1991):61) Therefore, organizational memory starts with the individual and continues with the organization. Once it is created, it gradually grows. In basic terms it can be said that organizational memory is the collective recollection of experience, meanings applied to experience, and inferences of meaning. Organizational memory can be acquired by routines and is located in organization rules, technologies, strategies, beliefs, culture and procedures. As it is mentioned before, the organizational memory has solid connection with individual. Individual memories adapt to the collective organizational memory while the organizational memory adapts to the individual memories.

Memory loss in companies or as known as in literature "Corporate Amnesia" is defined restriction of company's ability to develop learning capacity or failure of using the owned information efficiently. Corporate amnesia indicators show itself in such ways; loss of competence, fall of efficiency or repetition of the mistakes. There are two types of corporate amnesia. The first one is based on loss of memory in time and the second one is loss of memory based on the place. Loss of memory in time mostly occurs because of organizations' inefficiency in using some information. Loss of memory based on location occurs when the information is not shared with the organization's department and when it is not transferred from one point to another. The consequences of these kinds of company amnesias is the necessity to work hard inorder to re-gain information and they also miss the opportunity to create more information (Othman and Hashim, 2004: 276).

Factors which can cause loss of memory is given below (Pollitt, 2000: 8-10; Stoyko and Fang,2007:10)

- **Radical Change Ideas Like Benchmarking and Continuous Reconstruction etc.:** These kinds of applications contain irrelevant ideas to the past or contain fears about the past and the idea of looking to the past brings unsuccessfulness and characterizes as danger.
- **Changes in Information Systems:** The transition from paper to electronic system in the beginning then followed by transition from programming to another one causes continuous information loss, and as the consequence of irregular data storage, individuals experience some problems about reaching the correct information.
- ***Loss of Key Players or Documents by Reconstructions in the Firm and Creation of New Organizational Structure:** Individuals can get promoted or attendants can modify the document flow therefore recorded may be loss.
- **Employee Who Is Leaving the Current Position Due to Retirement or Better Job Opportunity:** If information is bonded to one single person, there may be loss of information.
- **Electronic or Software Based Information Losses:** Software or hardware which are used in the company may cause irreversible losses. Viruses, hardware or software based problems can be counted as common examples.

Consequences of Memory Loss for the Organizations

Many companies have to manage various changes and transformations from time to time. Routines may change, there may be newer working applications emerge. However, the most important point during those situations for the company is; to protect the application and values during the change. The companies, who are experiencing memory loss, suffer from time and cost inefficiencies and these losses slow down company's success level.

Main consequences of memory loss for the companies are listed below. (Pollitt, 2000: 13):

- Discontinuous, low learning policy; Retrying of five or ten years old policies or strategies. In this way companies do the same mistakes and harnesses continuously and it leads to a consecutive loop.
- Increasing vulnerability against fashion, artificial insufficiency and organizational solutions,
- Copying of innovative methods which were successful in other organizations and higher costs because of failure of adaptation.
- The failure to add value to information.
- The notion of rupture in relations and experience of inconsistency among the clients and with the other parties.

Effects of Information Technology on Organizational Memory

Information Technology is, set of tools that allows to access information. These tools can be written, non-written or verbally defined (such as programming, data communications, data conversion, storage and database systems, retrieval, systems analysis and design, systems control). In broad terms, information technology includes office automation, multimedia, and telecommunications. Like human brain, organizations also need storage for learning and comparing. In tha past, organizations were using papers for information storage. The difficult part of the written documents is accessing to them. That why indexing methodologies were developed. Organizations index their documents with respect to date, value or name. For example, when information is needed about last year's most valuable customer it can be extremely difficult to find it in the written documents. When the importance of this kind of documents increase, organizations started to created multiple documents for same data. For example; for the same customer, organizations created customer-value document, customer-year document and customer-project document. With the help of the developing technology, organizations are able to do the calculations faster. With the help of the calculator they learned how to calculate faster or with the help of the Content Management Systems, they learned how to store content and how to manage them. These improvements help organizations in time management and productivity. Both small and large companies need to scale out a plan to utilize opportunities brought by ''Information Technology''. Companies use IT in four ways ;(1) information processing tasks, (2) decision making tasks, (3) shared information through computing, and (4) innovation. (Ramey,2015; 1-10)

Information Technologies are used by companies for basic processing tasks. Printing payroll checks, creating documents for presentations, creating applications or designing websites for products or services are examples of those tasks. Information Technologies are also being used for support decision-masking tasks, and these tasks achieved through online analytical processing (OLAP). ''OLAP'' is the manipulation of information to support decision making. OLAP can range from performing simple queries on a database to determine which customers have overdue accounts, to employing sophisticated artificial intelligence tools such as neural networks and genetic algorithms to solve a complex problem or take advantage of an opportunity. You can also perform OLAP by using databases and data warehouses. (Ramey,2015; 2).

Information technology tools not only support information-processing tasks, decision-making tasks, and shared information through decentralized computing, but they also enable innovation. Tools like internet, present us with the opportunity to make research on any subject and the information acquired during the process can be used in creative design of services or products. Today, companies use IT to support their main business operations, to help internal communication and storing knowledge. In order to clarify this, three basic terms should be explained. Data, information and knowledge are some concepts that we use interchangeably in our daily lives. However, each of these concepts have different meanings with respect to information technologies. Data is the raw information. It can be meaningless without its own. (Bellinger, 2004: 21-33 Castro, & Mills, 2004:10-12). However data can be related with information. For example 1 and 7 is a data which can be stored in anywhere like paper or any database. If we combine days of the week with the 7 data then it is meaningful. Therefore, it needs to be connected. Information is meaningful data and without meaning it cannot be used. Knowledge is the combination of information and can be used by organizations. According to Marquardt, organizations loose data if they cannot create their own knowledge database. For creating knowledge database, organizations need structured systems that should be specific to organization. Whatsmore, organizations needs to create dynamic resource that may itself have the capacity to learn by the contribution of the individuals. Organizations don't have biological brains and memory, but can store information and knowledge with the help of the information and technology. Therefore storing, accessing and re-using terms are perfect metaphor for memory word (Walsh&Ungson,1991:55-57)

With the increasing environmental pressure and the increasing speed of the employee recruitment cycle, organizational memory has gained much more importance for the organizations. And this necessity is satisfied by the evolution of information technology.

Conceptualization of "IT supported organizational memory" is quite new in the literature yet. But the foundation can be seen in Konda (1992), Sandoe (1991), and Sandoe and Olfman (1992). Ackerman and Malone (1990) also, foresee that these systems (IT supported OM) will be the core functionality for the organizational memory. Quinn and Rohrbaugh also created a model that explains two concepts

(IT and Organizational Memory) together. In this model according to Quinn and Rohrbaugh, there are four steps;

(1) Internal Process, (2) Open Systems, (3) Rational Goal, (4) Human Relations.

1. **Internal Process:** Based on hierarchy, measurement, and documentation and information management. These processes bring stability and control. Hierarchies seem to function best when the task to be done is well understood and when time is not an important factor.
2. **Open Systems:** Based on an organic system, adaptability, readiness, growth, resource acquisition and external support. These processes bring innovation and creativity. People are not controlled but inspired.
3. **Rational Goal:** Based on profit, emphasis on rational action. It assumes that planning and goal setting results into productivity and efficiency. Tasks are clarified; objectives are set and action is taken.
4. **Human Relations:** Based on cohesion and morale with emphasis on human resource and training. People are seen not as isolated individuals, but as cooperating members of a common social system with a common stake in what happens.

Knowledge Capture Tools

As mentioned earlier, data, information and knowledge have a relation between each other. Within the information technology's perspective, the most basic storage unit is the data. Data can be stored with the help of Content Management Systems (CMS). Content management systems are a software application or combination of software applications that helps to create digital content. CMS systems are using databases to store data. CMS's are typically used for Enterprise Content Management (ECM) and Web Content Management (WCM). ECM's are used in many organizations for organizing and storing documents and also anyother content that has a relation with the organization. Documents management, HR content management, records management, digital asset management, workflow management are the features of the ECM tools. In time qualifications of the ECM systems are changed by the help of the organization's needs. In the year 2005, organizations used ECM for storing and reading the data. After 2006, ECM systems are also used for management of the organization. In those years, organizations stored data in an unstructured way which means that all of the information has the same value in the system. After 2008, ECM systems were used for different departments for different user models. For example, human resources (HR) use ECM for track employee information like, working hours, or storing key performance indicators (KPI), at the same time finance department use ECM for storing finance documents and profit sheets. After

2011, software companies created bigger and complex ECM tools that controls and manages nearly everything in the organization. Not only they can store data but also they can predict future by evaluating those data.

Professional and complex ECM tools generally present non-structural patterns, so that organizations have to create their own structures. In order to create structure, organizations, need to know themselves. They need to know how their operations work, how their flows work and what do they need. Therefore, many ECM software development company conduct the investigation of the organization and find their needs firstly. According to those needs they create the ECM structure. Creating structure is the most important part because it should fit to the organization. Following this, ECM companies give orientation about the ECM software usage. They teach how to add new data and how to manage and edit them. After that, organization data storage process begins. Organizations and ECM platforms needs to grow together like a new born baby. They need to learn together. Otherwise, at some point, ECM software needs bulk data storage.

Knowledge Repositories

Building knowledge includes activities ranging from market research to focus groups, surveys, competitive intelligence, and data mining applications. Building knowledge consists of six major activities: (Marquardt, 2002).

- Obtain knowledge.
- Reconstruct/synthesize knowledge.
- Analyze knowledge.
- Save and store.
- Transfer.
- Apply knowledge

Obtaining knowledge is the notion of existing information or data which is collected within or outside the organization. **Reconstruct/synthesize knowledge** can be realized by creating the new information, making a deeper research and via innovation processes. **Save and store,** online storage of the information in a systematic way in order to allow individuals in the organization to reach to information easily. **Analyze knowledge**; In order to make sense and restructure their own information, companies try various processes. Data-Mining Notion has been discoveredthrough these researches. **Transfer and Spread** with the help of technology, or by the combination of personal communication or the spread in the organization without knowing or being transferred. **Applying knowledge** is the using practice of the information among employees in the organization.

Retaining and sharing corporate knowledge has become a critical objective for companies, regardless of their size and industry. Knowledge Repository is an online database which systematically captures, organizes, and categorizes knowledge-based information. Knowledge repositories help organizations to keep knowledge and search and access it when it is needed. With the help of the ECM systems, knowledge repositories can be created in the organizations. There are several key features of creating knowledge repositories. **Centralization;** by definition knowledge repositories are for employees. That's why it must be centralized so that all of the members can access and share the data which comes from the information and knowledge. **Content management;** with the help of the content management tools (ECM) audio, video, document, pdf, finance sheets web links can be stored. The content must be linked with the keywords of the content for easy to use and easy to access. **Cost savings;** repositories can reduce the time for education or orientation. Like course materials, presentations or any training data can be stored in the repository. **Access control;** restricting content from the unauthorized users helps to secure data. That's why it needs to have login control. On the other hand, access control helps to control company's hierarchy. **Record management;** Repositories can integrate with learning management systems to blend seamlessly into learning and talent management programs.

Best Practices of Knowledge Repositories

Before creating a knowledge repository, a variety of best practices needed to be taken into consideration. Some of those steps are about user experience, some of them are about ease of use and some are about security issues. Each item has unique value of specific circumstances. (Elena C. Caprione (2010):26).

- **Ensure Quality Over Quantity:** As it mentioned before, knowledge repository is about storing information and knowledge. But it does not mean quantity is more important than quality. Every item in the knowledge repository for individuals and that's why quality is very important to understand and transfer. All the information in the knowledge repository has to be understood by the other users (employees). Information needs to be clearly defined in the knowledge repository. In order to do that, storage rules need to be set. by the others.
- **Provide Oversight and Control:** To ensure that, user access control mechanism needs to be set. Every user has different access-clearance. There are three different access types which are; no-access, read-access, and write-access. For example, public relations employee shouldn't see the finance department's information. So some items should have been restricted to the

other users. Read-access means user can read the specific item (document). Write-access means that user can change/update the item. So in order to provide control, only authorized personal can have an access to the repository in each department. There is one more different approach which is post-moderation or premoderation. Every submitted document in the repository can be saved after moderator's approval which is about pre-moderation. If the, moderator can remove the document after it is published then it is called post-moderation.

- **Protect Intellectual Property:** Intellectual properties such as patents, copyrights are the basic problem when it is about sharing and storing data. Organizations build copyright compliance and digital rights management in order to prevent such kind of problems.
- **Language Support:** Language support is needed if an organization operates in a multicontinental space. For example, if and organization services to both England and Germany, English and German language support has to be in the knowledge repository.
- **Update and Restore:** Updating and restoring is the one of the most important steps inknowledge repository. Since, by definition, information and knowledge are very dynamic concepts, and they rapidly and continuesly change.
- **Prevent Duplication:** Data duplication is a common problem for all databases and it needs to be prevented. It can be prevented by creating moderation. Adding moderation is the most basic and easy solution for duplication problem.

An Empirical Study

Organizations have faced several changes in recent years and those changes has affected them in the market. On the other hand, organizations need to compete with their rivals in the market. With the help of the information technologies, organizations learn to search and find the information faster and accurately.

In markets, competition turns to knowledge based competition. Therefore, acquiring information and increasing productivity becomes the most important element for the organizations. The simplest form of capital can be thought as information and information creates new economies in both macro and micro level. Organizations must constantly learn. More importantly, they need to save the information in their store or information pools. In the constantly changing environment conditions learning process is also affected from the change and innovations.

This research aims to create a platform (software) that stores information that learned in organization with the help of the employees (As known as knowledge repository).

This research is conducted by using "qualitative methodology" since the data gathered via interviews.

Research questions are stated below.

Research Question 1: What kind of system can be structured in order to keep the practically and theoretically learned information inside the organization?

Research Question 2: What should be the structure that would keep the information learned in the organization, which will create " knowledge repository" ?

Sampling

This research involves both corporate and small & medium and large sized organizations, which operate in Turkey. Most of the organization in my sampling are located in Istanbul European side and Anatolian side. An open ended interviews were conducted witheleven organizations, which operate in different industries. Part of the data gathering process was conducted online and the other part was done in company's offices with the authorized employees.

Procedure

As seen in the previous list, data gathered from eleven different organizations in five different sectors. Some of these interviews were conducted platforms such as Google Hangout and Skype. The others were conducted local offieces.

Table 1. Companies

Company Type	Employee Count	Interviewee	Company Name
Digital Agency	10+	Agency Manager	Company A
Software House	20+	Company Manager	Company B
Telekom Company	1000+	Product Owner	Company C
CRM Development Company	30+	Company Manager	Company D
Mobile App Development Company	10+	Company Manager	Company E
Software Development Company	10+	Company Co-Founder	Company F
Energy Company	1000+	IT Director	Company G
Survey Creation Start-up Company	5+	Co-Founder	Company H
Digital Agency	10+	Company Manager	Company I
Insurance Company	5+	Company Shareholder	Company J
Environmental Tech.	5+	Company Co-foudner	Company K

During the interviews the main purpose of this study was explained to the participants. Findings are not shared with the interviewees in order to prevent manipulation.

In order to increase the accuracy and reliability of the data, meetings are requested from the management personnel. Therefore interviews were conducted with eleven different companies with five company-manager two department manager and four company owner.

Below, there are the questions asked during the interwievs.

What kind of instructions and information are you teaching in your recruitment process?

Organizations will have to teach information during their recruitment process such as company orientations or technical details about the projects.

This information is easily learnable. But also easily forgotten by new employees who joined the company. The main purpose of this question is to examine and categorize the common pool of information which is transferred to the employees in recruitment process.

* After an employee quit your company, have you ever experienced any difficulty based on the necessity to reach an information that only he or she has? Did you regret not having the information that he/she has?

This question is the most important question in the research. It aims to find and examine the information that organizations lost and categorize them for the knowledge repositories. Another objective is to learn the importance and value for the company of data loss.

* What is the most frequent type of information that is lost inside your organization?

The purpose of this question is to examine and categorize the types of information that is lost inside the organizations.

What kind of methods are you following in order to regain the lost information?

Basic underlying purpose of this question is to find the existing solutions of the data loss in order to improve the knowledge repository.

* Are you using any kind of method or software to keep the learned information in thecompany?

The purpose of this question is to learn and examine what kind of software are used by the organizations.

FINDINGS OF THE STUDY

In this research, company's names are not mentioned in order to protect their privacy.

Company A

See Tabe 2.

Q 1: What kind of instructions and information are you teaching in your recruitment process?

A 1:

- We give information regarding working hours to the employees. As agency we give too much importance to the working hours. Our customers have to find authorized employee when its needed.
- We emphasis overtime working. As agency sometimes we work overtime in order to finish our work.
- We mention official holidays and vacation rules. Our employees have to get approval 2 months before their vacation.
- We mention how to store project related documents and tools. Archiving is very important for us employees have to archive project related documents both after and during the development.
- We mention our agency structure. We explain organizational hierarchicy. who are the superiors and subordinates.
- We mention our supply chain management and how it works.
- We mention our software development work-flow and how it proceeds in the firm.
- We give information about our suppliers.
- We mention our privacy policies; information that should not be shared and the consequences that might arise as a result of the violation of this rule.

Q 2: After an employee quit your company, have you ever experienced any difficulty based on the necessity to reach an information that only he or she has? Did you regret not having the information that he/she has?

Table 2. Company A description

Company Type	Digital Agency
Company Description	Creating Commercial movies, social media consulting and advertisement
Employee Count	15
Company Location	Istanbul
Interviewee	Head of the Agency
Interview location	Agency Office

A 2: In the agency our design documents amount and size are very big therefore back-ups are very important for us. Last year one of our old employees lost the location the documents and then he forgot to tell us before he quits. Because of that we need to design all project all over again and we couldn't able to reach him at that time. These experiences come back us with more workload at that time.

Q 3: What is the most type of information that is lost inside your organization?

A 3: We lose information mostly in project contents and product contents. Therefore, in our agency we refactor projects many times. Furthermore, we also need to archive all project related documents and information in each version. Most of the time our employees handle archives by looking to the agency archiving rules. But sometimes they forget to share the archive with the new employees. As a result, when they leave the organization, we loose the archives. As an example, we lost commercial movie raw files 5 years ago.

Q 4: What kind of methods are you following in order to regain the lost information?

A 4: When we need an information which is known by a former employee, we often try to reach that employee. If he/she is available at that time, that information is also learned by me (Agency owner) in order to prevent the information loss once again. If it is not possible, we work hard to recover that information. Sometimes recovery may not be possible due to time and cost. In those situations, we accept the fact of customer attrition

Q 5: Are you using any kind of method or software to keep the learned information in the company?

A 5: Generally, we use massive storage tools. But it needs to be designed properly. Otherwise it can be messy.

Those storage tools do not have a hierarchy by nature. As an agency, we have to create files and folders (Example: Google drive is a storage tool. We create files and folders for each customer).

Company B

See Table 3.

Q 1: What kind of instructions and information are you teaching in your recruitment process?

A 1:

- We mention about working hours to the employees. In our company we have different work hours and it depends to the job description. For example, field and sales personnel have more flexible work hours but

Table 3. Company B descriptions

Company Type	Software House
Company Description	Creating Mobile applications, working with both local and foreign customers
Employee Count	30
Company Location	Istanbul
Interviewee	Company Manager
Interview location	Company Office

developers have strict work hours and they need to synchronize their electronic cards.

- We share customer information. Who do you work with, what are the contact information, when he/she is available? We are customer-oriented firm therefore customer relationships are very important for us.
- We share software accounts and we are giving information about software that he/she will use.
- If the employee is a developer, we show project documents and project situation.
- We mention about our development work-flow and how it is continue in the firm.
- We teach how to use Apple TV. In our company we do presentations all the time in meeting room and we have a system that connects with every mac in the firm.

Q 2: After an employee quit your company, have you ever experienced any difficulty based on the necessity to reach an information that only he or she has? Did you regret not having the information that he/she has?

A 2: Yes, many. Generally, our biggest problems are about project-related. It happens especially in short term and low budget projects. After long period of time customer may want improvements on the project.

On the other hand, we are also keep learning software instructions again and again. For example, we learned technical software about server development and after some time our employee quits from his job and then we learned same software again. In fact we spent time for learning same software 5 times in 2 year.

Q 3: What is the most type of information that is lost inside your organization?

A 3: We lose information mostly on special software usage knowledge like how to use software and their account information like passwords and usernames.

Q 4: What kind of methods are you following in order to regain the lost information?

A 4: As a company we would not rather to reach old employees. First we consider possible options and outcomes to solve the problem. For example, if we lost the authentication information about some software we are opening a ticket to Software Company and requesting help from them. Or if we lost information about the usage of the software, we are spending more time on it in order to learn it again.

Q 5: Are you using any kind of method or software to keep the learned information in the company?

A 5: Generally, we use password management databases and customer management systems. Customers are really important for us therefore preventing customer-related problems before it happens is the key point.

Company C

See Table 4.

Q 1: What kind of instructions and information are you teaching in your recruitment process?

A 1:

- We mention about working hours to the employees.
- We give information about software and tools.
- We give information about equipment. For example, in our company everybody has their own data card. Almost every tool or machine in the company works with that data card.
- We mention about our development work-flow and how it is continuing in the firm.
- We are giving orientation about our organization.

Table 4. Company C description

Company Type	Telecom Company
Company Description	Vas services SMS, creating both BTB and BTC products
Employee Count	100 +
Company Location	Istanbul
Interviewee	Product Owner
Interview location	Online interview

Q 2: After an employee quit your company, have you ever experienced any difficulty based on the necessity to reach an information that only he or she has? Did you regret not having the information that he/she has?

A 2: In our organization, we develop SMS services and in those services our product owners and analysts are working with customers. If there is a problem regarding that service our analysts and development team is fixing that issue in the team. For example, last year we developed SMS package for students. After launching the service some pricing problem occurred and the solution found by our analyst. After some time, he quitted from his job and after some time we faced with similar problem again. But that time we didn't able to solve it and as a result we had to develop entire package all over again.

We are also facing workflow problems in monthly-bases. We are keep forgetting and broking our development methodologies and learning them all over again.

Q 3: What is the most type of information that is lost inside your organization?

A 3: Mostly workflows. We are performing different workflows to the different customers therefore we have very dynamic workflow categories.

Q 4: What kind of methods are you following in order to regain the lost information?

A 4: First we are calculating time and cost and if cost is affordable we start working.

Q 5: Are you using any kind of method or software to keep the learned information in the company?

A 5: We use four different content management application and one customer relation management software in order to maintain and save our work. We also use work-flow management software that we developed. One of our problem is we use many tools but all of them are different and all of them works independent from each other. It is hard to manage all of them. Sometimes we lose the connections between them.

Company D

See Table 5.

Q 1: What kind of instructions and information are you teaching in your recruitment process?

A 1:

- We mention about working hours to the employees.
- We give information about software and tools also we share passwords with them. We use password tools for that.

Table 5. Company D descriptions

Company Type	CRM Software Development Company
Company Description	Creating CRM application and services
Employee Count	30 +
Company Location	Istanbul
Interviewee	General Manager
Interview location	Company Office

- We use our own software product for customer management. And we teach that tools to new employees.
- We also teach Content Management software which employees can take vacation permissions, or see weekly schedules.

Q 2: After an employee quit your company, have you ever experienced any difficulty based on the necessity to reach an information that only he or she has? Did you regret not having the information that he/she has?

A 2: Generally, no.

Q 3: What is the most type of information that is lost inside your organization?

A 3: We taking many educations and trainings in the company. Sometimes those trainings is about the products we sell and sometimes they are related with software development methodologies. However sometimes we are taking the same course/training again. Therefore educations and trainings are the most common information loss for us.

Q 4: What kind of methods are you following in order to regain the lost information?

A 4: If there is no one in the firm that know the training we will take that training one more time. If there is one he/she will train others in several sessions.

Q 5: Are you using any kind of method or software to keep the learned information in the company?

A 5: We are using our own Content Management System.

Company E

See Table 6.

Q 1: What kind of instructions and information are you teaching in your recruitment process?

A 1:

- We mention about working hours to the employees.

Table 6. Company E descriptions

Company Type	Mobile Application Development Company
Company Description	Creating mobile application with different T.C. Government departments.
Employee Count	10 +
Company Location	Ankara
Interviewee	General Manager
Interview location	Online Interview

- We give information about our customers like location, contact info, phone, project status exc...
- If employee is related with sales we mention payment details, how to talk with clients, what platforms are we using for communications.

Q 2: After an employee quit your company, have you ever experienced any difficulty based on the necessity to reach an information that only he or she has? Did you regret not having the information that he/she has?

A 2: In our company sales representatives are changing frequently, therefore we lose customer-related data many times. For example, last year one of our old employee forgot to save customer information. Because of that we lost customer-project status and also we lost technical and commercial contract. After that we received many revises.

Q 3: What is the most type of information that is lost inside your organization?

A 3: In our company sales representatives are changing frequently because of that we are losing customer-related data.

Q 4: What kind of methods are you following in order to regain the lost information?

A 4: If the loss occurred because of an old employee we are trying to reach that employee. Otherwise first we make cost and time calculation if it is affordable then we start.

Q 5: Are you using any kind of method or software to keep the learned information in the company?

A 5: In general Turkish Republic Government departments uses their own platform. In the inside of our company we use Jira and Trello applications.

AS A CONCLUSION

According to the researches that have been done in Turkey on Information Technologies and Knowledge management, it is observed that the linkage between organizational learning and knowledge repositories is not strong enough.

As the result of this research, it is found that the companies need a platform (knowledge repository) which is easily adaptable to company and which simplifies and guides data saving process for them.

Structure of an Issue and Issue Types

In this research the term "ISSUE" is used for each learned information in the organization. When interview results have been analyzed, seven different types of "ISSUE" is developed. These developed ISSUES are grouped as follows;

Problem Solving

Based on the responses of the interviewed COMPANY C, its been realized that one of the biggest problem in organizations is problem solving and then forgetting the solution of the problem. Therefore, when organizations encounter with problems they need to save the both problem and the solution to the knowledge repository and it will help them when they encounter same kind of problem in the future. Because of that it's been released that "Problem Solving" has to be an ISSUE type

- **What Is the Problem or What Do We Want to Change:** First of all company need to save definition of the problem and this attribute will help company to search and find problem solving ISSUE when they encounter similar kind of problems
- **Why It Happens:** The information about how the problem occur will help company when they encounter similar problems.
- **Analyze Problem:** In this attribute company will save the mistakes, process and cost when the problem occurs.
- **What Is Solution or What Are the Potential Solutions:** In this attribute company will save the potential solutions and how they succeed when they apply the solution.
- **Feedbacks:** In this attribute company will save feedbacks and different perspectives of the problem solving process.

Organizational Training

Another problem of the organizations is, they keep forgetting trainings that are taken in the organization. According to the response of interview with COMPANY D strongly shows that companies need to store organization training's documents in their database. Because of that "Organizational Training" has to be an ISSUE type.

- **What Is the Training About:** What are the basics of the training and what is the title of the training?
- **Brief Summarize:** This section describes brief summary of the received training in the organization.
- **Key Points:** Important points will be recorded in this attribute.
- **What I Learned:** What I learned is the most important and the key point of this ISSUE. Therefore, users need to add most concentrated information in to this attribute.
- **Training Materials:** PowerPoint presentations and documents that are related to education will be saved to this section.

How It's Work (Equipment and Devices and Software)

After the interview with COMPANY B, its been noticed that organizations may lose knowledge about "device usage" or how to use certain software. Companies are suffering information loss about the use of software or device they use Therefore it's been decided to add, "How it's work" as an ISSUE

- **What Is Device or Software:** This section is the brief summary of the device and software
- **Usage Instructions:** How do I use this software or device. What are the authentication credentials?
- **Key Points:** What are the key points in the software or use of the device.
- **Feedbacks:** It includes user's feedback and key points.

Workflow

Based on the responses with the COMPANY C it's been noticed that organizations may lose workflow knowledge and it effects their production time.

Therefore, it's been decided to add "Workflow" as an ISSUE

    - **What Are the Steps of the Workflow:** What are the steps and how to use these steps in Workflow?
    - **What Are the Important Things of Each Step:** Important points and operation processes in each step.
    - **What Are the Feedbacks of Each Step:** Highlights and information about the process.

Software Instructions

Based on the responses of the interview with COMPANY B it's been realized that losing information about the software can effect company in a bad way. Usernames and password, usage of the software technical detail has to be stored into knowledge repository. Because each time company loses time and effort in order to learn it again. Therefore, it's been decided to add "Software instructions" as an ISSUE

- **What Is the Software About:** Brief information about the software. When do we need that software?
- **How Can We Use It:** How do I use this software. What are the authentication credentials?
- **Key points:** What are the key points in the software.
- **What Are the Feedbacks:** It includes feedbacks.

Project Instructions

Based on the responses of the interview with COMPANY A it's been realized that companies are storing project instructions and documents in their own databases or repositories. But the problem is they are not valuable individually. They need to be linked with customers and workflows. Therefore, it's been added "Project Instructions" as an ISSUE type.

- **Brief Information About the Project:** Information about the project will be entered in this section.
- **Who Is the Customer:** This attribute is for connecting customers with projects. Therefore, company can reach customer from the project instructions.
- **Deadlines:** This is the deadline of the project.
- **Workflow:** This attribute is for connecting workflows with projects. Therefore company can reach workflow information from the project instructions.
- **Notes:** This is for key point and notes for the project.

Customer Instructions

Based on the responses of interview with COMPANY E, it's been realized that customers and customer information are really important for the organizations.

- **Brief Information About the Customer:** Customer Email, Phone, will be recording in this section
- **How Can We Work With Him/Her:** Is it reachable at weekends? Which communication channel do I need to user in order to reach him/her.
- **What Project Related:** This attribute is for connecting project with customers. Therefore, company can reach project information from the customers.
- **Notes:** This is the notes about the customer.
- **Key Points:** In this section users can enter key points about the customer. Like birthdate.
- **Feedbacks:** It includes feedbacks.
- **Issue Date:** Each issue has date attribute so that company can see the distribution of the ISSUES by time.
- **Issue Read Amount:** Automatically organized by the system. Can be observed how many times that specific issue read by users.

Related Departments

Each issue can be assigned to individuals, groups or to whole department. Therefore, the departments in the organization have to be clarified and then created in the knowledge repository. In this way, employees who are in the same department can see the same issue.

Department examples that can be used in the company: IT, HR, Finance, Administration, Marketing, Production, Sales, Legal Department and General Firm

Usage of the Knowledge Repository

In order to use knowledge repository properly, there has to be some rules, otherwise it can be considered as waste of time. First of all, learned information in the company is required to record to knowledge repository. This process needs to be done continuously and in real time. Whatsmore, every opened issue should be monitored and updated. One of the most important part of the knowledge repository is the feedback mechanism. Users need to add their feedbacks about the ISSUES. Therefore, all issues must be kept live.

Table 7. Issue types

According to the researches that have been done in Turkey on Information Technologies and Knowledge management, it is observed that the linkage between organizational learning and knowledge repositories is not strong enough.	According to the researches that have been done in Turkey on Information Technologies and Knowledge management, it is observed that the linkage between organizational learning and knowledge repositories is not strong enough.
As the result of this research, it is found that the companies need a platform (knowledge repository) which is easily adaptable to company and which simplifies and guides data saving process for them. In Turkey, that kind of simple and -easy to use platforms- does not exist.	As the result of this research, it is found that the companies need a platform (knowledge repository) which is easily adaptable to company and which simplifies and guides data saving process for them. In Turkey, that kind of simple and -easy to use platforms- does not exist.
Structure of an Issue and Issue Types	**5.1. Structure of an Issue and Issue Types**
In this research the term "ISSUE" is used for each learned information in the organization. When interview results have been analyzed, seven different types of "ISSUE" is developed. These developed ISSUES are grouped as follows;	In this research the term "ISSUE" is used for each learned information in the organization. When interview results have been analyzed, seven different types of "ISSUE" is developed. These developed ISSUES are grouped as follows;
a) Problem Solving:	**a) Problem Solving:**
Based on the responses of the interviewed COMPANY C, its been realized that one of the biggest problem in organizations is problem solving and then forgetting the solution of the problem. Therefore, when organizations encounter with problems they need to save the both problem and the solution to the knowledge repository and it will help them when they encounter same kind of problem in the future. Because of that it's been released that "Problem Solving" has to be an ISSUE type	Based on the responses of the interviewed COMPANY C, its been realized that one of the biggest problem in organizations is problem solving and then forgetting the solution of the problem. Therefore, when organizations encounter with problems they need to save the both problem and the solution to the knowledge repository and it will help them when they encounter same kind of problem in the future. Because of that it's been released that "Problem Solving" has to be an ISSUE type
What is the problem or what do we want to change: First of all company need to save definition of the problem and this attribute will help company to search and find problem solving ISSUE when they encounter similar kind of problems	What is the problem or what do we want to change: First of all company need to save definition of the problem and this attribute will help company to search and find problem solving ISSUE when they encounter similar kind of problems

This research is prepared and conducted with the purpose of understanding the role of the information technology in organizational learning. As the result of literature surveys, organizational learning is a process and this process created by subdivision. These subdivisions are "Gain of Information", "Share of Information", "Distribution and Transfer of Information", "Usage of Information", "Preservation of Information", "Protection of Information" and "Re Usage of Information". Every subdivision interacts to itself and each other subdivision and this relation affect the organizational learning process. Knowledge repository prepared for this effect. The raw information to create an organizational level learning and knowledge repository is directly correlated between the samples gained from information firms and direct influence of organizational learning. As a result of meeting with firms at İstanbul and Ankara, the data are collected and analyzed. According to results, the issues to create the knowledge repository are determined. Firms runs variety of operation to gain information in last decade. They make serious investments to save the information, which is already learned, and reuse the information when it is need again. Organizations want to share the information, which is gained already. The process to share the information is crucial. The process is includes sharing between individual groups and also organizational level sharing. In other words, information needs sharing to survive. We want to learn how much importance organizations have in information sharing. The analyzed results show, in all subdivision share of the information are the most used subdivision for information technology.

In our era email, online communication applications, instantaneous messaging in mobile devices are the most used tools for communication. These days fast Internet infrastructure simplify information sharing for organizations. These technological developments significantly affect organizations. Preservation of information is one of the sensitive subhead for organizations. Organizations ready to take every precaution to avoid loss of information. Preservation of the information in the organization is the most important issue to protect the integrity and consistency of the information. To establish organizational learning; the last subhead is re-usage of the information. Re-usage of information is against to learning and spending money on already gained information. Re-usage of information is highly important in the lifecycle of the organizational learning. As a result, it can be stated that creation of a knowledge repository and keeping this repository active and updated, will be a benefit for organizations.

REFERENCES

Alan Frost - Organizational Memory and Knowledge Repositorieshttp. (n.d.). Retrieved from www.knowledge-management-tools.net/organizational-memory-and-knowledge.html

Alan Frost - The Different Types of Knowledge. (n.d.). Retrieved from http://www.knowledge-management-tools.net/different-types-of-knowledge.html

Barbiero, B. (2004). *Tacit knowledge. Dictionary of Philosophy of Mind.* Retrieved from http://philosophy.uwaterloo.ca/MindDict/tacitknowledge.html

Bellinger, G., Castro, D., & Mills, A. (2004). *Systems Thinking*. Retrieved from http://www.systems-thinking.org/

Bernstein, J. H. (2014). *The Data-Information-Knowledge-Wisdom Hierarchy*. Retrieved from http://inls151f14.web.unc.edu/files/2014/08/bernstein.pdf

Bernstein. (1985). *The Data-Information-Knowledge-Wisdom hierarchy*. Retrieved from http://inls151f14.web.unc.edu/files/2014/08/bernstein.pdf

Boyton & Zmud. (1987). *Information technology Planning in the 1980s*. Academic Press.

Caprione, E. C. (2010). *Museum Collections Management Systems*. Retrieved from http://rcaam.org/cms/wp-content/uploads/2011/05/Graduate-Studies-Thesis-Collections-Management-Elana-Carpinone.pdf

Collins, H. M. (2001). Tacit knowledge, trust and the Q Sapphire. *Social Studies of Science*, *31*(1), 71–85. doi:10.1177/030631201031001004

Cook, C., & Cook, M. (2000). *The convergence of knowledge management and Business intelligence*. Academic Press.

Davidson. (1993). Beyond Re-engineering. *IBM Systems Journals*.

Ekber & Keskin. (2005). *Örgütsel Hafıza ile Enformasyon Teknolojileri Arasındaki ilişkiler*. Retrieved from http://www2.bayar.edu.tr/yonetimekonomi/dergi/pdf/C12S22005/AEKHKAU.pdf

Gadu & El-Khameesy. (n.d.). *A Knowledge Management Framework Using Business Intelligence Solutions*. Retrieved from http://www.ijcsi.org/papers/IJCSI-11-5-1-102-107.pdf

Gamble & Blackwell. (2001). *Knowledge Management*. Author.

IBM - A practical framework for business intelligence and planning. (n.d.). Retrieved from http://www.ibm.com/midmarket/uk/en/att/pdf/practicalframework.pdf

Ives & Learmonth. (1984). *The Information System as a Competitive Weapon*. Academic Press.

Jennex, M. E. (2009). Knowledge Management, Organizational Memory, and Transfer Behavior. Academic Press.

Karabulut, K. (2014). *Blogger*. Retrieved from http://kaankarabulut.blogcu.com/ogrenen-organizasyonlar/7938311

Karehka, R. (2015). *Use of Information Technology*. Retrieved from http://www.useoftechnology.com/information-technology/

Kimiz-Dalkir. (2009). Knowledge Management. *Theory into Practice*.

King. (n.d.). *Knowledge Management and Organizational Learning*. Retrieved from http://www.uky.edu/~gmswan3/575/KM_and_OL.pdf

Kourie, D. (2008). Knowledge Management and Knowledge Management Technology. Academic Press.

Marquardt, M. J. (2002). *Building The Learning Organization (Mastering the 5 Elements For Corporate Learning)*. Palo Alto, CA: Davies Black Publishing.

Ocasio, W. (2001). *How do organizations think?* Academic Press.

Othman, R., & Hashim, N. A. (2004). *Typologizing Organizational Amnesia*. Academic Press.

Pollitt, C. (2000). *Institutional Amnesia: A Paradox of the Information Age*. Academic Press.

Senge, P. (1994). *Fifth Discipline*. New York: Doubleday.

Smith, E. A. (2001). The role of tacit and explicit knowledge in the workplace. *Journal of Knowledge Management*, *5*(4), 311–321. doi:10.1108/13673270110411733

Smith, M. K. (2001). *Peter senge learning organization*. Retrieved from http://infed.org/mobi/peter-senge-and-the- learning-organization/

Tolgay, F. (2010). *Öğrenen Organizasyonlar ve Bir Uygulama Yüksek Lisans Tezi*. İstanbul: Bahçeşehir University.

Training Industry Knowledge Repositories Knowledge Management Tools. (n.d.). Retrieved from https://www.trainingindustry.com/wiki/entries/knowledge-repositories.aspx

Tsang. (2004). *The Nature of Organizational Unlearning*. Retrieved from http://www.eolss.net/sample-chapters/c15/e1-29-04-05.pdf

Walsh, J. P., & Ungson, G. R. (1991). *Organizational Memory. The Academy of Management Journals*.

Walsh James, P. (1991). Organizational Memory. Academic Press.

Chapter 5
Enhanced Requirement Traceability Link Using Developer's Updated Activity

Raviraj Pandian
GSSS Institute of Engineering and Technology for Women, India

Anandha Kumar D.
Kalaignar Karunanidhi Institute of Technology, India

ABSTRACT

In the software development cycle, the requirement traceability link is one of the important factors. Information retrieval techniques typically produce links with low precision and/or recall because, due to their very nature, they depend on the textual similarity between requirements and source code. The developers may not evolve requirements in synchronization with source code. But, they frequently update other sources of information including CVS/SVN repositories, bug-tracking systems, mailing lists, forums, and blogs. These sources of information will be used to build improved requirement traceability-recovery approaches. After the source code was developed, the developer compiles the source code and commits the source code into versions. Then admin needs to compare the templates and versions based on similarity measurement. Based on textual comparison, the similarity is calculated. The admin can do the same process for the forum requirements.

DOI: 10.4018/978-1-5225-5522-3.ch005

INTRODUCTION

Researchers mine software repositories to get a better understanding of the complex and constantly evolving social-technical interactions that take place during a long software development project. For example, researchers use historical data to predict the most problematic modules requiring more attention from developers or to advise which developers are the most knowledgeable about a certain module. Requirement traceability is defined as "the ability to describe and follow the life of a requirement, in both a forwards and backwards direction. Traceability links between requirements of a system and its source code are helpful in reducing system comprehension effort (Mader, O. Gotel, and I. Philippow, 2008). They are also essential to ensure that a system's source code is consistent with its requirements and that all and only the specified requirements have been implemented by developers. Yet, during software maintenance and evolution, as developers add, remove, or modify features, requirement traceability links become obsolete because developers do not/cannot devote effort to update them. Yet, recovering later these traceability links is a daunting and costly task for developers. Consequently, the literature proposed methods, techniques, and tools to recover these traceability links semi-automatically or automatically.

Importance of Software Requirement Traceability

Preliminary to any software evolution task, a developer must comprehend the project landscape, in particular, the system architecture, design, implementation, and the relations between the various artifacts using any available documentation. Program comprehension occurs in a bottom-up manner, a top-down manner, or some combination thereof. Developers use different types of knowledge during program comprehension, ranging from domain-specific knowledge to general programming knowledge (Mader, O. Gotel, and I. Philippow, 2008). Traceability links between source code and sections of the documentation, e.g., requirements, aid both top-down and bottom-up comprehension. Requirement traceability is defined as the ability to describe and follow the life of a requirement, in both a forwards and backwards direction (i.e., from its origins, through its development and specification, to its subsequent deployment and use, and through all periods of on-going refinement and iteration in any of these phases)". Traceability links between the requirements of a system and its source code are helpful in reducing comprehension effort. This traceability information also helps in software maintenance and evolution tasks (X. Zou, R. Settimi, and J. Cleland-Huang 2010). For example, once a developer has traceability links, she can easily trace what software artifacts must be modified to implement a new requirement. Traceability links are also essential to ensure that a source code is consistent with its requirements and that all and only the specified requirements have been implemented by developers.

Despite the importance of traceability links, during software maintenance and evolution, as developers add, remove, or modify features, requirement traceability links become obsolete because developers do not/cannot devote effort to update them. This insufficient traceability information is one of the main factors that contributes to project over-runs, failure, and difficult to maintain. Insufficient traceability information results in the need for costly and laborious tasks of manual recovery and maintenance of traceability links. These manual tasks may be required frequently depending on how frequently software systems evolve or are maintained.

PROBLEM AND MOTIVATION

The precision and recall values of some requirements traceability approaches (RTAs) described in the literature are mainly: Vector Space Model (VSM), Latent Semantic Indexing (LSI), Rule-based, Jensen-Shannon similarity model (JSM), and Latent Dirichlet Allocation (LDA). It shows that, depending on the datasets, precision values vary from 0:9% to 95:9% and recall values vary from 3% to 99:8% (H. Kagdi, J. Maletic, and B. Sharif, 2007). For example, achieved 1:5% to 7:9% precision with VSM whereas achieved 50% to 80% precision with the same technique. Both group of researchers used standard VSM to obtain their results. The low precision and recall values are not only due to the use of one IR technique or another; the differences are due to the quality of RTAs' inputs, i.e., requirements, source code, and developers' programming knowledge.

In the previous study (D.Anandha Kumar, and Dr.P.Raviraj, 2013), the authors have performed an incremental literature review (ILR) to understand the cause of the variations in precision and recall values for different RTAs. We observed that there exist some factors that impact RTAs' inputs. We documented seven factors (see Figure 1), i.e., ambiguous requirement, vague requirement, conflicting requirement, granularity level, identifiers' quality, domain knowledge, and programming language knowledge. We also showed that controlling, avoiding, and -or mitigating the impact of these factors could yield better RTAs accuracy (H. Kagdi and J. Maletic, 2007). For each factor, we documented some preventive measures and -or techniques to improve the quality of RTA inputs. Regardless the importance of controlling/avoiding RTAs' input impacting factors, for some factors, e.g., identifiers' quality, it would not be feasible to completely control/avoid their impact on RTAs' inputs. Because the preventive measures and -or techniques to improve the quality of RTA inputs are not 100% automated. A developer must manually verify the quality of all these inputs at the end of a RT process. However, their model to combine different experts was not generalized and they did not consider adding more than two unique sources of information (H. Kagdi and J. Maletic, 2007).

In addition, to the best of our knowledge, adding more sources of information in the field of requirements traceability has not been analyzed yet.

OVERVIEW OF THE PROPOSED IDEA

Many tools have been built to extract the necessary information from historic software repositories, process and analyze it, and then visualize the results. Unfortunately, many of those tools are not publicly available or they use their own internal representations and input/output formats, which makes it difficult to reuse such tools for different purposes. In this project first they take the requirements into consideration. The requirements are based on JEDITOR. Based on the requirements the source code is compiled as versions. These versions and the requirement templates compare and get 3 types of attributes. After the similarity measurement the results are based on 3 attributes such as requirement with identity number, class with version number, and similarity value. Based on these three attributes log file should be generated and using the log file the trustrace is calculated. In the proposed system the same process is done with forums.

Tool Support

The methods and techniques presented in this chapter have been partially and-or fully implemented and integrated in FacTrace, for artifact TRACEability. FacTrace is an IR-based RT link recovery tool. It supports several IR techniques, namely VSM, LSI, LDA and JSM. FacTrace allows developers to select the source and target artifacts to recover traceability links between them. FacTrace uses an external Java parser to extract all the source code identifiers for further processing. A developer can set various parameters in FacTrace to achieve desired results. For example, she can

Figure 1.

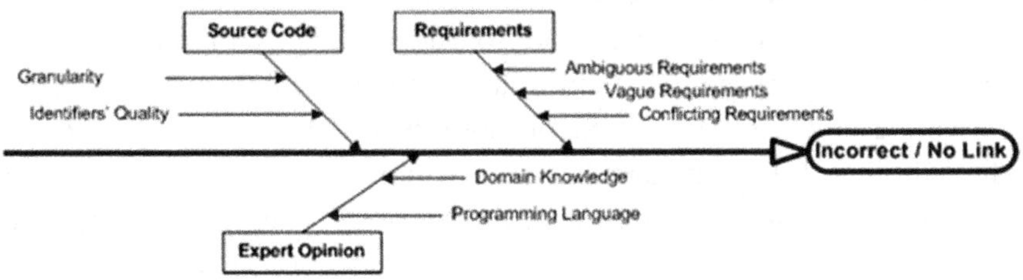

select the weighting schemes for an IR technique, IR technique, and thresholds etc. Threshold selection helps to retrieve only a set of traceability links whose similarity is above than a certain level.

FacTrace provides several modules that help from traceability recovery to traceability links verification (H. Kagdi and J. Maletic, 2007). FacTrace aids software engineers in different tasks, namely, requirement elicitation, requirement analysis, artifact traceability, and trust-based traceability. FacTrace has a graphical interface to perform different tasks. Following sections give you a brief description of different features of FacTrace. Requirement Elicitation: FacTrace currently supports Lime survey 2 to gather requirements. Customers' requirements will automatically be stored in a database. Customers can write or upload their requirements in FacTrace specified XML format. FacTrace performs similarity analysis for all the elicited requirements. Similarity analysis helps developers to see if a single customer or multiple customers wrote the same requirement twice. It helps to remove the duplicated requirements. The similarity analysis is backed-up by clustering approaches, i.e., agglomerative hierarchical clustering, to group similar requirements in a single cluster.

- **Requirement Analysis:** FacTrace enables users to perform requirement analysis in few mouse clicks. A developer can see all similar requirements and label them. She can write a label or simply click on a specific requirement; it will automatically be placed in a text area to save time. In addition, she can also categories each requirement as functional, nonfunctional, or an outlier (J.H. Hayes, G. Antoniol, and Y.-G. Gue´he´neuc, 2008). She can mark a requirement as duplicate if she thinks the current requirement is somehow semantically similar to another requirement. If any requirement has not been negotiated with a customer, developer can delete that requirement during requirement analysis. Traceability Management: FacTrace helps in recovering traceability links between different software artifacts. For example, traceability links among requirements, source code, and CVS/SVN change logs. FacTrace allows experts to create new manual traceability links as well. It supports different level of granularity for creating traceability links. A developer can write a description for each link and other identifiers specifications as well.
- **Traceability Links Verification:** To avoid bias when recovering traceability links, FacTrace allows developers to vote on the recovered link by an IR technique and-or proposed approaches. It allows adding up to five developers for voting on each link. If three or more than three developers accept a link, then a link will be considered as a valid link by FacTrace. A developer can change their voting option at any time. All other developers' voting is hidden to avoid bias. She can see source code files in the source code viewer of

FacTrace to verify each link. Requirement Elicitation / Traceability Reports: FacTrace provides easy to understand tabular reports for requirement elicitation and traceability links. Reports can be exported in XML and CSV format. Reports are dynamically generate (N. Ali, Y.-G. Gue´he´neuc, and G. Antoniol, 2011). All reports are updated as soon as a developer makes a change in a project.

Information Retrieval Process

IR-based RTAs process is typically divided into three main steps. Figure 1 shows the high-level diagram of IR-based RT links recovery process. First, all the textual information contained in the requirements and source code is extracted and preprocessed by splitting terms, removing stop words and remaining words are then stemmed to its grammatical root. Second, all the stemmed terms are weighted using a term weighting scheme, e.g., term frequency and inverse document frequency. Last, an IR technique computes the similarity between requirements and source code documents. Lastly, it generates a ranked list of potential traceability links (Mader, O. Gotel, and I. Philippow, 2008). A high similarity between two documents shows a potential semantic link between them. Below we will explain each step in details:

PROPOSED METHODOLOGY: MODULE DESCRIPTION

There are Four Modules are designed to implement the proposed idea as follows:

1. Document preprocessing
2. Constructing baseline link
3. Defining expert
4. Link recovery and expert voting

The description of the above Modules is as follows,

Document Preprocessing

In linking the source code and requirement, the class identifier and the preprocessed single word requirement is need to apply to information technique. There is a need that the software developers must use more significant name extracted form the customer's application area knowledge as class identifiers in source code as in the same context of requirement of that application. And also the identifiers should be preprocessed to be named as semantics of the requirement specification. These identifiers will play the role of term as key for making the requirement traceability link. The term must be in single natural language and same language to be used to name the class identifiers. This pre-processing step of requirement normalization will help the requirement traceability linking process enhancement.

- **Camel Case Conversion:** The requirement is preprocessed to make in to single word which is very useful for the similarity measure. This single word requirement is differentiate one form other is possible by camel case conversion. The camel case conversion is done by changing the first letter of each word as capitalized.
- **Remove Stop Words:** In the preprocessing task the unhelpful word like punctuation, article, prepositions etc for information retrieval technique. It reduces the lot of work load for the information retrieval technique. These stop word are only useful for the human understanding and it is not needed for the Information retrieval process.
- **Stemming:** Common words that will come through all over requirement are removed. For example, the database module requirement specification, almost all requirements will contain the word like "database" which is unhelpful for the information retrieval technique.
- **Remove Out of Context Reference:** In the requirement, there will be a stop list; stop list is the set of word unhelpful in the context of our requirement traceability linking process. For example, the customer who requires security software may give a requirement like "need for the protection to the entire system element like software, application, file, database, and internet". But the real need is "protection to system element". Unhelpful HTML page indexing in the context of requirement traceability linking process is removed.
- **Extracting Class Identifiers:** In requirement, the customer's viewpoint should be reduced to a single word. For example, for the banking customer, may request to make module of "putting money in the bank's customer's account" this requirement could be reduced as "deposit". This kind of extraction is need for the requirement traceability link. This extraction of requirement is much useful for the information retrieval technique. Here the similarity of the requirement and the source code would be the main constraint to link the both document to form a link. The source code's class identifier is the link component in requirement traceability, so this extraction will play an important pre-processing step.

Constructing Baseline Link

By using software repositories, e.g., CVS/SVN repositories and bug-tracking systems and the newly proposed forums as experts to trust more or less some baseline links recovered by an IR technique and, thus, to discard / rerank the links to improve the precision and recall of the IR based techniques.

Defining Expert

Information Retrieval techniques typically produce links with low precision and/or recall because, due to their very nature, they depend on the textual similarity between requirements and source code. The developers may not evolve requirements in synchronization with source code; they frequently update other sources of information, including CVS/SVN repositories, bug-tracking systems, mailing lists, forums, and blogs. The above said sources of information will be used to build improved requirement traceability-recovery approaches. In particular, forums are used as experts to improve the trust of baseline requirement traceability links

Link Recovery and Expert Voting

Link recovery and expert voting is supporting the accuracy improvement of the traceability links between requirements and source code recovered by an IR technique are due to 1) mining software repositories and considering the links recovered through these repositories as experts, 2) using a trust model inspired by web-trust models to combine these expert's opinions, and 3) weighting the expert's opinions on a per-link basis for each link recovered.

ALOGRITHMS USED

Porter Stemming

A consonant in a word is a letter other than A, E, I, O or U, and other than Y preceded by a consonant. (The fact that the term 'consonant' is defined to some extent in terms of itself does not make it ambiguous). So, in TOY the consonants are T and Y, and in SYZYGY they are S, Z and G. If a letter is not a consonant it is a *vowel.*

A consonant will be denoted by c, a vowel by v. A list ccc... of length greater than 0 will be denoted by C, and a list vvv... of length greater than 0 will be denoted by V. Any word, or part of a word, therefore has one of the four forms:

CVCV ... C

CVCV ... V

VCVC ... C

VCVC ... V

These may all be represented by the single form

[C]VCVC ... [V]

where the square brackets are denoting an arbitrary presence of their contents. Using $(VC)^m$ to denote VC repeated m times; this may again be written as

$[C](VC)^m[V]$.

m will be called the *measure* of any word or word part when represented in this form. The case m = 0 covers the null word. Some examples are shown in Table 1.

The *rules* for removing a suffix will be given in the form

(Condition) S1 -> S2

This means that if a word ends with the suffix S1 and the stem before S1 satisfies the given condition, S1 is replaced by S2. The condition is usually given in terms of m, e.g.

(m > 1) EMENT ->

Here S1 is 'EMENT' and S2 is null. This would map REPLACEMENT to REPLAC, since REPLAC is a word part for which m = 2.

The 'condition' part may also contain the following (see Table 2.)

Table 1.

m=0	TR, EE, TREE, Y, BY.
m=1	TROUBLE, OATS, TREES, IVY.
m=2	TROUBLES, PRIVATE, OATEN, ORRERY.

Table 2.

*S	-	The stem ends with S (and similarly for the other letters).
v	-	The stem contains a vowel.
*d	-	The stem ends with a double consonant (e.g. -TT, -SS).
*o	-	The stem ends cvc, where the second c is not W, X or Y (e.g. -WIL, -HOP).

And the condition part may also contain expressions with *and*, *or* and *not*, so that

(m>1 and (*S or *T))

Tests for a stem with m>1 ending in S or T, while

(*d and not (*L or *S or *Z))

Tests for a stem ending with a double consonant other than L, S or Z. Elaborate conditions like this are required only rarely.

In a set of rules written beneath each other, only one is obeyed, and this will be the one with the longest matching S1 for the given word. For example, see Table 3.

(Here the conditions are all null) CARESSES maps to CARESS; where SSES is the longest match for S1. Equally CARESS maps to CARESS (S1='SS') and CARES to CARE (S1='S').

In the rules below, examples of their application (successful or otherwise), are given on the right in lower case. The algorithm is as follows:

Step 1a: See Table 4.
Step 1b: See Table 5.

If the second or third of the rules in Step 1b is successful, the following is done (see Table 6).

Table 3.

SSES	->	SS
IES	->	I
SS	->	SS
S	->	

Table 4.

SSES	->	SS	caresses	->	caress
IES	->	I	ponies	->	poni
			ties	->	ti
SS	->	SS	caress	->	caress
S	->		cats	->	cat

Table 5.

(m>0) EED	->	EE	feed	->	feed
			agreed	->	agree
(*v*) ED	->		plastered	->	plaster
			bled	->	bled
(*v*) ING	->		motoring	->	motor
			sing	->	sing

Table 6.

AT	->	ATE	conflat(ed)	->	conflate
BL	->	BLE	troubl(ed)	->	trouble
IZ	->	IZE	siz(ed)	->	size
(*d and not (*L or *S or *Z))	->	single letter	hopp(ing)	->	hop
			tann(ed)	->	tan
			fall(ing)	->	fall
			hiss(ing)	->	hiss
			fizz(ed)	->	fizz
(m=1 and *o)	->	E	fail(ing)	->	fail
			fil(ing)	->	file

The rule to map to a single letter causes the removal of one of the double letter pair. The -E is put back on -AT, -BL and -IZ, so that the suffixes -ATE, -BLE and -IZE can be recognised later. This E may be removed in step 4.

Step 1c: See Table 7.

Table 7.

(*v*) Y	->	I	happy	->	happi
			sky	->	sky

Step 1: Deal with plurals and past participles. The subsequent steps are much more straightforward.
Step 2: See Table 8.

The test for the string S1 can be made fast by doing a program switch on the penultimate letter of the word being tested. This gives a fairly even breakdown of the possible values of the string S1. It will be seen in fact, that the S1-strings in step

Table 8.

(m>0) ATIONAL	->	ATE	relational	->	relate
(m>0) TIONAL	->	TION	conditional	->	condition
			rational	->	rational
(m>0) ENCI	->	ENCE	valenci	->	valence
(m>0) ANCI	->	ANCE	hesitanci	->	hesitance
(m>0) IZER	->	IZE	digitizer	->	digitize
(m>0) ABLI	->	ABLE	conformabli	->	conformable
(m>0) ALLI	->	AL	radicalli	->	radical
(m>0) ENTLI	->	ENT	differentli	->	different
(m>0) ELI	->	E	vileli	->	vile
(m>0) OUSLI	->	OUS	analogousli	->	analogous
(m>0) IZATION	->	IZE	vietnamization	->	vietnamize
(m>0) ATION	->	ATE	predication	->	predicate
(m>0) ATOR	->	ATE	operator	->	operate
(m>0) ALISM	->	AL	feudalism	->	feudal
(m>0) IVENESS	->	IVE	decisiveness	->	decisive
(m>0) FULNESS	->	FUL	hopefulness	->	hopeful
(m>0) OUSNESS	->	OUS	callousness	->	callous
(m>0) ALITI	->	AL	formaliti	->	formal
(m>0) IVITI	->	IVE	sensitiviti	->	sensitive
(m>0) BILITI	->	BLE	sensibiliti	->	sensible

2 are presented here in the alphabetical order of their penultimate letter. Similar techniques may be applied in the other steps.

Step 3: See Table 9.
Step 4: See Table 10.

The suffixes are now removed. All that remains is a little tidying up.

Table 9.

(m>0) ICATE	->	IC	triplicate	->	triplic
(m>0) ATIVE	->		formative	->	form
(m>0) ALIZE	->	AL	formalize	->	formal
(m>0) ICITI	->	IC	electriciti	->	electric
(m>0) ICAL	->	IC	electrical	->	electric
(m>0) FUL	->		hopeful	->	hope
(m>0) NESS	->		goodness	->	good

Table 10.

(m>1) AL	->	revival	->	reviv
(m>1) ANCE	->	allowance	->	allow
(m>1) ENCE	->	inference	->	infer
(m>1) ER	->	airliner	->	airlin
(m>1) IC	->	gyroscopic	->	gyroscop
(m>1) ABLE	->	adjustable	->	adjust
(m>1) IBLE	->	defensible	->	defens
(m>1) ANT	->	irritant	->	irrit
(m>1) EMENT	->	replacement	->	replac
(m>1) MENT	->	adjustment	->	adjust
(m>1) ENT	->	dependent	->	depend
(m>1 and (*S or *T)) ION	->	adoption	->	adopt
(m>1) OU	->	homologou	->	homolog
(m>1) ISM	->	communism	->	commun
(m>1) ATE	->	activate	->	activ
(m>1) ITI	->	angulariti	->	angular
(m>1) OUS	->	homologous	->	homolog
(m>1) IVE	->	effective	->	effect
(m>1) IZE	->	bowdlerize	->	bowdler

Step 5a: See Table 11.
Step 5b: See Table 12.

CONCLUSION AND FUTURE WORK

By mining software repositories one could support the traceability recovery process; considering heterogeneous sources of information to discard/re-rank the traceability links provided by an IR technique to improve its accuracy; and, could be used as an automatic, per-link experts' weighting technique to avoid the need of manually-built oracles to tune weights. For this whole process the essential thing is to applying pre-processing Techniques to the inputs data like source code and requirement.

The requirement traceability link is made between the pre-processed source code and requirement by finding the similarity between them. To trust the link of traceability the support for the link is to be collected from the user's updating activity. Then the purpose of finding consistency of source code to its requirement is solved.

Table 11.

(m>1) E	->	probate	->	probat
		rate	->	rate
(m=1 and not *o) E	->	cease	->	ceas

Table 12.

(m > 1 and *d and *L)	->	single letter	controll	->	control
			roll	->	roll

REFERENCES

Ali, N., Gue'he'neuc, Y.-G., & Antoniol, G. (2011). *Factors Impacting the Inputs of Traceability Recovery Approaches*. Springer-Verlag.

Gotel & Philippow. (2008). Enabling automated traceability maintenance by recognizing development activities applied to models. In *Proceedings of the 2008 23rd IEEE/ACM International Conference on Automated Software Engineering*. Washington, DC: IEEE Computer Society.

Hayes, J. H., Antoniol, G., & Gue'he'neuc, Y.-G. (2008). PREREQIR: Recovering Pre-Requirements via Cluster Analysis. *Proc. 15th Working Conf. Reverse Eng.*, 165-174.

Kagdi, H., & Maletic, J. (2007). Software repositories: A source for trace-ability links. *International Workshop on Traceability in Emerging Forms of Software Engineering (GCT/TEFSE^ 07)*, 32–39.

Kagdi, H., Maletic, J., & Sharif, B. (2007). Mining software repositories for traceability links. *ICPC '07, 15th IEEE International Conference*, 145–154.

Kumar & Raviraj. (2013). A Study on Requirement Traceability Methods in Software Engineering. *International Journal of Societal Applications of Computer Science*, *2*(11), 481–484.

Zou, X., Settimi, R., & Cleland-Huang, J. (2010). Improving automated requirements trace retrieval: A study of term-based enhancement methods. *Empirical Software Engineering*, *15*(2), 119–146. doi:10.100710664-009-9114-z

Chapter 6
4SRS-SoaML Method for Deriving a Service-Oriented Architecture From Use Cases Within a SPEM Approach

Carlos Salgado
Universidade do Minho, Portugal

Ricardo J. Machado
Universidade do Minho, Portugal

Rita S. P. Maciel
Universidade Federal da Bahia, Brazil

ABSTRACT

The transformation of requirements specification into an architectural design has been a crucial endeavor for the information systems analysis and design community, with ever-new challenges to tackle. Despite the wide and diverse existing proposals, the lack of a common structure and use of different strategies makes it close to impossible to analyze or compare these approaches. Therefore, the use of model-based methods benefits from a detailed specification in order to support their analysis and evolution, also in comparison to other approaches. Following work on the derivation of a logical architecture from business-process use-cases requirements in a service-oriented approach, the authors propose a detailed specification, within a SPEM approach, of a transformation method, which they further analyze and refurbish in order to meet current and future challenges.

DOI: 10.4018/978-1-5225-5522-3.ch006

INTRODUCTION

Transition from and consequent alignment between requirements and architectures has consistently been one of the main challenges during information system development, namely within Software Engineering (SE) solutions (Galster, Eberlein, & Moussavi, 2009). This is inherently a modelling activity, in which abstract models of information systems are derived from Requirements Engineering (RE) and then systematically developed from problem to solution space (France & Rumpe, 2007). Nevertheless, this activity counts on scarcely available and disparate techniques to support developers (Salgado, Machado, & Maciel, 2016b), and is confronted with ever-new challenges due to advances in research and practice.

Despite the extensive research in this topic, much is left to do regarding related model-based activities, where comparatively analyzing or evolving any of the numerous existing proposals remains a challenging task (Yue, Briand, & Labiche, 2011). In a previous work, supported in a set of selected proposals focused in model-based transformation approaches, a framework was presented for covering a set of related key issues (Salgado et al., 2016b) to answer these challenges. This framework allows classifying and categorizing the individual details of each approach, further facilitating the assessment and comparison of methods. This work also reinforces the need for any of these methods to be clearly modeled and specified, in order to better support its analysis and evolution.

Consequently, focusing on our 4SRS-SoaML method (Salgado, Teixeira, Santos, Machado, & Maciel, 2015), which is adapted to the derivation of a service-oriented logical architecture from business requirements, we deemed important to perform a detailed specification of its workings and constituents in a model-based approach. As this is one of the most recent approaches surrounding the conventional 4SRS method (R.J. Machado, Fernandes, Monteiro, & Rodrigues, 2005) and due to the growing extension of its associated research topics, we first propose to perform its specification in line with those previous research works.

This proposal intends to prepare the method to overcome doubts and difficulties associated to analysis and evolution according to previous proposals. These include future evolutions as higher control on its execution status, improved monitoring of the tasks, added support to the roles performing those tasks and a detailed view of the transversal use of the work products involved. Following our recent work (Salgado, Machado, & Maciel, 2016a) we will be using the Software and Systems Process Engineering Metamodel (SPEM) (OMG, 2008) for soundness and clarity reasons, thus leaving it open for future adjustments or adaptions to any other similar version.

Accordingly, succeeding this initial proposal for the detailed specification and analysis of the current 4SRS-SoaML method, we propose a new, refurbish version, of the set of steps and respectively associated micro-steps for this method. Supported in our extended experience and lessons learned with the use of this method, and its other related versions, in several projects, this work aims to better ground it to prepare future evolution proposals as well as their validation, and also to provision for the development of associated support tools.

This document follows in section 2 with background research information on the topics supporting this work and then, section 3, presents our initial analysis and proposal for the detailed specification of the 4SRS-SoaML method, within a SPEM approach. Following, section 4 presents the refurbished version of the method, according to current trends and extensive experience on the use of the method. Then, section 5 discusses and frames this later proposal inside the related work in the area, analyzing contributions, current research status and future work ahead. Finally, some conclusions are drawn for this work.

BACKGROUND

This section presents some background research on the topics supporting this work, namely on the evolution of the diverse approaches surrounding the 4SRS method for the transformation between requirements and architecture, and also on the relevance of service-oriented architectures for the development of business aligned solutions. The section closes with a quick glance on the importance of using standard, model-based approaches, for the development of artifacts in information systems.

The 4SRS Method

The 4SRS method originated as a technique to aid software engineers to transform user requirements models into the first logical architecture of the system (R.J. Machado et al., 2005). It was essentially based on the mapping of UML use case diagrams into UML object diagrams, where UML sequence, activity, and state diagrams and other artifacts could also be considered within the transformation decisions. Further integrated in a V-Model approach (Ferreira, Santos, Machado, Fernandes, & Gasevic, 2014), it supports and guides the design of information systems architectures by successive models derivation based on domain specific needs, promoting the alignment and traceability between the logical architecture and the requirements supporting models.

Successive research efforts led to diverse evolutions of this technique into a method that has already a considerable amount of work associated. These cover, among others, diverse topics as the refinement of architectures by application of a recursive approach (Ricardo J Machado, Fernandes, Monteiro, & Rodrigues, 2006), an extension to support the construction of class diagram that complements the logical architecture (Santos & Machado, 2010) and another applicable to product line architectural modeling (Azevedo, Machado, Muthig, & Ribeiro, 2009), and an adaption for automation purposes and study of the well-formedeness of relations (Azevedo, Machado, & Maciel, 2012). There is also significant work in a process-level perspective for product elicitation (Ferreira, Santos, Machado, & Gasevic, 2012) and on the use of SOA-participants instead of the conventional architectural elements for aligning business requirements with services quality characteristics (Salgado et al., 2015).

Service-Oriented Architectures

Service support helps reducing the gap between business and information systems, ensuring the connection between models of both sides, where the concepts of SOA apply both to business and system architectures, helping stakeholders to align their business requirements and IS architecture implementations. Delgado (Delgado, Guzmán, & Piattini, 2010) and Elvesaeter (Elvesaeter & Panfilenko, 2010) provide solutions for the service oriented development of business processes by relying on the SOA paradigm closeness to business models. These integrate concepts, methodologies and tools that combine the application of SOC and Model-Driven Development (MDD) paradigms to support BPM, namely through the use of OMG 'standards' to model business processes and services, such as BPMN (OMG, 2011) and SoaML (OMG, 2012).

Another solution to the problem of architecting the existing gap between the high-level configuration of a software system, describing business entities and relationships required by a software solution, and its low-level representation, in which the technological aspects determine the final shape of the system, is presented by López-Sanz (López-Sanz & Marcos, 2012). Here, the definition of a framework for the Model-Driven specification of Software Architectures, using concepts behind Service-Orientation for its definition, shows a tendency towards the use of a hybrid approach as the most suitable choice, following a 'pure' UML-based approach for architecture specification where SoaML is worth mentioning.

Software and Systems Process Engineering Meta-Model (SPEM)

The development of artifacts in information systems encompasses the application of several good practices and diversified knowledge as well as, eventually, the introduction of new ideas or strategies. This results on the possibility of existence of several distinct approaches or ways for their development. In order to be able to express, establish, or organize the structure of activities inherent to the development approach, it is convenient to use a standard way for expressing the process structure. In this context, the SPEM 2.0, standardized by the Object Management Group (OMG), is a process engineering meta-model that provides to process engineers a conceptual framework for "modeling, documenting, presenting, managing, interchanging, and enacting development methods and processes" (OMG, 2008).

SPEM is used to define software and systems development processes and their components, trying to accommodate a large range of development methods and processes of different styles. With SPEM 2.0, development teams are able to define how to apply the development methods and best practices throughout a project lifecycle, selecting and tailoring the development process as they require. In a recent study (Ruiz-Rube, Dodero, Palomo-Duarte, Ruiz, & Gawn, 2013), SPEM was considered the most widespread and popular language for representing development processes, with a high degree of acceptance of its metamodel, and its uses and applications. Despite some known weaknesses, SPEM is considered as a suitable language for representing development processes, and attending to this, we use it to describe our approach.

4SRS-SOAML METHOD SPECIFICATION

The four main steps of the 4SRS-SoaML method, as its name implies, are, respectively: Participant Creation, Participant Elimination, Participant Packaging and Aggregation, and Participant Association (Figure 1). Except for the first step, Participants Creation, all other three steps have further detailed micro-steps associated to their tasks.

Throughout this document, we assume the definition of Use Cases according to the RUP methodology (Kroll & Kruchten, 2003), and Participants and Services following the SoaML referential (OMG, 2012). Accordingly, a Participant is either a specific entity or kind of entity that provides or uses services, and can represent people, organizations, or information system components. In the business domain it may be a person, organization, or system, and in the systems domain it may be a system, application, or component. Participants may provide/consume any number of services, integrated in a SoaML ServicesArchitecture that shows how multiple participants work together, providing and using services to enable business goals or processes. One of the key benefits of SOA is the ability to enable a community, organization, or system of systems to work together more cohesively using services without getting overly coupled.

Figure 1. Sequence of the four steps of the 4SRS-SoaML

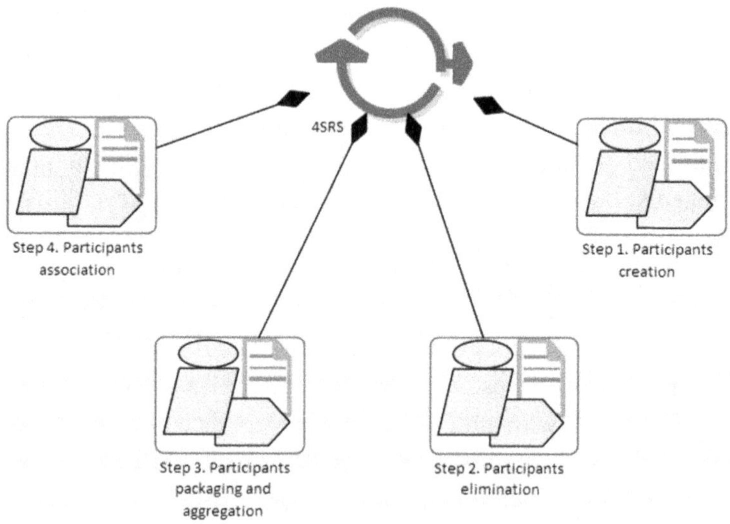

Step 1: Participants Creation

For intelligibility reasons we detail this first step into a solo micro-step, 1.i) Participant Creation, in order to align it with the three remaining steps, so identifying its associated performing role and work products (Figure 2). This is a fully automated task (Azevedo et al., 2012), which involves generating a set of Participants (P) of types i, c, d (interface, control and data, respectively), directly from the existing leaf Use-cases (UC), with no human intervention necessary.

Step 2: Participants Elimination

In what regards the second step, its original seven micro-steps composition have grown to eight in a proposal to detail the specification of the aggregated architectural elements (Ferreira et al., 2012), which are depicted in Figure 3 and following synthetized:

Micro-step 2.i) Use-Case Classification: Each UC is classified according to the nature of its P and the respective suffix it was tagged with, where more than one of each P type can be generated according to the textual description and model of the UC.

Figure 2. Detail of step 1. participant creation

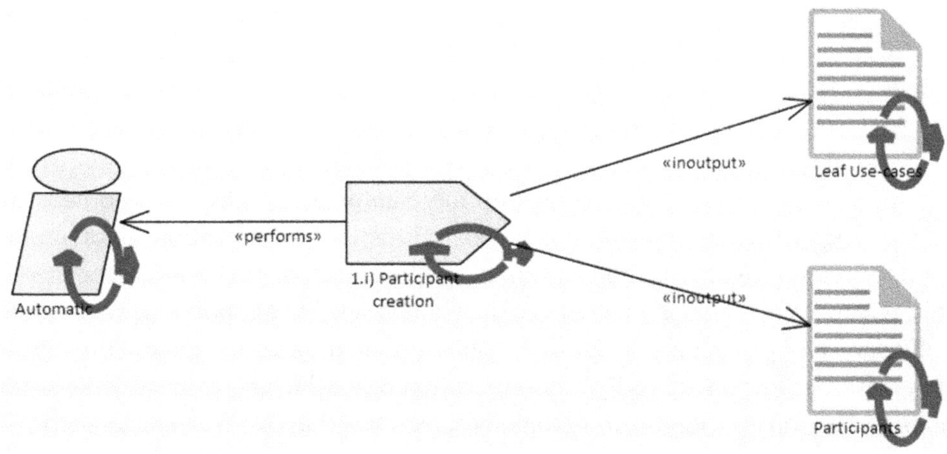

Micro-Step 2.ii) Local Elimination: Refers to determining which P must be eliminated in the context of a UC, guaranteeing its full representation, which is required since micro-step 2.i) disregards any representativeness concerns.

Micro-Step 2.iii) Participant Naming: P that survived the previous micro-step are given a name, which must reflect the role of the P within the entire UC and also its type (c, d or i), in order to semantically give hints on what it represents.

Micro-Step 2.iv) Participant Description: Provides an extended structure for the required description of the P's role for the service behavior, information which has as input the textual description of the original UC from the UC model.

Micro-Step 2.v) Participant Representation: Its purpose is to identify a P whose role can be represented by another P from the global architecture, thus signaling those P that can be eliminated without losing coherence within the architecture.

Micro-Step 2.vi) Global Elimination: Similar to micro-step 2.ii), it identifies which P must be eliminated in the context of the global model, where the P that is represented by itself or represents other P is maintained, while the rest are eliminated.

Micro-Step 2.vii) Participant Renaming: P which have not been eliminated are renamed and, in cases where the P under analysis results of the representation of more than one P, the new name must reflect their combined global execution in the project context.

Micro-Step 2.viii) Participant Specification: Similar to micro-step 2.iv), since it intends to describe P that, in micro-step 2.v), were considered to represent other P without losing any information and were meanwhile eliminated in micro-step 2.vi).

Added to the automatic creation of P in the previous step, there is also the possibility to generate one or more P of any one type if there is a need to separate or fragment a given UC functionality. This task, which has not been previously fully explored, would be included in micro-step 2.i), being sparkled according to the analysis performed by the systems analyst to each UC and executed under its responsibility.

Micro-steps 2.ii) and 2.vi) constitute mere automated tasks, with no need for further details, while the other micro-steps would benefit from additional tool support for its execution, especially micro-steps 2.iv), 2.v) and 2.viii). The task associated to micro-step 2.v) is the one that demands an added level of support since its actions and decisions span across the entire P list. All of the non-automatic micro-steps in this step are to be performed by a system analyst role, which here replaces the initial ambiguous 'software engineer' nomination, recalling that the UC were detailed by a business-process analyst role, which could be called upon for clarifications regarding the descriptions and functionality on any of them.

Step 3: Participants Packaging and Aggregation

Following, Step 3, Participant Packaging and Aggregation (Figure 4), stands as a first bridge to the architectural design, where the enduring P from the previous step, for which there is an advantage in being treated in a unified process, give origin to packages or aggregations of semantically consistent P represented in a super-participant (SP). A SP package represents a group of assigned P, which may or may not represent a software product from the services ecosystem in question. The SP aggregation performed can reflect identified product classes or other aggregated types of service suggested by reference architectures or models.

This step was not deeply explored in previous research efforts, having been divided into two micro-steps only in the recent presentation of the 4SRS-SoaML method (Salgado et al., 2015), as next described:

Micro-step 3.i) Super-participant Naming: performs the conventional identification and naming of the SP, according to the packaging/aggregation service provided.

Micro-step 3.ii) Super-participant Description: fills in a structure for the required description of the SP role for the packaged/aggregated service behavior, in a characterization similar to the description of a product class, where this information has as input the textual descriptions of the set of packaged/aggregated P.

Figure 3. Detail of step 2. participant elimination

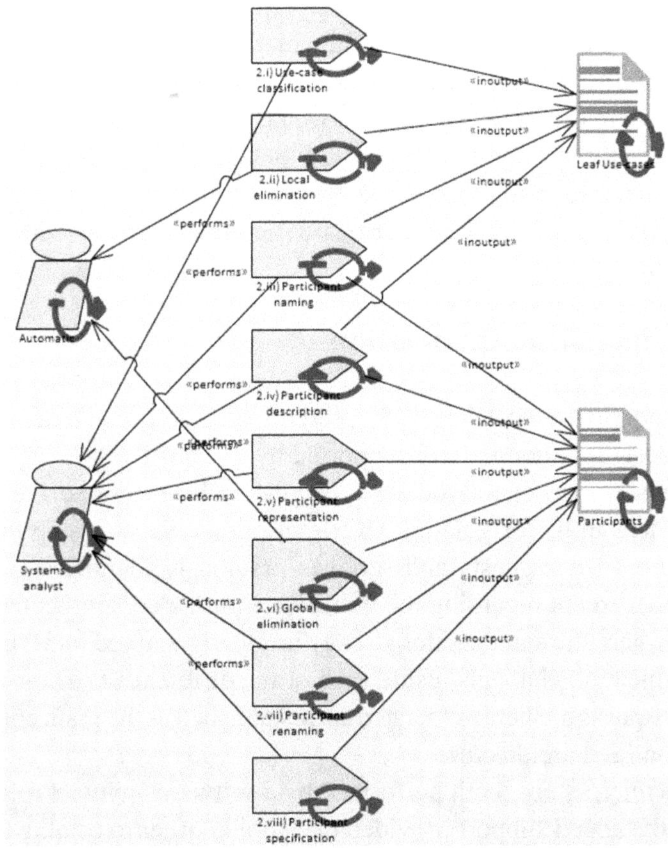

Figure 4. Detail of step 3. participant packaging and aggregation

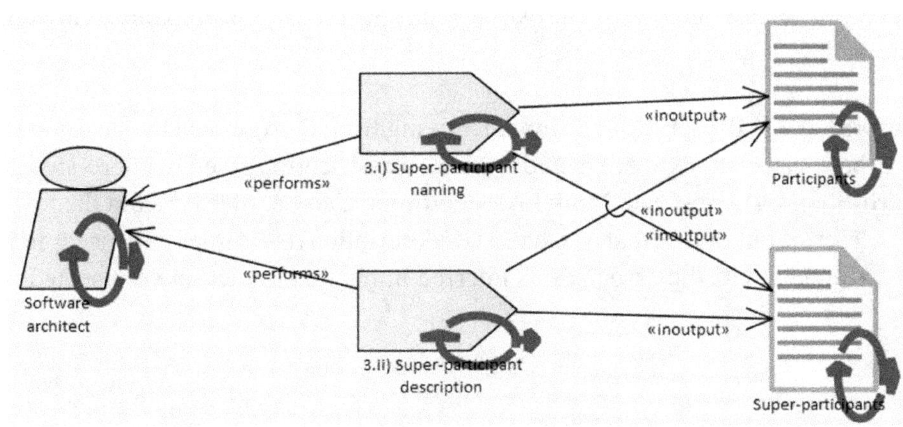

The act of selecting which P to package/aggregate demands architectural knowledge, so these micro-steps should be performed by a software architect role, handling the list of available P and deciding on the SP to create. As in the previous micro-steps 2.iv), 2.v) and 2.viii), these two micro-steps have no automation mechanisms, so, additional tool support would be most valuable to the software architect, especially during the execution of the 3.ii) micro-step. Another not fully explored question regarding this step is the possibility to have two or more levels of packaging/aggregation, where various SP could be encapsulated in another, higher-level, SP.

Step 4: Participants Association

The fourth and final step (Figure 5) presents also important decisions for the architecture design, although here supported by existing knowledge in the related elements. Namely, one can associate P originated by the same UC or based on textual references in the originating UC descriptions. So, this step formalizes the associations between requests and services previously identified in micro-steps 2.iv) and 2.viii), except regarding the P that were packaged/aggregated in the same SP in step 3, where the same tactics already implicitly applied to SP originated the inner communication channels inside each of the different SP. Their now exposed services and requests are here associated and established as the main communication channels in the final architecture.

These two micro-steps, both performed by a software architect role, would also benefit from the added support provided by a tool in order to be able to better span the entire P and SP lists, and also relate these to their associated originating UC. Similarly to the previous third step, this fourth step was not deeply explored in previous research efforts, so further work is needed in order to unveil the complete potential of the tasks involved. The two currently detailed micro-steps are followingly described:

Micro-Step 4.i) Direct Associations: Deriving from P originated by the same UC, these associations are depicted from the classification given in micro-step 2.i).

Micro-Step 4.ii) Use-Case Model Associations: Can be inferred from the textual descriptions of UC, that is, when a UC description refers implicitly or explicitly to another UC the associations inferred imply that the UC are connected.

Figure 5. Detail of step 4. participant association

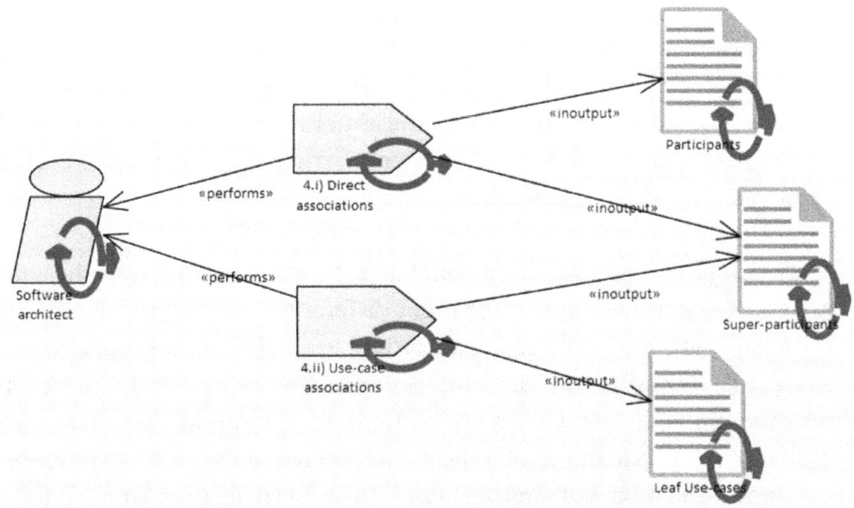

REFURBISHED 4SRS-SOAML METHOD SPECIFICATION

This first effort to obtain a detailed specification of the 4SRS-SoaML method, alongside its analysis based on our experience with the traditional 4SRS method and its variants, raised some questions regarding changes needed to increase the method's efficiency and efficacy. These questions relate to the organization of tasks, the handled work products or on the need to have added support for the involved analysts in its execution.

Consequently, we now propose a refurbished specification for the same four steps of the 4SRS-SoaML, still using SPEM, according to the performed analysis and future challenges ahead, and influenced by recent projects experience. Although we propose changes in micro-steps for every step, only one of the main steps has a name change, namely Step 2. Participants optimization (Figure 6). This is due to the reorganization of micro-steps within the first and second step, as we present next.

Step 1: Participants Creation

Although the first step was purely automatic, with the creation of Participants (P) of type i, c and d for each Use-case (UC), many were killed just after the UC classification by the systems analyst in the beginning of second step. So, in order to make the process more linear and efficient, also saving processing time and memory space, the first step now initiates with a micro-step covering the UC classification by the systems analyst, followed by an automatic micro-step responsible for P creation (Figure 7).

This change abolishes the need for the previous micro-step 2.ii) Local elimination, as the analyst role anticipates the UC classification task, preventing the creation of unneeded P. In order to further encapsulate the initial setup of P, two other micro-steps are migrated from the second to the first step, Participant Naming and Participant Description, as following described:

Micro-Step 1.i) Use-case Classification: Classify each UC regarding the nature of its P to be generated, among the eight different combinations or patterns ('', 'i', 'c', 'd', 'ic', 'di', 'cd', 'icd'), according to the UC description.

Micro-Step 1.ii) Participant Creation: Generate a set of P of types i, c, d, directly from the existing leaf UC, with no human intervention necessary, except when more than one of each P type must be generated according to the textual description and model of the UC, in case there is a need to separate or fragment a given functionality.

Micro-Step 1.iii) Participant Naming: P Originated from the previous micro-step are given a name, complementing the automatically tagged one, which must reflect the role of the P within the entire UC and also its type (c, d or i), in order to semantically give hints on what it represents.

Micro-Step 1.iv) Participant Description: Provides an extended structure for the required description of the P's role for the service behavior, information which has as main input the textual description of the original UC from the UC model.

Figure 6. Newly proposed sequence for the four steps of the 4SRS-SoaML

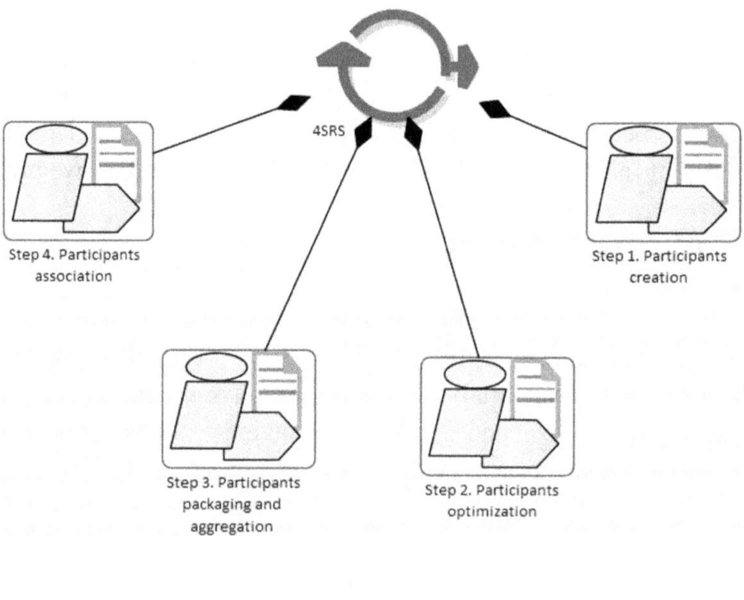

Step 2: Participants Optimization

Due to this concentration of tasks associated to P creation in the first step, the second step greatly diminishes its number of detailed micro-steps but not its global complexity, remaining the most crucial step in the method. Despite the renumbering of the micro-steps, nothing is changed in their functional side, as presented in Figure 8 and next synthesized:

Micro-Step 2.i) Participant Representation: Its purpose is to identify a P whose role can be represented by another P from the global architecture. This micro-step signals P that can be eliminated without losing coherence within the architecture, while incorporating them in the representing P.

Micro-step 2.ii) Global Elimination: Identifies which P must be eliminated in the context of the global model, where the P that is represented by itself or represents other P is maintained, while the rest are eliminated.

Micro-Step 2.iii) Participant Renaming: P which have not been eliminated are renamed and, in cases where the P under analysis results of the representation of more than one P, the new name must reflect its global execution in the project context.

Micro-Step 2.iv) Participant Specification: Describe P that, in micro-step 2.i), were considered to represent other P without losing any information and were meanwhile eliminated in micro-step 2.ii).

Figure 7. Detail of the newly proposed step 1. participant creation

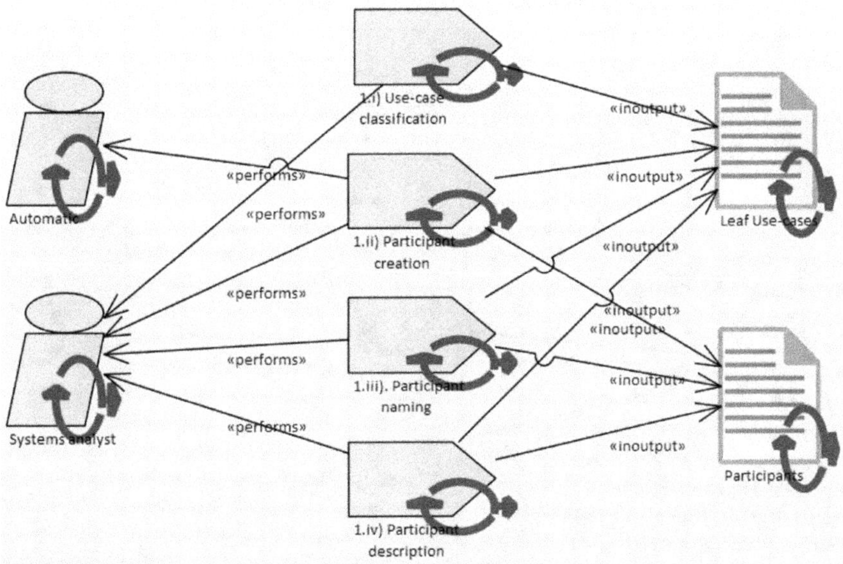

The new micro-step 2.ii) now constitutes the only automated task within this second step, although not completely, with the remaining three micro-steps being under responsibility of the systems analyst role. As previously noted, these micro-steps would greatly benefit from added tool support in order to aid its execution by the systems analyst in navigating throughout the list of P.

Step 3: Participants Packaging and Aggregation

As the inner details of Step 3 were not fully explored in previous research efforts, we now propose to further divide its functionality in additional micro-steps, especially in what relates to separating the packaging and aggregation actions. According to the conventional method, since packaging introduces a very light semantic cohesion between the P, it can be flexibly used to allow a temporary obtainment of more comprehensive and understandable P models. On the other hand, as aggregation imposes a strong semantic cohesion between P, it should only be used when it is explicitly assumed that the set of considered P is affected by a conscious design decision.

The current packaging and aggregation of P in SP implies the early association of P, anticipating some of the work to be performed in the fourth step. This opens a breach in the method's logic sequence, which should be avoided. Besides that, the current micro-steps do not take full advantage of SoaML elements as Catalog, ServiceInterface and Capability (OMG, 2012). Since Catalog extends the UML2

Figure 8. Detail of the newly proposed step 2. participant optimization

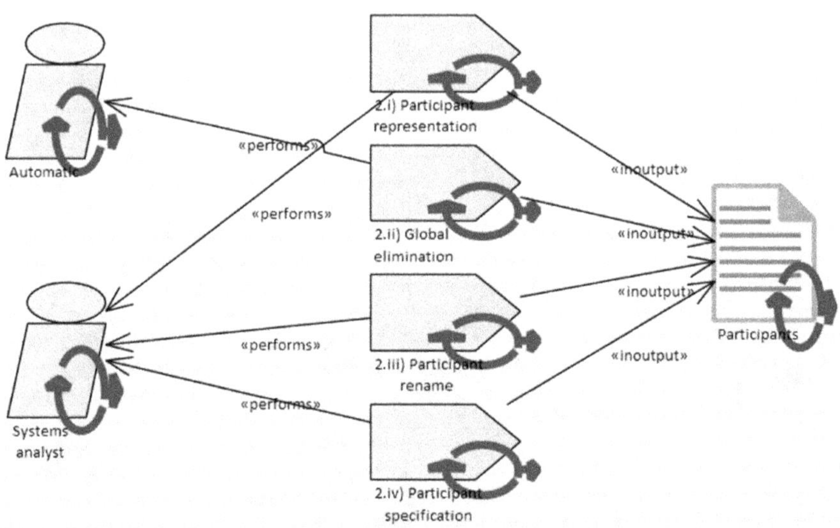

Package element, and ServiceInterface and Capability extend the UML2 Class element, P should be packaged through the use of Catalogs, while aggregation of P should be reflected in the definition of related ServiceInterfaces and Capabilities.

This due, the new proposed micro-steps for Step 3 are presented in Figure 9 and next described:

Micro-Step 3.i) Catalog Naming: Performs the identification and naming of the Catalogs to create packages of P, according to the desired wrapping of P, and with the possibility to have Catalogs inside a Catalog, as is the case with UML2 Packages.

Micro-Step 3.ii) Catalog Description: Fills in the required description of the Catalog, optionally categorizing or classifying elements by Category or CategoryValue, having as input the textual descriptions of the originating P from the previous step.

Micro-Step 3.iii) ServiceInterface/Capability Naming: Performs the identification and naming of the ServiceInterfaces/Capabilities to create aggregation of P, according to the intended aggregation service interface and responsibilities.

Micro-Step 3.iv) ServiceInterface/Capability Description: Defines the interface and responsibilities of a P to provide or consume a service, possibly including specific protocols, commands, and information exchange, or even specifying various protocols for using the functional capabilities defined by the servicer interface, so providing reusable protocol definitions in different P providing or consuming that same Service.

As in the previous step, the micro-steps from Step 3 would greatly benefit from added tool support in order to aid its execution by the software architect in managing throughout the list of P in order to create Catalogs and ServiceInterfaces/Capabilities.

Step 4: Participants Association

The fourth and final step still does not take full advantage of SoaML elements also, as for instance the ServiceChannel and ServiceContract. A ServiceChannel represents a plain communication path between Services and Requests within an architecture, while, on the other hand, a ServiceContract is the stricter formalization of a binding exchange of information, goods, or obligations between parties defining a service, which is used to model the specification for a specific service.

ServiceChannels are already being informally used inside the P aggregated in one SP, which is now part of the actions to take on the fourth step, while ServiceContracts are to be directed to associations between SP and P included in the ServiceInterface/Capability aggregations previously defined, usually connected to a higher-level

Figure 9. Detail of the newly proposed step 3. participant packaging and aggregation

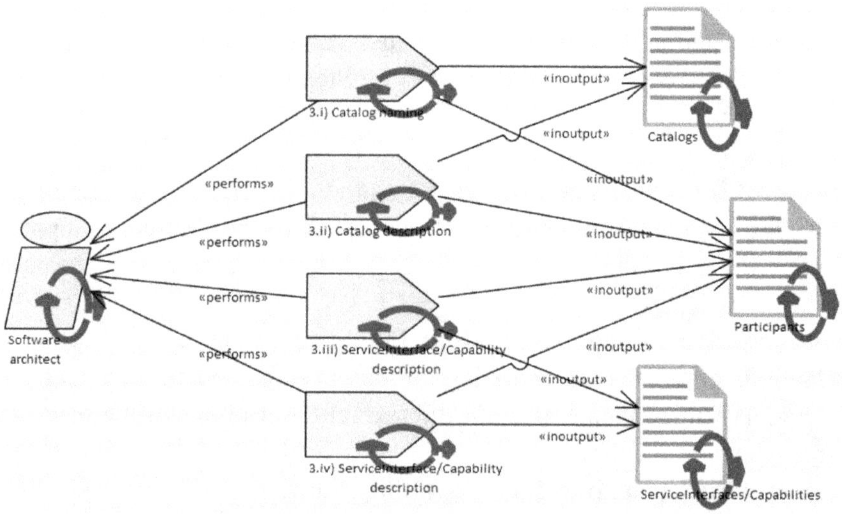

"business view". Despite the novelty of the use of these SoaML elements, the two existing micro-steps remain unchanged, as they can seamlessly accommodate their processing. Nevertheless, the two micro-steps associated to handling the SP in Step 3 now migrate to this step, as presented in Figure 10 and followingly described:

Micro-Step 4.i) Direct Associations: Deriving from P originated by the same UC, these associations are depicted from the classification given in micro-step 1.i).

Micro-Step 4.ii) Use-case Model Associations: Can be inferred from the textual descriptions of UC, that is, when a UC description refers implicitly or explicitly to another UC, the associations inferred imply that the UC are connected.

Micro-step 4.iii) Super-participant Naming: Performs the identification and naming of the SP, the new name must reflect its global execution in the project context according to the aggregation of P generated in the previous micro-steps.

Micro-Step 4.iv) Super-participant Description: Provides an extended structure for the required description of the SP's role for the service behavior, according to the aggregation of P generated in the previous micro-steps.

Again as in the previous step, micro-steps of this step would greatly benefit from added tool support in order to aid its execution by the software architect in managing throughout the lists of UC and P in order to create associations between P and SP. Another interesting added tool support would be on the generation of the final architecture schema, with all the associations between P and SP and related packages, as this represents a substantial, time consuming, manual task.

Figure 10. Detail of the newly proposed step 4. participant association

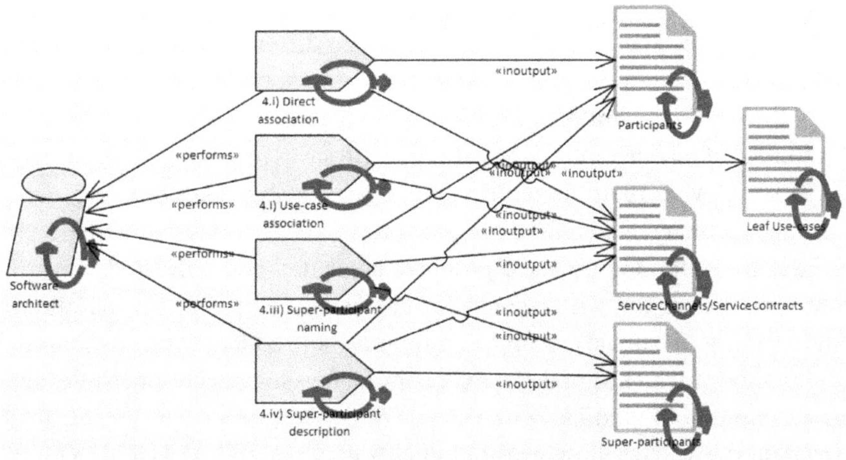

DISCUSSION

This specification covers the 4SRS-SoaML version of the 4SRS method, but also takes into account the evolutions occurred within the method during the past ten years research time. Despite the diverse directions followed within the different proposals, this current specification intends to be easily adaptable to be of use to any one of them, due to the use of SPEM modeling features. This specification prepares this method towards the ability to better ground future evolution proposals as well as their validation, and also to provision for the development of support tools.

The performed analysis on the method allowed identifying and solving small issues, as the one related to the creation of two or more Participants of each type when a Use-case type should be further divided. It was also important for recognizing issues which were not fully explored in previous research work as in Steps 3 and 4, and even for pertinent SoaML elements' use that were not yet been explored. Moreover, it permitted to balance the workload between the four steps and so to even the number and weight of tasks among them.

Another relevant upgrade was to clearly assign the roles and define the work products associated to each task in the micro-steps. The roles were assigned according to the RUP methodology. There, the business-process analyst is in charge of the Business Modeling discipline, having the responsibility to discover all business use cases, the systems analyst is in charge of Requirements, having to discover all requirement use cases, and the software architect is in charge of Analysis and Design, having to decide on technologies for the whole solution.

Related Research

Diverse approaches are currently available, using different strategies to handle the connection between requirements and architecture, according to each intervention setting. Although structurally alike, each approach has its proper insights. A review on a limited set of relevant model-based approaches was recently performed (Salgado et al., 2016b), with their transformation issues being analyzed and compared accordingly. As many of the initial research proposals, the reviewed CBSP technique and ATRIUM methodology were properly presented and validated, nevertheless there was no further known research activity involving them. On the other hand, although being active in the research community, both STREAM process and 4SRS-SoaML method still lack support of a proper tool for their execution, a relevant issue identified in previous studies.

In a related topic but following the cloud computing trend, MADCAT (Inzinger et al., 2014) is a methodology that tackles the practical problems faced when designing and deploying cloud applications. Also, incremental deployment of cloud services has been receiving particular importance, where successive increments must be integrated into existing cloud service architectures, requiring dynamic reconfiguration of software architectures to support integration and trigger deployments (Zuñiga-Prieto, Gonzalez-Huerta, Abrahao, & Insfran, 2014). Accordingly, microservices have recently appeared as a new architectural style that is native to the cloud, where organizations migrate or design these in order to promote building applications as a suite of small and cohesive services that are independently developed, deployed and scaled. Developers specify how to integrate them into the current application by describing both the integration logic and architectural impact of integration (Zúñiga-Prieto, Insfran, Abrahao, & Cano-Genoves, 2016).

CONTRIBUTIONS AND FUTURE WORK

As to contributions of this work, the added value of the SPEM specification, allowing for activity tailoring on any of the related versions of the 4SRS method, and for seamlessly analyze and compare them with any other similar methods, count as an innovative step forward regarding existing solutions in this topic. It also allows for better perceptions from the users and added flexibility in the techniques to work with the method. This is important to aid in the work towards reducing the gap between experts and novices, by supporting practical roadmaps, frameworks, and guidelines that can be more linear and easily taught to students, novices or experienced analysts outside a specific domain. These are key issues, as most approaches are hard to tackle at first and require a significant level of skill and expertise from the analysts to be used effectively.

Regarding future work, we plan to further detail the proposed tasks, developing guiding heuristics and strategies to guide their operationalization, while exploring other scenarios and comparisons between the user's performance and its adaptability regarding the use of different service model views. Also, an empirical evaluation of this approach in academic/industrial projects, where the plan is to test and evaluate the application of the presented method in a real setting, is also in our plans. The development of an aiding support tool to explore and process the different perspectives, by taking advantage of the SPEM foundations of this work is also essential at this point of this research, being currently in development phase. Moreover, we intend to continue to detail the alignment and traceability mechanisms of this solution inside the V-Model and PGR-CISQ Cube approach (Salgado et al., 2016a).

CONCLUSION

The transformation between requirements and architectures is a main concern in the development of information systems, where service-oriented architecture plays an important part in todays' research panorama. Also, the growing use of the SoaML notation can help to strengthen the link between business and technological worlds ever more interconnected and involved in issues of requirements elicitation, process modeling and business strategy. Our work integrates all of these topics and proposes a way to generate, align and maintain a service-oriented logical architecture for a desired information system, based on the elicitation of use cases and their transformation to a SoaML representation at the end of the 4SRS-SoaML method execution.

With the use of modeling features (SoaML, SPEM) as well as popular reference models (RUP) inside the area for this proposal, it allows for further development of the present solution and leaves an open door to future connections to other points of interest. The possibility to tailor this specification to other versions of the 4SRS method, the seamlessly adaptability to different audiences and types of projects, and as the ground for the development of support tools, constitute an added value contribution of this proposal.

The detailed specification and analysis of the existing 4SRS-SoaML method allowed identifying a number of issues that raised an opportunity to evolve the method. We believe that our new proposal for the detailed specification of the refurbished 4SRS-SoaML is better prepared to face future challenges and evolutions, where in a short-term view, we can identify cloud computing and microservices solutions, and also the development of a prototype support tool.

REFERENCES

Azevedo, S., Machado, R. J., & Maciel, R. S. P. (2012). On the use of model transformations for the automation of the 4SRS transition method. *Lecture Notes in Business Information Processing, 112*, 249–264. doi:10.1007/978-3-642-31069-0_22

Azevedo, S., Machado, R. J., Muthig, D., & Ribeiro, H. (2009). Refinement of Software Product Line Architectures through Recursive Modeling Techniques. *On the Move to Meaningful Internet Systems: OTM 2009 Workshops.*

Delgado, A., De Guzmán, I. G., & Piattini, M. (2010). From BPMN business process models to SoaML service models: a transformation-driven approach. In *2nd International Conference on Software Technology and Engineering (ICSTE)* (pp. 314–319). Academic Press.

Elvesaeter, B., & Panfilenko, D. (2010). Aligning business and IT models in service-oriented architectures using BPMN and SoaML. In *Proceedings of the 1st International Workshop on Model-Driven Interoperability* (pp. 61--68). ACM.

Ferreira, N., Santos, N., Machado, R. J., Fernandes, J. E., & Gasevic, D. (2014). A V-Model Approach for Business Process Requirements Elicitation in Cloud Design. In Advanced Web Services (pp. 551--578). Springer.

Ferreira, N., Santos, N., Machado, R. J., & Gasevic, D. (2012). Derivation of Process-Oriented Logical Architectures: An Elicitation Approach for Cloud Design. In A. J. O. Dieste and N. Juristo (Ed.), *13th International Conference on Product-Focused Software Development and Process Improvement - PROFES 2012* (Vol. 7343, pp. 44–58). Madrid, Spain: Springer-Verlag.

France, R., & Rumpe, B. (2007). Model-driven Development of Complex Software: A Research Roadmap. In *Proceedings of the Conference on Future of Software Engineering* (pp. 37--54). IEEE. 10.1109/FOSE.2007.14

Galster, M., Eberlein, A., & Moussavi, M. (2009). Comparing methodologies for the transition between software requirements and architectures. In *Conference Proceedings - IEEE International Conference on Systems, Man and Cybernetics* (pp. 2380--2385). IEEE.

Inzinger, C., Nastic, S., Sehic, S., Vogler, M., Li, F., & Dustdar, S. (2014). MADCAT: A methodology for architecture and deployment of cloud application topologies. *Proceedings - IEEE 8th International Symposium on Service Oriented System Engineering,* 13–22. 10.1109/SOSE.2014.9

Kroll, P., & Kruchten, P. (2003). *The rational unified process made easy: a practitioner's guide to the RUP*. Addison-Wesley.

López-Sanz, M., & Marcos, E. (2012). ArchiMeDeS: A model-driven framework for the specification of service-oriented architectures. *Information Systems*, *37*(3), 257–268. doi:10.1016/j.is.2011.11.002

Machado, R. J., Fernandes, J. M., Monteiro, P., & Rodrigues, H. (2005). Transformation of UML Models for Service-Oriented Software Architectures. *12th IEEE International Conference and Workshops on the Engineering of Computer-Based Systems (ECBS'05)*, 173–182. 10.1109/ECBS.2005.73

Machado, R. J., Fernandes, J. M., Monteiro, P., & Rodrigues, H. (2006). Refinement of Software Architectures by Recursive Model Transformations. In *Product-Focused Software Process Improvement* (pp. 422–428). Springer. doi:10.1007/11767718_38

OMG. (2008). *Software & Systems Process Engineering Meta-Model Specification (SPEM)*. Retrieved from http://www.omg.org/spec/SPEM/2.0/

OMG. (2011). *Business Process Model and Notation*. Retrieved from http://www.omg.org/spec/BPMN/2.0

OMG. (2012). *Service oriented architecture Modeling Language (SoaML) Specification*. Retrieved from http://www.omg.org/spec/SoaML/1.0.1/

Ruiz-Rube, I., Dodero, J. M., Palomo-Duarte, M., Ruiz, M., & Gawn, D. (2013). Uses and applications of Software & Systems Process Engineering Meta-Model process models. A systematic mapping study. *Journal of Software: Evolution and Process*, *25*(9), 999–1025.

Salgado, C. E., Machado, R. J., & Maciel, R. S. P. (2016a). A Three-Dimensional Approach for a Quality-Based Alignment Between Requirements and Architecture. In *International Conference on Exploring Services Science* (Vol. 2, pp. 112-125). Springer.

Salgado, C. E., Machado, R. J., & Maciel, R. S. P. (2016b). MATRA : A Framework for Assessing Model-based Approaches on the Transformation between Requirements and Architecture. In Enterprise, Business-Process and Information Systems Modeling (pp. 1-12). Springer.

Salgado, C. E., Teixeira, J., Santos, N., Machado, R. J., & Maciel, R. S. P. (2015). A SoaML Approach for Derivation of a Process-Oriented Logical Architecture from Use Cases. In *Exploring Services Science* (pp. 80–94). Springer.

Santos, M. Y., & Machado, R. J. (2010). On the derivation of class diagrams from use cases and logical software architectures. *Proceedings - 5th International Conference on Software Engineering Advances,* 107–113. 10.1109/ICSEA.2010.24

Yue, T., Briand, L. C., & Labiche, Y. (2011). A systematic review of transformation approaches between user requirements and analysis models. *Requirements Engineering*, *16*(2), 75–99. doi:10.100700766-010-0111-y

Zuñiga-Prieto, M., Gonzalez-Huerta, J., Abrahao, S., & Insfran, E. (2014). Towards a model-driven dynamic architecture reconfiguration process for cloud services integration. *CEUR Workshop Proceedings*, *1331*, 52–61.

Zúñiga-Prieto, M., Insfran, E., Abrahao, S., & Cano-Genoves, C. (2016). Incremental Integration of Microservices in Cloud Applications. *Information Systems Development: Complexity in Information Systems Development (ISD2016 Proceedings)*, 93–105.

Chapter 7
Quantitative Evaluation of the Accomplishment of Operational Plans of the Organization and Context-Free Grammar Operational Planning Language

Valeri Pougatchev
University of Technology, Jamaica

ABSTRACT

The innovative and effective solutions for the strategic and operational planning management of organizations are discussed. The author reviews current and past challenges of the strategic and operational planning and describes two novel solutions with practical implementation for improving these processes. The first one is a numerical indicator V-index that represents the level of accomplishment of operational plans of the entire organization, its units, and members of staff. The V-index serves operational plans with hierarchical and non-hierarchical structures. The second solution is a novel context-free grammar operational planning language for a formal definition of the planning process. All examples and case-study presentation are based on fragments of the faculty/departments/programs of some fictional educational institution (university).

DOI: 10.4018/978-1-5225-5522-3.ch007

INTRODUCTION

In the beginning of this research we identify two main goals to be achieved:

1. *Develop a numerical indicator ("V-index") of the accomplishment of the unit/ persons operational plans, which provides transparency of viewing of the organization's and staff's achievements at all levels.*

This parameter also facilitates a process of year-by-year strategic analysis of the success of the organization, its units, employees by managers and provides an effective control of organizational plans.

2. *Design a formal precise defined universal language to facilitate communication between all stakeholders of the organizational planning processes.*

This language guarantees that everyone uses the same terminology, measurement requirements, and has the same vision on the planning process. It also facilitates an effective mechanism for creating an overall operational plan of the organization with a holistic balance between its different items. The content of this language is, actually, a set of organizational planning rules and performs all communications between personnel activity and computing machines without being subject to limitations of any specific computational platform (hardware, software, operational system, etc.).

Solutions presented in this study do not depend on the size of the organization; they can be implemented in the entire organization or partially in some units. For practitioners, the chapter provides a source code of scripts, which describe processes discussed here and can be used for practical simulation on readers' own computers.

This research is unique because there are no other studies which investigate proposed goals.

Who is this chapter for?

- Readers, who are involved in the strategic/operational planning processes of the organization as managers, and their employees – all staff of the organization.
- Employees of the office of strategy management, if there are any at the organization.
- Information communication technology (ICT) specialists, with software development, database management design, and system administration background.

- Researchers and designers, which are focused on up-to-date technology in the Theory of Management and Computer Science.
- Any practitioners, who are interested to implement proposed solutions.

A REVIEW OF CHALLENGES IN THE STRATEGIC PLANNING MANAGEMENT OF THE ORGANIZATIONS AND PROPOSED QUANTITATIVE SOLUTIONS

We are living in a time when management theories are developing under the great impact of quantitative mathematical methods and computing. The three main areas of the quantitative approach are – management science (another name for operations research), operational management, and management information systems (Griffin, 1990). This approach includes the content covered in Table 1.

The major contribution of the quantitative approach for management is in the area of decision-making, particularly as it relates to organizational planning and controlling (Robbins, 1991; Hellriegel & Slocum, 1992). It places an emphasis on computers in decision support systems (Higgins, 1991). During this time, it was clear that quantitative management approaches successfully supplied managers with tools and techniques to increase effectiveness and efficiency (Raymond, 1964), unfortunately, with one condition. To apply a quantitative approach to decision-making, individuals with mathematical, statistical, engineering, economics, software engineering, and business background skills are needed. From our point of view, a team approach to decision-making is required, where each member is an expert in areas mentioned above. These debates have been continuing from the late 40s to the middle of 90s, where the introduction of computers made a great impact on our culture. Osborn characterized this time as a *'new industrial revolution'* (Osborn, 1979). Toffler (Toffler, 1980) called the advent of microelectronics as a part of *'the third wave of change'* in human history, and Naisbitt (Naisbitt, 1982) predicted a transformation of an industrial society to an *'information society'*.

Table 1.

o Mathematical statistics, o Optimization and information models, o Waiting line theory,	o Linear programming, o Time series analysis, o The probability theory,	o Decision theory, o Computer simulations o

In the past, managers usually referred to the term *'long-range planning'*. More recently, they use the term *'strategic planning'*. Although many still use these terms interchangeably, strategic planning and long-range planning are different. Long-range planning is generally considered to be a policy or set of policies implemented over a period of several years, with the assumption that the projection of (or extrapolation from) the past and the current situation is sufficient to ensure the implementation of future activities. In other words, long-range planning assumes that the environment is stable while strategic planning assumes that a system must be responsive to a dynamic and changing environment. The term *'strategic planning'* is meant to capture the nature (comprehensive, holistic, thoughtful or fundamental) of this type of planning.

Strategic and operational planning is a critical management process of the organization. It shows to the senior management its current position as well as the positions of all units and individuals, on its/their way to achieving its/their strategic and individual goals. An understanding of this management requirement by the senior leaders of the organization is a prerequisite for the successful achievement of its targets (Penny, 2001).

The process of operational planning has to be based on a strong structure of targets/objectives/goals, cascading and aligning them with a holistic hierarchy system throughout the organization. No target or objective can be presented in the system independently – all of them are interrelated horizontally and vertically from the bottom to the top and vice versa.

Role of the Operational Plan's Accomplishment in the Organization's Strategic Vision

The success of each organization generally is based on many components and the ability of the organization to achieve their targets can be considered as one of the main indicators of its success. In this study, we follow the definitions given by U.S. Department of Energy and Oak Ridge Associated Universities (2001):

- *Strategic Planning* is a process of developing a mission and long-range objectives and determining in advance how they will be accomplished.
- *Operational Planning* is a process of setting short-range objectives and determining in advance how they will be accomplished.
- *Strategy (Organization Targets)* is a plan for pursuing the mission and achieving objectives.
- *Mission statement* (like organizations) tends to stand for long periods of time. But they should be examined and debated periodically, both by those to whom the organization 'reports' and by those accountable for carrying them

out. A whole hierarchy of missions exists in a large organization, and each level derives its mission from the mission of the parent.

The last definition reflects the main ideas of organization's mission statement – to be dynamic, well-structured on all levels of organization's hierarchy, and be inheritable.

From our point of view, an effective management process should be based on a Balanced Scorecard (BSC), first proposed by Kaplan & Norton (Kaplan & Norton, 1992). The BSC reflects the balance between short and long-term objectives. They emphasize that the companies that can translate their strategy into their measurement system, are able to execute their strategy. Hence, a freely adjustable system must provide:

- An understanding of the organization's vision of the future.
- A holistic model of the strategy, that allows all employees to see how they contribute to the success of the organization.
- A reflection of all objectives in the scorecard. If the objectives and measurements are identified, successful implementation is likely to occur. If not, investments and initiatives will be wasted.
- The holistic balance of the organization planning strategy – on the horizontal and vertical perspective.

The targets (individual plans) of each member of staff can be considered as a part of the unit's operational plan along with his/her colleagues' targets with some weights (*horizontal alignment*). At the same time, each individual target can be considered as a part of the operational plan of units above and weighted as a part of the supervisor's operational/strategic plan (*vertical alignment*). Here each target has two weights – one for horizontal alignment (the sum of these weights must equal to 100%) and the second one - for reflecting a part (in percents) of the objective/target weight from the level above. This aspect will be described later in this chapter when we discuss an algorithm for calculating a *Total Accomplishment* of the objectives/ targets by the unit/individual.

Cascading corporate goals throughout t the organization allows alignment of the entire workforce to the overall strategy. This ensures that everyone is focused on the organization's business objectives.

One of the main goals of the well-built management system is to be able to provide *transparency* of viewing of the organization's and staff's achievements at all levels. Everybody should feel that he/she is a member of one team and he/she is able to see his/her contribution to the common success. It is easier for employees to understand what and why some goals need to be accomplished. If employees are part of the process, they will accept it. If they know there is no employee participation - it doesn't matter how good the plan, it will not succeed. There will be chaos in the organization.

STRUCTURE OF THE OPERATIONAL PLANS OF THE ORGANIZATION AND V-INDEX

Hierarchy Structure of Operational Plans and Vertical/Horizontal Alignments of Their Items

No two businesses in the world are exactly the same; each uses a unique set of tools and processes to manage their customers. We need to ensure that an effective management process can easily be adjusted and conformed to specific company needs. Each part of it also exists to carry out some commensurate task or mission of its own. An understanding of this unique mission by the senior management of the organization is a prerequisite for the strategic planning process to achieve its targets Each organization has to control their movement according to their *Vision* while following their *Mission*:

Let us show how to evaluate and measure the progress of the achievements of the institution targets. Hereinafter, *measurability* is the main essential feature of well-written goals, objectives, and targets; they must be quantifiable. In Figure 1 an indicator $\boldsymbol{S}_i$ (light circle) identifies a position of the organization for comparison with the target position $\boldsymbol{T}_i$ (dark circle). The distance Ω_i between the centers (positive, negative, or is equal to zero) of the circles $\boldsymbol{S}_i$ and $\boldsymbol{T}_i$ can be considered as a measure of the success of the organization in achieving its targets. Later in this chapter, will be proposed an algorithm, which calculates a total accomplishment of the organization's plan. With $\boldsymbol{S}_i$ and $\boldsymbol{T}_i$, we associate real numbers and calls them as V - indices. At each appraisal period, the position of the organization may be:

Figure 1. Example of achieving targets by the University during 5 years strategic planning (Pougatchev & Kulkarni, 2011)

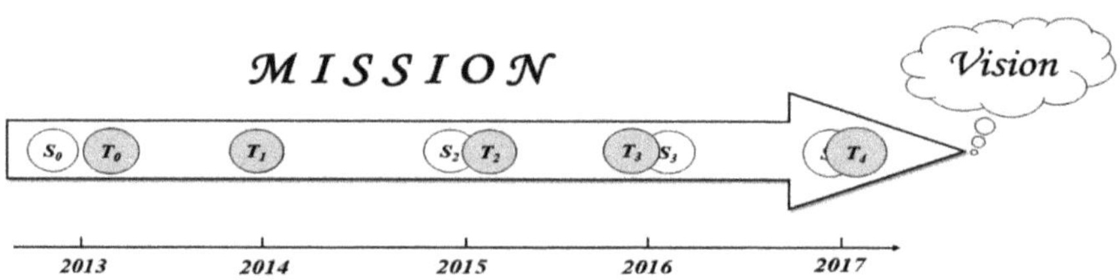

- **Unaccomplished:** In this case, a circle S_i is to the left of target T_i. The organization hasn't achieved all its goals for that period (2013, 2015, and 2017 in Figure 1). We have $\Omega < 1$ (<100%).
- **Accomplished:** In this case, the centre of circle S_i perfectly matches that of T_i. The organization has achieved its goals in 2014 year. We have $\Omega = 1$ (= 100%).
- **Overfullfilled:** In this case, the circle S_i is to the right side of T_i. The organization has not only achieved its targets but has exceeded the set of achievements (as in 2016). We have $\Omega > 1$ (>100%).

Hereinafter we need to give definitions for some of the terms (see Table 2).

Operational plans (OPs) of the organization and its units have the hierarchical structure of their objectives (items of the OP). The hierarchy of objectives is a managerial concept that enables managers to view the different levels or magnitudes of a decision within an organization in terms of a hierarchy of objectives to be achieved. Accordingly, definition of the operational plan, given by U.S. Department of Energy and Oak Ridge Associated Universities (2001) the OP can be considered as a *set* of items (objectives) with hierarchical links between each other.

The success of accomplishment of the entire organization's plan depends on how well this plan is presented and specified on each level of the organization's hierarchy; highlighting what exactly must be done by each unit and individual. To support it, the organization has to have a structural mechanism for balancing all '*chains*' of its hierarchical plans. Kaplan and Norton stated: *'The annual planning process provides an architecture around which the alignment process can be executed'* (Kaplan & Norton, 2005).

Table 2.

Definition 2.1 The Object of Responsibility (OOR) is a member of the organization staff or unit, which is responsible for accomplishing some objectives/targets.
Examples: • Prof. Elma White – member of academic staff of some department (OOR as a member of the academic staff) • School of engineering (OOR as a unit of the institution)
Definition 2.2 V-index is the Total Accomplishment by the OOR/OORs its/their goals/objectives/ targets within the appraisal period.
Note: Actually V-index is a measure of the total accomplishment of the operational plan by the OOR given its objectives/targets within the appraisal period.
Definition 2.3 *Ω is a Total Accomplishment of the organization targets in the process of achieving their targets within* appraisal period.

We present strict definitions for *Vertical* and *Horizontal alignments* between elements of organization's operational plan (Pougatchev & Kulkarni, 2013-2014) shown in Table 3.

Organization goals do not just happen. They are orchestrated at the top of its hierarchy and executed at individual levels. It means any organization's goals are completed by individuals by their day-to-day efforts, which should be guided by a structure that provides clear direction and support from managers. Individual goals are derived from organization's/units' objectives and create a foundation for success. In this case, individuals know how and what they do, fits with the work of others and this is important since their efforts are interwoven with others in their units (Pougatchev & Kulkarni, 2011).

Each target *must be personalized.* It means a good strategic plan should have comprehensive and clear targets. Each target must be associated with some OOR, which is assigned to accomplish it. There are no targets without strict relation to the person or unit who/which must do it. Targets on intermediate levels (between

Table 3.

Definition 2.4 *Vertical hierarchical alignment (VHA)* is any link between nodes at the two neighboring levels (level up and level down) in the organization operational plan, which actually delegates/inherits some pieces of plan and have to be done at these levels.
Examples: • *Faculty of Engineering & Computing (FENC) operational plan describes a research activity: "Publish 10 papers in the international reviewed journals".* • *The Department of Computing Science (DCS), which also belongs to the FENC, must publish 5 papers in the international journals. This is an example of inheritance (deriving) some items on level below from the 'parent' plan.*
Definition 2.5 *Non-hierarchical alignment (nHA)* is any link between nodes at two different levels or two different nodes of hierarchy in the organization operational plan, where OOR shares some items of its operational plan with other OOR(s).
Examples: • *DCS participates in research with other departments, even from other faculties.* • *A member of academic staff from one department writes a research paper in collaboration with a member of academic staff from another department* • *"Bachelor of Science in Computing & Information Technology" (BSCIT)* programme, *which belongs to DCS, describes its own research activity: "Publish three papers in the international reviewed journals". At the same time the "Bachelor of Science in Computing with Management Studies" (BSCMS)* programme, *which belongs to DCS as well, describes its own research activity: "Publish one paper in an international refereed journal". This paper must be written in cooperation with BSCIT programme.*
Definition 2.6 *Horizontal alignment* is a link between any pieces of OOR's plan on one level.
Example: • *One person must align his/her targets for the upcoming appraisal period to achieve 100% accomplishment.*

organization targets and final executor) have their own hierarchical structure. The sentence *'Each target must be associated with some object'*, means that object-executor of the target is a person or unit, who/which is charged to accomplish it by his/her supervisor, or possibly the supervisor himself if he has not decided who will be in charge for that job. It means that the role of the supervisor is to mobilize his/her staff for accomplishing some objective/target. Otherwise, he/she will be personally responsible for that job.

Operational Planning Service

Proper measurement and evaluation of targets' accomplishment is the key to compare the performance of the operational plans and processes. Combining multiple criteria of evaluations into a single number is quite common practice in academic institutions. Consider the method of expressing a *grade point average* (GPA, a single number) as an indicator of student's academic performance. The GPA is simply determined by averaging the grades of all courses (such as scores in mathematics, physics, or chemistry by individual criteria evaluations) which the student achieves.

Each element of an operational plan (at all levels) has two parameters (both are positive numbers, each lesser or equal to 1) – *weight*, which indicates a part of target within the list of targets at that level must be done in the planning period, and *real weight*, achieved by OOR during the appraisal period. The products of values of these two attributes give a digit number *'V-index'* - real achievement of executing an element of the operational plan. If this value is equal to *1*, it means that particular element of the plan was *accomplished* at 100%. If that value is lesser than *1*, it means that element of the operational plan was not completed (*unaccomplished*), as it was initially planned. If the value of the *V*-index is greater than *1*, it means that element of the operational plan has not only achieved its targets but has exceeded the set of achievements (*overfullfilled*).

V-Index as a Numerical Indicator of the Accomplishment of the Unit/Person Operational Plans

We start with the top level *'Goals'*. The operational plan on the top level has several goals - 'G_1', 'G_2', ..., 'G_n' with weights ("*planning weights*") 'w_1', 'w_2', ..., 'w_n' and "*real weights*" (real achievements of goals by OOR) are - 'r_1', 'r_2',..., 'r_n'. Using the methods of *Linear Algebra*, it is reasonable to consider a set of values of *weights* and *real* attributes as the set of coordinates of the *vectors*. Generally speaking, according to this idea, we have:

- *Vector of goals* $\overrightarrow{VG} = [w_1(G_1), \ldots, w_n(G_n)]$, where *n* is a number of goals from the operational plan with $\sum_{i=1}^{n} w_i(G_i) = 1$

Vector of real achievements of goals

$$\overrightarrow{VRAG} = [r_1(G_1), \ldots, r_n(G_n)]$$

where

$$r_i(G_i) \leq 1$$

or

$$r_i(G_i) > 1$$

- If $r_i(G_i) = 1$ it means, that i^{th} goal is completed at 100%,
- if $r_i(G_i) < 1$ it means, that this goal is completed lesser than 100%, and if it is equal to *0,* which means – not completed.
- if $r_i(G_i) > 1$ it means, that this goal is overfulfilled than that it was planned initially.

Inner products of vectors $\overrightarrow{VG}$ and $\overrightarrow{VRAG}$ gives

$$\boldsymbol{\Omega} = \langle\overrightarrow{VG}, \overrightarrow{VRAG}\rangle = \sum_{i=1}^{n} w_i(G_i) r_i(G_i) \tag{2.1}$$

According definition 2.3, $\boldsymbol{\Omega}$ is a measure of the total accomplishment of the operational plan by the educational institution as per its goals.

- Each coordinate $r_i\,(G_i)$ of the vector $\overrightarrow{VRAG}$ expresses a real achievement of accomplishing the goal G_i . Because each goal consists of one or several objectives, we have to go one level down to objectives level for the goal 'G_i'. At this level, we have a set of objectives $\{O_j\}$, where $j = \{1, \ldots, i_l\}$. We can consider a *vector of objectives*

$$\overrightarrow{VO_i} = [w_1(O_1), \ldots, w_{i_1}(O_{i_1})]$$

where

$$\sum_{j=1}^{i_1} w_j(O_j) = 1$$

and *vector of real achievements of objectives {O_j}*

$$\overrightarrow{VRAO_i} = [r_1(O_1), \ldots, r_{i_1}(O_{i_1})]$$

The $r_j(O_j)$ compares to *1* in the same manner as it was presented in equation (2.1).

Inner products of vectors $\overrightarrow{VO_i}$ and $\overrightarrow{VRAO_i}$ gives

$$\mathrm{r_i(G_i)} = \Omega_{G_i} = \langle \overrightarrow{VO_i}, \overrightarrow{VRAO_i} \rangle = \sum_{j=1}^{i_1} w_j(O_j) r_j(O_j)$$

The equation (2.1) can be rewritten as

$$\boldsymbol{\Omega} = \langle \overrightarrow{VG}, \overrightarrow{VRAG} \rangle = \sum_{i=1}^{n} w_i(G_i) r_i(G_i) =$$

$$\sum_{i=1}^{n} w_i(G_i) \Omega_{G_i} = \sum_{i=1}^{n} w_i(G_i) \Big(\sum_{j=1}^{i_1} w_j(O_j) r_j(O_j) \Big) \tag{2.2}$$

- Each coordinate $r_j\,(O_j)$ of vector $\overrightarrow{VRAO_i}$ expresses a real achievement of accomplishing of the *university targets*, which are related to objective 'O_j'. We have to go on one level down to targets level for the objective 'O_j'. Suppose 'j_1' is a number of targets for that objective. On this level, we can consider a *vector of targets*

$$\overrightarrow{VT}_j = [w_1(T_1), \ldots, w_{j_1}(T_{j_1})]$$

where

$$\sum_{t=1}^{j_1} w_t(T_t) = 1$$

and set of real achievements of targets *{T_t}* we consider as a *vector of real achievements of targets*

$$\overrightarrow{VRAT_j} = [r_1(T_1), \ldots, r_{j_1}(T_{j_1})]$$

where $r_j(T_j) \leq 1$, $r_j(T_j) > 1$, or $r_j(T_j) = 1$ (see above). *An inner product* of vectors $\overrightarrow{VT_j}$ and $\overrightarrow{VRAT}_j$

$$\Omega_{O_j} = \langle \overrightarrow{VT_j}, \overrightarrow{VRAT_j} \rangle = \sum_{t=1}^{j_1} w_t(T_t) r_t(T_t)$$

is a measure of the accomplishment of the university objective 'Oj''. The equation (2.2) can be rewritten as

$$\boldsymbol{\Omega} = \sum_{i=1}^{n} w_i(G_i) \Big(\sum_{j=1}^{i_1} w_j(O_j) r_j(O_j) \Big) =$$

$$= \sum_{i=1}^{n} w_i(G_i) \Big(\sum_{j=1}^{i_1} w_j(O_j) \Big(\sum_{t=1}^{j_1} w_t(T_t) r_t(T_t) \Big) \Big)$$

The level we have just considered is the lowest level of the *institutional strategic plan*. It is not necessary to show mathematical formulas on levels below because of the similar recursive nature of the algorithm and due to lack of space. The details and discussions/interpretations were extensively presented in previous publication (Pougatchev & Kulkarni, 2011).

- Each *division/unit* has a set of targets obtained from the upper-level *(institution targets)*. This is not a strict mapping of data because each *department/unit* has some specific *view* on targets obtained from the level above. For instance, let us consider the university target *'Student enrollment in university programmes'*. It is obvious, that *division of academic affairs* has some specific plans to support that target, but *the division of the university registrar* has another plan to provide success of its accomplishment. Here it is possible to say that full definition of targets to be accomplished is a combination of the definition of the target at levels above plus strict definition for that specific unit. This is very important because it provides a direct link between all university targets and their details for each unit of the university. It is a *vertical alignment* link from the top of the hierarchy of the university operational plan, to the bottom – to the *object of responsibility (OOR)*.

Using this approach, it is easy for the senior management of the university to get an absolutely precise answer (for example) to the question (*vertical analysis*) – *'Why our university has published just 20 journal papers, instead of 40, as was planned?'* The system can give a structured answer (accountability) which department (going through all levels) and which member of staff must do it, how many they did and who has not done it at all.

According to the above, it is possible to provide a *horizontal analysis* as well. For instance, if the manager would like to obtain the analysis of how publishing journal papers is going at some (for example – school/department) level, he/she can get details, online information which can present each school/department separately and/or in comparison with others, or in comparison with previous appraisal period.

The *V-index* gives the opportunity to have a long-term strategic analysis, how some specific OOR (person/unit) moves as per his/her/its vision.

Theoretically, there is no difference between the educational institution (organization), its units and some particular employee. All of them are objects for evaluation. This is very important because it opens a way for each OOR to create their own vision, which is the subset of the institution (organization)' vision. Everybody fills himself as a part of one organization and clearly sees his/her individual contribution to organization's common goals. From another side, the organization considers its own employees and units as '*atoms*' of its own '*body*', which could grow only if its every atom makes a real contribution.

CONTEXT-FREE GRAMMAR OPERATIONAL PLANNING LANGUAGE

The first task in process of creating an operational plan of the organization is to have *a universal standard language* of communication between different items of operational plans, created by managers or individuals from different (linked or not linked) or the same units of the organization. For example, when the employee and the manager operate on two different definitions of the same issue of the plan, the result of such "planning" will be failed or will not reflect a reality.

Operational planning processes should use a formal precisely defined language, like our '*natural*' languages, which is designed to facilitate communication between all stakeholders of the organizational planning process. However, this language differs from the natural language in two important ways. First, it has a narrower expressive domain, in that it facilitates only the communication of content of the objectives/targets and their accomplishment between all participants of the organization who are really involved into organization's business. Second, this language also enables the communication of personnel activity and computing machines without any limitations for some specific computational platform (hardware, software, operational system, etc.) Thus, the design of that language must respond to different requirements than a natural language.

Language designers need to have a basic vocabulary, a language structure (which must be able to capture a number of organizational planning rules), meaning, and other pragmatic features that aid in the understanding of how language works and provides a full control of the accomplishment of the operational plans. This vocabulary most naturally expresses itself in the form of language design *principles*, many of which are borrowed from linguistics and mathematics. The principles that underlie the design of that language fall into two main categories (Tucker, *et al.*, 2002): *syntax*, and *type systems* and *semantics*.

- **Syntax:** This design category helps designers understand what constitutes a correctly written operational plan. That is, what is the grammar for the process of creating the OP. The operational planning designers have borrowed strongly from the work of linguists in this area. For that design, we use the linguistic formalism called a *Context-Free Grammar* (CFG). This is done both for simplicity and clarity and to enable a more rigorous treatment of the concepts.
- **Type Systems and Semantics:** This area addresses types of values that the OP can manipulate and the meaning (semantic) of its fragments. Below we show that type systems and semantics are also best understood using a formal approach. This approach makes these processes independent of any particular

machine or operating system architecture – it is a fully abstract definition of the language. Portability is fundamentally important in that language design because machines and operating systems change; tying a language too closely to the features of a single machine automatically ensures its obsolescence.

With this in mind, note that the syntax is a structure of the language. In the 1950s, Noam Chomsky developed the idea of context-free grammars, and John Backus, with contributions by Peter Naur, developed a notational system for describing these grammars. They were used for creating the syntax of one of the first programming language Algol60. Later it was called Backus-Naur forms (BNFs for short), which have subsequently been used in the definition of many programming languages. Actually, as a BNF, this is a *meta-language*, which is used for describing other languages. We utilize this idea to describe an operational-planning language (OPL) that defines a set of rules for encoding documents in a format that is both human and machine-readable.

Some features of the CFG that have a recursive structure and make them useful in a variety of planning procedures in the organization are presented below.

A CFG for the OPL has four components:

1. A set of *terminals* symbols, which are the elementary symbols (represent themselves) of the language defined by the grammar. In production roles, presented below (3.1 – 3.21) terminals are: '*_subordinate:*', '*_itemID:*', '*_itemDef:*', '*_v-index:*', '*_vertical*', '*_person_horizont:*', '*_dueDate:*' etc. In this chapter, these elements are case-sensitive and presented using lower-case and italic fonts.
2. A set of *non-terminals* symbols, sometimes called '*syntax variables*'. Each non-terminal symbol needs to be further expanded and represents a set of strings of terminals. In (3.1 – 3.21) these are variables: *<OP>*, *<ITEM>*, *<WEIGHT>*, etc. In this chapter, these elements are presented using upper-case and italic fonts.
3. A set of *production rules*, where each production rule consists of a non-terminals symbol, called the *head* or *left side* of the production and is located on the left side of the rule, before the symbol '*::=*', and a sequence of terminals and/or

Table 4.

Definition 3.1 *Operational planning language is a Context-Free Grammar Operational Planning Language (CFGOPL) if it satisfies some context-free grammar*

non-terminals, called the *body* or *right side* of the production rule. In other words, the left side of a production rule is a single variable symbol, and the right side is a combination of terminals and variable symbols. The symbol '*::=*' is used for the derivation of the left side to the right side.

4. A designation of one of the non-terminal as the *start* symbol. In this case it is a non-terminal <*OP*> symbol.

For notational convenience, production rules with the same non-terminal as the head can have their bodies grouped, with the alternative bodies separated by the symbol '|', which we read as 'or', e.g.

'*ε* | <*DATE*>'. Here ε is an empty string. The following symbols are pretty standard:

- *[ ]* enclose an optional part of the rule,
- *{ }* mean the enclosed can be repeated any number of times (including zero).

The definition of the CFG has a set of production rules, which consists of twenty one rules and presented below as follows:

- An <*OP*> non-terminal start symbol - the operational plan (OP) of the entire organization. The semantic diagram (SD) of that symbol is in Appendix 1.

<OP> ::= ε | <ITEM> (3.1)

- The <*ITEM*> non-terminal symbol (nTS) - item of the OP. The SD is in Appendix 2.

<ITEM> ::= _itemID: <ITEM_ID> _itemDef: <DEFINITION>_unit: <UNIT>

_v-index: <V-INDEX>_level_horizont: <WEIGHT> _dueDate: <DATE>

_doneDate: [ε | <DATE>] (3.2)

serviced_by: [ε | { <ITEM_SUB> _vertical: <WEIGHT> }] |

[ε | { <PERSON> _vertical: <WEIGHT> _person_horizont: <WEIGHT> _realDone: <WEIGHT>}]

- The <ITEM_SUB> nTS – subordinate item of the <ITEM> nTS. The SD is in Appendix 3.

<ITEM_SUB> ::= _itemID_sub: <ITEM_ID> _itemDef: <DEFINITION>_unit: <UNIT> (3.3)

_v-index: <V-INDEX>_level_horizont: <WEIGHT> _dueDate: <DATE> _doneDate: [ε | <DATE>]

- The <ITEM_ID> nTS - identification number (ID). The SD is in Appendix 4.

<ITEM_ID> ::= { <DIGIT> } (3.4)

- The <DEFINITION> nTS of the item or unit definitions. The SD is in Appendix 5.

<DEFINITION> ::= [<LETTER> | <DIGIT>]

(<LETTER> { [<LETTER> | <DIGIT>] | <SYMBOL> }) |

(< DIGIT > { [<LETTER> | <DIGIT>] | <SYMBOL> }) | (3.5)

(< SYMBOL > { [<LETTER> | <DIGIT>] | <SYMBOL> })

- The <WEIGHT> nTS of the item of the OP. The SD is in Appendix 6.

<WEIGHT> ::= <REAL_NUMBER> (3.6)

- The <DATE> nTS - the due date or date of completion of the item. The SD is in Appendix 7.

<DATE> ::= <YEAR>.<MONTH>.<DAY>

<YEAR> ::= <DIGIT> <DIGIT> <DIGIT> <DIGIT>

<MONTH> ::= <DIGIT> <DIGIT> (3.7)

<DAY> ::= *<DIGIT>* *<DIGIT>*

- The *<PERSON>* nTS – employee's detailed information. The SD is in Appendix 8.

<PERSON>::= _person_ID: <ID> _title: <TITLE>

_first_name: <PERSON_NAME>_mid_name: [ε | <PERSON_NAME>] (3.8)

_last_name: <PERSON_NAME> _category: <STAFF_CATEGORY>

_position: <PERSON_POSITION> _unit: <UNIT> _v-index: <V-INDEX>

- The *<TITLE>* nTS – the title of the employee. The SD is in Appendix 9.

<TITLE> ::= _titleID: <ID> _titleName: [Prof | Dr | Mr. | Mrs. | Ms.] (3.9)

- The *<PERSON_NAME>* nTS – person's name. The SD is in Appendix 10.

<PERSON_NAME> ::= <LETTER> { [' | <LETTER> | -] } (3.10)

- The *<STAFF_CATEGORY>* in case of educational institution nTS – staff category. The SD is in Appendix 11.

<STAFF_CATEGORY>::= _catID: {<DIGIT> } _catName: { <LETTER> } (3.11)

- The *<PERSON_POSITION>* nTS – position of the person. The SD is in Appendix 12.

<PERSON_POSITION>::= _posID: {<DIGIT> } _posName: <LETTER>

{ [<LETTER> | <DIGIT>] } (3.12)

- The *<UNIT>* nTS – unit. The SD is in Appendix 13.

<UNIT> ::= _unitID: <ID> _unitDef: <DEFINITION> (3.13)

- The *<V-INDEX>* nTS – V-index. The SD is in Appendix 14.

<V-INDEX> ::= <REAL_NUMBER> (3.14)

- The <REAL_NUMBER> nTS – real number. The SD is in Appendix 14.

<REAL_NUMBER> ::= <INTEGER_PART> . <FRACTION> (3.15)

- The <INTEGER_PART> nTS – integer part of the number. The SD is in Appendix 14.

<INTEGER_PART>::= <DIGIT> | (<INTEGER_PART> < DIGIT>) (3.16)

- The <FRACTION> nTS – fraction part of the number. The SD is in Appendix 14.

<FRACTION> ::= <DIGIT> | <FRACTION> <DIGIT> (3.17)

- The <LETTER> nTS – letter. The SD is in Appendix 15. (3.18)

<LETTER> ::= A | B | C | D | E | F | G | H | I | J | K | L | M | N | O | P | Q | R | S | T | U | V | W | X | Y | Z

a | b | c | d | e | f | g | h | i | j | k | l | m | n | o | p | q | r | s | t | u | v | w | x | y | z

- The <DIGIT> nTS – digit. The SD is in Appendix 16.

<DIGIT> ::= 0 | 1 | 2 | 3 | 4 | 5 | 6 | 7 | 8 | 9 (3.19)

- The <SYMBOL> nTS – symbol. The SD is in Appendix 17.

<SYMBOL> ::= ! | @ | # | $ | % | * | ^ | & | (|) | - | _ | + | = | { | (3.20)

} | [|] | \ | / |: | ; | " | ' | < | > |, | . | ? | ε

- The <ID> nTS – ID. The SD is in Appendix 18.

<ID> ::= (<LETTER> { [<LETTER> | <DIGIT>] }) | (<DIGIT> { [<LETTER> | <DIGIT>] }) (3.21)

An important application of CFG occurs in the specification and compilation of the operational planning language into a hierarchical model of objects – a model which describes a hierarchical structure of the operational plans and communication processes between computers with different computational platforms. The independence of the computational platform and type of database storage is a predominant idea of that approach. Using a case study for some fiction operational plan of the fiction university, below in this chapter, we consider *the parsing process* of the CFG, which describes operational plans for several units and members of staff. The *syntax analyzer (Parser)* computer program provides a parsing process for identifying the significant pieces of the text (tokens) of the OP, which were written using CFGOPL, as elements and use them for the automated process of building a database structure. It is possible to generate relational, hierarchical based databases, or extensible markup language (XML) files (W3C Information and Knowledge Domain, 2016). An implementation of this idea using a relational database management system (RDBMS) Microsoft® SQL-Server® 2014 is presented below.

Versioning of the Context-Free Grammar Operational Planning Language: The CFGOPL should be very dynamic and is similar to a living organism. The idea of versioning allows keeping a holistic picture of this language during a time period. Actually, the version number has a structure - *<major updates>*. *<intermediate updates>*. *<minor updates>*, which are numbers started from 1 and incrementing up by step 1. The first version of the language, which is described in this chapter, is the version 1.0.0. Here are definitions of each level of versioning:

1. *<minor updates>*. This level reflects small updates, which are caused by recognizing small errors, and bugs, during the process of executing the CFGOPL, which can be fixed by the designer(s) of this language in conjunction with other researchers.
2. *<intermediate updates>*. This level reflects:
    a. Deployment of new non-terminal symbols with new functionalities.
    b. Updating of the relational database structure, which is related to the current CFGOPL - creating new tables, updating links between tables, renaming tables and/or their columns.
3. *<major updates>*. This level reflects strategic major updates of the language – the transformation of the CFGOPL into database structure with different (not relational) structure.

The CFGOPL Team of Researchers and Enthusiasts (CFGOPL-TRE) maintains a history of all versions and amendments of the language in a *LogHistory* file for effective control and meaningful analysis. The CFGOPL-TRE may be transformed into a *world-wide open source consortium* in future.

Below is a case-study example of operational planning data, which describes a proposed mechanism using *syntax analyzer (parser)* and *derivation tree.*

Case-Study With Fictional Data

Suppose there is a hypothetical *University of Technology (UTech)*, which has an *academic affairs division (AAD).* All deans of faculties of the university report to the head of AAD (e.g. in the UTech the head of AAD is a deputy president of the university). For a sake of simplicity, consider a fragment of the operational plan (the hierarchical structure is in Appendix 19) just of one faculty - *Faculty of Engineering and Computing* (FENC), which consists of two schools – *School of Engineering* (SE) and *School of Computing and Information Technology* (SCIT). FENC belongs to AAD. Suppose the SCIT has two programmes:

- *Bachelor of Science in Computing & Information Technology (BSCIT),*
- *Bachelor of Science in Computing with Management Studies (BSCMS)*

and the SE has also two programmes:

- *Bachelor of Science in Electrical Engineering (BSEE)*
- *Bachelor of Science in Mechanical Engineering (BSME)*

Using this example, we can discuss in details how to obtain the percentage of real achievements of the individual targets of the academic staff and, based on these values, how to obtain *V*-indices for completing operational plans of the programmes, schools, and faculty. These values indicate where these individuals/ units/university stand at present and how should they move forward to achieve their goals at the earliest.

For the detail description of the operational plan (Appendix 19) there is a list of items of the FENC's operational plan (Appendix 20) and the list of academic and administrative staff of the FENC (Appendix 21).

Using hierarchical structure diagram of the FENC operational plan (Appendix 19) and using CFGOPL (rules 3.1 – 3.21) consider some fragments of the FENC operational plan.

Derivation Process of the Operational Plan of the University

In this example, we consider an operational plan of the Faculty of Engineering and Computing (FENC), which is a part of the Academic Affairs Division (AAD).

Consider the UTech's operational plan with $ID = I_{UTech}$. Suppose that one component of that plan is an item "*Provide high quality, innovative academic and research programmes*". It must be done by academic affairs division ($ID = AAD_1$) and is associated with the weight 40% of all planning activities of the university (vertical alignment). It can be presented as shown in Table 5.

Hereafter, the statements '*_doneDate/_v-index: ε*' means that the item is not done and *V*-index is equal to 0. For simplicity sake, in the statement (3.2.1) consider only part of the UTech's OP, which is related to AAD. In this case, consider only one subordinate item AAD_1 of the plan. For simplicity, assign the string (not integer) values for the '*_itemID*' for the university as an 'I_{utech}' and 'AAD_1' for the part of the operational plan of the academic affairs division.

To confirm that (3.2.1) statement definition for item 'I_{utech}' is satisfied in the CFGOPL, the string has to be derived from the production rules (3.1 – 3.21) in a sequence of steps, beginning with the start symbol *<OP>*, as shown below. This process is called *'Derivation process'*.

1. The rule 3.1 can be used for a definition of the I_{utech}
   <OP>::= <ITEM>
2. Substitute non-terminal symbols *<ITEM>* in its definition, described by rule 3.2, the statement will be presented as follows (hereafter substituted fragments are presented using bold font):

<ITEM> ::= ***_itemID: <ITEM_ID> _itemDef: <DEFINITION> _unit: <UNIT> _v-index:***
<V-INDEX> _level_horizont: <WEIGHT> _dueDate: <DATE> _doneDate: ε _serviced_by: <ITEM_SUB> _vertical: <WEIGHT>

3. Substitute non-terminal symbols ***<ITEM_ID>, <DEFINITION>, <UNIT>, <V-INDEX>, WEIGHT>,*** and ***<DATE>*** in their definition, described by rules 3.4, 3.5, 3.13, 3.14, 3.6, 3.7 the previous statement will be presented as follows:

Table 5.

<OP>::= _itemID: I_{utech} _itemDef: Operational plan of the University of Technology for 2016-2017 Academic Year _unit: _unitID: Utech _unitDef: University of Technology _v-index: 0.0 _level_ horizont: 100.0 _dueDate: 2017.07.31 _doneDate: ε _serviced_by: _itemID_sub: AAD_1 _itemDef: Provide High quality, innovative academic and research programmes _unitID: AAD _unitDef: Academic Affairs Division _v-index: 0.0 _level_ horizont: 70.0 _dueDate: 2017.07.31 _doneDate: ε _vertical: 40.0 _serviced_by:	(3.2.1)

<ITEM>::= _itemID: **{<LETTER>}** _itemDef: **{<LETTER>}** _unit: **_unitID: <ID> _unitDef: <DEFINITION>** _v-index: **<REAL_NUMBER>** _level_horizont: **<REAL_NUMBER>**

_dueDate: **<YEAR>.<MONTH>.<DAY>**

_serviced_by: **_itemID_sub: <ITEM_ID> _itemDef: <DEFINITION> _unit: <UNIT> _v-index: <V-INDEX> _level_horizont: <WEIGHT> _dueDate: <DATE> _doneDate: ε _vertical: <REAL_NUMBER>**

_serviced_by: ε _vertical: **<REAL_NUMBER>**

4. Continuing the process of derivation based on production rules 3.1 – 3.21 we obtain

<ITEM> ::= _itemID: I_{utech} _itemDef: Operational plan of the University of Technology for 2016-2017 Academic Year _unit: _unitID: **<LETTER>{[<LETTER>| <DIGIT>]}** _unitDef: **{<LETTER>}** _v-index: **<INTEGER_PART>.<FRACTION>** _level_horizont: **<INTEGER_PART>.<FRACTION>** _dueDate: **<DIGIT><DIGIT><DIGIT><DIGIT>. <DIGIT><DIGIT>.<DIGIT><DIGIT>**

_serviced_by: _itemID_sub: **{<LETTER>}** _itemDef: **{<LETTER>}** _unit: **_unitID: <ID> _unitDef: <DEFINITION>** _v-index: **<REAL_NUMBER>** _level_horizont: **<REAL_NUMBER>** _dueDate: **<YEAR>.<MONTH>.<DAY>** _vertical: **<INTEGER_PART>. <FRACTION>**

5. <ITEM> ::= _itemID: I_{utech} _itemDef: Operational plan of the University of Technology for 2016-2017 Academic Year _unit: _unitID: **Utech** _unitDef: **University of Technology** _v-index: **0.0** _level_horizont: **100.0** _dueDate: **2017.07.31**

_serviced_by: _itemID_sub: **AAD_1** _itemDef: **Provide High quality, innovative academic and research programmes** _unitID: **<LETTER>{[<LETTER>|<DIGIT>]}** _unitDef: **{<LETTER>}** _v-index: **<INTEGER_PART>.<FRACTION>** _level_horizont: **<INTEGER_PART>.<FRACTION>** _dueDate: **<DIGIT> <DIGIT> <DIGIT> <DIGIT>. <DIGIT> <DIGIT>. <DIGIT> <DIGIT>** _vertical: 40.0

and finally, after last substitution, we are getting a string, which has no non-terminal symbols:

6. <ITEM> ::= _itemID: I_{utech} _itemDef: Operational plan of the University of Technology for 2016-2017 Academic Year _unit: _unitID: UTech _unitDef: University of Technology _v-index: 0.0 _level_horizont: 100.0 _dueDate: 2017.07.31

_serviced_by: _itemID_sub: AAD$_1$ _itemDef: Provide High quality, innovative academic and research programmes _unit: _unitID: AAD _unitDef: Academic Affairs Division _v-index: 0.0 _level_horizont: 70.0 _dueDate: 2017.07.31 _vertical: 40.0

The last statement does not have the terminal symbol '*_doneDate:*' with '*ε*' value. Based on the definition given above, this is an empty string. The value of the terminal symbol and the value of the '*_v-index:*' which is equal to '*0.0*', mean, that items, described in this statement are not accomplished as yet – they are in the process of accomplishment. The last string is equivalent to the string 3.2.1. It means that item above, which describes (on the top level) an operational plan of the university is satisfied with context-free grammar operational planning language.

The derivation process ('*derivation tree*'), presented below in steps 1-6 (Figure 2), is a process of derivation '*parent*' item '*Operational plan of the University of Technology for 2016-2017 Academic Year*' of the University's OP, which consists on the level of plan's hierarchy by another item with the same definition and belongs to the Academic Affairs Division unit, which is the subordinate unit to the Utech unit. It is an *"Item-to-Items" (ItoIs)* relationship with only one subordinate item.

Below is another part of the operational plan with the *ItoIs* relationships containing three subordinate items and minimum comments, where it is possible. Suppose the item AAD_1, of the academic affairs division which was derived in the previous example in the direction to the faculty of engineering and computing (FENC) has three main items in its OP – I_1 with 8% of the *Vertical Alignment* (VA) to AAD_1

Figure 2. The derivation tree from the CFGOPL definition for the top level of the operational plan of the university

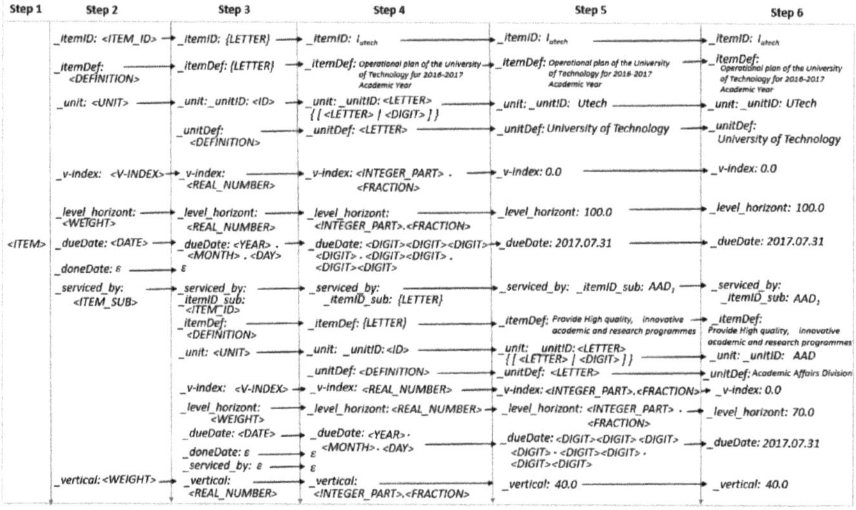

item, I_2 with 5% of the VA to AAD_1, and I_3 with 4% of the VA to AAD_1 (IDs and definitions were taken from Appendices 20, 21). We have a statement:

_itemID: AAD_1 _itemDef: Provide High quality, innovative academic and research programmes _unit: _unitID: AAD _unitDef: Academic Affairs Division _v-index: 0.0 _level_horizont: 70.0 _dueDate: 2017.07.31 _vertical: 40.0
_serviced_by: _itemID_sub: 1 _itemDef: Provide High quality, innovative academic and research programmes _unit: _unitID: FENC _unitDef: Faculty of Engineering and Computing _v-index: 0.0 _level_horizont: 40.0 _dueDate: 2017.07.31 _vertical:8.0
_serviced_by: _itemID_sub: 2 _itemDef: Efficient and Effective Academic and Administrative Processes _unit: _unitID: FENC _unitDef: Faculty of Engineering and Computing _v-index: 0.0 _level_horizont: 40.0 _dueDate: 2017.07.31 _vertical:5.0
_serviced_by: _itemID_sub: 3 _itemDef: Provide opportunities for learning and research _unit: _unitID: FENC _unitDef: Faculty of Engineering and Computing _v-index: 0.0 _level_horizont: 20.0 _dueDate: 2017.07.31 _vertical:4.0

The item I_1 *(ID = 1)* which belongs to the FENC level has six subordinate items – I_{44} *(ID = 44)* on FENC level, I_6 *(ID = 6)* and I_7 *(ID = 7)* on the SCIT level, and I_{14} *(ID = 14)*, I_{15} *(ID = 15)*, and I_{16} *(ID = 16)* on the SE level, can be written as a string:

_itemID: 1 _itemDef: Provide High quality, innovative academic and research programmes _unit: FENC _unitDef: Faculty of Engineering and Computing _v-index: 0.0 _level_horizont: 40.0 _dueDate: 2017.07.31
_serviced_by: _itemID_sub: 44 _itemDef: Improve access to courses through innovative matriculation strategies _unit: _unitID: FENC _unitDef: Faculty of Engineering and Computing _v-index: 0.0 _level_horizont: 100.0 _dueDate: 2017.07.31 _vertical:2.0
_serviced_by: _itemID_sub: 6 _itemDef: Increase number and improve quality of Graduate Research students at 30% _unit: _unitID: SCIT _unitDef: School of Computing and Information Technology _v-index: 0.0 _level_horizont: 40.0 _dueDate: 2017.07.31 _vertical:18.0
_serviced_by: _itemID_sub: 7 _itemDef: Increase number and improve quality of Graduate Research students at 30% _unit: _unitID: SCIT _unitDef: School of Computing and Information Technology _v-index: 0.0 _level_horizont: 25.0 _dueDate: 2017.07.31 _vertical:20.0
_serviced_by: _itemID_sub: 14 _itemDef: Number of new cross faculty programmes _unit: _unitID: SE _unitDef: School of Engineering _v-index: 0.0 _level_horizont: 15.0 _dueDate: 2017.07.31 _vertical:20.0

_serviced_by: _itemID_sub: 15 _itemDef: Increase number and improve quality of Graduate Research students at 20% _unit: _unitID: SE _unitDef: School of Engineering _v-index: 0.0 _level_horizont: 20.0 _dueDate: 2017.07.31 _vertical:20.0

_serviced_by: _itemID_sub: 16 _itemDef: Develop a strategic plan to link expertise in research, services and programmes _unit: _unitID: SE _unitDef: School of Engineering _v-index: 0.0 _level_horizont: 25.0 _dueDate: 2017.07.31 _vertical:20.0

Moving one the level down (schools level), it is interesting to consider an item I_{14} which belongs to item I_1 on the level of hierarchy above (FENC level). This item can be written as a string:

_itemID: 14 _itemDef: Number of new cross faculty programmes _unit: _unitID: SE _unitDef: School of Engineering _v-index: 0.0 _level_horizont: 15.0 _dueDate: 2017.07.31 _vertical:20.0

_serviced_by: _itemID_sub: 13 _itemDef: Engage in cross-faculty research and delivery of courses _unit: _unitID: SE _unitDef: School of Engineering _v-index: 0.0 _level_horizont: 100.0 _dueDate: 2017.07.31 _vertical:10.0

_serviced_by: _itemID_sub: 27 _itemDef: Participating in a new Solar Energy Project _unit: _unitID: BSEE _unitDef: Bachelor of Science in Electrical Engineering _v-index: 0.0 _level_horizont: 15.0 _dueDate: 2017.07.31 _vertical:15.0

_serviced_by: _itemID_sub: 28 _itemDef: Participation in a Sustainable Energy, Caribbean Sustainable Energy project _unit: _unitID: BSEE _unitDef: Bachelor of Science in Electrical Engineering _v-index: 0.0 _level_horizont: 10.0 _dueDate: 2017.07.31 _vertical:20.0

_serviced_by: _itemID_sub: 31 _itemDef: Engage in cross-faculty research _unit: _unitID: BSME _unitDef: Bachelor of Science in Mechanical Engineering _v-index: 0.0 _level_horizont: 15.0 _dueDate: 2017.07.31 _vertical:30.0

_serviced_by: _itemID_sub: 32 _itemDef: Engage in cross-faculty delivery of courses _unit: _unitID: BSME _unitDef: Bachelor of Science in Mechanical Engineering _v-index: 0.0 _level_horizont: 15.0 _dueDate: 2017.07.31 _vertical:25.0

The last definition for the I_{14} *(ID = 14)* has some structural peculiarities (see Appendix 19). An item I_{13} *(ID = 13)* must be completed by two employees – P_3 (Miss Tiana Green from the head office of the SCIT), and P_{19} (Dr. Alexander Cook from the head office of the SE). This is a case when one item is served by employees, which are from different schools. Another peculiarity, which indicates a *'violation of operational plans hierarchy'* is here – the employee P_3 (Miss Tiana Green) serves two different items - I_{10} and I_{13} from different schools. The solution, proposed here, considers these cases as a normal scenario shown in Table 6.

The full definition for the item I_{13} can be derived from the production rule 3.2 of the CFGOPL, where the item must be accomplished by two employees (see Table 7).

Substituting non-terminal symbols ***<ITEM_ID>, <DEFINITION>, <UNIT>, <V-INDEX>, <WEIGHT>, <DATE>***, and ***<PERSON>*** in their definition, described by rules 3.4, 3.5, 3.13, 3.14, 3.6, 3.7, and 3.8 the previous statement will be presented as follows (see Table 8).

Continuing the process of substituting non-terminal symbols indicated by the bold font by their actual values (terminal symbols) (see Table 9).

Continuing the derivation process, we have Table 10.

Table 6.

Notes: • *An employee can participate (alone or as a member of a team) in the execution of any item at any level of the organization operational plan.* • *Each item of the operational plan can be executed only by subordinate items or by employees. The mixed team, which consists of some items and some employees at the same time is not allowed.*

Table 7.

<ITEM> ::= _itemID: <ITEM_ID> _itemDef: <DEFINITION> _unit: <UNIT> *_v-index: <V-INDEX> _level_horizont: <WEIGHT> _dueDate: <DATE> _doneDate: ε* *_serviced_by:* *{ <PERSON> _vertical: <WEIGHT> _person_horizont: <WEIGHT> }*	(3.2.2)

Table 8.

<ITEM> ::= _itemID: ***<LETTER>*** *_itemDef:* ***{ <LETTER> }*** *_unit:* ***_unitID: <UNIT_ID> _unitDef: <DEFINITION>*** *_v-index:* ***<REAL_NUMBER>*** *_level_horizont:* ***<REAL_NUMBER>*** *_dueDate:* ***<YEAR>.<MONTH>.<DAY>*** ***_serviced_by:*** ***_person_ID: <ID> _title: <TITLE>*** ***_first_name: <PERSON_NAME>_mid_name: [ε | <PERSON_NAME>] _last_name: <PERSON_NAME> _category: <STAFF_CATEGORY>*** ***_position: <PERSON_POSITION> _unit: <UNIT> _v-index: <V-INDEX>*** *_vertical:* ***<REAL_NUMBER>*** *_person_horizont:* ***<REAL_NUMBER>_*** ***_person_ID: <ID> _title: <TITLE>*** ***_first_name: <PERSON_NAME>_mid_name: [ε | <PERSON_NAME>]*** ***_last_name: <PERSON_NAME> _category: <STAFF_CATEGORY>*** ***_position: <PERSON_POSITION> _unit: <UNIT> _v-index: <V-INDEX>*** *_vertical:* ***<REAL_NUMBER>*** *_person_horizont:* ***<REAL_NUMBER>***	(3.2.3)

Table 9.

<table>
<tr>
<td><ITEM> ::= _itemID: 13 _itemDef: Participating in a new Solar Energy Project _unit: _unitID: <ID> _unitDef: { <LETTER> }
_v-index: <INTEGER_PART>.<FRACTION>_level_horizont: <INTEGER_PART>.<FRACTION> _dueDate: <DIGIT><DIGIT><DIGIT><DIGIT>.<DIGIT><DIGIT>.<DIGIT><DIGIT>
_serviced_by:
_person_ID: P_3 _titleID: <ID> _titleName: [Prof | Dr | Mr. | Mrs. | Ms.] _first_name: { <LETTER> } _mid_name: ε _last_name: { <LETTER> } _category: _catID: {<DIGIT> } _catName: { <LETTER> } _position: _posID: {<DIGIT> } _posName: <LETTER> { [<LETTER> | <DIGIT>] } _unit: _unitID: <ID> _unitDef: <DEFINITION> _v-index: <REAL_NUMBER> _vertical: <INTEGER_PART>.<FRACTION> _person_horizont: <INTEGER_PART>.<FRACTION>
_person_ID: P_{19} _titleID: <ID> _titleName: [Prof | Dr | Mr. | Mrs. | Ms.] _first_name: { <LETTER> } _mid_name: ε _last_name: { <LETTER> } _category: _catID: {<DIGIT> } _catName: { <LETTER>} _position: _posID: {<DIGIT> } _posName: <LETTER> { [<LETTER> | <DIGIT>] } _unit: _unitID: <ID> _unitDef: <DEFINITION> _v-index: <REAL_NUMBER> _vertical: <INTEGER_PART>.<FRACTION> _person_horizont: <INTEGER_PART>.<FRACTION></td>
<td>(3.2.4)</td>
</tr>
</table>

Table 10.

<table>
<tr>
<td><ITEM> ::= _itemID: 13 _itemDef: Participating in a new Solar Energy Project _unit: _unitID: SE _unitDef: School of Engineering _v-index: 0.0_level_horizont: 100.0 _dueDate: 2017.07.31
_serviced_by:
_person_ID: P_3 _titleID: 3 _titleName: Miss. _first_name: Tiana _last_name: Green _category: _catID: 1 _catName: Academic _position: _posID: 6 _posName: Professor _unit: _unitID: SCIT _unitDef: School of Computing and Information Technology _v-index: 0.0 _vertical: 60.0 _person_horizont: 40.0
_person_ID: P_{19} _titleID: 4 _titleName: Dr. _first_name: Alexander _last_name: Cook _category:: _catID: 1 _catName: Academic _position: _posID: 6 _posName: Professor _unit: _unitID: BSEE _unitDef: Bachelor of Science in Electrical Engineering _v-index: 0.0 _vertical: 50.0 _person_horizont: 60.0</td>
<td>(3.2.5)</td>
</tr>
</table>

Hereafter, we consider the process of execution of items of operational plans by employees as *an operational planning service*. This process starts from the bottom level (executives' level) of the OP's hierarchy and moves up level by level until it finishes on the top level of hierarchy for the operational plan of entire university/organization. On the bottom level, at the appraisal period, appraisee and appraiser together evaluate an accomplishment of items of the appraisee's individual plan. After that, using integrated management information system software the supervisor enters the results of evaluation into Database Management System (DBMS). The type of the DBMS – *'relational'*, *'hierarchical'* or other types are not discussed in this chapter. In this research, we use a Microsoft® SQL-Server® relational DBMS. All entered data are utilized by automatic recurrent calculating procedures for obtaining V-indices for each individual, units, and the entire organization. The technical aspects of procedures are presented below.

Transformation CFGOPL Definition Into Relational Database Structure and CFGOPL Remote Service

This section presents a process of the transformation the CFGOPL definitions of the plans into the relational database structure. The derivation process and set of production rules 3.1 – 3.21 allow to identify significant elements of the CFGOPL and apply them for creating SQL script schema definitions of the tables and their relationships of the database.

Production Rules (PRs) 3.1 and 3.2 describe a CFG of the operational plan at the top level of the university. The PR 3.2 gives the definition for any item of the plan. It is important to note that the PR 3.2 has multiple links to elements *'_serviced_by'* and identifies an alternative link to two types of the sub-elements *<ITEM>* and *<PERSON>,* which have multiple values. It is not so difficult to recognize programmatically that there two different database entities – an *Items* and *Persons* with relationship link between them using a *'_itemID'* and *'_person_ID'* terminal symbols. The last one has been derived from the PR 3.8. The transformation program recognizes that non-terminals symbols *<ITEM>* and *<PERSON>* can be a basis for creating tables *'Items'* and *'Persons'* in the database. The terminal symbols which belong to them can be considered as names of columns of these tables.

In this case, the CFGOPL structure, described by 3.1 and 3.2 production rules, can be used as an input data for the transformation process to the database computer program. Using 3.1- 3.21 PRs it is possible to generate programmatically a DB structure without data – just database schema definition. To populate tables with real data from the operational plans of the organization it is possible to use the production rules, the derivation process, and the operational planning data of the organization using its information system. It may be the web or form-based applications (let call it – *'CFGtransToDB'*), which uses XML files or some other information resources like spreadsheets or text files. The *'CFGtransToDB'* transformation program has to offer at least two different handling processes – generating only SQL schema definition (without data content – see Appendix 22) or generating a script for insert/update/delete data (an example of such script is presented in Appendix 24) in the database (see Figure 3).

The structure, algorithms and source code of the *'CFGtransToDB'* program is not a subject of discussion for this chapter and can be developed by professional programmers. To simplify the process of development and programming the CFGOPL - Team of Researchers and Enthusiasts (TRE) should provide a remote web-service as a reusable object which encapsulates *CFGOPL Parser* and *SQL script data generator* with an open interface for all developers and practitioners. The remote web-service (W3C Working Group, 2004) can be presented as a windows communication foundation (WCF) server (Sharp, 2010) with opportunities to join different computer systems, working under different computational platforms and protocols of communication such as *HTTP/HTTPS, TCP/IP, FTP,* etc. In this case, any computers (mainframes, desktops/laptops, smartphones, tablets, etc.) will be able to use that service. The last fact is very important since applying this approach, the practitioners are free to integrate CFGOPL into their corporate information systems (without knowledge of the programming code details) and coordinate their plans with information systems of other partner organizations. The CFGOPL-TRE through its website should present an interface of the *'CFGtransToDB'* service.

RECURRENT PROCEDURES FOR CALCULATING *V*-INDICES AT ALL LEVELS OF THE ORGANIZATION

For readers, who would like to simulate algorithms and procedures on their computers, create a model of the SQL-Server database *'OP_2017'* using SQL scripts and structure, described in Appendices 19-24.

In section 2.1, we presented a definition of the *V*-index, which calculates a total accomplishment of the organization's plan, its parts and individuals, the hierarchical structure of the plans, and mechanism of alignments of the items of

Figure 3. Transformation CFGOPL definition and real operational data from the organization information system into the relational database

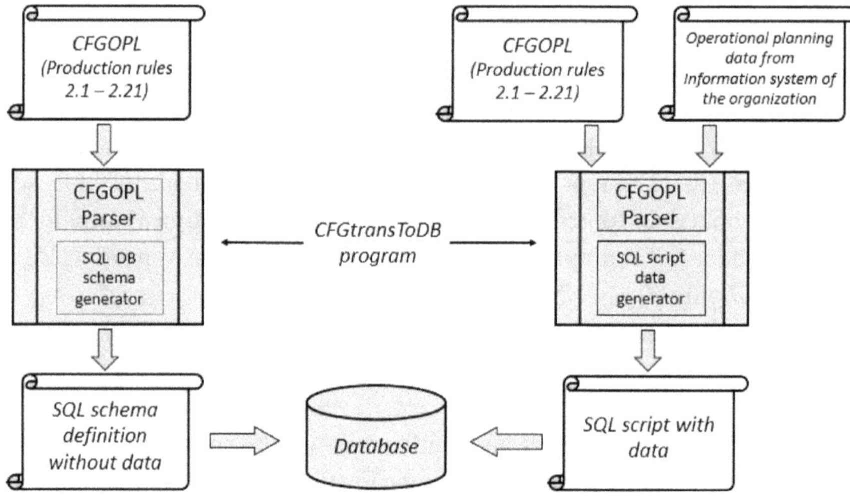

the plan on *'horizontal'* and *'vertical'* levels. In parts 2.2 and 2.3 a mathematical recurrent algorithm of the process (Pougatchev & Kulkarni 2013-2014) was given. This section of the chapter presents real working procedures, which implement theoretical solutions using two SQL procedures – '*vIndexForItemsByPerson*' and '*calcOfvIndicesForGeneralOP*'.

Based on a real accomplishment (this data is presented is *INSERT* SQL script for the table *'Item_Persons',* column *'[_realDone]'* in Appendix 24) of the individual plans for the appraisal period by staff these two procedures calculate a *V*-indices for:

- Each member of the faculty staff, which indicate rates of accomplishments of individual plans
- Each unit of the entire faculty (programmes, schools/departments, and faculty)

The accomplishment items of the plan depend on accomplishments of their subordinate. On the lowest level of items' hierarchy, each item has to be accomplished by members of the faculty staff (see the structure of the FENC operational plan - Appendix 19). Hence, the recurrent procedures should start from the process of calculating of the *V*-indices for items served by individuals.

The source code of the SQL procedure '*vIndexForItemsByPerson*' is presented below. This procedure is a sub-procedure and is included in the body of the *'calcOfvIndicesForGeneralOP'* SQL procedure. For readers who familiar with Structured Query Language (SQL) of relational database systems, the SQL code is self-described enough and does not need additional comments.

Figure 4. The source code of the 'vIndexForItemsByPerson' SQL procedure

```
-- ==============================================
-- Author:        Valeri Pougatchev
-- Create date: April 09, 2017
-- Description: Calculating v-indices for Items of the Faculty
--                of Engineering and Computing Operational
--                Plan accomplished by Staff of the Faculty
-- ==============================================
ALTER PROCEDURE [dbo].[vIndexForItemsByPerson]
SET NOCOUNT ON;

DECLARE @itemID int, @vItem int, @vOut numeric(5, 2)
DECLARE @i int, @nRows int, @endItem int

SELECT @endItem = COUNT(*) FROM Items

SET @i = 0  SET @vItem = 0
WHILE (@i <= @endItem)
BEGIN
    SET @i = @i + 1

    SELECT @nRows = COUNT(*)
    FROM Items_Persons AS ip  WHERE ip._itemID = @i

    IF @nRows = 0
    BEGIN
        UPDATE Items
        SET [_v-index] = NULL
        WHERE _itemID = @i
    END
    ELSE
    BEGIN
        SELECT @vItem = SUM(ip._vertical*ip._realDone)
        FROM Items_Persons AS ip WHERE ip._itemID = @i
        GROUP BY ip._itemID

        SET @vOut = @vItem/100.00

        UPDATE Items
        SET [_v-index] = @vOut
        WHERE _itemID = @i
    END

    SET @vOut = 0.00  SET @vItem = 0.00
END
```

Figure 5. The source code of the 'calcOfvIndicesForGeneralOP' SQL procedure

```sql
-- ==================================================
-- Author:        Valeri Pougatchev
-- Create date: April 10, 2017
-- Description: Recalculating of all vIndices of the
--                General Operational Plan (GOP)
--                of the organization
-- ==================================================
ALTER PROCEDURE [dbo].[calcOfvIndicesForGeneralOP]
SET NOCOUNT ON;

/* clear previous vIndices for all items of the General Operational
Plan */
UPDATE Items SET [_v-index] = NULL

/* calculating of the vIndices for items of the GOP accomplished by
personnel of the organization*/
EXEC [vIndexForItemsByPerson]

/* based on vIndices of items accomplished by personnel of the
organization, the part below
  calculates vIndices for all others items (which are 'parent' items for
already calculated) and
  other items, which are parent for the items on levels up in the total
hierarchy of
  the organization's GOP
*/
DECLARE @endItemID int, @i int, @count int
DECLARE @vInd numeric(5, 2)
DECLARE @numberOfNullvIndices int
DECLARE @itemID int, @vIndRes numeric(5, 2)
DECLARE @vert numeric(5, 2), @gTotal numeric(5, 2)
DECLARE @child int, @val numeric(5, 2)
DECLARE @total numeric(7, 2), @ind1 int, @ind2 int DECLARE
@cursorOpen1 bit, @cursorOpen2 bit
DECLARE @loop1 bit, @loop2 bit

SELECT @endItemID = COUNT(*) FROM Items

SET @cursorOpen1 = 0 SET @count = 0
SET @total = 0.00       SET @i = 0
SET @cursorOpen2 = 0 SET @loop1 = 0
SET @vert = 0.00        SET @cursorOpen1 = 0
SET @loop2 = 0          SET @val = 0.00
SET @gTotal = 0.00

SELECT @numberOfNullvIndices = COUNT(*)
FROM Items
WHERE [_v-index] IS NULL

WHILE (@i < @numberOfNullvIndices)
BEGIN
    SET @ind1 = 1

    IF CURSOR_STATUS('global','c1') <> -3
    BEGIN
        CLOSE c1
        DEALLOCATE c1
    END

    DECLARE c1 CURSOR FOR
        SELECT _itemID, [_v-index] FROM Items

    OPEN c1

    SET @cursorOpen1 = 1

    WHILE (@ind1 < @endItemID + 1)
    BEGIN
        FETCH NEXT FROM c1 INTO @itemID, @vInd

        SET @vInd = ISNULL(@vInd, -1.00)

        IF CURSOR_STATUS('global','c2') <> -3
          BEGIN
              CLOSE c2
              DEALLOCATE c2
          END

        IF (@vInd = -1.00)
        BEGIN
            DECLARE c2 CURSOR FOR
                SELECT _itemID_sub
                FROM Item_Item
                WHERE _itemID = @itemID

            OPEN c2

            SET @cursorOpen2 = 1
            SET @ind2 = 0

            WHILE (@ind2 < @endItemID)
            BEGIN
                FETCH NEXT FROM c2 INTO @child

                IF (@@FETCH_STATUS <> 0) BREAK

                SELECT @val = CAST((ISNULL([_v-index], -1.00)) AS
                        numeric(5, 2))
                FROM Items
                WHERE _itemID = @child

                IF (@val = -1.00)
                BEGIN
                    SET @total = 0

                    BREAK
                END
                ELSE
                BEGIN
                    SELECT @vert = _vertical
                    FROM Item_Item
                    WHERE (_itemID = @itemID) AND (_itemID_sub
                            = @child)

                    SET @total = @total + @val*@vert
                END

                SET @ind2 = @ind2 + 1
            END

            SET @gTotal = @total/100

            IF (@gTotal <> 0)
            BEGIN
                UPDATE Items
                SET [_v-index] = @gTotal
                WHERE _itemID = @itemID
            END

            SET @total = 0.00

            IF (@cursorOpen2 = 1)
            BEGIN
                SET @cursorOpen2 = 0

                CLOSE c2
                DEALLOCATE c2
            END
        END

        SET @ind1 = @ind1 + 1

    END
    SET @i = @i + 1
END

CLOSE c1
DEALLOCATE c1
```

SQL procedures, shown in the Figures 4, 5 calculate *V*-indices for all items of the faculty operational plan, store these results in the database in table *'Items'* and give an opportunity to calculate *V*-indices for each unit (programmes, schools of the faculty) and for the entire operational plan of the faculty using the *'vIndexForUnit'* SQL procedure. The source SQL code of that procedure is presented in Figure 6.

The SQL procedure has one input parameter *('@unitID')*, which represents an ID of the requested unit, and one output parameter *('@out')*, which indicates a *V*-index for the requested unit. The SQL code is quite simple and does not need comments.

Figure 6. The source code of the 'vIndexForUnit' SQL procedure

```
-- ============================================
-- Author:       Valeri Pougatchev
-- Create date: April 10, 2017
-- Description: Calculates a V-index for the requested unit
-- ============================================
ALTER PROCEDURE [dbo].[vIndexForUnit]
    @unitID int,
    @out varchar(100) OUTPUT
AS
BEGIN
    DECLARE @vIndexForUnit numeric(5,2), @vItem int, @uDef varchar(100)

    SELECT @vItem = SUM(i.[_v-index] * iu._level_horizont)
    FROM Units AS u INNER JOIN Items_Units AS iu ON u._unitID = iu._unitID
                    INNER JOIN Items AS i ON iu._itemID = i._itemID
    WHERE u._unitID = @unitID GROUP BY u._unitID

    SET @vIndexForUnit = @vItem/100.00

    SELECT @uDef = LTRIM(RTRIM(_unitDef)) FROM Units WHERE _unitID = @unitID

    SET @out = 'vIndex for the ' + @uDef + ' : ' + CAST(@vIndexForUnit AS CHAR(10))
END
```

Two SQL procedures *'vIndexForPerson'* and *'calcOfvIndicesForPersons'* calculate V-indices for one individual and all staff of the faculty accordingly. The source codes for these procedures are presented in Figure 7 (A, B).

USING V-INDEX FOR THE ANALYSIS OF THE ACCOMPLISHMENT OF THE FACULTY OPERATIONAL PLAN, BASED ON THE CASE STUDY

In this section, we show how the *V*-index reflects the percentage of real achievements of the individual targets of the institution's staff of the departments and units. Based on these values, it is possible to obtain the percentage completion of the programmes, departments, faculties' operational plans as well as the university's yearlong strategic plan. Using the case-study presented above and the strategic planning analysis (SPA) introduced in section 2.1, the reader is ready for a detailed discussion of what their major weaknesses and strengths are. Based on that, midterm corrections could be applied, if necessary. These values indicate where individuals/units/organization stand at present and how should they move forward to achieve their goals most expeditiously (Pougatchev & Kulkarni, 2011).

The indicator of the OOR's plan accomplishment is one of the key indicators of the total performance of the OOR in the performance-based management system (PBMS), which is based on the principle of well known *'360 - degree evaluation',* where an overall score of the member of staff performance depends on the *supervisor's*, *self's*, *'peer's'*, *customer's*, etc. evaluations as well as the accomplishment of individual

Figure 7. The source code of the 'vIndexForPerson' and 'calcOfvIndicesForPersons' SQL procedures

(A)

```
==========================================
-- Author:       Valeri Pougatchev
-- Create date: April 10, 2017
-- Description: Calculates a V-index for the requested person
==========================================
ALTER PROCEDURE [dbo].[vIndexForPerson]
-- Add the parameters for the stored procedure here
    @_person_ID int,
    @out varchar(100) OUTPUT
AS
BEGIN
    DECLARE @vIndexForPerson numeric(5,2)
    DECLARE @vPerson int, @uFullName varchar(100)

    SELECT @vPerson = SUM(ip._person_horizont * ip._realDone)

    FROM Titles AS t INNER JOIN Persons AS p
                        ON t._titleID = p._titleID
                    NNER JOIN Items_Persons AS ip
                        ON p._person_ID = ip._person_ID
    WHERE p._person_ID = @_person_ID

    GROUP BY p._person_ID

    SELECT ip._itemID
    FROM Titles AS t INNER JOIN Persons AS p
                        ON t._titleID = p._titleID
                    INNER JOIN Items_Persons AS ip
                        ON p._person_ID = ip._person_ID
    WHERE p._person_ID = @_person_ID

    SET @vIndexForPerson = @vPerson/100.00

    SELECT @uFullName = LTRIM(RTRIM(t._titleName)) + ' ' +
        LTRIM(RTRIM(p._first_name)) + ' ' +
        LTRIM(RTRIM(ISNULL(p._mid_name, ''))) + ' ' +
        LTRIM(RTRIM(p._last_name))
    FROM Titles AS t INNER JOIN Persons AS p
                        ON t._titleID = p._titleID
    WHERE p._person_ID = @_person_ID

    SET @out = 'vIndex for the ' + @uFullName + ' : ' +
                CAST(@vIndexForPerson AS CHAR(10))
END
```

(B)

```
==========================================
-- Author:       Valeri Pougatchev
-- Create date: April 11, 2017
-- Description: Calculates a V-indices for all persons
==========================================
ALTER PROCEDURE [dbo].[calcOfvIndicesForPersons]
/* clear previous vIndices for all persons of the Entire OP */
UPDATE Persons SET [_v-index] = NULL

DECLARE @vIndexForPerson numeric(5,2)
DECLARE  @_person_ID numeric(5, 2)
DECLARE @cursorOpen1 bit, @endItemID int, @i int
DECLARE  @uFullName varchar(100), @vPerson int

SELECT @endItemID = COUNT(*) FROM Items

SET @i = 0

IF CURSOR_STATUS('global','c1') <> -3
BEGIN
    CLOSE c1   DEALLOCATE c1
END

DECLARE c1 CURSOR FOR SELECT _person_ID FROM Persons

OPEN c1

SET @cursorOpen1 = 1

WHILE (@i < @endItemID + 1)
BEGIN
    FETCH NEXT FROM c1 INTO @_person_ID

    SELECT @vPerson = SUM(ip._person_horizont * ip._realDone)
    FROM Titles AS t
        INNER JOIN Persons AS p ON t._titleID = p._titleID
        INNER JOIN Items_Persons AS ip
                        ON p._person_ID = ip._person_ID
    WHERE p._person_ID = @_person_ID  GROUP BY p._person_ID

    SET @vIndexForPerson = @vPerson/100.00

    UPDATE Persons SET [_v-index] = @vIndexForPerson
    WHERE _person_ID = @_person_ID

    SET @i = @i + 1
END

CLOSE c1   DEALLOCATE c1
```

plans. The discussion of the building of the PBMS is not a part of this chapter and can be found in many publications, including (Pougatchev *et al.*, 2009).

Consider a strategic planning analysis (SPA) of the success of operational planning accomplishments within two (previous and current) appraisal periods for each member of staff, units (programmes), schools, and entire faculty. The Figure 1 in section 2.1 graphically introduces two circles – T_i (dark circle) *'target position'*, and S_i (light circle) identifies a *'current position'* of the OOR in terms of accomplishments of the operational plans. Table 11 presents a success of targets accomplishment by members of academic staff in comparison with the previous year. For simplicity, the table presents just fragment of that information. The data from the previous year are not described here.

Total accomplishments of targets for each individual are data, which characterizes an efficiency of activity of each member of faculty staff on the way of achieving its/his/her targets and objectives of the unit its/he/she belongs to. By analyzing this information, the supervisor can:

Table 11.

<table>
<tr><th rowspan="2"></th><th colspan="2">Previous Acad. Year</th><th colspan="2">Current Acad. Year</th><th rowspan="2">Indicator of the progress</th></tr>
<tr><th>V-index</th><th>V - 100</th><th>V-index</th><th>V - 100</th></tr>
<tr><td>Miss Tiana Green</td><td>92</td><td>92-100=-8</td><td>46</td><td>46-100=-54</td><td>|-8|-|-54|=-46</td></tr>
<tr><td>Dr. Shaniel Walker</td><td>80</td><td>80-100=-20</td><td>66.5</td><td>66.5 -100=-33.5</td><td>|-20|-|-12|=+8</td></tr>
<tr><td colspan="6">……………………………………………………………………</td></tr>
<tr><td>Dr. Mikael Reid</td><td>55</td><td>55–100=45</td><td>68</td><td>68-100=-32</td><td>|45|-|-32|=+13</td></tr>
</table>

- See the real contribution of each member of staff in achieving goals of the unit's OP.
- Compare the contribution of each member of staff.
- See the progress of members of staff in their strategic goals (if any) year by year plans, which should exist.

Table 12 presents successful accomplishment of objectives by these academic programmes in comparison with the previous year.

Values of *V - 100* for BSCIT, BSCMS, BSEE, and BSME programmes present a distance between circles S_i and T_i of archived targets. By making an analysis of this information, Heads of schools can see:

- A real contribution of each programme in achieving goals of the school's OP.
- Compare the contribution of each programme.
- A progress of each programme in their strategic plans.

Table 13 presents successful accomplishment of objectives of schools of the faculty and the faculty itself in comparison with the previous year.

Table 12.

<table>
<tr><th rowspan="2"></th><th colspan="2">Previous Acad. Year</th><th colspan="2">Current Acad. Year</th><th rowspan="2">Indicator of the progress</th></tr>
<tr><th>V -index</th><th>V - 100</th><th>V -index</th><th>V - 100</th></tr>
<tr><td>BSCIT</td><td>75.4</td><td>75.4-100=-24.6</td><td>70.89</td><td>78.8-100=-21.2</td><td>|-24.6|-|-21.2|= +3.4</td></tr>
<tr><td>BSCMS</td><td>81.3</td><td>81.3-100=-18.7</td><td>93.8</td><td>93.8-100=-16.2</td><td>|-18.7|-|-16.2|= +2.5</td></tr>
<tr><td>BSEE</td><td>68.7</td><td>68.7-100=-31.3</td><td>53.9</td><td>53.9-100=-46.1</td><td>|-31.3|-|-46.1|=-14.8</td></tr>
<tr><td>BSME</td><td>88</td><td>88-100=-12</td><td>51.4</td><td>51.4-100=-48.6</td><td>|-12|-|-48.6|=-36.6</td></tr>
</table>

Table 13.

	Previous Acad. Year		*Current Acad. Year*		*Indicator of the progress*
	V -index	*V - 100*	*V -index*	*V - 100*	
SCIT	65.4	65.4-100=-34.6	98.48	98.48-100=-1.52	|-34.6|-|-1.52|=+33.08
SE	75.3	75.3-100=-24.7	55.86	55.86-100=-44.14	|-24.7|-|-44.14|= -19.44
FENC	78.7	78.7-100=-21.3	68.9	68.9-100=-31.1	|-21.3|-|-31.1|= -9.8

A value of the V-index for the SCIT shows that this school has made an improvement on the accomplishment of its plans of 33.08 points. The value of the V-index for the school of Engineering indicates that it has not accomplished its plans, and is equal just to 55.86 points, which is less than the previous year with 19.44 points. The Head of schools and Dean of faculty can see the real position of schools on the way of year-by-year strategic movement process as an analog of what we described for the entire educational institution. The sequence of these numbers shows for management of the schools and faculty in which direction the schools have been moving.

CONCLUSION

Quantitative solutions described in this chapter provide for the control, analysis, and transparency of the planning processes in an organization at all levels of the organization's hierarchy. This study has a practical implementation in the original software application developed by the author.

The chapter introduces a novel numeric indicator (*V*-index) of accomplishments of the plans of the institution, units, and individuals. The original recursive algorithm of calculating of the *V*-index has been developed. The *V*-index allows the senior management to make a year-by-year strategic analysis of targets' achievements of the organization.

The chapter introduces an absolutely new approach to the definition of the operational planning processes – Context-Free Grammar Operational Planning Language (CFGOPL). The CFGOPL is the flat text file (can be modified by any text-based editor), case-sensitive and independent of the computing platform, hardware, and programming implementation.

In this chapter, we share the source codes of his solutions using Microsoft® SQL-Server® relational database system. All SQL script codes, presented in this chapter, are successfully tested and can be used by readers for simulation processes on his/her computers. The practitioners who would like to test procedures shown in this chapter should have a Windows operating system (Windows 8/8.1/10) and MS SQL Server 2014 professional. The chapter presents a first 1.0.0 version of the CFGOPL and welcomes everybody to participate in its discussions/suggestions and recommendations for its improvement.

The solutions, which are presented in this study, do not depend on the size of the organization; they can be implemented in an entire organization or partially in some of its units.

ACKNOWLEDGMENT

The author would like to thank Dr. Conall Kelly and Prof. Alexandra Rodkina of the University of the West Indies, Mona campus, Jamaica, for proof reading and helpful comments.

REFERENCES

W3C Information and Knowledge Domain. (2016). Retrieved from http://www.w3.org/XML/

W3C Working Group. (2004). *Web Services Architecture.* W3C Working Group Note 11 February 2004. Retrieved from http://www.w3.org/TR/2003/WD-ws-arch-20030808/

Griffin, R. W. (1990). *Management* (3rd ed.). Boston, MA: Houghton Mifflin.

Hellriegel, D., & Slocum, J. W. Jr. (1992). *Management* (6th ed.). Reading, MA: Addison-Wesley.

Higgins, J. M. (1991). *The Management Challenge: An Introduction to Management.* New York, NY: Macmillan.

Kaplan, R., & Norton, D. (2005, October). The Office of Strategy Management. *Harvard Business Review*, 72–80. http://hbswk.hbs.edu/item/5305.html PMID:16250626

Kaplan, R. S., & Norton, D. P. (1992, January-February). The balanced scorecard - measures that drive performance. *Harvard Business Review*, 75–85. PMID:10119714

Naisbitt, J. (1982). *Megatrends.* Warner Books.

Osborn, A. (1979). *Running Wild – The next Industrial revolution.* Osborn/McGraw-Hill.

Penny, J. (2001). Differential item functioning an international 360—degree assessment: Evidence of gender stereotype, environmental complexity, and organizational contingency. *European Journal of Work and Organizational Psychology, 10*(3), 245–271. doi:10.1080/13594320143000663

Pougatchev, V., Glasgow, S., Ellis, J., & Johnson, N. (2009). Online Performance Based Management and Evaluation System as an Instrument to Manage the Quality of Institutional Performance at the University of Technology, Jamaica. *Journal of Research in Innovative Teaching, National University, San Diego, CA, USA, 2*(1), 53–78. Retrieved from http://www.nu.edu/assets/resources/pageResources/7638_JournalofResearch09.pdf

Pougatchev, V., & Kulkarni, A. (2011). V-index as a Measure of the Targets/ Objectives Accomplishment of the Strategic and Operation Plans for an Educational Institution Unit (Case Study). Journal of Research in Innovative Teaching, 4(1).

Pougatchev, V., & Kulkarni, A. (2013). Online Strategic and Operational Planning Procedures in the Integrated Management Information Systems for Educational Institutions. In *ICT Management in Non-Profit Organizations* (pp. 192-222). IGI Global. Retrieved from http://www.igi-global.com/book/ict-management-non-profit-organizations/97312

Raymond, C. K. (1964). Theories of choice in business. In G. Fisk (Ed.), *The Frontiers of Management Psychology* (pp. 3–17). New York, NY: Harper and Row.

Robbins, S. P. (1991). *Management* (3rd ed.). Englewood Cliffs, NJ: Prentice-Hall.

Sharp, J. (2010). Windows® Communication Foundation 4 Step by Step. O'Reilly Media, Inc.

Toffler, A. (1980). *The Third Wave*. Bantam Books.

Tucker, A. B., & Noonan, R. E. (2002). *Programming languages: Principals and paradigms* (1st ed.). New York: McGraw-Hill.

U.S. Department of Energy and Oak Ridge Associated Universities. (2001). *The Performance-Based Management Handbook. Volume 1. Establishing and Maintaining a Performance-Based Management Program.* Author.

APPENDIX 1

Figure 8. Syntactic diagram for a non-terminal symbol <OP>

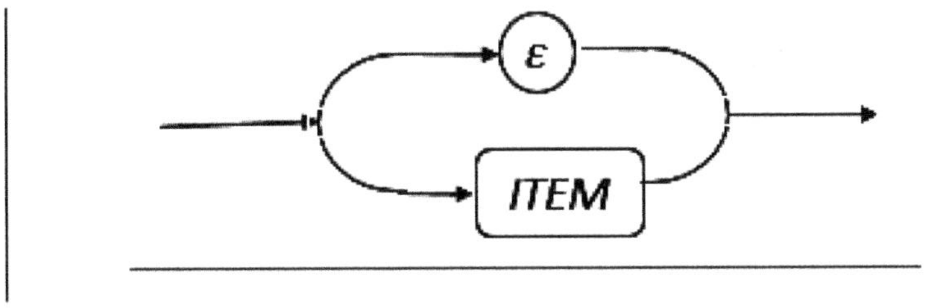

APPENDIX 2

Figure 9. Syntactic diagram for a non-terminal symbol <ITEM>

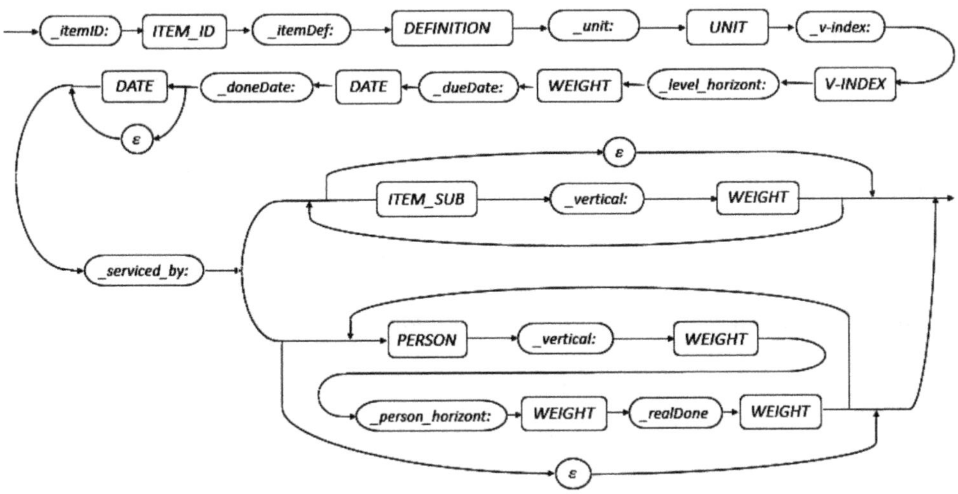

APPENDIX 3

Figure 10. Syntactic diagram for a non-terminal symbol <ITEM_SUB>

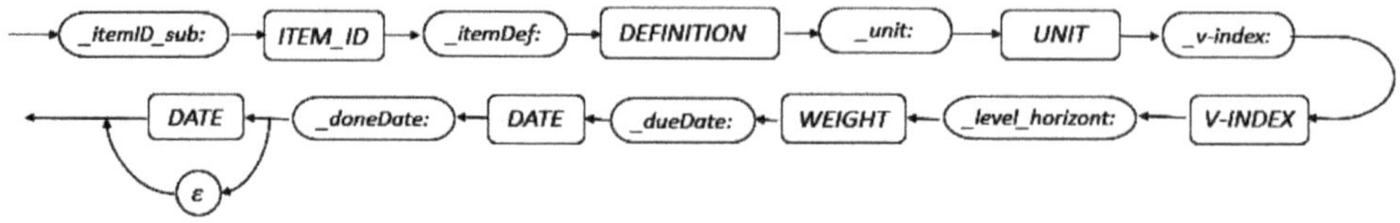

APPENDIX 4

Figure 11. Syntactic diagram for a non-terminal symbol <ITEM_ID>

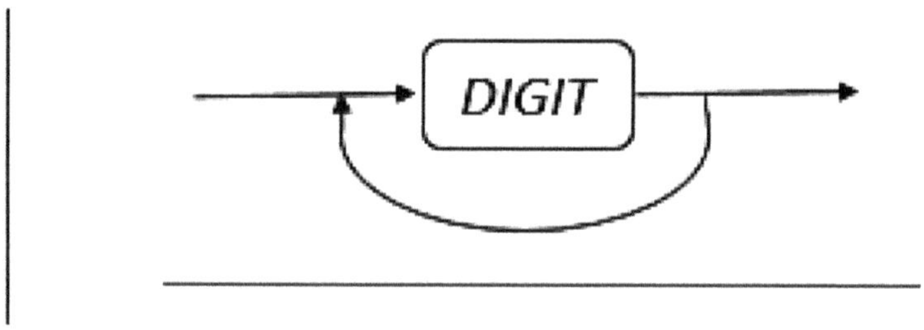

APPENDIX 5

Figure 12. Syntactic diagram for a non-terminal symbol <DEFINITION>

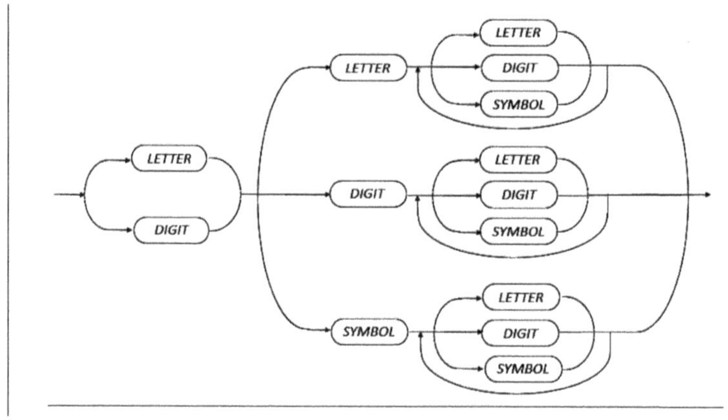

APPENDIX 6

Figure 13. Syntactic diagram for a non-terminal symbol <WEIGHT>

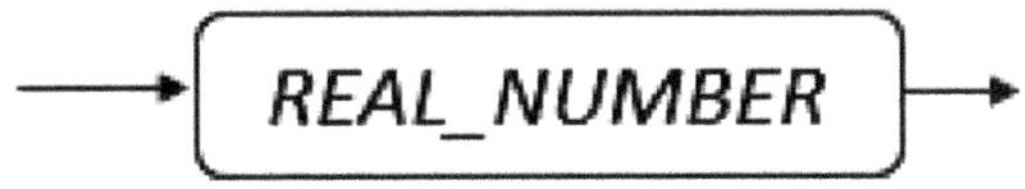

APPENDIX 7

Figure 14. Syntactic diagram for a non-terminals symbol <DATE>

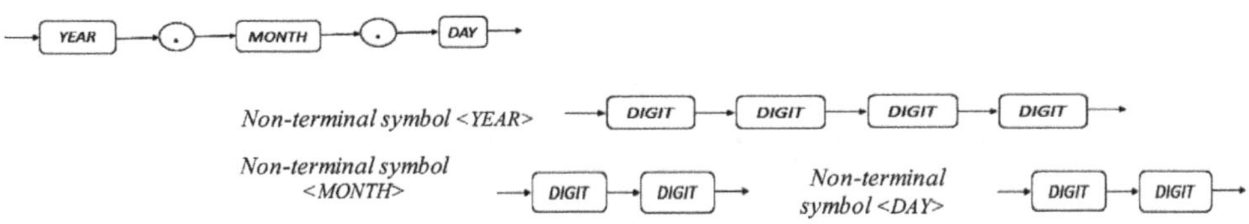

APPENDIX 8

Figure 15. Syntactic diagram for a non-terminal symbol <PERSON>

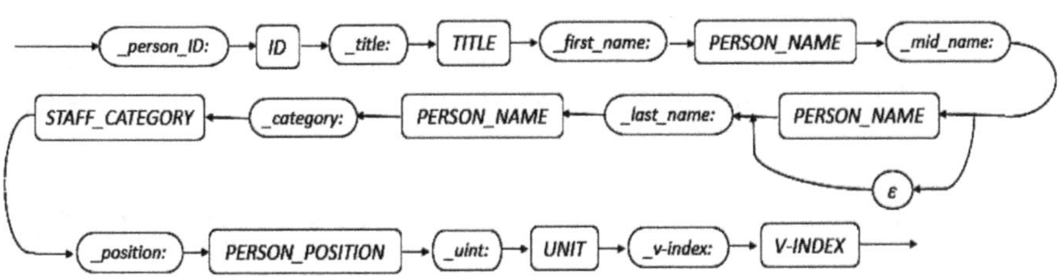

APPENDIX 9

Figure 16. Syntactic diagram for a non-terminal symbol <TITLE>

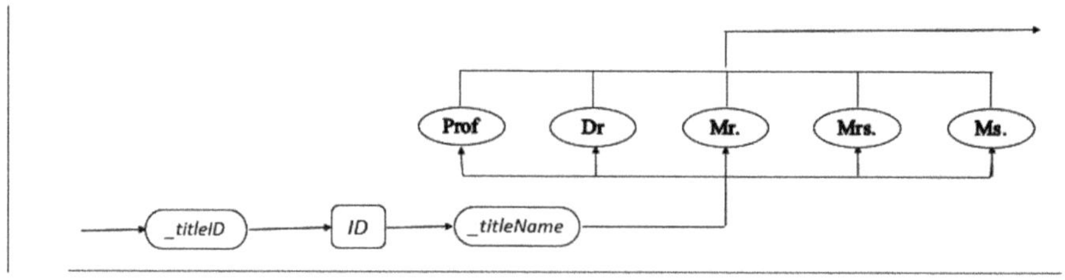

APPENDIX 10

Figure 17. Syntactic diagram for a non-terminal symbol <PERSON_NAME>

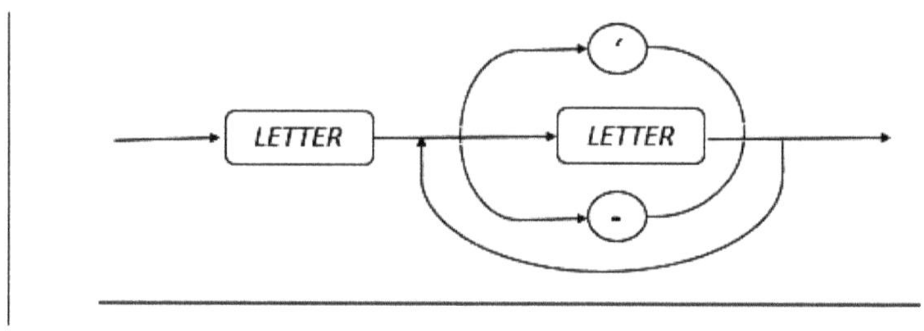

APPENDIX 11

Figure 18. Syntactic diagram for a non-terminals symbol <STAFF_CATEGORY>

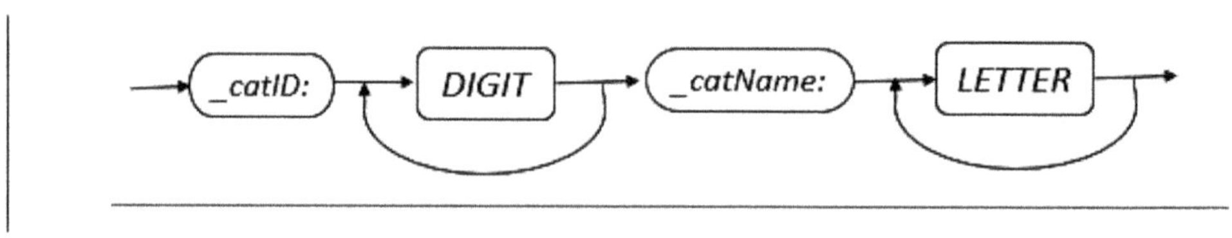

APPENDIX 12

Figure 19. Syntactic diagram for a non-terminal symbol <PERSON_POSITION>

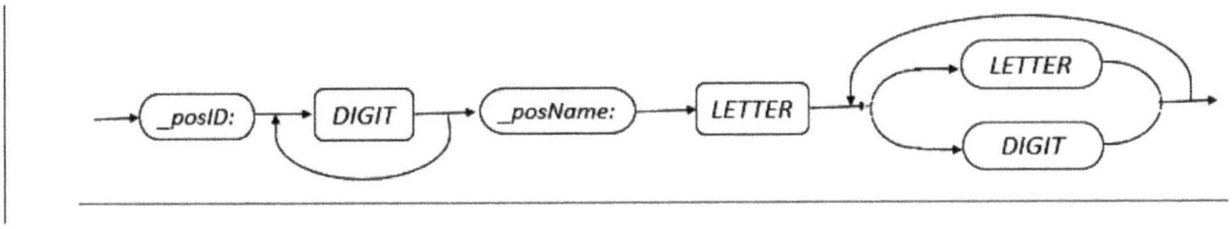

APPENDIX 13

Figure 20. Syntactic diagram for a non-terminal symbol <UNIT>

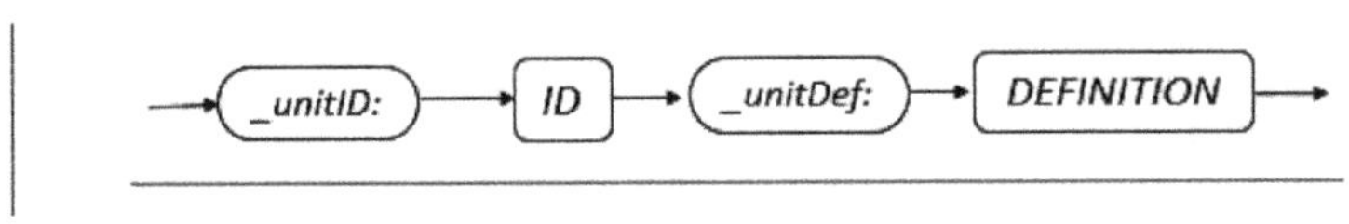

APPENDIX 14

Figure 21. Syntactic diagram for a non-terminal symbol <V-INDEX>

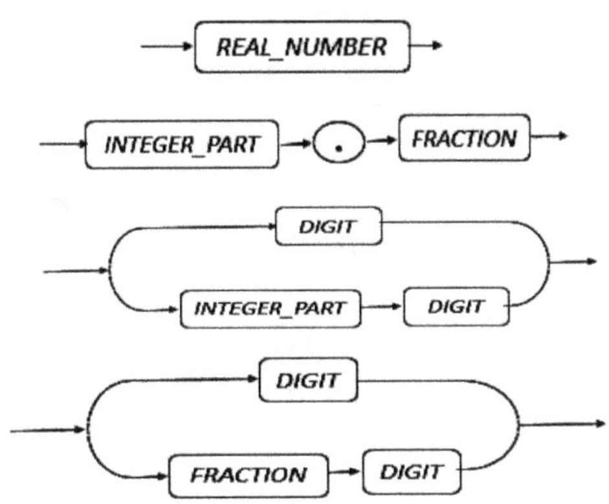

Syntactic diagram for a non-terminal symbol <REAL_NUMBER>

Syntactic diagram for a non-terminal symbol <INTEGER_PART>

Syntactic diagram for a non-terminal symbol <FRACTION>

APPENDIX 15

Figure 22. Syntactic diagram for a non-terminal symbol <LETTER>

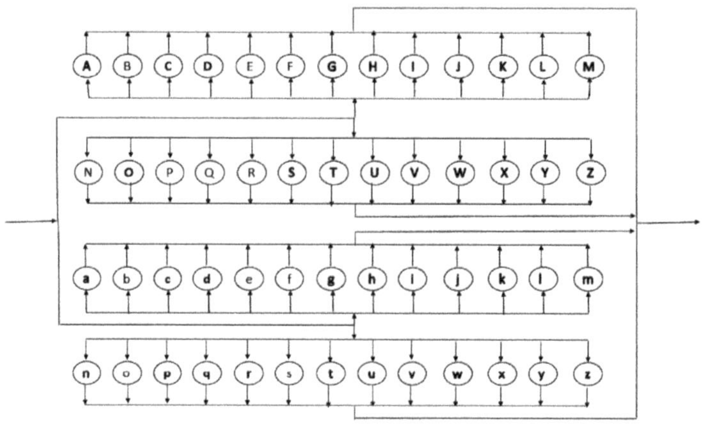

APPENDIX 16

Figure 23. Syntactic diagram for a non-terminal symbol <DIGIT>

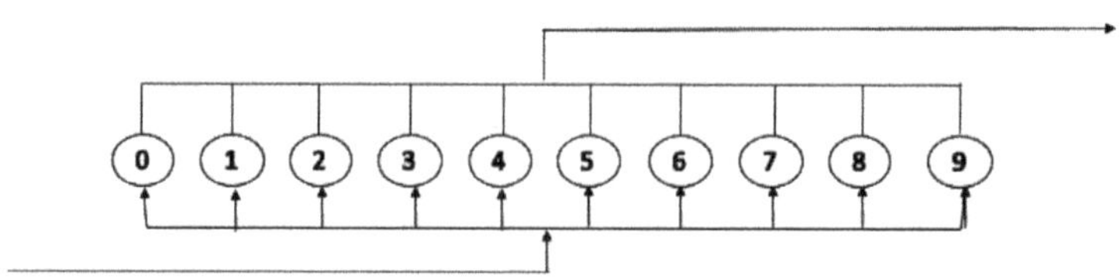

APPENDIX 17

Figure 24. Syntactic diagram for a non-terminal symbol <SYMBOL>

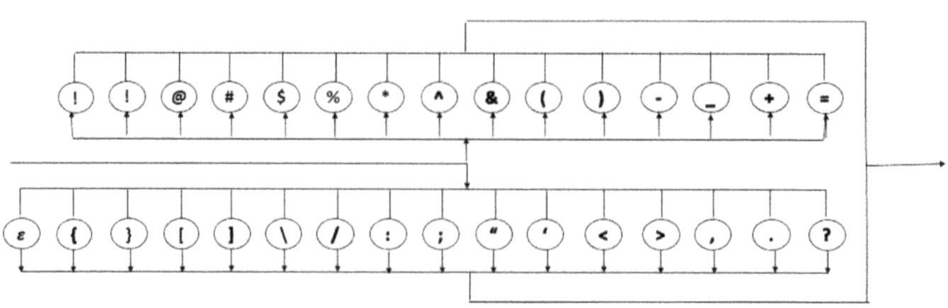

APPENDIX 18

Figure 25. Syntactic diagram for a non-terminal symbol <ID>

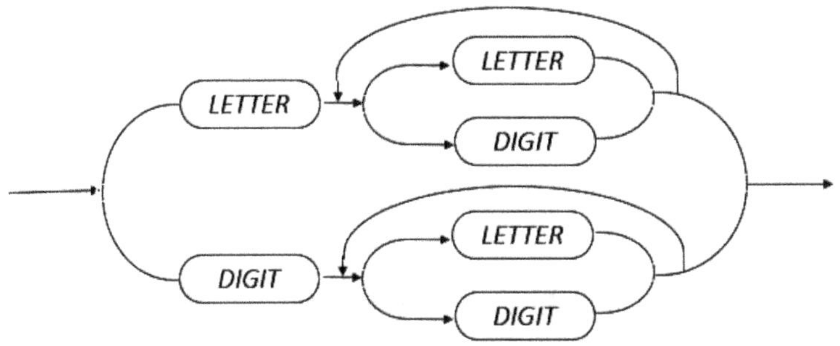

APPENDIX 19

Legend of the diagram:

Figure 26. Hierarchical structure diagram of the FENC operational plan

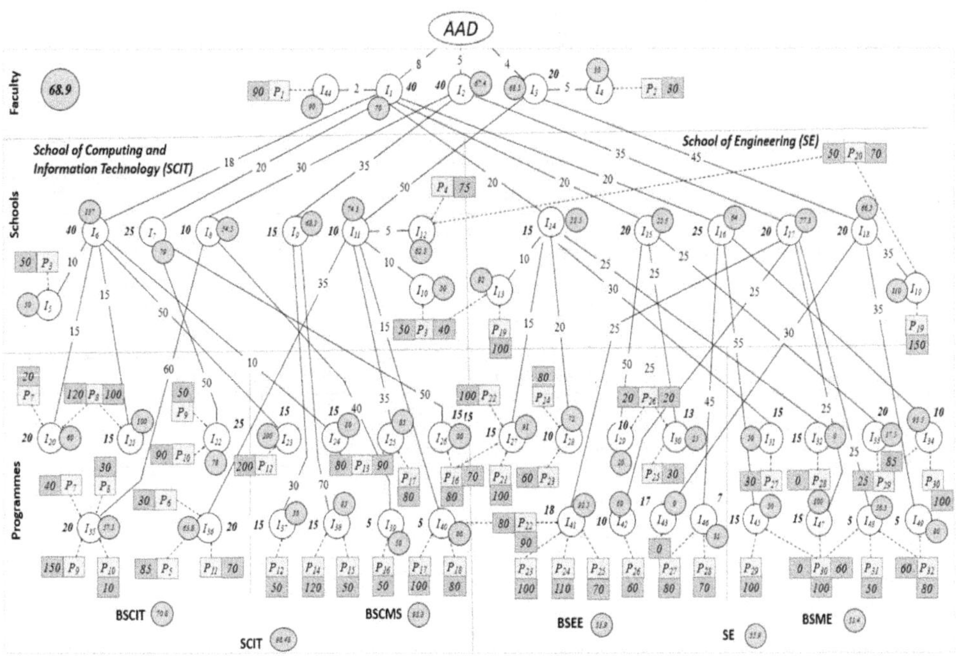

- The oval depicts an item of the operational plan with item's ID inside
- The rectangle depicts ID of the person (right side) and percentage of completing of the item (left side of the rectangle)
- The lines between Items depict a vertical alignment between items (with a weight of the child item)

APPENDIX 20

See Table 14.

Table 14. List of items of the FENC's operational plan

ID in DB	ID in Diagram	Definition
1	I_1	*"Provide High quality, innovative academic and research programmes"*
2	I_2	*"Efficient and Effective Academic and Administrative Processes"*
3	I_3	*"Provide opportunities for learning and research"*
4	I_4	*"Total number of students enrolled in faculty 100%"*
5	I_5	*"Increase the percentage on school level performance"*
6	I_6	*"Increase number and improve quality of Graduate Research students at 30%"*
7	I_7	*"Develop a strategic plan to link expertise in research, services and programmes"*
8	I_8	*"Explore and increase funding for research and innovation by 15%"*
9	I_9	*"Increase the flexible teaching and learning opportunities to meet diverse learner needs"*
10	I_{10}	*"Review courses and programmes to address attributes of the ideal graduate"*
11	I_{11}	*"Promote continuous curriculum renewal to develop the skill set necessary for the learning environment"*
12	I_{12}	*"Review courses and programmes to address attributes of the ideal graduate"*
13	I_{13}	*"Engage in cross-faculty research and delivery of courses"*
14	I_{14}	*"Number of new cross faculty programmes"*
15	I_{15}	*"Increase number and improve quality of Graduate Research students at 20%"*
16	I_{16}	*"Develop a strategic plan to link expertise in research, services and programmes"*
17	I_{17}	*"Increase the flexible teaching and learning opportunities to meet diverse learner needs"*
18	I_{18}	*"Review courses and programmes to address attributes of the ideal graduate"*
19	I_{19}	*"Review courses in Mechanical programme to address attributes of the ideal graduate"*
20	I_{20}	*"Increase the percentage on school level performance"*
21	I_{21}	*"Increase the percentage on BSCIT programme level performance for Master of Science Degree"*
22	I_{22}	*"Plan and execute a research strategy for BSCIT programme to gain access to expertise"*
23	I_{23}	*"Increase the percentage on BSCMS programme level performance for Master of Science Degree"*
24	I_{24}	*"Increase the percentage on BSCMS programmer level performance for Doctorate Degree"*
25	I_{25}	*"Review courses and programmes to address attributes of the ideal graduate for BSCMS programme"*
26	I_{26}	*"Plan and execute a research strategy for BSCMS programme to gain access to expertise"*

continued on following page

Table 14. Continued

ID in DB	ID in Diagram	Definition
27	I_{27}	"Participating in a new Solar Energy Project"
28	I_{28}	"Participation in a Sustainable Energy, Caribbean Sustainable Energy project"
29	I_{29}	"For electrical engineering programme increase number and improve quality of Graduate Research (Master of Science) students at 10%"
30	I_{30}	"For electrical engineering programme increase number and improve quality of Graduate Research (Doctorate degree) students at 5%"
31	I_{31}	"Engage in cross-faculty research"
32	I_{32}	"Engage in cross-faculty delivery of courses"
33	I_{33}	"For mechanical engineering programme increase number and improve quality of Graduate Research (Master of Science) students at 10%"
34	I_{34}	"Plan and execute a research strategy to gain access to expertise"
35	I_{35}	"Increase external funding of research for BSCIT programme"
36	I_{36}	"Review courses and BSCIT programme to address attributes of the ideal graduate"
37	I_{37}	"Increase the flexible teaching and learning opportunities to meet diverse learner needs (scheduling, distance, blended, on-line)"
38	I_{38}	"Increased use of experienced-based learning, articulation, multiple locations for BSCMS programme"
39	I_{39}	"Increase external funding of research for BSCMS programme"
40	I_{40}	"Review IT and programming courses for BSCMS programme"
41	I_{41}	"Increase the flexible teaching and learning opportunities to meet diverse learner needs (scheduling, distance, blended) for Electrical engineering programme"
42	I_{42}	"Increase the flexible teaching and learning opportunities to meet diverse learner needs (on-line, increased use of experienced-based learning, articulation, multiple locations)"
43	I_{43}	"Review courses for Electrical engineering programme using up-to date computer technology"
44	I_{44}	"Improve access to courses through innovative matriculation strategies"
45	I_{45}	"Develop a strategic plan to link expertise in research"
46	I_{46}	"Develop a strategic plan to link expertise in services for Mechanical programme"
47	I_{47}	"Increase the flexible teaching and learning opportunities to meet diverse learner needs (scheduling, distance, blended) for Mechanical engineering programme"
48	I_{48}	"Increase a distance and blended learning opportunities to meet diverse learner needs for Mechanical engineering programme"
49	I_{49}	"Review courses for Mechanical engineering programme using up-to date computer technology"

APPENDIX 21

See Table 15.

Table 15. List of the academic and administrative staff of the FENC involved in the operational plan

ID	Name	ID	Name	ID	Name
P_1	Mrs. Simone McKlein	P_{12}	Mr. Malik Campbell	P_{23}	Mr. Orlando Irving
P_2	Mrs. Shanika Walker	P_{13}	Dr. Xavier Stephens	P_{24}	Dr. Rushawn Johnson
P_3	Miss Tiana Green	P_{14}	Mr. Brandon Hamilton	P_{25}	Mrs. Sheray Jackson
P_4	Mrs. Adrianna Green	P_{15}	Mr. Raymond Reid	P_{26}	Mr. Dontae Hylton
P_5	Dr. Andrew Price	P_{16}	Dr. Shaniel Walker	P_{27}	Mrs. Simone McKlein
P_6	Dr. Jolene Johnson	P_{17}	Mrs. Shermani Chambers	P_{28}	Mrs. Mickalia Powell
P_7	Mrs. Jordana Harrison	P_{18}	Mrs. Aaliyah Lindsay	P_{29}	Mr. Byran Barracks
P_8	Mrs. Brianna Smith	P_{19}	Dr. Alexander Cook	P_{30}	Dr. Mikael Reid
P_9	Prof. Orville Francis	P_{20}	Prof. Tina-Ann Francies	P_{31}	Mr. Sean Williams
P_{10}	Mrs. Bianca Wallace	P_{21}	Prof. Dean Smith	P_{32}	Dr. John Smith
P_{11}	Miss. Kavia Whyte	P_{22}	Dr. Katherine Taylor		

APPENDIX 22

SQL script, which generates a database OP2017

```
USE [master] GO
/****** Object: Database [OP_2017] ******/
CREATE DATABASE [OP_2017]
CONTAINMENT = NONE ON PRIMARY
(NAME = N'OP_2017', FILENAME = N'C:\Program Files\Microsoft SQL Server\
    MSSQL12.MSSQLSERVER2014\MSSQL\DATA\OP_2017.mdf', SIZE =
    5120KB, MAXSIZE = UNLIMITED, FILEGROWTH = 1024KB)
LOG ON
(NAME = N'OP_2017_log', FILENAME = N'C:\Program Files\Microsoft SQL
    Server\MSSQL12.MSSQLSERVER2014\MSSQL\DATA\OP_2017_log.ldf',
    SIZE = 2048KB, MAXSIZE = 2048GB, FILEGROWTH = 10%) GO
ALTER DATABASE [OP_2017] SET COMPATIBILITY_LEVEL = 120 GO
IF (1 = FULLTEXTSERVICEPROPERTY('IsFullTextInstalled')) begin EXEC
    [OP_2017].[dbo].[sp_fulltext_database] @action = 'enable' end GO
```

```
ALTER DATABASE [OP_2017] SET ANSI_NULL_DEFAULT OFF GO
ALTER DATABASE [OP_2017] SET ANSI_NULLS OFF GO
ALTER DATABASE [OP_2017] SET ANSI_PADDING OFF GO
ALTER DATABASE [OP_2017] SET ANSI_WARNINGS OFF GO
ALTER DATABASE [OP_2017] SET ARITHABORT OFF GO
ALTER DATABASE [OP_2017] SET AUTO_CLOSE OFF GO
ALTER DATABASE [OP_2017] SET AUTO_SHRINK OFF GO
ALTER DATABASE [OP_2017] SET AUTO_UPDATE_STATISTICS ON GO
ALTER DATABASE [OP_2017] SET CURSOR_CLOSE_ON_COMMIT OFF GO
ALTER DATABASE [OP_2017] SET CURSOR_DEFAULT GLOBAL GO
ALTER DATABASE [OP_2017] SET CONCAT_NULL_YIELDS_NULL OFF GO
ALTER DATABASE [OP_2017] SET NUMERIC_ROUNDABORT OFF GO
ALTER DATABASE [OP_2017] SET QUOTED_IDENTIFIER OFF GO
ALTER DATABASE [OP_2017] SET RECURSIVE_TRIGGERS OFF GO
ALTER DATABASE [OP_2017] SET DISABLE_BROKER GO
ALTER DATABASE [OP_2017] SET AUTO_UPDATE_STATISTICS_ASYNC OFF
    GO
ALTER DATABASE [OP_2017] SET DATE_CORRELATION_OPTIMIZATION
    OFF GO
ALTER DATABASE [OP_2017] SET TRUSTWORTHY OFF GO
ALTER DATABASE [OP_2017] SET ALLOW_SNAPSHOT_ISOLATION OFF GO
ALTER DATABASE [OP_2017] SET PARAMETERIZATION SIMPLE GO
ALTER DATABASE [OP_2017] SET READ_COMMITTED_SNAPSHOT OFF GO
ALTER DATABASE [OP_2017] SET HONOR_BROKER_PRIORITY OFF GO
ALTER DATABASE [OP_2017] SET RECOVERY FULL GO
ALTER DATABASE [OP_2017] SET MULTI_USER GO
ALTER DATABASE [OP_2017] SET PAGE_VERIFY CHECKSUM GO
ALTER DATABASE [OP_2017] SET DB_CHAINING OFF GO
ALTER DATABASE [OP_2017] SET FILESTREAM(NON_TRANSACTED_ACCESS
    = OFF) GO
ALTER DATABASE [OP_2017] SET TARGET_RECOVERY_TIME = 0 SECONDS
    GO
ALTER DATABASE [OP_2017] SET DELAYED_DURABILITY = DISABLED GO
EXEC sys.sp_db_vardecimal_storage_format N'OP_2017', N'ON' GO
USE [OP_2017] GO
/****** Object: Table [dbo].[Category] ******/
SET ANSI_NULLS ON GO SET QUOTED_IDENTIFIER ON GO SET ANSI_
    PADDING ON GO
CREATE TABLE [dbo].[Category] ([_catID] [smallint] NOT NULL, [_catName]
    [char](30) NULL,
```

```
CONSTRAINT [PK_Category] PRIMARY KEY CLUSTERED ([_catID] ASC)
WITH (PAD_INDEX = OFF, STATISTICS_NORECOMPUTE = OFF, IGNORE_
    DUP_KEY = OFF, ALLOW_ROW_LOCKS = ON, ALLOW_PAGE_LOCKS
    = ON) ON [PRIMARY]) ON [PRIMARY] GO SET ANSI_PADDING OFF GO
/****** Object: Table [dbo].[Item_Item] ******/
SET ANSI_NULLS ON GO SET QUOTED_IDENTIFIER ON GO
CREATE TABLE [dbo].[Item_Item] ([_itemID] [int] NOT NULL, [_itemID_sub]
    [int] NOT NULL, [_vertical] [numeric](5, 2) NULL,
CONSTRAINT [PK_Item_Item] PRIMARY KEY CLUSTERED ([_itemID] ASC,
    [_itemID_sub] ASC)
WITH (PAD_INDEX = OFF, STATISTICS_NORECOMPUTE = OFF, IGNORE_
    DUP_KEY = OFF, ALLOW_ROW_LOCKS = ON, ALLOW_PAGE_LOCKS
    = ON) ON [PRIMARY]) ON [PRIMARY] GO
/****** Object: Table [dbo].[Items] ******/
SET ANSI_NULLS ON GO SET QUOTED_IDENTIFIER ON GO SET ANSI_
    PADDING ON GO
CREATE TABLE [dbo].[Items] ([_itemID] [int] NOT NULL, [_itemDef] [varchar]
    (500) NULL, [_v-index] [numeric](5, 2) NULL,
CONSTRAINT [PK_Items] PRIMARY KEY CLUSTERED ([_itemID] ASC)
WITH (PAD_INDEX = OFF, STATISTICS_NORECOMPUTE = OFF, IGNORE_
    DUP_KEY = OFF, ALLOW_ROW_LOCKS = ON, ALLOW_PAGE_LOCKS
    = ON) ON [PRIMARY]) ON [PRIMARY] GO SET ANSI_PADDING OFF GO
/****** Object: Table [dbo].[Items_Persons] ******/
SET ANSI_NULLS ON GO SET QUOTED_IDENTIFIER ON GO SET ANSI_
    PADDING OFF GO
CREATE TABLE [dbo].[Items_Persons] ([_itemID] [int] NOT NULL, [_person_ID]
    [char](30) NOT NULL, [_vertical] [numeric](5, 2) NULL,
[_person_horizont] [numeric](5, 2) NULL, [_realDone] [numeric](5, 2) NULL,
CONSTRAINT [PK_Items_Persons] PRIMARY KEY CLUSTERED ([_itemID]
    ASC, [_person_ID] ASC)
WITH (PAD_INDEX = OFF, STATISTICS_NORECOMPUTE = OFF, IGNORE_
    DUP_KEY = OFF, ALLOW_ROW_LOCKS = ON, ALLOW_PAGE_LOCKS
    = ON) ON [PRIMARY]) ON [PRIMARY] GO SET ANSI_PADDING OFF GO
/****** Object: Table [dbo].[Items_Units] ******/
SET ANSI_NULLS ON GO SET QUOTED_IDENTIFIER ON GO
CREATE TABLE [dbo].[Items_Units] ([_itemID] [int] NOT NULL, [_unitID] [int]
    NOT NULL, [_level_horizont] [numeric](5, 2) NULL,
CONSTRAINT [PK_Items_Units] PRIMARY KEY CLUSTERED ([_itemID] ASC,
    [_unitID] ASC)
```

```
WITH (PAD_INDEX = OFF, STATISTICS_NORECOMPUTE = OFF, IGNORE_
    DUP_KEY = OFF, ALLOW_ROW_LOCKS = ON, ALLOW_PAGE_LOCKS
    = ON) ON [PRIMARY]) ON [PRIMARY] GO
/****** Object: Table [dbo].[Persons] ******/
SET ANSI_NULLS ON GO SET QUOTED_IDENTIFIER ON GO SET ANSI_
    PADDING ON GO
CREATE TABLE [dbo].[Persons]([_person_ID] [char](30) NOT NULL, [_first_
    name] [char](50) NULL, [_mid_name] [char](50) NULL, [_last_name]
    [char](50) NULL, [_titleID] [smallint] NULL, [_category] [smallint] NULL,
    [_position] [smallint] NULL, [_unitID] [smallint] NULL, [_v-index] [numeric]
    (5, 2) NULL,
CONSTRAINT [PK_Persons] PRIMARY KEY CLUSTERED ([_person_ID] ASC)
WITH (PAD_INDEX = OFF, STATISTICS_NORECOMPUTE = OFF, IGNORE_
    DUP_KEY = OFF, ALLOW_ROW_LOCKS = ON, ALLOW_PAGE_LOCKS
    = ON) ON [PRIMARY]) ON [PRIMARY] GO SET ANSI_PADDING OFF GO
/****** Object: Table [dbo].[Position] ******/
SET ANSI_NULLS ON GO SET QUOTED_IDENTIFIER ON GO SET ANSI_
    PADDING ON GO
CREATE TABLE [dbo].[Position] ([_posID] [smallint] NOT NULL, [_posName]
    [varchar](50) NULL,
CONSTRAINT [PK_Position] PRIMARY KEY CLUSTERED ([_posID] ASC)
WITH (PAD_INDEX = OFF, STATISTICS_NORECOMPUTE = OFF, IGNORE_
    DUP_KEY = OFF, ALLOW_ROW_LOCKS = ON, ALLOW_PAGE_LOCKS
    = ON) ON [PRIMARY]) ON [PRIMARY] GO SET ANSI_PADDING OFF GO
/****** Object: Table [dbo].[Titles] ******/
SET ANSI_NULLS ON GO SET QUOTED_IDENTIFIER ON GO SET ANSI_
    PADDING ON GO
CREATE TABLE [dbo].[Titles] ([_titleID] [smallint] NOT NULL, [_titleName]
    [char](30) NULL,
CONSTRAINT [PK_titleID] PRIMARY KEY CLUSTERED ([_titleID] ASC)
WITH (PAD_INDEX = OFF, STATISTICS_NORECOMPUTE = OFF, IGNORE_
    DUP_KEY = OFF, ALLOW_ROW_LOCKS = ON, ALLOW_PAGE_LOCKS
    = ON) ON [PRIMARY]) ON [PRIMARY] GO SET ANSI_PADDING OFF GO
/****** Object: Table [dbo].[Units] ******/
SET ANSI_NULLS ON GO SET QUOTED_IDENTIFIER ON GO SET ANSI_
    PADDING ON GO
CREATE TABLE [dbo].[Units] ([_unitID] [int] NOT NULL, [_unitDef] [varchar]
    (100) NULL,
CONSTRAINT [PK_Units] PRIMARY KEY CLUSTERED ([_unitID] ASC)
```

```
WITH (PAD_INDEX = OFF, STATISTICS_NORECOMPUTE = OFF, IGNORE_
    DUP_KEY = OFF, ALLOW_ROW_LOCKS = ON, ALLOW_PAGE_LOCKS
    = ON) ON [PRIMARY]) ON [PRIMARY] GO SET ANSI_PADDING OFF GO
ALTER TABLE [dbo].[Item_Item] WITH CHECK ADD CONSTRAINT [FK_Item_
    Item_Items] FOREIGN KEY([_itemID])
REFERENCES [dbo].[Items] ([_itemID]) GO
ALTER TABLE [dbo].[Item_Item] CHECK CONSTRAINT [FK_Item_Item_Items]
    GO
ALTER TABLE [dbo].[Item_Item] WITH CHECK ADD CONSTRAINT [FK_Item_
    Item_Items1] FOREIGN KEY([_itemID_sub])
REFERENCES [dbo].[Items] ([_itemID]) GO
ALTER TABLE [dbo].[Item_Item] CHECK CONSTRAINT [FK_Item_Item_Items1]
    GO
ALTER TABLE [dbo].[Items_Persons] WITH CHECK ADD CONSTRAINT [FK_
    Items_Persons_Items] FOREIGN KEY([_itemID])
REFERENCES [dbo].[Items] ([_itemID]) GO
ALTER TABLE [dbo].[Items_Persons] CHECK CONSTRAINT [FK_Items_Persons_
    Items] GO
ALTER TABLE [dbo].[Items_Persons] WITH CHECK ADD CONSTRAINT [FK_
    Items_Persons_Persons] FOREIGN KEY([_person_ID])
REFERENCES [dbo].[Persons] ([_person_ID]) GO
ALTER TABLE [dbo].[Items_Persons] CHECK CONSTRAINT [FK_Items_Persons_
    Persons] GO
ALTER TABLE [dbo].[Items_Units] WITH CHECK ADD CONSTRAINT [FK_
    Items_Units_Items] FOREIGN KEY([_itemID])
REFERENCES [dbo].[Items] ([_itemID]) GO
ALTER TABLE [dbo].[Items_Units] CHECK CONSTRAINT [FK_Items_Units_
    Items] GO
ALTER TABLE [dbo].[Items_Units] WITH CHECK ADD CONSTRAINT [FK_
    Items_Units_Units] FOREIGN KEY([_unitID])
REFERENCES [dbo].[Units] ([_unitID]) GO
ALTER TABLE [dbo].[Items_Units] CHECK CONSTRAINT [FK_Items_Units_
    Units] GO
ALTER TABLE [dbo].[Persons] WITH CHECK ADD CONSTRAINT [FK_Persons_
    Category] FOREIGN KEY([_category])
REFERENCES [dbo].[Category] ([_catID]) GO
ALTER TABLE [dbo].[Persons] CHECK CONSTRAINT [FK_Persons_Category] GO
ALTER TABLE [dbo].[Persons] WITH CHECK ADD CONSTRAINT [FK_Persons_
    Position] FOREIGN KEY([_position])
REFERENCES [dbo].[Position] ([_posID]) GO
```

```
ALTER TABLE [dbo].[Persons] CHECK CONSTRAINT [FK_Persons_Position] GO
ALTER TABLE [dbo].[Persons] WITH CHECK ADD CONSTRAINT [FK_Persons_
    Titles] FOREIGN KEY([_titleID])
REFERENCES [dbo].[Titles] ([_titleID]) GO
ALTER TABLE [dbo].[Persons] CHECK CONSTRAINT [FK_Persons_Titles] GO
```

APPENDIX 23

See Figure 27.

Figure 27. The structure of the OP_2017 database

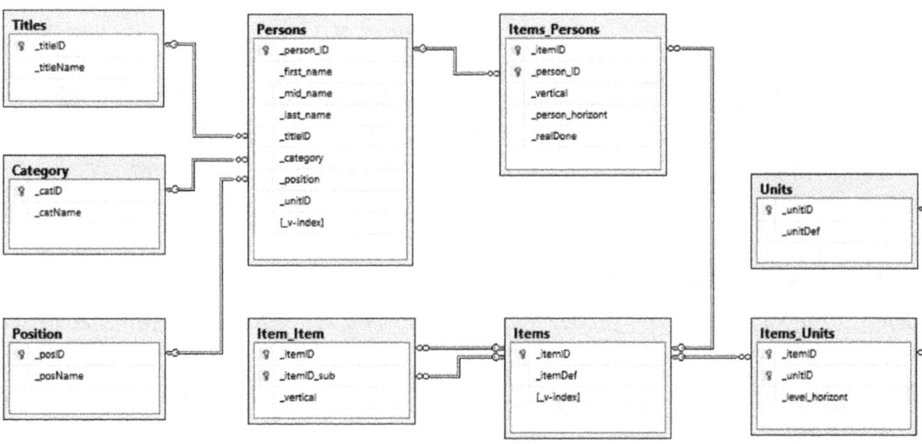

APPENDIX 24

SQL script, which inserts data into the OP_2017 database.

```
USE [OP_2017]
GO
INSERT [dbo].[Category] ([_catID], [_catName]) VALUES (1, N'Academic')
INSERT [dbo].[Category] ([_catID], [_catName]) VALUES (2, N'Technical')
INSERT [dbo].[Category] ([_catID], [_catName]) VALUES (3, N'Administrative')
INSERT [dbo].[Category] ([_catID], [_catName]) VALUES (4, N'Ancillary')
INSERT [dbo].[Position] ([_posID], [_posName]) VALUES (1, N'Assistant lecturer')
INSERT [dbo].[Position] ([_posID], [_posName]) VALUES (2, N'Lecturer')
INSERT [dbo].[Position] ([_posID], [_posName]) VALUES (3, N'Senior lecturer')
INSERT [dbo].[Position] ([_posID], [_posName]) VALUES (4, N'Associate
    Professor')
INSERT [dbo].[Position] ([_posID], [_posName]) VALUES (5, N'Professor')
INSERT [dbo].[Position] ([_posID], [_posName]) VALUES (6, N'Head of School')
INSERT [dbo].[Position] ([_posID], [_posName]) VALUES (7, N'Head of
    Department')
INSERT [dbo].[Position] ([_posID], [_posName]) VALUES (8, N'Programme
    Director')
INSERT [dbo].[Position] ([_posID], [_posName]) VALUES (9, N'Dean')
INSERT [dbo].[Position] ([_posID], [_posName]) VALUES (10, N'Administrative
    support')
INSERT [dbo].[Position] ([_posID], [_posName]) VALUES (11, N'Executive
    assistant')
INSERT [dbo].[Position] ([_posID], [_posName]) VALUES (12, N'Faculty
    administrator')
INSERT [dbo].[Position] ([_posID], [_posName]) VALUES (13, N'Technician')
INSERT [dbo].[Position] ([_posID], [_posName]) VALUES (14, N'Technologist')
INSERT [dbo].[Position] ([_posID], [_posName]) VALUES (15, N'Technical officer')
INSERT [dbo].[Titles] ([_titleID], [_titleName]) VALUES (1, N'Mr.') INSERT
    [dbo].[Titles] ([_titleID], [_titleName]) VALUES (2, N'Mrs.')
INSERT [dbo].[Titles] ([_titleID], [_titleName]) VALUES (3, N'Miss') INSERT
    [dbo].[Titles] ([_titleID], [_titleName]) VALUES (4, N'Dr.')
INSERT [dbo].[Titles] ([_titleID], [_titleName]) VALUES (5, N'Prof.')
INSERT [dbo].[Persons] ([_person_ID], [_first_name], [_mid_name], [_last_name],
    [_titleID], [_category], [_position], [_unitID], [_v-index]) VALUES (N'1',
    N'Simone ', NULL, N'McKlein ', 2, 3, 12, 1, 90.00)
```

INSERT [dbo].[Persons] ([_person_ID], [_first_name], [_mid_name], [_last_name], [_titleID], [_category], [_position], [_unitID], [_v-index]) VALUES (N'10', N'Bianca ', NULL, N'Wallace', 2, 1, 2, 3, 66.00)
INSERT [dbo].[Persons] ([_person_ID], [_first_name], [_mid_name], [_last_name], [_titleID], [_category], [_position], [_unitID], [_v-index]) VALUES (N'11 ', N'Kavia ', NULL, N'Whyte', 3, 1, 1, 3, 70.00)
INSERT [dbo].[Persons] ([_person_ID], [_first_name], [_mid_name], [_last_name], [_titleID], [_category], [_position], [_unitID], [_v-index]) VALUES (N'12', N'Malik ', NULL, N'Campbell', 1, 1, 2, 4, 110.00)
INSERT [dbo].[Persons] ([_person_ID], [_first_name], [_mid_name], [_last_name], [_titleID], [_category], [_position], [_unitID], [_v-index]) VALUES (N'13', N'Xavier ', NULL, N'Stephens', 4, 1, 4, 4, 85.00)
INSERT [dbo].[Persons] ([_person_ID], [_first_name], [_mid_name], [_last_name], [_titleID], [_category], [_position], [_unitID], [_v-index]) VALUES (N'14 ', N'Brandon', NULL, N'Hamilton', 1, 3, 10, 4, 120.00)
INSERT [dbo].[Persons] ([_person_ID], [_first_name], [_mid_name], [_last_name], [_titleID], [_category], [_position], [_unitID], [_v-index]) VALUES (N'15', N'Raymond', NULL, N'Reid', 1, 3, 10, 4, 50.00)
INSERT [dbo].[Persons] ([_person_ID], [_first_name], [_mid_name], [_last_name], [_titleID], [_category], [_position], [_unitID], [_v-index]) VALUES (N'16', N'Shaniel', NULL, N'Walker', 4, 1, 5, 4, 66.50)
INSERT [dbo].[Persons] ([_person_ID], [_first_name], [_mid_name], [_last_name], [_titleID], [_category], [_position], [_unitID], [_v-index]) VALUES (N'17', N'Shermani ', NULL, N'Chambers ', 2, 1, 3, 4, 90.00)
INSERT [dbo].[Persons] ([_person_ID], [_first_name], [_mid_name], [_last_name], [_titleID], [_category], [_position], [_unitID], [_v-index]) VALUES (N'18', N'Aaliyah', NULL, N'Lindsay', 2, 2, 13, 4, 80.00)
INSERT [dbo].[Persons] ([_person_ID], [_first_name], [_mid_name], [_last_name], [_titleID], [_category], [_position], [_unitID], [_v-index]) VALUES (N'19', N'Alexander', NULL, N'Cook', 4, 1, 6, 5, 130.00)
INSERT [dbo].[Persons] ([_person_ID], [_first_name], [_mid_name], [_last_name], [_titleID], [_category], [_position], [_unitID], [_v-index]) VALUES (N'2', N'Shanika ', NULL, N'Walker ', 2, 3, 10, 1, 30.00)
INSERT [dbo].[Persons] ([_person_ID], [_first_name], [_mid_name], [_last_name], [_titleID], [_category], [_position], [_unitID], [_v-index]) VALUES (N'20', N'Tina-Ann', NULL, N'Francies', 5, 1, 5, 5, 60.00)
INSERT [dbo].[Persons] ([_person_ID], [_first_name], [_mid_name], [_last_name], [_titleID], [_category], [_position], [_unitID], [_v-index]) VALUES (N'21', N'Dean', NULL, N'Smith', 5, 1, 5, 6, 100.00)

INSERT [dbo].[Persons] ([_person_ID], [_first_name], [_mid_name], [_last_name], [_titleID], [_category], [_position], [_unitID], [_v-index]) VALUES (N'22', N'Katherine', NULL, N'Taylor', 4, 1, 4, 6, 88.00)
INSERT [dbo].[Persons] ([_person_ID], [_first_name], [_mid_name], [_last_name], [_titleID], [_category], [_position], [_unitID], [_v-index]) VALUES (N'23 ', N'Orlando', NULL, N'Irving', 1, 1, 2, 6, 84.00)
INSERT [dbo].[Persons] ([_person_ID], [_first_name], [_mid_name], [_last_name], [_titleID], [_category], [_position], [_unitID], [_v-index]) VALUES (N'24', N'Rushawn', NULL, N'Johnson ', 4, 1, 4, 6, 98.00)
INSERT [dbo].[Persons] ([_person_ID], [_first_name], [_mid_name], [_last_name], [_titleID], [_category], [_position], [_unitID], [_v-index]) VALUES (N'25', N'Sheray', NULL, N'Jackson', 2, 1, 3, 6, 58.00)
INSERT [dbo].[Persons] ([_person_ID], [_first_name], [_mid_name], [_last_name], [_titleID], [_category], [_position], [_unitID], [_v-index]) VALUES (N'26', N'Dontae', NULL, N'Hylton', 1, 1, 3, 6, 36.00
INSERT [dbo].[Persons] ([_person_ID], [_first_name], [_mid_name], [_last_name], [_titleID], [_category], [_position], [_unitID], [_v-index]) VALUES (N'27', N'Simone', NULL, N'McKlein', 2, 1, 2, 7, 44.00)
INSERT [dbo].[Persons] ([_person_ID], [_first_name], [_mid_name], [_last_name], [_titleID], [_category], [_position], [_unitID], [_v-index]) VALUES (N'28', N'Mickalia', NULL, N'Powell', 2, 1, 3, 6, 49.00)
INSERT [dbo].[Persons] ([_person_ID], [_first_name], [_mid_name], [_last_name], [_titleID], [_category], [_position], [_unitID], [_v-index]) VALUES (N'29', N'Byran', NULL, N'Barracks', 1, 1, 2, 7, 80.50)
INSERT [dbo].[Persons] ([_person_ID], [_first_name], [_mid_name], [_last_name], [_titleID], [_category], [_position], [_unitID], [_v-index]) VALUES (N'3', N'Tiana', NULL, N'Green', 3, 1, 6, 2, 46.00)
INSERT [dbo].[Persons] ([_person_ID], [_first_name], [_mid_name], [_last_name], [_titleID], [_category], [_position], [_unitID], [_v-index]) VALUES (N'30', N'Mikael', NULL, N'Reid', 4, 1, 4, 7, 68.00)
INSERT [dbo].[Persons] ([_person_ID], [_first_name], [_mid_name], [_last_name], [_titleID], [_category], [_position], [_unitID], [_v-index]) VALUES (N'31', N'Sean', NULL, N'Williams ', 1, 1, 2, 7, 50.00)
INSERT [dbo].[Persons] ([_person_ID], [_first_name], [_mid_name], [_last_name], [_titleID], [_category], [_position], [_unitID], [_v-index]) VALUES (N'32', N'John', NULL, N'Smith', 4, 1, 4, 7, 68.00)
INSERT [dbo].[Persons] ([_person_ID], [_first_name], [_mid_name], [_last_name], [_titleID], [_category], [_position], [_unitID], [_v-index]) VALUES (N'4 ', N'Adrianna', NULL, N'Green', 2, 3, 10, 2, 75.00)

INSERT [dbo].[Persons] ([_person_ID], [_first_name], [_mid_name], [_last_name], [_titleID], [_category], [_position], [_unitID], [_v-index]) VALUES (N'5', N'Andrew ', NULL, N'Price', 4, 1, 5, 3, 85.00)

INSERT [dbo].[Persons] ([_person_ID], [_first_name], [_mid_name], [_last_name], [_titleID], [_category], [_position], [_unitID], [_v-index]) VALUES (N'6', N'Jolene', NULL, N'Johnson', 4, 1, 4, 3, 30.00)

INSERT [dbo].[Persons] ([_person_ID], [_first_name], [_mid_name], [_last_name], [_titleID], [_category], [_position], [_unitID], [_v-index]) VALUES (N'7', N'Jordana', NULL, N'Harrison', 2, 1, 2, 2, 32.00)

INSERT [dbo].[Persons] ([_person_ID], [_first_name], [_mid_name], [_last_name], [_titleID], [_category], [_position], [_unitID], [_v-index]) VALUES (N'8', N'Brianna', NULL, N'Smith', 2, 1, 2, 2, 69.00)

INSERT [dbo].[Persons] ([_person_ID], [_first_name], [_mid_name], [_last_name], [_titleID], [_category], [_position], [_unitID], [_v-index]) VALUES (N'9 ', N'Orville ', NULL, N'Francis', 5, 1, 5, 2, 120.00)

Below is a template of the SQL Insert script to populate a table Items. To generate full script, the "_itemID" and "_itemDef" elements must be replaced by values "ID in DB" and "Definition" accordingly to a List of items of the FENC's operational plan, presented in Appendix 20.

INSERT [dbo].[Items] ([_itemID], [_itemDef], [_v-index]) VALUES (_itemID, N'_itemDef', NULL)

INSERT [dbo].[Item_Item] ([_itemID], [_itemID_sub], [_vertical]) VALUES (1, 6, CAST(18.00 AS Numeric(5, 2)))

INSERT [dbo].[Item_Item] ([_itemID], [_itemID_sub], [_vertical]) VALUES (1, 7, CAST(20.00 AS Numeric(5, 2)))

INSERT [dbo].[Item_Item] ([_itemID], [_itemID_sub], [_vertical]) VALUES (1, 14, CAST(20.00 AS Numeric(5, 2)))

INSERT [dbo].[Item_Item] ([_itemID], [_itemID_sub], [_vertical]) VALUES (1, 15, CAST(20.00 AS Numeric(5, 2)))

INSERT [dbo].[Item_Item] ([_itemID], [_itemID_sub], [_vertical]) VALUES (1, 16, CAST(20.00 AS Numeric(5, 2)))

INSERT [dbo].[Item_Item] ([_itemID], [_itemID_sub], [_vertical]) VALUES (1, 44, CAST(2.00 AS Numeric(5, 2)))

INSERT [dbo].[Item_Item] ([_itemID], [_itemID_sub], [_vertical]) VALUES (2, 8, CAST(30.00 AS Numeric(5, 2)))

INSERT [dbo].[Item_Item] ([_itemID], [_itemID_sub], [_vertical]) VALUES (2, 9, CAST(35.00 AS Numeric(5, 2)))

INSERT [dbo].[Item_Item] ([_itemID], [_itemID_sub], [_vertical]) VALUES (2, 17, CAST(35.00 AS Numeric(5, 2)))

```
INSERT [dbo].[Item_Item] ([_itemID], [_itemID_sub], [_vertical]) VALUES (3, 4, CAST(5.00 AS Numeric(5, 2)))
INSERT [dbo].[Item_Item] ([_itemID], [_itemID_sub], [_vertical]) VALUES (3, 11, CAST(50.00 AS Numeric(5, 2)))
INSERT [dbo].[Item_Item] ([_itemID], [_itemID_sub], [_vertical]) VALUES (3, 18, CAST(45.00 AS Numeric(5, 2)))
INSERT [dbo].[Item_Item] ([_itemID], [_itemID_sub], [_vertical]) VALUES (6, 5, CAST(10.00 AS Numeric(5, 2)))
INSERT [dbo].[Item_Item] ([_itemID], [_itemID_sub], [_vertical]) VALUES (6, 20, CAST(15.00 AS Numeric(5, 2)))
INSERT [dbo].[Item_Item] ([_itemID], [_itemID_sub], [_vertical]) VALUES (6, 21, CAST(15.00 AS Numeric(5, 2)))
INSERT [dbo].[Item_Item] ([_itemID], [_itemID_sub], [_vertical]) VALUES (6, 23, CAST(50.00 AS Numeric(5, 2)))
INSERT [dbo].[Item_Item] ([_itemID], [_itemID_sub], [_vertical]) VALUES (6, 24, CAST(10.00 AS Numeric(5, 2)))
INSERT [dbo].[Item_Item] ([_itemID], [_itemID_sub], [_vertical]) VALUES (7, 22, CAST(50.00 AS Numeric(5, 2)))
INSERT [dbo].[Item_Item] ([_itemID], [_itemID_sub], [_vertical]) VALUES (7, 26, CAST(50.00 AS Numeric(5, 2)))
INSERT [dbo].[Item_Item] ([_itemID], [_itemID_sub], [_vertical]) VALUES (8, 35, CAST(60.00 AS Numeric(5, 2)))
INSERT [dbo].[Item_Item] ([_itemID], [_itemID_sub], [_vertical]) VALUES (8, 39, CAST(40.00 AS Numeric(5, 2)))
INSERT [dbo].[Item_Item] ([_itemID], [_itemID_sub], [_vertical]) VALUES (9, 37, CAST(30.00 AS Numeric(5, 2)))
INSERT [dbo].[Item_Item] ([_itemID], [_itemID_sub], [_vertical]) VALUES (9, 38, CAST(70.00 AS Numeric(5, 2)))
INSERT [dbo].[Item_Item] ([_itemID], [_itemID_sub], [_vertical]) VALUES (11, 10, CAST(10.00 AS Numeric(5, 2)))
INSERT [dbo].[Item_Item] ([_itemID], [_itemID_sub], [_vertical]) VALUES (11, 12, CAST(5.00 AS Numeric(5, 2)))
INSERT [dbo].[Item_Item] ([_itemID], [_itemID_sub], [_vertical]) VALUES (11, 25, CAST(35.00 AS Numeric(5, 2)))
INSERT [dbo].[Item_Item] ([_itemID], [_itemID_sub], [_vertical]) VALUES (11, 36, CAST(35.00 AS Numeric(5, 2)))
INSERT [dbo].[Item_Item] ([_itemID], [_itemID_sub], [_vertical]) VALUES (11, 40, CAST(15.00 AS Numeric(5, 2)))
INSERT [dbo].[Item_Item] ([_itemID], [_itemID_sub], [_vertical]) VALUES (14, 13, CAST(10.00 AS Numeric(5, 2)))
```

```
INSERT [dbo].[Item_Item] ([_itemID], [_itemID_sub], [_vertical]) VALUES (14,
    27, CAST(15.00 AS Numeric(5, 2)))
INSERT [dbo].[Item_Item] ([_itemID], [_itemID_sub], [_vertical]) VALUES (14,
    28, CAST(20.00 AS Numeric(5, 2)))
INSERT [dbo].[Item_Item] ([_itemID], [_itemID_sub], [_vertical]) VALUES (14,
    31, CAST(30.00 AS Numeric(5, 2)))
INSERT [dbo].[Item_Item] ([_itemID], [_itemID_sub], [_vertical]) VALUES (14,
    32, CAST(25.00 AS Numeric(5, 2)))
INSERT [dbo].[Item_Item] ([_itemID], [_itemID_sub], [_vertical]) VALUES (15,
    29, CAST(50.00 AS Numeric(5, 2)))
INSERT [dbo].[Item_Item] ([_itemID], [_itemID_sub], [_vertical]) VALUES (15,
    30, CAST(25.00 AS Numeric(5, 2)))
INSERT [dbo].[Item_Item] ([_itemID], [_itemID_sub], [_vertical]) VALUES (15,
    33, CAST(25.00 AS Numeric(5, 2)))
INSERT [dbo].[Item_Item] ([_itemID], [_itemID_sub], [_vertical]) VALUES (16,
    45, CAST(55.00 AS Numeric(5, 2)))
INSERT [dbo].[Item_Item] ([_itemID], [_itemID_sub], [_vertical]) VALUES (16,
    46, CAST(45.00 AS Numeric(5, 2)))
INSERT [dbo].[Item_Item] ([_itemID], [_itemID_sub], [_vertical]) VALUES (17,
    41, CAST(25.00 AS Numeric(5, 2)))
INSERT [dbo].[Item_Item] ([_itemID], [_itemID_sub], [_vertical]) VALUES (17,
    42, CAST(25.00 AS Numeric(5, 2)))
INSERT [dbo].[Item_Item] ([_itemID], [_itemID_sub], [_vertical]) VALUES (17,
    47, CAST(25.00 AS Numeric(5, 2)))
INSERT [dbo].[Item_Item] ([_itemID], [_itemID_sub], [_vertical]) VALUES (17,
    48, CAST(25.00 AS Numeric(5, 2)))
INSERT [dbo].[Item_Item] ([_itemID], [_itemID_sub], [_vertical]) VALUES (18,
    19, CAST(35.00 AS Numeric(5, 2)))
INSERT [dbo].[Item_Item] ([_itemID], [_itemID_sub], [_vertical]) VALUES (18,
    43, CAST(30.00 AS Numeric(5, 2)))
INSERT [dbo].[Item_Item] ([_itemID], [_itemID_sub], [_vertical]) VALUES (18,
    49, CAST(35.00 AS Numeric(5, 2)))
INSERT [dbo].[Items_Persons] ([_itemID], [_person_ID], [_vertical], [_person_
    horizont], [_realDone])
VALUES (4, N'2 ', CAST(100.00 AS Numeric(5, 2)), CAST(100.00 AS Numeric(5,
    2)), CAST(30.00 AS Numeric(5, 2)))
INSERT [dbo].[Items_Persons] ([_itemID], [_person_ID], [_vertical], [_person_
    horizont], [_realDone])
VALUES (5, N'3', CAST(100.00 AS Numeric(5, 2)), CAST(30.00 AS Numeric(5, 2)),
    CAST(50.00 AS Numeric(5, 2)))
```

```
INSERT [dbo].[Items_Persons] ([_itemID], [_person_ID], [_vertical], [_person_horizont], [_realDone])
VALUES (10, N'3 ', CAST(100.00 AS Numeric(5, 2)), CAST(30.00 AS Numeric(5, 2)), CAST(50.00 AS Numeric(5, 2)))
INSERT [dbo].[Items_Persons] ([_itemID], [_person_ID], [_vertical], [_person_horizont], [_realDone])
VALUES (12, N'20', CAST(50.00 AS Numeric(5, 2)), CAST(50.00 AS Numeric(5, 2)), CAST(50.00 AS Numeric(5, 2)))
INSERT [dbo].[Items_Persons] ([_itemID], [_person_ID], [_vertical], [_person_horizont], [_realDone])
VALUES (12, N'4 ', CAST(50.00 AS Numeric(5, 2)), CAST(100.00 AS Numeric(5, 2)), CAST(75.00 AS Numeric(5, 2)))
INSERT [dbo].[Items_Persons] ([_itemID], [_person_ID], [_vertical], [_person_horizont], [_realDone])
VALUES (13, N'19', CAST(40.00 AS Numeric(5, 2)), CAST(40.00 AS Numeric(5, 2)), CAST(100.00 AS Numeric(5, 2)))
INSERT [dbo].[Items_Persons] ([_itemID], [_person_ID], [_vertical], [_person_horizont], [_realDone])
VALUES (13, N'3', CAST(60.00 AS Numeric(5, 2)), CAST(40.00 AS Numeric(5, 2)), CAST(40.00 AS Numeric(5, 2)))
INSERT [dbo].[Items_Persons] ([_itemID], [_person_ID], [_vertical], [_person_horizont], [_realDone])
VALUES (19, N'19', CAST(50.00 AS Numeric(5, 2)), CAST(60.00 AS Numeric(5, 2)), CAST(150.00 AS Numeric(5, 2)))
INSERT [dbo].[Items_Persons] ([_itemID], [_person_ID], [_vertical], [_person_horizont], [_realDone])
VALUES (19, N'20', CAST(50.00 AS Numeric(5, 2)), CAST(50.00 AS Numeric(5, 2)), CAST(70.00 AS Numeric(5, 2)))
INSERT [dbo].[Items_Persons] ([_itemID], [_person_ID], [_vertical], [_person_horizont], [_realDone])
VALUES (20, N'7', CAST(60.00 AS Numeric(5, 2)), CAST(40.00 AS Numeric(5, 2)), CAST(20.00 AS Numeric(5, 2)))
INSERT [dbo].[Items_Persons] ([_itemID], [_person_ID], [_vertical], [_person_horizont], [_realDone])
VALUES (20, N'8 ', CAST(40.00 AS Numeric(5, 2)), CAST(20.00 AS Numeric(5, 2)), CAST(120.00 AS Numeric(5, 2)))
INSERT [dbo].[Items_Persons] ([_itemID], [_person_ID], [_vertical], [_person_horizont], [_realDone])
VALUES (21, N'8 ', CAST(100.00 AS Numeric(5, 2)), CAST(30.00 AS Numeric(5, 2)), CAST(100.00 AS Numeric(5, 2)))
```

```
INSERT [dbo].[Items_Persons] ([_itemID], [_person_ID], [_vertical], [_person_
    horizont], [_realDone])
VALUES (22, N'10', CAST(70.00 AS Numeric(5, 2)), CAST(70.00 AS Numeric(5,
    2)), CAST(90.00 AS Numeric(5, 2)))
INSERT [dbo].[Items_Persons] ([_itemID], [_person_ID], [_vertical], [_person_
    horizont], [_realDone])
VALUES (22, N'9 ', CAST(30.00 AS Numeric(5, 2)), CAST(30.00 AS Numeric(5,
    2)), CAST(50.00 AS Numeric(5, 2)))
INSERT [dbo].[Items_Persons] ([_itemID], [_person_ID], [_vertical], [_person_
    horizont], [_realDone])
VALUES (23, N'12', CAST(100.00 AS Numeric(5, 2)), CAST(40.00 AS Numeric(5,
    2)), CAST(200.00 AS Numeric(5, 2)))
INSERT [dbo].[Items_Persons] ([_itemID], [_person_ID], [_vertical], [_person_
    horizont], [_realDone])
VALUES (24, N'13', CAST(100.00 AS Numeric(5, 2)), CAST(50.00 AS Numeric(5,
    2)), CAST(80.00 AS Numeric(5, 2)))
INSERT [dbo].[Items_Persons] ([_itemID], [_person_ID], [_vertical], [_person_
    horizont], [_realDone])
VALUES (25, N'13', CAST(50.00 AS Numeric(5, 2)), CAST(50.00 AS Numeric(5,
    2)), CAST(90.00 AS Numeric(5, 2)))
INSERT [dbo].[Items_Persons] ([_itemID], [_person_ID], [_vertical], [_person_
    horizont], [_realDone])
VALUES (25, N'17', CAST(50.00 AS Numeric(5, 2)), CAST(50.00 AS Numeric(5,
    2)), CAST(80.00 AS Numeric(5, 2)))
INSERT [dbo].[Items_Persons] ([_itemID], [_person_ID], [_vertical], [_person_
    horizont], [_realDone])
VALUES (26, N'16 ', CAST(100.00 AS Numeric(5, 2)), CAST(35.00 AS Numeric(5,
    2)), CAST(80.00 AS Numeric(5, 2)))
INSERT [dbo].[Items_Persons] ([_itemID], [_person_ID], [_vertical], [_person_
    horizont], [_realDone])
VALUES (27, N'16 ', CAST(30.00 AS Numeric(5, 2)), CAST(30.00 AS Numeric(5,
    2)), CAST(70.00 AS Numeric(5, 2)))
INSERT [dbo].[Items_Persons] ([_itemID], [_person_ID], [_vertical], [_person_
    horizont], [_realDone])
VALUES (27, N'21', CAST(35.00 AS Numeric(5, 2)), CAST(100.00 AS Numeric(5,
    2)), CAST(100.00 AS Numeric(5, 2)))
INSERT [dbo].[Items_Persons] ([_itemID], [_person_ID], [_vertical], [_person_
    horizont], [_realDone])
VALUES (27, N'22', CAST(35.00 AS Numeric(5, 2)), CAST(20.00 AS Numeric(5,
    2)), CAST(100.00 AS Numeric(5, 2)))
```

```
INSERT [dbo].[Items_Persons] ([_itemID], [_person_ID], [_vertical], [_person_
    horizont], [_realDone])
VALUES (28, N'23', CAST(40.00 AS Numeric(5, 2)), CAST(40.00 AS Numeric(5,
    2)), CAST(60.00 AS Numeric(5, 2)))
INSERT [dbo].[Items_Persons] ([_itemID], [_person_ID], [_vertical], [_person_
    horizont], [_realDone])
VALUES (28, N'24 ', CAST(60.00 AS Numeric(5, 2)), CAST(40.00 AS Numeric(5,
    2)), CAST(80.00 AS Numeric(5, 2)))
INSERT [dbo].[Items_Persons] ([_itemID], [_person_ID], [_vertical], [_person_
    horizont], [_realDone])
VALUES (29, N'26', CAST(100.00 AS Numeric(5, 2)), CAST(25.00 AS Numeric(5,
    2)), CAST(20.00 AS Numeric(5, 2)))
INSERT [dbo].[Items_Persons] ([_itemID], [_person_ID], [_vertical], [_person_
    horizont], [_realDone])
VALUES (30, N'25', CAST(50.00 AS Numeric(5, 2)), CAST(30.00 AS Numeric(5,
    2)), CAST(30.00 AS Numeric(5, 2)))
INSERT [dbo].[Items_Persons] ([_itemID], [_person_ID], [_vertical], [_person_
    horizont], [_realDone])
VALUES (30, N'26', CAST(50.00 AS Numeric(5, 2)), CAST(35.00 AS Numeric(5,
    2)), CAST(20.00 AS Numeric(5, 2)))
INSERT [dbo].[Items_Persons] ([_itemID], [_person_ID], [_vertical], [_person_
    horizont], [_realDone])
VALUES (31, N'27', CAST(100.00 AS Numeric(5, 2)), CAST(40.00 AS Numeric(5,
    2)), CAST(50.00 AS Numeric(5, 2)))
INSERT [dbo].[Items_Persons] ([_itemID], [_person_ID], [_vertical], [_person_
    horizont], [_realDone])
VALUES (32, N'28', CAST(100.00 AS Numeric(5, 2)), CAST(30.00 AS Numeric(5,
    2)), CAST(0.00 AS Numeric(5, 2)))
INSERT [dbo].[Items_Persons] ([_itemID], [_person_ID], [_vertical], [_person_
    horizont], [_realDone])
VALUES (33, N'29 ', CAST(100.00 AS Numeric(5, 2)), CAST(20.00 AS Numeric(5,
    2)), CAST(25.00 AS Numeric(5, 2)))
INSERT [dbo].[Items_Persons] ([_itemID], [_person_ID], [_vertical], [_person_
    horizont], [_realDone])
VALUES (34, N'29', CAST(30.00 AS Numeric(5, 2)), CAST(30.00 AS Numeric(5,
    2)), CAST(85.00 AS Numeric(5, 2)))
INSERT [dbo].[Items_Persons] ([_itemID], [_person_ID], [_vertical], [_person_
    horizont], [_realDone])
VALUES (34, N'30', CAST(70.00 AS Numeric(5, 2)), CAST(30.00 AS Numeric(5,
    2)), CAST(100.00 AS Numeric(5, 2)))
```

```
INSERT [dbo].[Items_Persons] ([_itemID], [_person_ID], [_vertical], [_person_horizont], [_realDone])
VALUES (35, N'10 ', CAST(25.00 AS Numeric(5, 2)), CAST(30.00 AS Numeric(5, 2)), CAST(10.00 AS Numeric(5, 2)))
INSERT [dbo].[Items_Persons] ([_itemID], [_person_ID], [_vertical], [_person_horizont], [_realDone])
VALUES (35, N'7'', CAST(25.00 AS Numeric(5, 2)), CAST(60.00 AS Numeric(5, 2)), CAST(40.00 AS Numeric(5, 2)))
INSERT [dbo].[Items_Persons] ([_itemID], [_person_ID], [_vertical], [_person_horizont], [_realDone])
VALUES (35, N'8 ', CAST(25.00 AS Numeric(5, 2)), CAST(50.00 AS Numeric(5, 2)), CAST(30.00 AS Numeric(5, 2)))
INSERT [dbo].[Items_Persons] ([_itemID], [_person_ID], [_vertical], [_person_horizont], [_realDone])
VALUES (35, N'9 ', CAST(25.00 AS Numeric(5, 2)), CAST(70.00 AS Numeric(5, 2)), CAST(150.00 AS Numeric(5, 2)))
INSERT [dbo].[Items_Persons] ([_itemID], [_person_ID], [_vertical], [_person_horizont], [_realDone])
VALUES (36, N'11', CAST(50.00 AS Numeric(5, 2)), CAST(100.00 AS Numeric(5, 2)), CAST(70.00 AS Numeric(5, 2)))
INSERT [dbo].[Items_Persons] ([_itemID], [_person_ID], [_vertical], [_person_horizont], [_realDone])
VALUES (36, N'5', CAST(25.00 AS Numeric(5, 2)), CAST(100.00 AS Numeric(5, 2)), CAST(85.00 AS Numeric(5, 2)))
INSERT [dbo].[Items_Persons] ([_itemID], [_person_ID], [_vertical], [_person_horizont], [_realDone])
VALUES (36, N'6 ', CAST(25.00 AS Numeric(5, 2)), CAST(100.00 AS Numeric(5, 2)), CAST(30.00 AS Numeric(5, 2)))
INSERT [dbo].[Items_Persons] ([_itemID], [_person_ID], [_vertical], [_person_horizont], [_realDone])
VALUES (37, N'12', CAST(100.00 AS Numeric(5, 2)), CAST(60.00 AS Numeric(5, 2)), CAST(50.00 AS Numeric(5, 2)))
INSERT [dbo].[Items_Persons] ([_itemID], [_person_ID], [_vertical], [_person_horizont], [_realDone])
VALUES (38, N'14', CAST(50.00 AS Numeric(5, 2)), CAST(100.00 AS Numeric(5, 2)), CAST(120.00 AS Numeric(5, 2)))
INSERT [dbo].[Items_Persons] ([_itemID], [_person_ID], [_vertical], [_person_horizont], [_realDone])
VALUES (38, N'15', CAST(50.00 AS Numeric(5, 2)), CAST(100.00 AS Numeric(5, 2)), CAST(50.00 AS Numeric(5, 2)))
```

INSERT [dbo].[Items_Persons] ([_itemID], [_person_ID], [_vertical], [_person_horizont], [_realDone])
VALUES (39, N'16', CAST(100.00 AS Numeric(5, 2)), CAST(35.00 AS Numeric(5, 2)), CAST(50.00 AS Numeric(5, 2)))
INSERT [dbo].[Items_Persons] ([_itemID], [_person_ID], [_vertical], [_person_horizont], [_realDone])
VALUES (40, N'17', CAST(30.00 AS Numeric(5, 2)), CAST(50.00 AS Numeric(5, 2)), CAST(100.00 AS Numeric(5, 2)))
INSERT [dbo].[Items_Persons] ([_itemID], [_person_ID], [_vertical], [_person_horizont], [_realDone])
VALUES (40, N'18 ', CAST(30.00 AS Numeric(5, 2)), CAST(100.00 AS Numeric(5, 2)), CAST(80.00 AS Numeric(5, 2)))
INSERT [dbo].[Items_Persons] ([_itemID], [_person_ID], [_vertical], [_person_horizont], [_realDone])
VALUES (40, N'22 ', CAST(40.00 AS Numeric(5, 2)), CAST(40.00 AS Numeric(5, 2)), CAST(80.00 AS Numeric(5, 2)))
INSERT [dbo].[Items_Persons] ([_itemID], [_person_ID], [_vertical], [_person_horizont], [_realDone])
VALUES (41, N'22', CAST(25.00 AS Numeric(5, 2)), CAST(40.00 AS Numeric(5, 2)), CAST(90.00 AS Numeric(5, 2)))
INSERT [dbo].[Items_Persons] ([_itemID], [_person_ID], [_vertical], [_person_horizont], [_realDone])
VALUES (41, N'23 ', CAST(25.00 AS Numeric(5, 2)), CAST(60.00 AS Numeric(5, 2)), CAST(100.00 AS Numeric(5, 2)))
INSERT [dbo].[Items_Persons] ([_itemID], [_person_ID], [_vertical], [_person_horizont], [_realDone])
VALUES (41, N'24', CAST(25.00 AS Numeric(5, 2)), CAST(60.00 AS Numeric(5, 2)), CAST(110.00 AS Numeric(5, 2)))
INSERT [dbo].[Items_Persons] ([_itemID], [_person_ID], [_vertical], [_person_horizont], [_realDone])
VALUES (41, N'25', CAST(25.00 AS Numeric(5, 2)), CAST(70.00 AS Numeric(5, 2)), CAST(70.00 AS Numeric(5, 2)))
INSERT [dbo].[Items_Persons] ([_itemID], [_person_ID], [_vertical], [_person_horizont], [_realDone])
VALUES (42, N'26', CAST(100.00 AS Numeric(5, 2)), CAST(40.00 AS Numeric(5, 2)), CAST(60.00 AS Numeric(5, 2)))
INSERT [dbo].[Items_Persons] ([_itemID], [_person_ID], [_vertical], [_person_horizont], [_realDone])
VALUES (43, N'27', CAST(100.00 AS Numeric(5, 2)), CAST(30.00 AS Numeric(5, 2)), CAST(0.00 AS Numeric(5, 2)))

INSERT [dbo].[Items_Persons] ([_itemID], [_person_ID], [_vertical], [_person_horizont], [_realDone])
VALUES (44, N'1 ', CAST(100.00 AS Numeric(5, 2)), CAST(100.00 AS Numeric(5, 2)), CAST(90.00 AS Numeric(5, 2)))
INSERT [dbo].[Items_Persons] ([_itemID], [_person_ID], [_vertical], [_person_horizont], [_realDone])
VALUES (45, N'29', CAST(50.00 AS Numeric(5, 2)), CAST(50.00 AS Numeric(5, 2)), CAST(100.00 AS Numeric(5, 2)))
INSERT [dbo].[Items_Persons] ([_itemID], [_person_ID], [_vertical], [_person_horizont], [_realDone])
VALUES (45, N'30 ', CAST(50.00 AS Numeric(5, 2)), CAST(20.00 AS Numeric(5, 2)), CAST(0.00 AS Numeric(5, 2)))
INSERT [dbo].[Items_Persons] ([_itemID], [_person_ID], [_vertical], [_person_horizont], [_realDone])
VALUES (46, N'27', CAST(40.00 AS Numeric(5, 2)), CAST(30.00 AS Numeric(5, 2)), CAST(80.00 AS Numeric(5, 2)))
INSERT [dbo].[Items_Persons] ([_itemID], [_person_ID], [_vertical], [_person_horizont], [_realDone])
VALUES (46, N'28', CAST(60.00 AS Numeric(5, 2)), CAST(70.00 AS Numeric(5, 2)), CAST(70.00 AS Numeric(5, 2)))
INSERT [dbo].[Items_Persons] ([_itemID], [_person_ID], [_vertical], [_person_horizont], [_realDone])
VALUES (47, N'30', CAST(100.00 AS Numeric(5, 2)), CAST(20.00 AS Numeric(5, 2)), CAST(100.00 AS Numeric(5, 2)))
INSERT [dbo].[Items_Persons] ([_itemID], [_person_ID], [_vertical], [_person_horizont], [_realDone])
VALUES (48, N'30', CAST(35.00 AS Numeric(5, 2)), CAST(30.00 AS Numeric(5, 2)), CAST(60.00 AS Numeric(5, 2)))
INSERT [dbo].[Items_Persons] ([_itemID], [_person_ID], [_vertical], [_person_horizont], [_realDone])
VALUES (48, N'31', CAST(35.00 AS Numeric(5, 2)), CAST(100.00 AS Numeric(5, 2)), CAST(50.00 AS Numeric(5, 2)))
INSERT [dbo].[Items_Persons] ([_itemID], [_person_ID], [_vertical], [_person_horizont], [_realDone])
VALUES (48, N'32', CAST(30.00 AS Numeric(5, 2)), CAST(60.00 AS Numeric(5, 2)), CAST(60.00 AS Numeric(5, 2)))
INSERT [dbo].[Items_Persons] ([_itemID], [_person_ID], [_vertical], [_person_horizont], [_realDone])
VALUES (49, N'32 ', CAST(100.00 AS Numeric(5, 2)), CAST(40.00 AS Numeric(5, 2)), CAST(80.00 AS Numeric(5, 2)))

```
INSERT [dbo].[Units] ([_unitID], [_unitDef]) VALUES (1, N'Faculty of Engineering
    and Computing')
INSERT [dbo].[Units] ([_unitID], [_unitDef]) VALUES (2, N'School of Computing
    and Information Technology')
INSERT [dbo].[Units] ([_unitID], [_unitDef]) VALUES (3, N'Bachelor of Science
    in Computing and Information Technology Programme')
INSERT [dbo].[Units] ([_unitID], [_unitDef]) VALUES (4, N'Bachelor of Science
    in Computing and Management Studies Programme')
INSERT [dbo].[Units] ([_unitID], [_unitDef]) VALUES (5, N'School of Engineering')
INSERT [dbo].[Units] ([_unitID], [_unitDef]) VALUES (6, N'Bachelor of Science
    in Electrical Engineering ')
INSERT [dbo].[Units] ([_unitID], [_unitDef]) VALUES (7, N'Bachelor of Science
    in Mechanical Engineering ')
INSERT [dbo].[Items_Units] ([_itemID], [_unitID], [_level_horizont]) VALUES
    (1, 1, CAST(40.00 AS Numeric(5, 2)))
INSERT [dbo].[Items_Units] ([_itemID], [_unitID], [_level_horizont]) VALUES
    (2, 1, CAST(40.00 AS Numeric(5, 2)))
INSERT [dbo].[Items_Units] ([_itemID], [_unitID], [_level_horizont]) VALUES
    (3, 1, CAST(20.00 AS Numeric(5, 2)))
INSERT [dbo].[Items_Units] ([_itemID], [_unitID], [_level_horizont]) VALUES
    (6, 2, CAST(40.00 AS Numeric(5, 2)))
INSERT [dbo].[Items_Units] ([_itemID], [_unitID], [_level_horizont]) VALUES
    (7, 2, CAST(25.00 AS Numeric(5, 2)))
INSERT [dbo].[Items_Units] ([_itemID], [_unitID], [_level_horizont]) VALUES
    (8, 2, CAST(10.00 AS Numeric(5, 2)))
INSERT [dbo].[Items_Units] ([_itemID], [_unitID], [_level_horizont]) VALUES
    (9, 2, CAST(15.00 AS Numeric(5, 2)))
INSERT [dbo].[Items_Units] ([_itemID], [_unitID], [_level_horizont]) VALUES
    (11, 2, CAST(10.00 AS Numeric(5, 2)))
INSERT [dbo].[Items_Units] ([_itemID], [_unitID], [_level_horizont]) VALUES
    (14, 5, CAST(15.00 AS Numeric(5, 2)))
INSERT [dbo].[Items_Units] ([_itemID], [_unitID], [_level_horizont]) VALUES
    (15, 5, CAST(20.00 AS Numeric(5, 2)))
INSERT [dbo].[Items_Units] ([_itemID], [_unitID], [_level_horizont]) VALUES
    (16, 5, CAST(25.00 AS Numeric(5, 2)))
INSERT [dbo].[Items_Units] ([_itemID], [_unitID], [_level_horizont]) VALUES
    (17, 5, CAST(20.00 AS Numeric(5, 2)))
INSERT [dbo].[Items_Units] ([_itemID], [_unitID], [_level_horizont]) VALUES
    (18, 5, CAST(20.00 AS Numeric(5, 2)))
```

```
INSERT [dbo].[Items_Units] ([_itemID], [_unitID], [_level_horizont]) VALUES
    (20, 3, CAST(20.00 AS Numeric(5, 2)))
INSERT [dbo].[Items_Units] ([_itemID], [_unitID], [_level_horizont]) VALUES
    (21, 3, CAST(15.00 AS Numeric(5, 2)))
INSERT [dbo].[Items_Units] ([_itemID], [_unitID], [_level_horizont]) VALUES
    (22, 3, CAST(25.00 AS Numeric(5, 2)))
INSERT [dbo].[Items_Units] ([_itemID], [_unitID], [_level_horizont]) VALUES
    (24, 4, CAST(15.00 AS Numeric(5, 2)))
INSERT [dbo].[Items_Units] ([_itemID], [_unitID], [_level_horizont]) VALUES
    (25, 4, CAST(15.00 AS Numeric(5, 2)))
INSERT [dbo].[Items_Units] ([_itemID], [_unitID], [_level_horizont]) VALUES
    (26, 4, CAST(15.00 AS Numeric(5, 2)))
INSERT [dbo].[Items_Units] ([_itemID], [_unitID], [_level_horizont]) VALUES
    (27, 6, CAST(15.00 AS Numeric(5, 2)))
INSERT [dbo].[Items_Units] ([_itemID], [_unitID], [_level_horizont]) VALUES
    (28, 6, CAST(10.00 AS Numeric(5, 2)))
INSERT [dbo].[Items_Units] ([_itemID], [_unitID], [_level_horizont]) VALUES
    (29, 6, CAST(10.00 AS Numeric(5, 2)))
INSERT [dbo].[Items_Units] ([_itemID], [_unitID], [_level_horizont]) VALUES
    (30, 6, CAST(13.00 AS Numeric(5, 2)))
INSERT [dbo].[Items_Units] ([_itemID], [_unitID], [_level_horizont]) VALUES
    (31, 7, CAST(15.00 AS Numeric(5, 2)))
INSERT [dbo].[Items_Units] ([_itemID], [_unitID], [_level_horizont]) VALUES
    (32, 7, CAST(15.00 AS Numeric(5, 2)))
INSERT [dbo].[Items_Units] ([_itemID], [_unitID], [_level_horizont]) VALUES
    (33, 7, CAST(20.00 AS Numeric(5, 2)))
INSERT [dbo].[Items_Units] ([_itemID], [_unitID], [_level_horizont]) VALUES
    (34, 7, CAST(10.00 AS Numeric(5, 2)))
INSERT [dbo].[Items_Units] ([_itemID], [_unitID], [_level_horizont]) VALUES
    (35, 3, CAST(20.00 AS Numeric(5, 2)))
INSERT [dbo].[Items_Units] ([_itemID], [_unitID], [_level_horizont]) VALUES
    (36, 3, CAST(20.00 AS Numeric(5, 2)))
INSERT [dbo].[Items_Units] ([_itemID], [_unitID], [_level_horizont]) VALUES
    (37, 4, CAST(15.00 AS Numeric(5, 2)))
INSERT [dbo].[Items_Units] ([_itemID], [_unitID], [_level_horizont]) VALUES
    (38, 4, CAST(15.00 AS Numeric(5, 2)))
INSERT [dbo].[Items_Units] ([_itemID], [_unitID], [_level_horizont]) VALUES
    (39, 4, CAST(5.00 AS Numeric(5, 2)))
INSERT [dbo].[Items_Units] ([_itemID], [_unitID], [_level_horizont]) VALUES
    (40, 4, CAST(5.00 AS Numeric(5, 2)))
```

INSERT [dbo].[Items_Units] ([_itemID], [_unitID], [_level_horizont]) VALUES (41, 6, CAST(18.00 AS Numeric(5, 2)))
INSERT [dbo].[Items_Units] ([_itemID], [_unitID], [_level_horizont]) VALUES (42, 6, CAST(10.00 AS Numeric(5, 2)))
INSERT [dbo].[Items_Units] ([_itemID], [_unitID], [_level_horizont]) VALUES (43, 6, CAST(17.00 AS Numeric(5, 2)))
INSERT [dbo].[Items_Units] ([_itemID], [_unitID], [_level_horizont]) VALUES (45, 7, CAST(15.00 AS Numeric(5, 2)))
INSERT [dbo].[Items_Units] ([_itemID], [_unitID], [_level_horizont]) VALUES (46, 6, CAST(7.00 AS Numeric(5, 2)))
INSERT [dbo].[Items_Units] ([_itemID], [_unitID], [_level_horizont]) VALUES (47, 7, CAST(15.00 AS Numeric(5, 2)))
INSERT [dbo].[Items_Units] ([_itemID], [_unitID], [_level_horizont]) VALUES (48, 7, CAST(5.00 AS Numeric(5, 2)))
INSERT [dbo].[Items_Units] ([_itemID], [_unitID], [_level_horizont]) VALUES (49, 7, CAST(5.00 AS Numeric(5, 2)))

Chapter 8
Drafting Enterprise Models

Hector Florez
Universidad Distrital Francisco Jose de Caldas, Colombia

Mario Sanchez
Universidad de los Andes, Colombia

Jorge Villalobos
Universidad de los Andes, Colombia

ABSTRACT

Enterprise models are created to analyze, document, and communicate the state of an enterprise under multiple perspectives. In addition to being large and complex, the construction of these models presents several difficulties: firstly, they require information provided by sources that might be inaccurate, incomplete, or even obsolete; secondly, although they should be structured, it is not possible to completely define their metamodel a priori. To support this construction process, the usage of enterprise model drafts is proposed, which should have the capacity to conform to changing metamodels and should also support incomplete or imperfect information. Unfortunately, current frameworks and tools have limitations for supporting these two features. Therefore, a set of strategies for the construction of modeling environments that make it possible to properly handle drafts is also proposed. These strategies include the support of metamodel flexibility during the modeling process and an approach to model imperfect information.

DOI: 10.4018/978-1-5225-5522-3.ch008

INTRODUCTION

Enterprise Modeling refers to the practices to build and use Enterprise Models to represent multiple aspects of an enterprise. The purpose of enterprise models is to document, communicate, analyze organizational structures, business processes, information systems, and infrastructure with the aim of improving these elements (Buschle, Ullberg, Franke, Lagerström, & Sommestad, 2010; Iacob & Jonkers, 2006; Kurpjuweit & Winter, 2007; Lankhorst, 2013). While enterprise models can be small, simple, and well-focused, most are typically the opposite; they are large, complex, and cover a large number of areas and lines of business. Such extensive and complex models are useful for enterprise analysis purposes because they enable holistic approaches for understanding an organization, combining both business and technological aspects (Lagerström, Franke, Johnson, & Ullberg, 2009; Lankhorst, 2013).

However, this complexity has strong implications for the construction of the models. The construction process starts with the selection of a framework of reference that defines the structure of the model, and which is typically based on a metamodel. Then, modelers have to discover and classify multiple sources of enterprise information (e.g., people, documents, meetings) which can be located anywhere in the company, or may even be external (e.g., regulations, policy documents). Afterwards, modelers perform different kinds of observations on sources of enterprise information (e.g., interviews, reviews, meeting minutes), extract information, and introduce these into the model.

It is at this point that problems start to appear. First of all, there is the issue of compatibility between the facts and the metamodel selected as the underlying structure for the enterprise model. If the metamodel does not offer an adequate metatype to represent a certain fact, that fact will either have to be omitted from the model, or it will have to be adjusted in order to match the metatypes existing in the metamodel. For example, standard metamodels commonly have a metatype to represent infrastructure devices, but do not include a specific metatype to represent load balancers. Thus, models sacrifice a bit of semantics when they represent load balancers using the simpler infrastructure device concept. The second problem has to do with the quality of the sources and the observations, which may have different levels of precision and reliability. For example, it is possible to find sources with contradictory information, opposite points of view, obsolete information, and conflicts of interest which can generate inconsistency in the model.

A natural way to handle the construction of enterprise models is to use drafts, that is, to a model in phases without having committed to a definitive metamodel from the beginning. Furthermore, drafts may lack complete information and even be imperfect (imprecise, inconsistent, vague, uncertain) (Florez, Sanchez, & Villalobos,

2014b; Florez, Sánchez, & Villalobos, 2013). The problem is that current enterprise modeling environments, as well as general purpose modeling frameworks and tools, lack the capabilities to support what was just described: typically there is little or no support for flexible or changing metamodels, nor is there support for imperfection in the models, or to trace the modeling processes.

Models have to be perfectly structured during the entirety of the modeling process.

The objective of this chapter is to propose mechanisms to support the construction of drafts for enterprise modeling, while addressing problems highlighted in existing tools. This proposal is based on three core elements: 1) a strategy to support flexible metamodels which makes it possible to easily change the metamodels even after the modeling process has started; 2) the necessary elements to model imperfection caused by the information gathering process and the quality of the sources; and 3) the support for documenting the construction and evolution of the models. This documentation, which presents information about the sources, observations, and facts used by modelers to build the drafts, is valuable to build the definitive versions of the models. The whole proposal described has been implemented in *iArchiMate*, which is a modeling tool for the creation of enterprise model drafts based on ArchiMate (The Open Group, 2012).

This chapter is structured as follows: The section *Background* explains Model Driven Engineering and Enterprise Modeling, as well as related work. The section *Issues regarding enterprise modeling* presents the problems related to modeling flexibility and modeling imperfection in the enterprise context to be addressed in this chapter. The section *Approach for drafting enterprise models* discusses our approach for supporting modeling flexibility and modeling imperfection based on the creation of drafts of enterprise models. The section *Conclusion* offers our conclusions and the future work based on the results presented here.

BACKGROUND

Model Driven Engineering

Model Driven Engineering (MDE) is an approach to address technologies regarding Domain Specific Modeling Languages (DSML) as well as transformation and generation engines (Schmidt, 2006). The core concepts of MDE are models that represent systems, and metamodels that define the languages in which the models are expressed. MDE uses models for supporting design, construction, operation, maintenance, and modification of systems. DSMLs formalize the structure of particular domains and they are described using metamodels that contain the domain concepts and rules. Said metamodels are the base for creating models of systems that belong to the described domain. In this context, a model is a simplified, abstract representation of a system under study, which allows reasoning about the system. It focuses on desired and relevant details in order to achieve an intended purpose, while a metamodel is a specification model that defines concepts and their associated constrains, as well specifying their relationships in a particular domain.

The Object Management Group (OMG)[1] defined a four level architecture for structuring models and metamodels in the MDE context. In this architecture, relations can be *instanceOf* and *conformsTo*. The former is used to relate the system with the model, while the latter is used to relate a model with the corresponding metamodel and to relate a metamodel with the corresponding metametamodel. The *conformsTo* relation indicates that model's elements, attributes, and relations must accomplish the concepts and rules defined in the conforming metamodel. This usually means that a model's element must be an instance of a metatype defined in the conforming metamodel; relations between model's elements must be relation instances between metatypes, subject to the cardinality rules as described. The element's attributes must be the only ones defined for the corresponding metatypes. In the architecture, the first level refers to the system under study, which is represented by a model. The model corresponds to the second level and conforms to one metamodel, which defines the concepts and relations of the domain, and is placed in the third level. The metamodel conforms to one metametamodel placed in the fourth level, which conforms to itself.

Enterprise Modeling

As was mentioned in the introduction, the term Enterprise Modeling refers to the set of practices to build, maintain, and utilize well-structured representations of diverse aspects of an enterprise, including business and IT aspects, to guide projects, analyze and improve said enterprise (Braun & Winter, 2005). The core element of this is the *enterprise model* itself, which organizes information in a manner that should be usable for the purposes defined by the enterprise modeling initiative. This means that enterprise models are built differently depending on the objective of the project and the kind of analyses that are intended to be performed: in some cases, general information about the whole enterprise is required; in others, very detailed information about some particular areas is what is necessary.

Regardless of their usage, enterprise models share some basic characteristics. First of all, they tend to be *large* enough to be beyond the capacity of a single person. This is because typical enterprise models involve several areas and dimensions of an enterprise, which may range from technical to pure business aspects, and cover different product lines as well as support areas (e.g., human resources, infrastructure, etc.). This broad scope results in *complex* models where the number of relations is high compared to the number of nodes. Finally, enterprise models are *well structured*, which means that their structure respects well-defined and verifiable rules, typically formalized using a metamodel. Moreover, it means that it is possible to describe algorithms to operate within these models based on their abstract structure. Automatic analysis methods, which may calculate indicators or enriched enterprise models, are a perfect example of this (Florez, Sanchez, & Villalobos, 2014a).

From a practical point of view, enterprise models also have special characteristics that separate them from models used in other areas such as MDE. In the first place, enterprise models are *descriptive* instead of *prescriptive,* a fact stemming from the fact that they are typically intended to be used by humans (e.g., business and IT analysts) as documentation of the enterprise. Furthermore, enterprise models do not typically conform to well known or standard metamodels (Bjekovi, Proper, & Sottet, 2013; Braun & Winter, 2005). On the contrary, standardized or popular metamodels are used in the earliest stages of enterprise modeling projects, but they are rapidly modified and improved to make them suitable for the projects' purposes. Thus, when metamodels evolve, conforming models need to *co-evolve* in order to regain their conformity relationship (Florez, Sanchez, Villalobos, & Vega, 2012; Rose, Kolovos, Paige, & Polack, 2010). For example, if the main purpose of the project is to understand, analyze and improve IT support for business processes, a standard such as Business Process Model and Notation (BPMN)(Object Management Group, 2011) may be complemented with information systems and infrastructure architecture concepts. These additional concepts may be completely ad hoc, or they may be borrowed from other existing standards such as ArchiMate, which is closely tied to TOGAF (The Open Group, 2011) and is thus particularly useful for cross-dimensional modeling (Lankhorst, 2013).

Moreover, achieving quality of enterprise modelsis very desirable. Quality might be estimated based on the criteria: a) the enterprise model is useful after the modeling activity is done; b) stakeholders are satisfied with the enterprise modeling process and the enterprise model. Thus, an enterprise model should satisfy the following criteria (Sandkuhl, Stirna, Persson, & Wißotzki, 2014):

- **Completeness:** All desired facts of the domain are included in the enterprise models.
- **Correctness:** The elements of the enterprise model conform to the reality under study.
- **Flexibility:** Ease in which the enterprise model can face changes of the domain.
- **Integration:** Consistency between sub-models that conform the enterprise model.

- **Simplicity:** Minimum amount of elements in the model to represent the reality under study.
- **Understandability:** Stakeholders can understand the model easily
- **Usability:** Ease in which the enterprise model can be used.

Nevertheless, a special trait of enterprise models is that they cannot everbe considered complete. As enterprise modeling starts to deliver its promises and starts generating value, new requirements typically arise. This not only creates the need to expand the existing models, but also to extend the underlying metamodels both in small aspects (e.g., creating additional attributes) as large aspects (e.g., adding entire new dimensions with complex relationships towards existing elements). When modeling platforms are not particularly suitable for handling metamodel flexibility, this situation creates enormous problems that heavily limit the potential gains brought by enterprise modeling.

Beyond what has already been described, the construction of enterprise models presents some further practical complications. The first one lies in the means to gather the data that ultimately forms the model. One approach is to gather said data through *direct observation*, that is, by directly observing the elements in the enterprise that are then represented in the models. The other approach is by *indirect observation*, which requires the participation of several *sources* (e.g., people, documents, reports) and additional activities. In this case, modelers consult the sources through *observations* (e.g., interviews, meetings, surveys, reviewing meeting acts) and obtain *facts* to be included in the model as elements, relations or attributes.

The other practical difficulty is related to the quality of the information obtained for creating the enterprise models, which is never perfect. On the contrary, sources may provide information that either has problems or simply incorrect. In Florez et al. (2013), sources, which provide information that cannot be used to create the model accurately have been called *imperfect sources* and have been classified as *incorrect*; these are sources that provide false information. *Imprecise* sources are those that provide ranges of values instead of a unique value for one specific numeric attribute. *Inconsistent* sources provide more than one value for one attribute or relation, and *vague* sources provide linguistic values (i.e., qualitative values in a given scale) instead of a numeric value for one specific numeric attribute (e.g., availability= "High"). Sources that provide one value with a certainty degree are labeled *uncertain*, whereas *incomplete* sources does not provide any information.

In this chapter, an approach to create enterprise models in a flexible way is presented. This approach is based on the drafting enterprise models. Said drafts are partial versions of the enterprise model, which can be refined without any technological limitation. In addition, drafts can conform to evolving metamodels; conforming drafts can co-evolve when a metamodel evolves based on the new features of the metamodel. Furthermore, drafts are able to include imperfect information, such as when information gathered from sources lacks consistency, precision, or even reliability. Finally, drafts might include supporting information regarding the decisions made by modelers, when including elements, attributes, or relations. This information is very important in the modeling process because modelers can make better decisions based on such information when the draft is being refined or complemented. In the end, a draft can become the enterprise model when it completely satisfies the modeling objective and it does not include imperfect or supporting information.

Related Work

Some previous literature is related to the work presented in this chapter, especially because these prior endeavors tackle the problem of metamodel flexibility so necessary for creating drafts of enterprise models. Erol and Neumann (2013) present a proposal for collaborative drafting of business processes models. In this work, the authors assert that modeling, in a general sense, is a process that could consist the following activities: 1) elicitation, which refers to the act of collecting information from domain experts; 2) modeling, which is the transformation of the informal specification into a formal specification; and 3) validation, which refers to the act of evaluating the congruence of the formal specification regarding the informal specification. Based on these activities, this work presents a case study of a wiki supported models drafting process, including a wiki engine developed to support collaboration in processes for building models. One wiki page can contain fields of different types; then, a new field type for business process models can be added. Created pages and fields can be changed and extended in the modeling process. In this proposal, all types of content are handled in the context of a generic page object. Our proposal follows a similar one to this proposal because we use generic types to allow flexible modeling and metamodeling.

In Sánchez-Cuadrado, De Lara, and Guerra (2012), the authors present a framework capable of creating a metamodel from model fragments that are constructed by end-users using sketching tools, such as *Visio* or *PowerPoint*. This approach is directed to domain experts that do not know MDE, but use informal drawing tools. The proposed framework transforms the models made with these informal tools into untyped model fragments which are annotated by engineers to indicate what actions to take when the metamodel is induced. By means of these model fragments and annotations, changes can be automatically applied in the metamodel, but only if they do not break the conformity. Otherwise, the user is queried for additional information. The proposal presented in this chapter also provides mechanisms to document how the information was gathered by modelers in order to know how to make further changes. Also, the user can decide how and when the model or metamodel have to be changed. Finally, this proposal is limited since it can only support EMF models and metamodels, although it can import and export models to work with other enterprise modeling tools.

Gabrysiak, Giese, Lüders, and Seibel (2011) discuss how metamodels can be used in a flexible way and present a classification of approaches based on how dynamic metamodels are in different tools. Typically, modeling approaches fall into only one of the categories they propose. Our proposal, however, belongs to several categories. Regarding the first category, which is the definition of metamodels before modeling, our strategy is based on the ArchiMate metamodel; it supports the creation of attributes, new relations, and new elements that are not defined in the metamodel. With respect to the second category, which is modeling captured insights, the strategy presented in this chapter provides support to flexible modeling through drafts of models in the enterprise context.

In Cicchetti, Ruscio, Kolovos, and Pierantonio (2011), authors use test-driven development (TDD) techniques to build metamodels iteratively. In this proposal, test cases from the metaclasses are attached in a metamodel. Said test cases are executable models that perform transformations. When a test case informs that the metamodel is inadequate, the metamodel needs to be upgraded. The proposal of this chapter allows validation whether or not the model conforms ontologically to the ArchiMate metamodel. In the case of errors, the model or metamodel might be manually upgraded.

In De Lara and Guerra (2010), a metamodeling environment called MetaDepth is presented. This environment allows metamodeling with an arbitrary number of ontological levels and permits a dual ontological and linguistic instantiation based on a linguistic metamodel proposed by authors. Then, models at all levels are linguistic instances of said linguistic metamodel. Additionally, each level can provide linguistic extensions, and potency annotations can be used to manage these multiple levels MetaDepth also manages models but in the deeper levels, thus suggesting a top-down strategy. Finally, MetaDepth is integrated with the Epsilon language, particularly, with EVL so that it can express constraints. Similar to MetaDeph, the proposal presented in this chapter handles a linguistic metamodel that provides a structure for modeling imperfect information; however, it is based on ArchiMate as modeling language.

Another approach to defining formal conditions for uncertainty in order to reduce refinement processes between models and transformations is presented by Salay, Chechik, Famelis, and Gorzny (2015). This approach is based on checking the correctness of uncertainty-reducing refinements of specific model and partial model refinement transformations. The approach in this chapter tackles not only uncertainty but also other kinds of information such as imprecision and inconsistency.

Bruneliere et al. (2015) offer a generic metamodel extension approach for quick and efficient adaptations required by modeling tools. Based on this proposal, modeling tools do not require transformation processes when metamodels evolve. This paper provides metamodel extension operations involving addition, updating and filtering changes to existing metamodels. In this proposal, flexibility is guaranteed when the metamodel evolves with some specific changes. The approach presented allows metamodels to evolve, but keeps models independent of the nature of changes of the domain metamodel.

An approach to reasoning with partial models that are able to include uncertainty is proposed in Famelis, Salay, and Chechik (2012). The approach handles uncertainty by using annotations, changing a complete model into a partial model. The proposal of this chapter, so far, is not able to make further tasks based on uncertain information. The model can only store this kind of information and allow modelers to refine it by consulting how the uncertain information was gathered. However, this approach provides mechanisms to represent other kinds of information.

In Zolotas, Matragkas, Kolovos, and Paige (2015), a flexible modeling approach is presented, and it allows for the capturing of requirements for software applications through the use of tendered contracts, thus promoting clients to support documentation requirements. This approach is based on a flexible graph definition language to allow users to draw models and include annotations in them. The flexibility offered in this approach is similar to the flexibility in the approach proposed in this chapter because it uses supporting data instead of annotations. However, supporting data can be included even when models include imperfect information.

ISSUES REGARDING ENTERPRISE MODELING

When creating enterprise models, two issues become very important to address since lead to the creation of imperfect enterprise models: the lack of metamodel flexibility and the presence of imperfect information.

Lack of Metamodel Flexibility

The rationale for requiring support for Enterprise Modeling drafts is that it is impossible to know every detail about the structure of the models before completing the projects. While some aspects may not be known in the beginning, the metamodel is very likely to change. Unfortunately, most enterprise modeling environments typically lack the capacity to modify the metamodels in an easy, efficient, and natural way after the modeling phase has started. This also applies to general purpose modeling frameworks, such as Eclipse Modeling Framework (EMF)(Eclipse, n.d.-a)

The first reason behind these limitations can be traced to the fact that these tools and environments are based on a strong conformance relation that usually has to be permanently guaranteed. This means that each model must conform, in every moment, to the metamodel (Rose et al., 2010). As a result, elements in models have to be instances of metatypes defined in the metamodels; relationships between elements in the models must be instances of relationships between metatypes and should follow the cardinality rules described there. Additionally, the element's attributes must be those defined for the corresponding metatypes. On top of that, modeling environments are typically designed around requirements for the creation of models and leave the manipulation of metamodels on a secondary plane (Rose, Kolovos, & Paige, 2012).

All of these problems are particularly evident in the EMF framework, which is very prominently used in the modeling community. As it happens, in EMF there are some strong requirements with respect to the metamodels: 1) metamodels have to be completely described before any modeling can be done (L. M. Rose et al., 2012); 2) problems of non-conformity are considered errors and require immediate resolution; and 3) changing metamodels after models they have been created requires the application of non-trivial model migration techniques. In addition to that, before modeling begins, but after the metamodels are finished, there is a code generation phase that creates the classes required by the tools that will manipulate the models (e.g., parsers, editors, interpreters, etc.). This makes metamodels even more static because in order to alter them, it is necessary to replay complicated activities which include code generation, compilation, configuration, and eventually some kind of programming.

The second reason behind the aforementioned limitations is that some frameworks and tools, including EMF, combine the linguistic and the ontological validation of conformance. On the one hand, linguistic validation refers to the activities to assert that a model is described using the primitive and structural elements defined in a metamodel (De Lara & Guerra, 2010; Kuhne, 2006). In this case, a metamodel can be understood as a linguistic framework for the definition of models. On the other hand, ontological validation verifies that the elements in a model, as well as their attributes and relationships, are ontological instances of the metatypes defined in the metamodel. In this case a metamodel describes a reality and the way its elements may be related. In the former perspective, model elements are linguistic instances of the metatypes; in the latter, model elements are ontological instances of the metatypes. Combining these two perspectives makes it impossible to create a model that conforms to a metamodel from one perspective and not from the other. Furthermore, the technological complexity associated with handling the linguistic perspective has created limitations in EMF for its ontological perspective. In particular, the code-generation technique used to create the framework of classes to define and validate models has performance benefits, but it is almost completely static and makes it impossible to easily change metamodels at runtime.

Imperfect Enterprise Models

Based on the information provided by enterprise sources, modelers may deal with multiple possible values for a specific attribute, or multiple possible targets of a specific relation. Therefore, modelers should include all possible information gathered to avoid a loss of information which would produce an inaccurate model. This can generate wrong results in further uses of the model for business analysis or decision making processes. For instance, consider a situation where the CTO (Chief Technology Officer) of a company asserts that the availability of the CRM is 96%, but an IT operator argues that the availability is 99%. In the case of numeric attributes, modelers have six alternatives:

1. Model just one numeric value, either by selecting the best value (e.g., the greatest availability, *99%*), or by doing some calculation (e.g., the average, *97.5%*).
2. Describe availability as a range of numeric values (e.g., *[96% – 99%]*).
3. Include availability as a set of values (e.g., (96%, 99%)).
4. Assign a linguistic value to describe availability as a category (e.g., *"High"*), instead of with a percentage value.
5. Assign a certainty degree to a value, depending on the reliability of the source (e.g., *96%* with an *80%*.
6. Leave an empty value until the modeler has more information.

If a modeler takes the first alternative, the model is complete, but it might be incorrect. Alternatives 2, 3, 4, and 5 imply making changes to the metamodel. The final alternative is undesired, as it leaves the model incomplete.

Imperfection can also be present in one to one relations with multiple elements, which are possible sources or targets. For instance, the *CTO* may assert that the Application Service *MySQL Database Service* is realized either by the Application Component *Windows Server*, or the *Linux Server*, but it is unsure by which one in particular. In this case, the modeler has four courses of action:

1. Select just one component (e.g., *MySQL Database Service} →Linux Server*).
2. Create two realization relations, each one with the same probability (e.g., *MySQL Database Service→Windows Server* and *MySQL Database Service →Linux Server*).

3. Create two realization relations, and assign a certainty degree to each one of them.
4. Model neither of the relations until the modeler has more information.

When the modeler takes the first course of action, the model is complete, but again, it might not be accurate.

To be able to model imperfection, it is necessary to describe the imprecision, inconsistency, vagueness, uncertainty, and incompleteness of the sources alongside the information they provide (Florez et al., 2013). Thus, depending on the sources, the model can have five types of imperfection:

- **Imprecision:** An attribute has a range of possible numeric values instead of a single one when sources are imprecise or inconsistent. This range is described in terms of minimum and maximum numeric values.
- **Inconsistency:** One or more attributes or relations have multiple values. Regarding attributes, the modeler assigns a set of values when the sources are imprecise or inconsistent. Regarding relations, the modeler can place multiple relations with the same name between two elements when the sources are inconsistent or uncertain.
- **Vagueness:** An attribute has assigned a linguistic (i.e., qualitative) value instead of a numeric value. This can happen when the sources are imprecise, inconsistent, uncertain, or vague.
- **Uncertainty:** Attributes or relations have a certainty degree as they come from imprecise, inconsistent, or uncertain sources.
- **Incompleteness:** The model contains empty values for some attributes, or if an element is placed as absent, which implies that there is no warranty for its existence in the enterprise. This can happen when the modeler does not have enough information, or when the information collected comes from unreliable sources.

APPROACH FOR DRAFTING ENTERPRISE MODELS

In order to create enterprise models based on drafts, this chapter presents an approach that focues on supporting modeling flexibility as well as supporting modeling imperfection.

Supporting Metamodel Flexibility

In order to address the problems described, a strategy based on making a distinction between and a separation of linguistic conformance and ontological conformance has been developed. In this strategy, linguistic conformance should be permanently verified against a static intermediate metamodel whose goal is to provide a linguistic framework for the definition of models. In addition, ontological conformance is verified against a *domain metamodel,* which can be modified or even replaced at runtime. Furthermore, ontological conformance is not mandatory. That is, at any given time, a model must conform to the linguistic metamodel, but it may not conform to the domain metamodel. The core of this strategy is thus the intermediate linguistic metamodel and the mechanisms to validate the ontological conformance dynamically.

An Intermediate Metamodel

In order to support the strategy based on making the distinction between linguistic and ontological conformance, a metamodel called *GIMM (Generic Intermediate Metamodel)* has been created as a linguistic framework for the definition of models (Gómez, Sánchez, Florez, & Villalobos, 2014). In this sense, *GIMM* provides the necessary primitives to define models in a way that is completely independent of the domain.

Figure 1 presents the elements that are part of the metamodel. First of all, *GIMM* defines the metatype called Model, which contains all other elements. The abstract type Component is specialized by the types Group, which serves to group elements in the model by specific features (e.g., groups of business processes and application services). It includes Element in order to represent instances of the model. The type Relation serves to represent relations between elements, and the type Attribute serves to represent the actual values of attributes contained in elements and relations of the model. The type Attribute has an attribute named type with the attribute type AttributeTypeValue that is an enumeration, which contains the name of all possible types of attributes in the model (e.g., int, double, string).

Moreover, the most important aspect of this metamodel is that each Element has an attribute called typeName. This attribute, which is just a string, is used to indicate to which metatype each element belongs in an ontological metamodel. In the following section, we explain how this attribute is used to verify the conformance of models from an ontological point of view.

Figure 1. Generic intermediate metamodel GIMM

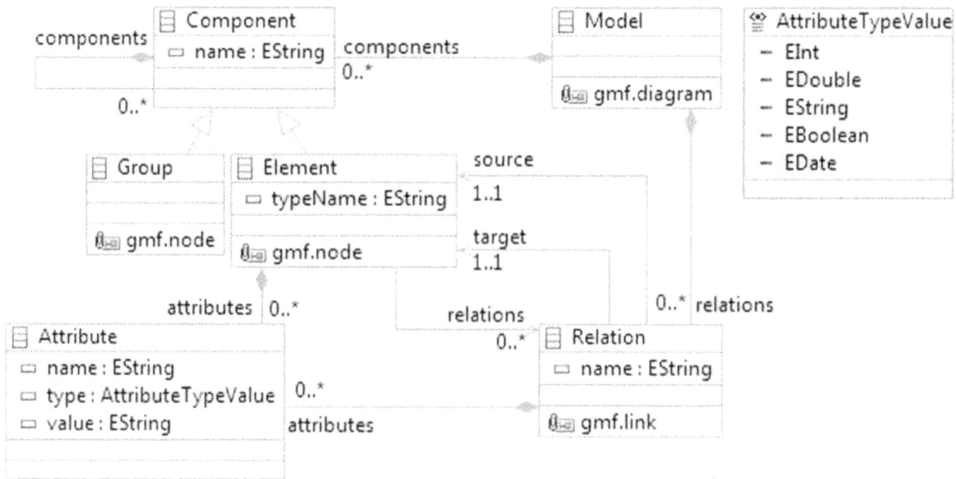

Dynamically Generated Validation Rules

The second aspect of the strategy is the mechanisms to validate the linguistic and the ontological conformance of *GIMM*-based models. In the former case, the solution is trivial: since *GIMM* is a metamodel that is not intended to be modified, the typical validation mechanisms can be used without requiring any special treatment. The ontological validation is handled with the dynamic generation of validation rules to evaluate the conformance of the model with respect to the domain metamodel. Since these rules are generated when the domain metamodel is modified, metamodel flexibility is ultimately supported.

There are currently two types of rules generated. The first type is called *ontological rules* because they are specifically targeted towards validating ontological conformance to the domain metamodel. For example, one of these rules serves to verify that the attribute typeName of each Element in the model has a value that matches the name of a metatype in the domain metamodel.

The second type of rules serves to check if the model is properly constructed with respect to *GIMM* in order to guarantee a successful ontological validation. For example, they check that the values of the attributes typeName are properly formed (no blanks, no symbols, etc.) in order to establish matches with the metatype names in the domain metamodel.

Modeling Imperfection for Enterprise Models

As mentioned before, modelers must consult multiple sources and make observations in order to gather the facts that are ultimately reified in the enterprise models (Florez et al., 2014b, 2013). However, the nature of enterprises makes it likely for modelers to obtain inaccurate information even from the best available sources. Modelers thus face the dilemma of what to do with the imperfection. One alternative is to make the most of the available information and create the best possible model. The problem with this strategy is that it hides the fact that the information had problems and thus may lead others to use it as if it were perfect (complete, precise, and 100% certain). The other alternative is to make the imperfection explicit in the model. This makes the problems evident for anyone who attempts to use said models, and it transfers the responsibility of deciding how to handle the imperfection to them the. For example, they may decide to gather more information to fix the problems, or they might decide to ignore it. Either way, they are making an informed decision.

In Enterprise Modeling, sources have different levels of precision and reliability. For example, it is possible to find sources with contradictory information or opposite points of view, conflicts of interest, lacking information, and other situations that may obstruct the construction of enterprise models. In addition, it is possible to find information that was true in the past, though sources cannot confirm if the information remains valid. As a result, depending on the quality of the informationprovided, enterprise sources can be classified into the following categories: incorrect, imprecise, inconsistent, vague, and uncertain. In addition, it is possible that a source omits certain information, or does not have the required knowledge to answer some questions. Therefore, the corresponding observation is *incomplete* because it does not produce a fact (Florez et al., 2013).

Modeling imperfection and creating imperfect models requires having the primitives to represent imperfect elements, attributes or relations. In order to achieve this, a strategy for modeling imperfection is based on the strategy for flexible modeling and metamodeling already presented. A metamodel called *iMM (Metamodel of Imperfection)* is proposed as an extension of *GIMM* for including the necessary concepts to represent imperfection. In this way, imperfect enterprise models should only conform linguistically to *iMM* and may ontologically conform to any domain metamodel.

iMM complements the metatypes defined in *GIMM* with the ones marked in red as presented in Figure 2. The types ImperfectAttribute and ImperfectRelation are specializations of the typesAttribute and Relation respectively. These types represent imperfect attributes and imperfect relations in the model. Both types include the attribute named imperfectionType, which defines the kind of imperfection of the attribute and relation. For instance, if the attribute is imprecise, its imperfectionType must contain the value NumericRange and if the relation is uncertain, its imperfectionType must contain the value InstanceCertaintyDegree. The values of imperfection types are specified in *iMM* through the enumerations ImperfectAttributeTypeValue and ImperfectRelationTypeValue respectively. The type AbsentElement is a specialization of the type Element and serves to represent elements whose existence is not confirmed. Finally, the types Element and Relation contain the attribute typeName. In the former, the attribute comes from *GIMM*, but it is upgraded in order to define the ArchiMate element type (e.g., BusinessProcess). In the latter, the attribute is included and serve to define the ArchiMate relation type (e.g., UsedBy). The type for elements and relations are specified by the enumerations ElementTypeName and RelationTypeName respectively.

Drafts of Enterprise Models

Based on the proposals for flexible modeling and for modeling imperfection, it is possible to support the construction of platforms for creating drafts of enterprise

Figure 2. Metamodel of imperfection iMM

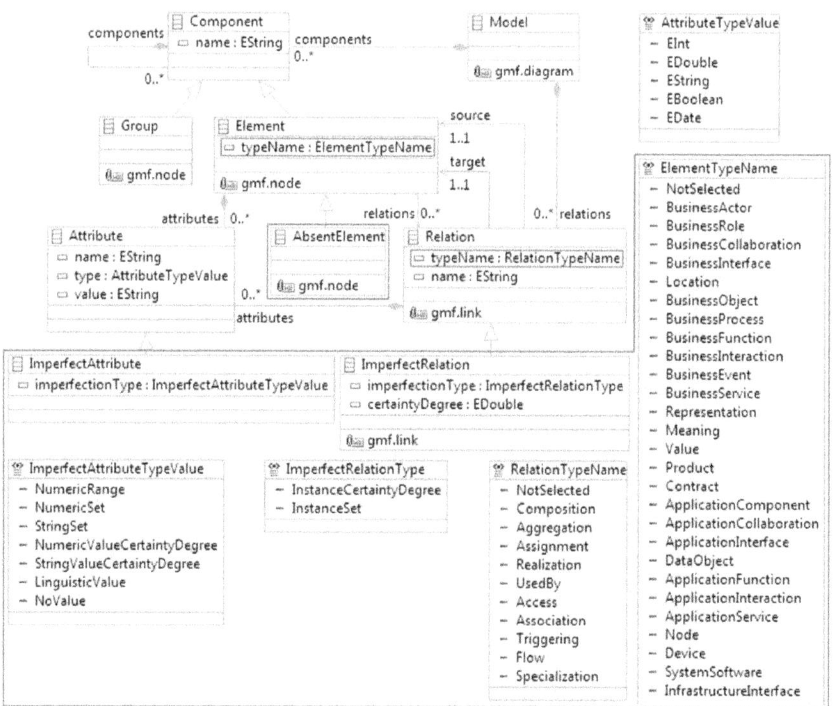

models. These platforms should support all the characteristics that drafts require in order to be useful in the enterprise modeling context: firstly, they should support metamodel flexibility; secondly, they should support model imperfection; and lastly, they should support the management of meta-data about the modeling process. In this chapter, this additional information is called *supporting data*, which contains details about the sources, observations, and facts involved in the modeling process. It should be useful to guide the removal of imperfections.

The purpose of this section is to show how the two approaches previously presented are useful for supporting drafts in the enterprise model domain. For this, the modeling tool *iArchiMate* is presented. This tool is useful for the creation of enterprise model drafts. It is based on standard frameworks such as the Eclipse Modeling Framework Project (EMF)(Eclipse, n.d.-a), the Graphical Modeling Framework Project (GMF)(Eclipse, n.d.-d), EuGENia (Eclipse, n.d.-c) and the Epsilon Validation Language (EVL)(Eclipse, n.d.-b). Furthermore, *iArchiMate* is based on the ArchiMate metamodel (The Open Group, 2012) and is compatible with Archi (Archi, n.d.), which is one of the most popular modeling tools compatible with this standard.

ArchiMate in iArchiMate

ArchiMate has become the standard language for describing and visualizing enterprise models involving different domains. It has been designed to provide a complete graphical representation of enterprises over time and is closely linked to TOGAF (The Open Group, 2011). ArchiMate is a visual language with concepts for specifying inter-related architectures and specific viewpoints for selected stakeholders (The Open Group, 2012). ArchiMate is defined in a metamodel small but sufficient to fulfill most enterprise modeling tasks. This is achieved because the ArchiMate metamodel includes concepts that cover most practical modeling cases (The Open Group, 2012). ArchiMate incorporates three kinds of aspects: 1) active structure elements, which are concepts that perform behavior (e.g., Business Actor); 2) behavior elements, which are concepts that represents activity units (e.g., Business Process); and 3) passive structure elements, which are passive entities manipulated through behavioral elements (e.g., Business Object). In addition, ArchiMate divides its concepts into three layers aligned with TOGAF's architectures. The business layer provides concepts that are supported by business processes from the enterprise. The application layer gives necessary support to the business layer through application components and services, and the technology layer provides required infrastructure needed to execute software application.

In order to illustrate drafts of enterprise models, an enterprise scenario has been built based on the case of an academic book publisher. The enterprise model of this scenario has been created using ArchiMate as modeling language and *iArchiMate* as the modeling tool. The enterprise model of this scenario has 184 business elements, 13 application elements, 13 infrastructure elements, 28 motivation elements, and 432 relations arranged in 12 views. Business elements include business actors, business collaborations, business events, business functions, business interactions, business objects, business processes, business roles, contracts, locations, products, and values. Application elements include application components and application services. Infrastructure elements are comprised of communication paths, devices, infrastructure services, networks, nodes, and system software. Motivation elements involve assessments, drivers, goals, principles, requirements, and stakeholders. The views of the model are:

- **Business Motivation:** In this view, the model presents the goals of the Enterprise that are related to principles, requirements, assessments, and drivers.
- **Business Processes:** This view includes the business processes of the enterprise focusing on those that are the most important for the business such as Book Selection, Book Design, Book Correction, Book Warehousing and Shipping, and Book Sales.
- **Canvas:** This view sorts different business elements in the categories of the canvas business model.
- **Capabilities:** In this view, business capabilities are modeled taking into account their related business processes, business actors, business roles, and IT systems.
- **Competitors:** Based on the business goals, this view models the enterprise competitors.
- **Layered:** This view presents the relation between various elements that belongs to the ArchiMate layers infrastructure, technology, or business. Elements from the infrastructure layer include devices, system software, and infrastructure services. Elements from the application layer are application components and application services. Finally, elements from the business layer are just business processes.
- **Market:** In this view, the locations where the enterprise exerts its business are modeled.
- **Resources:** This view includes the resources of the enterprise such as employees, factories, IT systems among others.
- **Stakeholders:** This view shows enterprise primary and secondary stakeholders.

- **Technical Infrastructure:** This view presents all IT elements of the enterprise with their corresponding relations.
- **Value Chain:** In this view, the enterprise capabilities and its corresponding business processes are presented.

iArchiMate handles *linguistic conformance* using EMF's validation engine and *ontological conformance* using *iArchiMate*'s validation engine. Furthermore, *iArchiMate*'s validation engine includes several rules for validating the correct format for imperfect elements, attributes and relations.

Figures 3 and 4 present the results of applying the linguistic and ontological validation. Figure 3 shows a fragment of the publisher scenario model, which includes some problems detected during the validation process. Figure 4 presents the *Problems view* with the details about the errors and warnings discovered.

1. The element *CRM* does not have any ArchiMate concept assigned to the attribute typeName; consequently, the relations from the *SQL Server Database Service* and *Glassfish Application Server* to the *CRM* present warnings.
2. The relation from the *Glassfish Application Server* to the *DMS* does not have any ArchiMate relation assigned to the attribute typeName.
3. The relation from the *WindowsServer* to the *SQL Server Database Service* cannot be a Composition relation.
4. The relation from the *JBoss Application Server* to the *BI* cannot be a Realization relation.

Figure 3. Fragment of the model after the validation process

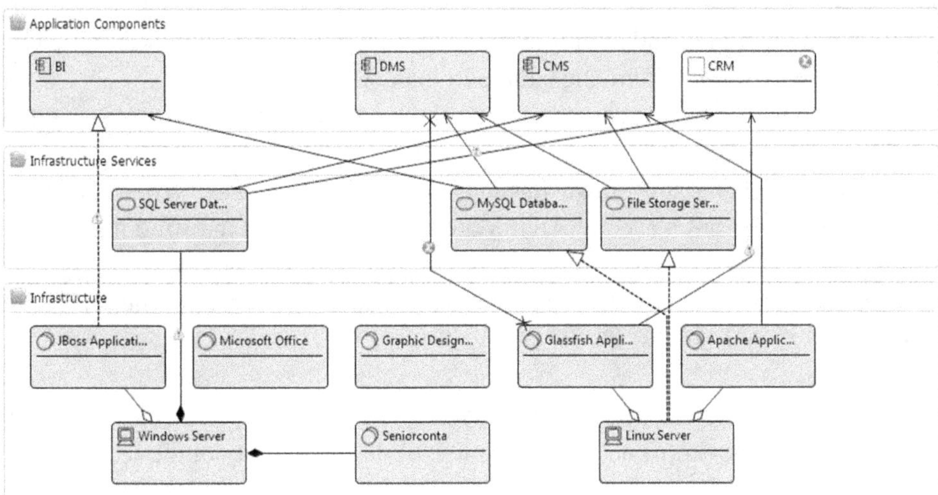

Figure 4. Problems view with the validation results

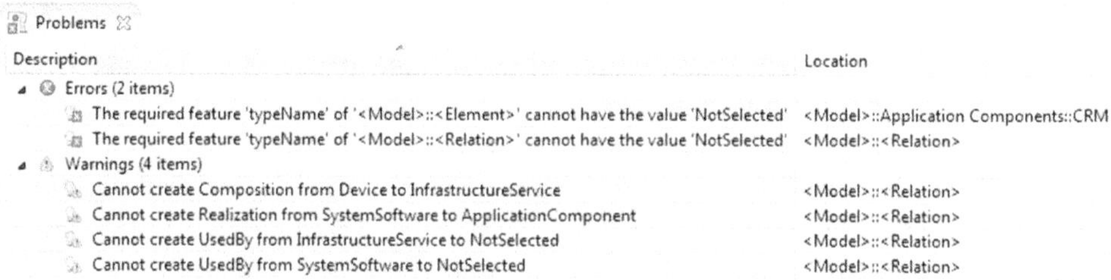

Imperfect Models in iArchiMate

iArchiMate allows for the creation of imperfect models through the inclusion of imperfect elements, relations, and attributes (in elements or relations) using a specific notation.

- Imprecise attributes have a minimum and a maximum value that are placed in square brackets, and separated by a dash (e.g., *[1-2]*).
- Inconsistent attributes are described with a set of values inside of parentheses and separated by commas (e.g., *(A, B, C)*).
- Uncertain attributes are represented with a pair of elements enclosed by curly brackets and separated by a comma, where the first element represents the actual value of the attribute, and the second element represents its degree of certainty (e.g., *{A, 0.9}*).
- Vague attributes include a linguistic value inside of less than and greater than signs (e.g. *<High>*).
- Empty attributes have a question mark (*?*) as value. Inconsistent relations are drawn in blue and are represented as a set of relations with the same type (e.g., Realization) from one source to many targets.
- Uncertain relations are drawn in blue and have their certainty degree specified as an attribute.
- *Absent* elements are drawn in blue with unfilled squares. When an absent element does not have any ArchiMate type, its icon is a question mark.

Continuing with the enterprise publisher scenario, consider the following situations.

- The CTO asserts: a) the availability of the Device*Windows Server* is *High*, but he does not know an accurate value; b) the availability of the Device*Linux*

Server is *95%* and its provider is *DELL*; and c) the version and availability of the ApplicationComponent *BI* is *2.1.2* and 90% respectively.
- A technology operator indicates that the availability of the *Linux Server* is 98% and its provider is *SUN*.
- The CIO (Chief Information Officer) communicates: a) the ApplicationService *Profile Service* is not yet running, but he is not sure if this service is already installed and b) the ApplicationService *Analytics Service*, *Dashboard Service*, and *Customer Management Service* are used by the BusinessProcess *Indicator Management* with a certainty degree of 95%, 80%, and 85% respectively.
- A development engineer states: a) the availability of the *BI* is *0.8%*, b) the version of the ApplicationComponent *CRM* is unknown, and c) the *Linux Server* aggregates the Firewall *Shorewall*.
- A contract establishes that the version of the *BI* is *2.1.6*

Based on the previous information provided by different sources, the modeler creates the model including some imperfect elements, attributes and relations. Figure 5 presents a fragment of the layered view that includes only the elements containing imperfection and their related elements. Then, the model includes the following imperfect information:

1. The *Windows Server* includes the vague attribute availability with value *High* based on the information provided by the *CTO*.
2. The *Linux Server*contains the: a) imprecise attribute availability with minimum value *0.95* and maximum value *0.98,* and b) the inconsistent attribute provider with values *DELL* and *SUN*. Both attributes are based on the information provided by the *CTO* and a technology operator.
3. The *BI* contains: a) the inconsistent attribute version with values *2.1.2* and *2.1.6* based on the information provided by the *CTO* and a contract, and b) the vague attribute availability with value *Medium* based on the information provided by the *CTO* and a development engineer.
4. The *CRM* contains the incomplete attribute version based on a development engineer.
5. The *Profile Service* is placed as an absent element based on the information communicated by the*CIO*.
6. The firewall *Shorewall* is placed as an absent element based on the information provided by a development engineer because the element *Firewall* is not defined by ArchiMate.
7. The uncertain relations UsedBy from Analytics *Service*, *Dashboard Service*, and *Customer Management Service* to *Indicator Management* based on the information provided by the *CIO*.

Figure 5. Fragment of layered view of the imperfect model

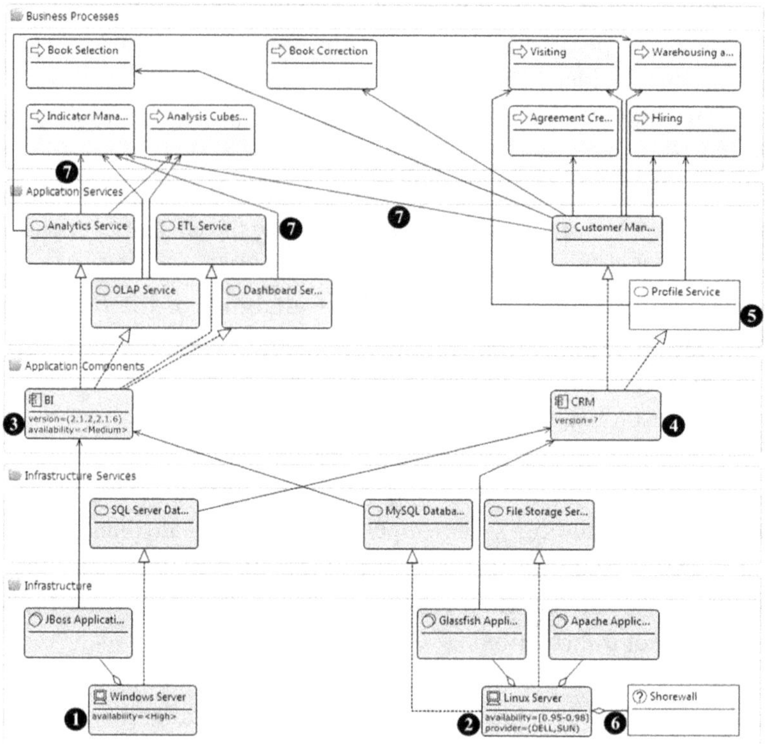

iArchiMate also validates imperfect information to verify whether attributes and relations have the proper format depending on the values assigned to the attribute imperfectionType. For instance, Figure 6 presents an example of validation for imperfect information and Figure 7 presents the *Problems view* with detail about errors and warnings. This validation discovered the following problems.

1. Imperfect relations UsedBy from *CustomerManagementService* and *Dashboard Service* to *Indicator Management* have the value *InstanceCertaintyDegree* as imperfectionType, but they do not have any certainty degree assigned.
2. Imperfect attribute availability in *Windows Server* is vague; however, its value includes square brackets instead of less than and greater than signs.
3. The *CRM* includes the imperfect attribute version, which has no value; nevertheless, the imperfectionType assigned to this attribute is *NumericRange*.
4. The *Linux Server* has the imprecise attribute availability, but the range of values assigned is separated by comma instead of by dash.

5. In *BI*, the inconsistent attribute version has a collection enclosed by brackets instead of parentheses.
6. The *Shorewall*, which represents a firewall, is an absent element; thus, it does not have any ArchiMate type selected. For the same reason, the Aggregation relation from *Linux Server* to *Shorewall* presents a warning.

Figure 6. Fragment of layered view of the imperfect model after the validation process

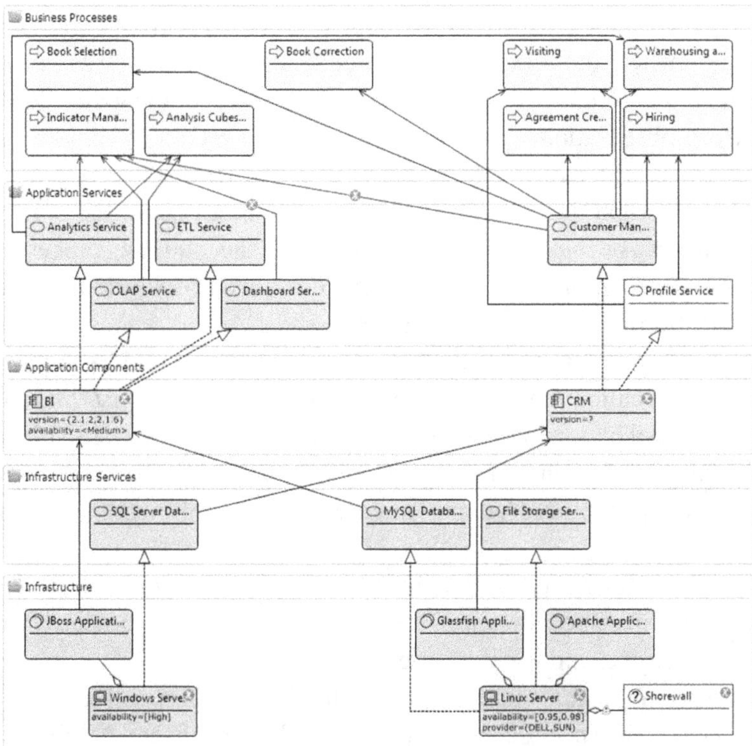

Figure 7. Problems view with the validation results of the imperfect model

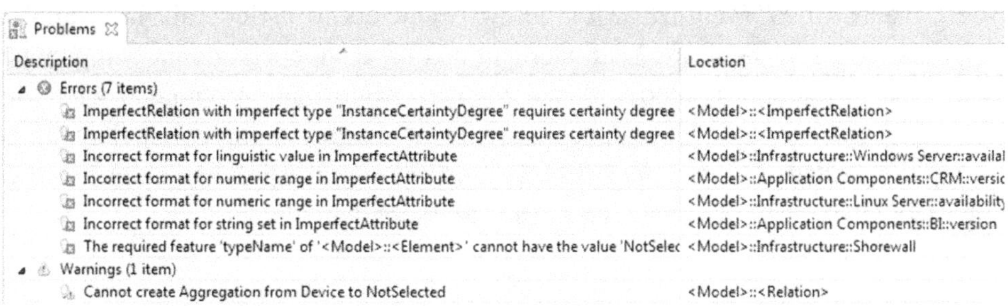
Problems

Description	Location
Errors (7 items)	
ImperfectRelation with imperfect type "InstanceCertaintyDegree" requires certainty degree	<Model>::<ImperfectRelation>
ImperfectRelation with imperfect type "InstanceCertaintyDegree" requires certainty degree	<Model>::<ImperfectRelation>
Incorrect format for linguistic value in ImperfectAttribute	<Model>::Infrastructure::Windows Server::availal
Incorrect format for numeric range in ImperfectAttribute	<Model>::Application Components::CRM::versic
Incorrect format for numeric range in ImperfectAttribute	<Model>::Infrastructure::Linux Server::availabilit
Incorrect format for string set in ImperfectAttribute	<Model>::Application Components::BI::version
The required feature 'typeName' of '<Model>::<Element>' cannot have the value 'NotSelec	<Model>::Infrastructure::Shorewall
Warnings (1 item)	
Cannot create Aggregation from Device to NotSelected	<Model>::<Relation>

Supporting Data for Drafts

The final element of the proposal for handling model drafts is to include *supporting data*. This is additional data about the information gathering process and information provided by sources. Based on this supporting data, modelers can understand the reasons why such a draft has been created; later on, they can identify new sources to observe to obtain the required information for refining the draft.

The supporting data can contain: 1) *Sources* such as *People*, *Meetings* (attended by the correspondingpeople), *Documents*, and *Direct Observations* (information regarding the enterprise provided by the modeler); 2) *Observations*, which determine the time stamp where the source was consulted; and 3) *Facts* such as *Instance Fact*, *Attribute Fact*, and *Relation Fact*, which allow for the documentation of the values obtained from observations. Based on the supporting data, modelers can obtain specific information for refining the draft. Once the modeler refines one element in the draft by completing it or by removing its imperfection, the corresponding supporting data can be removed as well. At the end of the modeling process, when the draft does not have incomplete or imperfect elements and does not have supporting data, the draft becomes the final enterprise model.

In order to include supporting data in enterprise models, *iMM* was extended into a new metamodel called *Extended Metamodel of Imperfection (EiMM)* (see Figure 8). This metamodel has the necessary metatypes to represent sources, observations, and facts related to elements of the enterprise model draft. *EiMM* includes all the elements that are part of *iMM*, complemented with the following additional types:

1. SupportingData serves as container for all other additional elements.
2. Source and its specializations DirectObservation, Document, Person, and Meeting serve to represent sources.
3. Observationrepresents interviews, document revisions, and meeting minutes.
4. Fact, which is specialized by the types InstanceFact, AttributeFact, and RelationFact serve to create registers with information obtained about elements, attributes, or relations of the enterprise.

By means of *EiMM*, *iArchiMate* allows modelers to include all the available supporting data in the draft. Each element can have supporting data components to specify all the data related with the enterprise information obtained when the modeler decides to include: a) the correspondent element as imperfect element; or b) imperfect attributes, or imperfect relations in the correspondent element; or c) imperfect attributes in one relation of the correspondent element.

Figure 8. Extended metamodel of imperfection EiMM

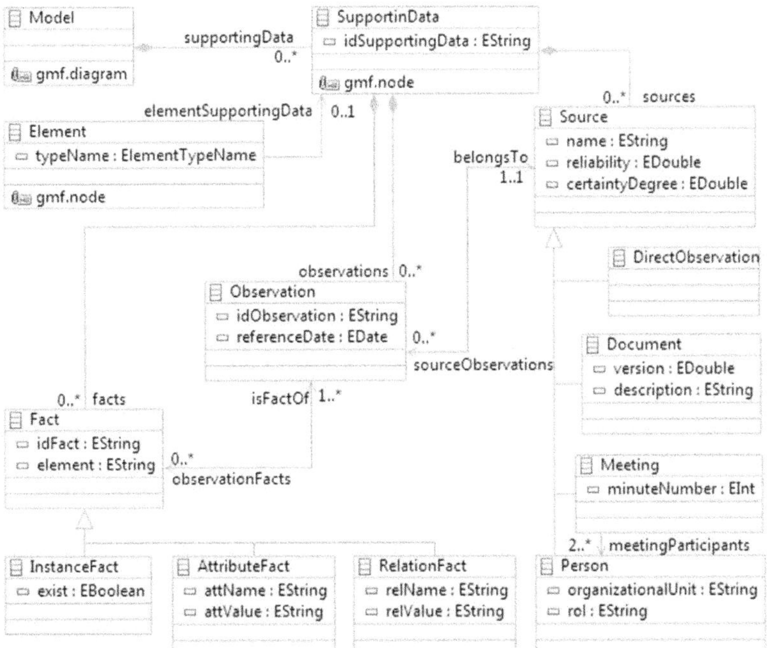

Continuing with the publisher scenario, consider that the modeler wants to include supporting data in those elements that contain imperfect information. The modeler then includes one supporting data component for the following elements in the draft: *Windows Server, Linux Server,BI,CRM* that include imperfect attributes; *Analytics Service,Dashboard Service,Customer Management Service* that include imperfect relations; and *Profile Service,* which is an absent element. Figure 9presents the supporting data components for the *Windows Server,Linux Server, BI*, and *CRM*.

iArchiMate also includes a graphic editor for creating supporting data, which can be opened by double clicking on a supporting data component placed in the draft. This editor permits the inclusion of elements related with supporting data where each element is differentiated by icons. It contains the required attributes for documenting all possible information regarding the enterprise information obtained by the enterprise sources. In addition, relations are drawn by dashed arrows and can only be placed from sources to observations and from observations to facts. Figure 10 presents the supporting data for the application component *BI*. It contains the following sources: the Person*CTO*, the Document*Contract*, and thePerson*Development Engineer*. The *CTO* provides in the Observation *Interview1*, the AttributeFact *AttFact1* that includes information about the version and the AttributeFact*AttFact2* that includes information about the availability. The Observation *Review1* of the

Figure 9. Fragment of the layered view with supporting data

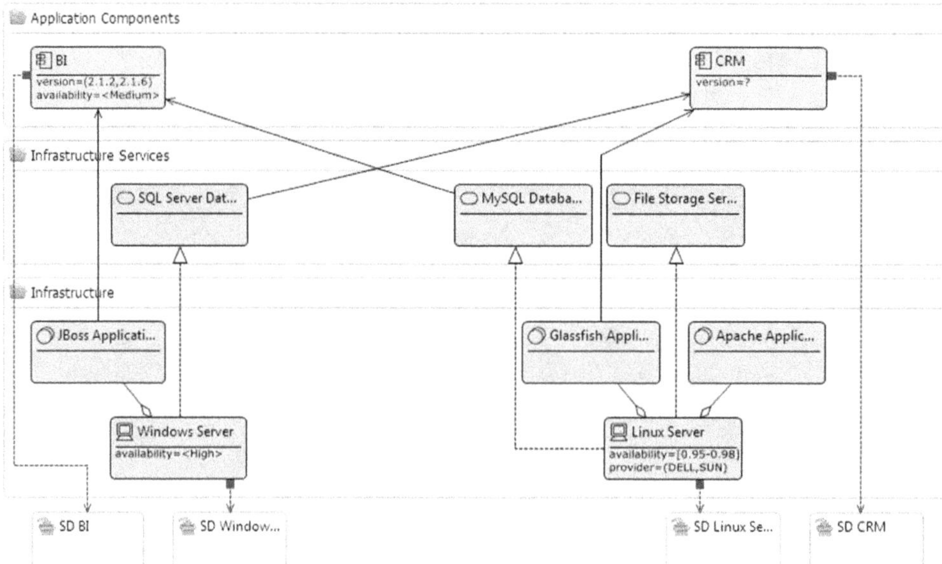

Contract provides the AttributeFact *AttFact* that specifies information about the version. The *Development Engineer* in the Observation *Interview2* provides the AttributeFact*AttFact4* that includes information about the availability.

Thus, supporting data helps modelers to understand why elements, attributes, and relations are imperfect in the draft. With this information, modelers can identify other sources in order to gather new useful information for refining the draft. Nevertheless, in some cases, modelers might not obtain additional information, in which case the draft can keep imperfect information.

CONCLUSION

Enterprise Modeling as a field and as a series of practices to connect business and technology in organizations is rapidly gaining importance worldwide. The models that are at the center of these practices have several characteristics that set them apart from models used in other fields such as MDE and MDA; they are large (can have upwards of 10.000 nodes), complex, and continuously evolving. Since these models are mostly intended to be a reflection of the organizations, they should be updated as the organization changes in order to properly reflect its reality.

Figure 10. Supporting data of the application component BI

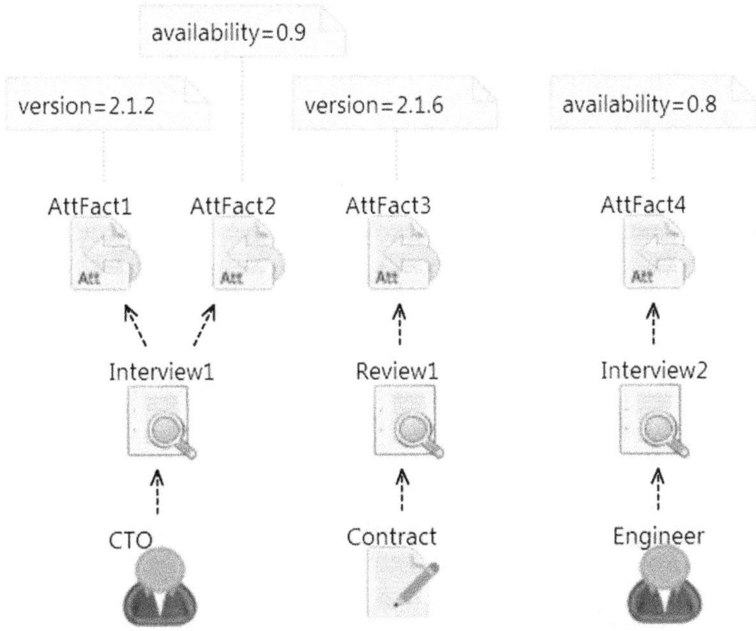

The construction of such enterprise models is challenging using traditional modeling environments. On the one hand, the metamodels cannot be known a priori because models are constructed in an organic way, following the changing needs and structures of the organization. On the other hand, not all the necessary information is available or has an optimal quality during every phase of the modeling process. Models may thus have different imperfections that may be progressively eliminated as new information is made available.

In this chapter, drafts of enterprise models have been presented as useful artifacts to aid in the construction of complete models. However, supporting drafts must overcome the aforementioned limitations of modeling environments. For this purpose, a solution strategy that covers three main aspects was presented. To support flexibility at the metamodel level, the follow have been proposed: the separation between linguistic and ontological conformance, the usage of an intermediate metamodel to define a linguistic framework, and the dynamic generation of validation rules to check ontological conformance. To support the inherent imperfection of enterprise models, the chapter presented an extension to the intermediate metamodel allowing for the inclusion of imperfect facts in the models; in this way, imperfect information is not mistakenly made perfect by introducing it in the models using normal mechanisms. Finally, a further extension to the intermediate metamodel was proposed to model meta-data about the drafts and the imperfections. Because of this, it becomes easier for modelers to trace the origin of every imperfection and work towards its removal. *iArchiMate*, a tool to implement all of the aforementioned elements was also presented and its usage was illustrated.

Future work will study two main topics: the evolution of drafts and the impact of drafts in the enterprise modeling process. Regarding the former, we want to provide the mechanisms to trace the evolution of the drafts taking in to account all versions allowing recovering elements, attributes, and relations from each draft version.About the latter, we wish to study the consequences of creating enterprise models using drafts.

REFERENCES

Archi. (n.d.). *ArchiMate Modeling Tool.* Retrieved from http://www.archimatetool.com/

Bjekovi, M., Proper, H. A., & Sottet, J.-S. (2013). Enterprise Modelling Languages - Just Enough Standardisation? In *Business Modeling and Software Design: Third International Symposium, BMSD 2013*. Springer.

Braun, C., & Winter, R. (2005). A comprehensive enterprise architecture metamodel and its implementation using a metamodeling platform. *Enterprise Modelling and Information Systems Architectures*, 64–79.

Bruneliere, H., Garcia, J., Desfray, P., Khelladi, D. E., Hebig, R., Bendraou, R., & Cabot, J. (2015). On Lightweight Metamodel Extension to Support Modeling Tools Agility. In *European Conference on Modelling Foundations and Applications* (pp. 62–74). Academic Press. 10.1007/978-3-319-21151-0_5

Buschle, M., Ullberg, J., Franke, U., Lagerström, R., & Sommestad, T. (2010). A tool for enterprise architecture analysis using the PRM formalism. In *Forum at the Conference on Advanced Information Systems Engineering (CAiSE)* (pp. 108–121). Academic Press.

Cicchetti, A., Ruscio, D. D., Kolovos, D. S., & Pierantonio, A. (2011). A test-driven approach for metamodel development. *Emerging Technologies for the Evolution and Maintenance of Software Models*, 319–342.

De Lara, J., & Guerra, E. (2010). Deep meta-modelling with metadepth. In Objects, Models, Components, Patterns (pp. 1–20). Springer. doi:10.1007/978-3-642-13953-6_1

Eclipse. (n.d.a). *Eclipse Modeling Framework Project (EMF).* Retrieved January 1, 2016, from http://www.eclipse.org/modeling/emf/

Eclipse. (n.d.b). *Epsilon Validation Language.* Retrieved January 1, 2016, from http://www.eclipse.org/epsilon/doc/evl/

Eclipse. (n.d.c). *EuGENia.* Retrieved from http://www.eclipse.org/epsilon/doc/eugenia/

Eclipse. (n.d.d). *Graphical Modeling Framework Project (GMF).* Retrieved January 1, 2016, from http://www.eclipse.org/modeling/gmp/

Erol, S., & Neumann, G. (2013). A Case-Study of Wiki-Supported Collaborative Drafting of Business Processes Models. In *Business Informatics (CBI), 2013 IEEE 15th Conference on* (pp. 382–390). IEEE.

Famelis, M., Salay, R., & Chechik, M. (2012). Partial models: Towards modeling and reasoning with uncertainty. In *Software Engineering (ICSE), 2012 34th International Conference on* (pp. 573–583). Academic Press.

Florez, H., Sánchez, M., & Villalobos, J. (2013). Embracing Imperfection in Enterprise Architecture Models. *CEUR Workshop Proceedings*, *1023*, 8–17.

Florez, H., Sanchez, M., & Villalobos, J. (2014a). Extensible Model-Based Approach for Supporting Automatic Enterprise Analysis. In *Proceedings. IEEE 18th international Enterprise Distributed object computing conference* (pp. 32–41). Institute of Electrical and Electronics Engineers Inc.

Florez, H., Sanchez, M., & Villalobos, J. (2014b). iArchiMate: A Tool for Managing Imperfection in Enterprise Models. In *18th IEEE International Enterprise Distributed Object Computing Conference Workshops and Demonstrations (EDOCW)* (pp. 201–210). IEEE.

Florez, H., Sanchez, M., Villalobos, J., & Vega, G. (2012). Coevolution Assistance for Enterprise Architecture Models. In *Models And Evolution (ME 2012) Workshop at The ACM/IEEE 15th International Conference on Model Driven Engineering Languages And Systems (MoDELS 2012).* ACM. 10.1145/2523599.2523605

Gabrysiak, G., Giese, H., Lüders, A., & Seibel, A. (2011). How can metamodels be used flexibly? In *Proceedings of FlexiTools Workshop at ICSE 2011* (p. 5). Academic Press.

Gómez, P., Sánchez, M., Florez, H., & Villalobos, J. (2014). An approach to the co-creation of models and metamodels in Enterprise Architecture Projects. *Journal of Object Technology*, *13*(3), 2:1. doi:10.5381/jot.2014.13.3.a2

Iacob, M.-E., & Jonkers, H. (2006). Quantitative analysis of enterprise architectures. *Interoperability of Enterprise Software and Applications.*

Kuhne, T. (2006). Matters of (meta-) modeling. *Software & Systems Modeling*, *5*(4), 369–385. doi:10.100710270-006-0017-9

Kurpjuweit, S., & Winter, R. (2007). Viewpoint-based Meta Model Engineering. In *Proceedings of the 2nd International Workshop on Enterprise Modelling and Information Systems Architectures* (pp. 143–161). Academic Press.

Lagerström, R., Franke, U., Johnson, P., & Ullberg, J. (2009). A method for creating enterprise architecture metamodels--applied to systems modifiability analysis. *International Journal of Computer Science and Applications*, *6*(5), 89–120.

Lankhorst, M. (2013). *Enterprise architecture at work: Modelling, communication and analysis*. Springer. doi:10.1007/978-3-642-29651-2

Object Management Group. (2011). *Business Process Model and Notation*. BPMN.

Rose, L., Kolovos, D., Paige, R., & Polack, F. (2010). Model migration with epsilon flock. *Theory and Practice of Model Transformations*, 184–198.

Rose, L. M., Kolovos, D. S., & Paige, R. F. (2012). Eugenia live: a flexible graphical modelling tool. In *Proceedings of the 2012 Extreme Modeling Workshop* (pp. 15–20). Academic Press. 10.1145/2467307.2467311

Salay, R., Chechik, M., Famelis, M., & Gorzny, J. (2015). A Methodology for Verifying Refinements of Partial Models. *Journal of Object Technology*, *14*(3), 1–3. doi:10.5381/jot.2015.14.3.a3

Sánchez-Cuadrado, J., De Lara, J., & Guerra, E. (2012). Bottom-up meta-modelling: an interactive approach. In *Proceedings of the 15th international conference on Model Driven Engineering Languages and Systems* (pp. 3–19). Academic Press. 10.1007/978-3-642-33666-9_2

Sandkuhl, K., Stirna, J., Persson, A., & Wißotzki, M. (2014). Quality of Enterprise Models. In Enterprise Modeling: Tackling Business Challenges with the 4EM Method (pp. 203–216). Berlin: Springer Berlin Heidelberg. doi:10.1007/978-3-662-43725-4_12

Schmidt, D. (2006). Guest editor's introduction: Model-driven engineering. *Computer*, *39*(2), 25–31. doi:10.1109/MC.2006.58

The Open Group. (2011). *TOGAF Version 9.1*. Van Haren Publishing.

The Open Group. (2012). *ArchiMate 2.0 Specification*. Van Haren Publishing.

Zolotas, A., Matragkas, N. D., Kolovos, D. S., & Paige, R. F. (2015). Flexible Modelling for Requirements Engineering. In FlexMDE@ MoDELS (pp. 32–41). Academic Press.

KEY TERMS AND DEFINITIONS

ArchiMate: Modeling language for describing and visualize enterprise models involving several enterprise domains sorted the aspects active structure, passive structure, behavior, and motivations, as well as in the layer, business, application, infrastructure, motivation, and implementation.

Draft of an Enterprise Model: Not finished enterprise model that might include imperfection features to be refined when new useful information is gathered from enterprise sources.

Enterprise Modeling: Practice to create, maintain, and use models in order to represent certain aspects of the enterprise.

iArchiMate: Enterprise modeling tool for creating drafts of ArchiMate models.

Imperfect Models: Models that include imprecision, inconsistency, vagueness, uncertainty, and incompleteness.

Linguistic Conformance: Relation between a model and its corresponding metamodel in terms of structure.

Ontological Conformance: Relation between a model and its corresponding metamodel in terms of semantics.

Validation Rules: Artifacts that verifies the accomplishment of linguistic and ontological conformance of models.

ENDNOTE

1 http://www.omg.org/

Compilation of References

Adeyemi, S., & Aremu, M. A. (2008). Impact assessment of business Process re-engineering on organizational performance. *European Journal of Soil Science*, *7*(1), 115–125.

Alan Frost - Organizational Memory and Knowledge Repositorieshttp. (n.d.). Retrieved from www.knowledge-management-tools.net/organizational-memory-and-knowledge.html

Alan Frost - The Different Types of Knowledge. (n.d.). Retrieved from http://www.knowledge-management-tools.net/different-types-of-knowledge.html

Ali, N., Gue'he'neuc, Y.-G., & Antoniol, G. (2011). *Factors Impacting the Inputs of Traceability Recovery Approaches*. Springer-Verlag.

Al-Mashara, M., Iran, Z., & Zairi, M. (2001). Business process re-engineering: A survey of international experience. *Business Process Management Journal*, *7*(5), 437–455. doi:10.1108/14637150110406812

Amaldi, E., Capone, A., Cesana, M., & Filippini, I. (2012). On the design of wireless sensor networks for mobile target detection. *IEEE/ACM Transactions on Networking*, *20*(3), 784–797. doi:10.1109/TNET.2011.2175746

Archi. (n.d.). *ArchiMate Modeling Tool.* Retrieved from http://www.archimatetool.com/

Aremu, M. A., & Saka, S. T. (2006). The impact of information technology on library, Management: A Marketing Perspective. Advances in Management, 5(1), 141 – 150.

Arratia, A. (2016, October 7). *Getting started with R.* Retrieved from: http://computationalfinance.lsi.upc.edu/?page_id=87

Attaran, M. (2004). Exploring the relationship between information technology and business process re-engineering. *Information & Management, 41*(5), 585–596. doi:10.1016/S0378-7206(03)00098-3

Azevedo, S., Machado, R. J., & Maciel, R. S. P. (2012). On the use of model transformations for the automation of the 4SRS transition method. *Lecture Notes in Business Information Processing, 112*, 249–264. doi:10.1007/978-3-642-31069-0_22

Azevedo, S., Machado, R. J., Muthig, D., & Ribeiro, H. (2009). Refinement of Software Product Line Architectures through Recursive Modeling Techniques. *On the Move to Meaningful Internet Systems: OTM 2009 Workshops.*

Barbiero, B. (2004). *Tacit knowledge. Dictionary of Philosophy of Mind.* Retrieved from http://philosophy.uwaterloo.ca/MindDict/tacitknowledge.html

Beckford, J. (1998). *Quality, a critical introduction.* London: Routledge.

Bellinger, G., Castro, D., & Mills, A. (2004). *Systems Thinking*. Retrieved from http://www.systems-thinking.org/

Bernstein, J. H. (2014). *The Data-Information-Knowledge-Wisdom Hierarchy.* Retrieved from http://inls151f14.web.unc.edu/files/2014/08/bernstein.pdf

Bernstein. (1985). *The Data-Information-Knowledge-Wisdom hierarchy.* Retrieved from http://inls151f14.web.unc.edu/files/2014/08/bernstein.pdf

Bjekovi, M., Proper, H. A., & Sottet, J.-S. (2013). Enterprise Modelling Languages - Just Enough Standardisation? In *Business Modeling and Software Design: Third International Symposium, BMSD 2013*. Springer.

Boyton & Zmud. (1987). *Information technology Planning in the 1980s.* Academic Press.

Braun, C., & Winter, R. (2005). A comprehensive enterprise architecture metamodel and its implementation using a metamodeling platform. *Enterprise Modelling and Information Systems Architectures*, 64–79.

Bruneliere, H., Garcia, J., Desfray, P., Khelladi, D. E., Hebig, R., Bendraou, R., & Cabot, J. (2015). On Lightweight Metamodel Extension to Support Modeling Tools Agility. In *European Conference on Modelling Foundations and Applications* (pp. 62–74). Academic Press. 10.1007/978-3-319-21151-0_5

Buavaraporn, N. (2010). *Business process improvement methodology adoption for improving service quality: Case study of financial institutions in Thailand* (PhD thesis). University of Nottingham, Nottingham, UK.

Buschle, M., Ullberg, J., Franke, U., Lagerström, R., & Sommestad, T. (2010). A tool for enterprise architecture analysis using the PRM formalism. In *Forum at the Conference on Advanced Information Systems Engineering (CAiSE)* (pp. 108–121). Academic Press.

Caprione, E. C. (2010). *Museum Collections Management Systems*. Retrieved from http://rcaam.org/cms/wp-content/uploads/2011/05/Graduate-Studies-Thesis-Collections-Management-Elana-Carpinone.pdf

Chen, Y. (2001). *Empirical Modelling for Participative Business Process Re-engineering* (Thesis). University of Warwick, Warwick, UK.

Chin, J.-C., Dong, Y., Hon, W.-K., Ma, C. Y.-T., & Yau, D. K. Y. (2010). Detection of Intelligent Mobile Target in a Mobile Sensor Network. *IEEE/ACM Transactions on Networking*, *18*(1), 41–52. doi:10.1109/TNET.2009.2024309

Chow, C.-Y., Mokbel, M. F., & He, T. (2011). A Privacy-Preserving Location Monitoring System for Wireless Sensor Networks. *IEEE Transactions on Mobile Computing*, *10*(1), 94–107. doi:10.1109/TMC.2010.145

Cicchetti, A., Ruscio, D. D., Kolovos, D. S., & Pierantonio, A. (2011). A test-driven approach for metamodel development. *Emerging Technologies for the Evolution and Maintenance of Software Models*, 319–342.

Cohen, K., & Zhao, Q. (2015). Asymptotically Optimal Anomaly Detection via Sequential Testing. *IEEE Transactions on Signal Processing*, *63*(11), 2929–2941. doi:10.1109/TSP.2015.2416674

Collins, H. M. (2001). Tacit knowledge, trust and the Q Sapphire. *Social Studies of Science*, *31*(1), 71–85. doi:10.1177/030631201031001004

Cook, C., & Cook, M. (2000). *The convergence of knowledge management and Business intelligence*. Academic Press.

Covert, M. (1997). *Successfully Performing Business Process Re-engineering*. Visible Systems Corporation.

Cross, F. K., Feather, J. J., & Lynch, L. R. (1994). Corporate renaissance, the art of re-engineering. Cambridge, MA: Blackwell Publisher.

Davenport, T. H., & Short, J. E. (1990). The new industrial engineering: Information technology and business process redesign. *Slogan Management Review,* 11 – 27.

Davidson. (1993). Beyond Re-engineering. *IBM Systems Journals.*

De Lara, J., & Guerra, E. (2010). Deep meta-modelling with metadepth. In Objects, Models, Components, Patterns (pp. 1–20). Springer. doi:10.1007/978-3-642-13953-6_1

Delgado, A., De Guzmán, I. G., & Piattini, M. (2010). From BPMN business process models to SoaML service models: a transformation-driven approach. In *2nd International Conference on Software Technology and Engineering (ICSTE)* (pp. 314–319). Academic Press.

Dodaro, G. L. and Crwley, B. P. (1997). *Business process re-engineering assessment guide.* United States General Accounting Office-Accounting and Information management Division, 3rd Version.

Eclipse. (n.d.a). *Eclipse Modeling Framework Project (EMF).* Retrieved January 1, 2016, from http://www.eclipse.org/modeling/emf/

Eclipse. (n.d.b). *Epsilon Validation Language.* Retrieved January 1, 2016, from http://www.eclipse.org/epsilon/doc/evl/

Eclipse. (n.d.c). *EuGENia.* Retrieved from http://www.eclipse.org/epsilon/doc/eugenia/

Eclipse. (n.d.d). *Graphical Modeling Framework Project (GMF).* Retrieved January 1, 2016, from http://www.eclipse.org/modeling/gmp/

Economist 662f. (2014). R v. Stata v. others. [Web log comment]. Retrieved from: https://www.econjobrumors.com/topic/r-v-stata-v-others

Eddelbuettel, D. (2017, April 25). *CRAN Task View: Empirical Science.* Retrieved from: https://cran.r-project.org/web/views/Finance.html

Ekber & Keskin. (2005). *Örgütsel Hafıza ile Enformasyon Teknolojileri Arasındaki ilişkiler.* Retrieved from http://www2.bayar.edu.tr/yonetimekonomi/dergi/pdf/C12S22005/AEKHKAU.pdf

Elvesaeter, B., & Panfilenko, D. (2010). Aligning business and IT models in service-oriented architectures using BPMN and SoaML. In *Proceedings of the 1st International Workshop on Model-Driven Interoperability* (pp. 61--68). ACM.

Erol, S., & Neumann, G. (2013). A Case-Study of Wiki-Supported Collaborative Drafting of Business Processes Models. In *Business Informatics (CBI), 2013 IEEE 15th Conference on* (pp. 382–390). IEEE.

Famelis, M., Salay, R., & Chechik, M. (2012). Partial models: Towards modeling and reasoning with uncertainty. In *Software Engineering (ICSE), 2012 34th International Conference on* (pp. 573–583). Academic Press.

Ferreira, N., Santos, N., Machado, R. J., & Gasevic, D. (2012). Derivation of Process-Oriented Logical Architectures: An Elicitation Approach for Cloud Design. In A. J. O. Dieste and N. Juristo (Ed.), *13th International Conference on Product-Focused Software Development and Process Improvement - PROFES 2012* (Vol. 7343, pp. 44–58). Madrid, Spain: Springer-Verlag.

Ferreira, N., Santos, N., Machado, R. J., Fernandes, J. E., & Gasevic, D. (2014). A V-Model Approach for Business Process Requirements Elicitation in Cloud Design. In Advanced Web Services (pp. 551--578). Springer.

Florez, H., Sanchez, M., & Villalobos, J. (2014a). Extensible Model-Based Approach for Supporting Automatic Enterprise Analysis. In *Proceedings. IEEE 18th international Enterprise Distributed object computing conference* (pp. 32–41). Institute of Electrical and Electronics Engineers Inc.

Florez, H., Sanchez, M., Villalobos, J., & Vega, G. (2012). Coevolution Assistance for Enterprise Architecture Models. In *Models And Evolution (ME 2012) Workshop at The ACM/IEEE 15th International Conference on Model Driven Engineering Languages And Systems (MoDELS 2012)*. ACM. 10.1145/2523599.2523605

Florez, H., Sánchez, M., & Villalobos, J. (2013). Embracing Imperfection in Enterprise Architecture Models. *CEUR Workshop Proceedings*, *1023*, 8–17.

Florez, H., Sanchez, M., & Villalobos, J. (2014b). iArchiMate: A Tool for Managing Imperfection in Enterprise Models. In *18th IEEE International Enterprise Distributed Object Computing Conference Workshops and Demonstrations (EDOCW)* (pp. 201–210). IEEE.

France, R., & Rumpe, B. (2007). Model-driven Development of Complex Software: A Research Roadmap. In *Proceedings of the Conference on Future of Software Engineering* (pp. 37--54). IEEE. 10.1109/FOSE.2007.14

Gabrysiak, G., Giese, H., Lüders, A., & Seibel, A. (2011). How can metamodels be used flexibly? In *Proceedings of FlexiTools Workshop at ICSE 2011* (p. 5). Academic Press.

Gadu & El-Khameesy. (n.d.). *A Knowledge Management Framework Using Business Intelligence Solutions*. Retrieved from http://www.ijcsi.org/papers/IJCSI-11-5-1-102-107.pdf

Galster, M., Eberlein, A., & Moussavi, M. (2009). Comparing methodologies for the transition between software requirements and architectures. In *Conference Proceedings - IEEE International Conference on Systems, Man and Cybernetics* (pp. 2380--2385). IEEE.

Gamble & Blackwell. (2001). *Knowledge Management*. Author.

Gómez, P., Sánchez, M., Florez, H., & Villalobos, J. (2014). An approach to the co-creation of models and metamodels in Enterprise Architecture Projects. *Journal of Object Technology*, *13*(3), 2:1. doi:10.5381/jot.2014.13.3.a2

Google. Trends. (2004-2017). Retrieved from https://trends.google.com/trends/explore?date=all&q=python,%2Fm%2F0212jm,SAS

Gotel & Philippow. (2008). Enabling automated traceability maintenance by recognizing development activities applied to models. In *Proceedings of the 2008 23rd IEEE/ACM International Conference on Automated Software Engineering*. Washington, DC: IEEE Computer Society.

Griffin, R. W. (1990). *Management* (3rd ed.). Boston, MA: Houghton Mifflin.

Hammer, M. (1990). Re-engineering Work: Don't Automate, Obliterate. *Harvard Business Review*, 104–112.

Hammer, M., & Champy, J. (1993). *Re-engineering the Corporation: A Manifesto for Business Revolution*. New York: Harper Business.

Hayes, J. H., Antoniol, G., & Gue'he'neuc, Y.-G. (2008). PREREQIR: Recovering Pre-Requirements via Cluster Analysis. *Proc. 15th Working Conf. Reverse Eng.*, 165-174.

Heizer, J., & Render, B. (2011). *Operations Management* (10th ed.). Prentice Hall.

Higgins, J. M. (1991). *The Management Challenge: An Introduction to Management*. New York, NY: Macmillan.

Housel, T., & Bell, A. (2001). Surges and sediments: Shaping the reception of re-engineering. *Information & Management*, *38*(4), 239–251. doi:10.1016/S0378-7206(00)00069-0

Iacob, M.-E., & Jonkers, H. (2006). Quantitative analysis of enterprise architectures. *Interoperability of Enterprise Software and Applications*.

IBM - A practical framework for business intelligence and planning. (n.d.). Retrieved from http://www.ibm.com/midmarket/uk/en/att/pdf/practicalframework.pdf

Inzinger, C., Nastic, S., Sehic, S., Vogler, M., Li, F., & Dustdar, S. (2014). MADCAT: A methodology for architecture and deployment of cloud application topologies. *Proceedings - IEEE 8th International Symposium on Service Oriented System Engineering*, 13–22. 10.1109/SOSE.2014.9

ISO 9001. (2008). Introduction and Support Package: Guidance on the Concept and Use of the Process Approach for management systems. ISO/TC 176/SC 2/N 544R3.

Ives & Learmonth. (1984). *The Information System as a Competitive Weapon*. Academic Press.

Jaehoon Jeong, Shuo Guo, Tian He, & Du, D. H. C. (2011). Autonomous Passive Localization Algorithm for Road Sensor Networks. *IEEE Transactions on Computers*, *60*(11), 1622–1637. doi:10.1109/TC.2010.260

Jennex, M. E. (2009). Knowledge Management, Organizational Memory, and Transfer Behavior. Academic Press.

Jeong, J., Guo, S., Gu, Y., He, T., & Du, D. H. C. (2011). Trajectory-Based Data Forwarding for Light-Traffic Vehicular Ad Hoc Networks. *IEEE Transactions on Parallel and Distributed Systems*, *22*(5), 743–757. doi:10.1109/TPDS.2010.103

Kagdi, H., & Maletic, J. (2007). Software repositories: A source for trace-ability links. *International Workshop on Traceability in Emerging Forms of Software Engineering (GCT/TEFSE^ 07)*, 32–39.

Kagdi, H., Maletic, J., & Sharif, B. (2007). Mining software repositories for traceability links. *ICPC '07, 15th IEEE International Conference*, 145–154.

Kaplan, R. S., & Norton, D. P. (1992, January-February). The balanced scorecard - measures that drive performance. *Harvard Business Review*, 75–85. PMID:10119714

Kaplan, R., & Norton, D. (2005, October). The Office of Strategy Management. *Harvard Business Review*, 72–80. http://hbswk.hbs.edu/item/5305.html PMID:16250626

Karabulut, K. (2014). *Blogger*. Retrieved from http://kaankarabulut.blogcu.com/ogrenen-organizasyonlar/7938311

Karehka, R. (2015). *Use of Information Technology*. Retrieved from http://www.useoftechnology.com/information-technology/

Kimiz-Dalkir. (2009). Knowledge Management. *Theory into Practice*.

King. (n.d.). *Knowledge Management and Organizational Learning*. Retrieved from http://www.uky.edu/~gmswan3/575/KM_and_OL.pdf

Kourie, D. (2008). Knowledge Management and Knowledge Management Technology. Academic Press.

Krill, P. (2016). *Businesses stick with Java, Python, and C*. Retrieved from https://search.proquest.com/docview/1808338164?pq-origsite=summon

Kroll, P., & Kruchten, P. (2003). *The rational unified process made easy: a practitioner's guide to the RUP*. Addison-Wesley.

Kuhne, T. (2006). Matters of (meta-) modeling. *Software & Systems Modeling*, *5*(4), 369–385. doi:10.100710270-006-0017-9

Kumar & Raviraj. (2013). A Study on Requirement Traceability Methods in Software Engineering. *International Journal of Societal Applications of Computer Science*, *2*(11), 481–484.

Kurpjuweit, S., & Winter, R. (2007). Viewpoint-based Meta Model Engineering. In *Proceedings of the 2nd International Workshop on Enterprise Modelling and Information Systems Architectures* (pp. 143–161). Academic Press.

Lagerström, R., Franke, U., Johnson, P., & Ullberg, J. (2009). A method for creating enterprise architecture metamodels--applied to systems modifiability analysis. *International Journal of Computer Science and Applications*, *6*(5), 89–120.

Lai, I.-W., Ascheid, G., Meyr, H., & Chiueh, T.-D. (2011). Efficient Channel-Adaptive MIMO Detection Using Just-Acceptable Error Rate. *IEEE Transactions on Wireless Communications*, *10*(1), 73–83. doi:10.1109/TWC.2010.101810.091129

Lambert, K. (2013). *Fundamentals of Python: Data Structures*. Retrieved from https://ebookcentral.proquest.com/lib/valpo-ebooks/reader.action?docID=3136674

Lankhorst, M. (2013). *Enterprise architecture at work: Modelling, communication and analysis*. Springer. doi:10.1007/978-3-642-29651-2

Laudon, K. C., & Laudon, J. P. (2006). *Management information system: Managing the digital firm* (10th ed.). Upper Saddle River, NJ: Prentice Hall.

Lenk, K. (1997). Business process re-engineering in public sector. In Beyond BPR in public administration. Amsterdam: IOS Press.

Liu, L., Zhang, X., & Ma, H. (2011). Localization-Oriented Coverage in Wireless Camera Sensor Networks. *IEEE Transactions on Wireless Communications*, *10*(2), 484–494. doi:10.1109/TWC.2010.01.080956

López-Sanz, M., & Marcos, E. (2012). ArchiMeDeS: A model-driven framework for the specification of service-oriented architectures. *Information Systems*, *37*(3), 257–268. doi:10.1016/j.is.2011.11.002

Machado, R. J., Fernandes, J. M., Monteiro, P., & Rodrigues, H. (2005). Transformation of UML Models for Service-Oriented Software Architectures. *12th IEEE International Conference and Workshops on the Engineering of Computer-Based Systems (ECBS'05)*, 173–182. 10.1109/ECBS.2005.73

Machado, R. J., Fernandes, J. M., Monteiro, P., & Rodrigues, H. (2006). Refinement of Software Architectures by Recursive Model Transformations. In *Product-Focused Software Process Improvement* (pp. 422–428). Springer. doi:10.1007/11767718_38

Manganelli, R. L., & Klein, M. M. (1994). *The re-engineering Handbook: A step-by-step guide to business transformation*. New York: American Management Association.

Markham, K. (2015, February 2). *Should you teach Python or R for data science?* Retrieved from: http://www.dataschool.io/python-or-r-for-data-science/

Marquardt, M. J. (2002). *Building The Learning Organization (Mastering the 5 Elements For Corporate Learning)*. Palo Alto, CA: Davies Black Publishing.

Miao, P., Chenb, H., Xiao, Y., Ozdemir, S., Vasilakos, A. V., & Wue, J. (2011). Impacts of sensor node distributions on coverage in sensor networks. *Journal of Parallel and Distributed Computing*, *71*(12), 1578–1591. doi:10.1016/j.jpdc.2011.04.011

Mohamed, O. (2017 February 27). R software for statistical computing: useful in finance? [Web log comment]. Retrieved from: https://www.researchgate.net/post/R_software_for_statistical_computing_useful_in_finance#view=58bd86c196b7e4950c77810e

Moore, B. (2014, January 4). *Analyse Your Bank Statements Using R*. Retrieved from: https://www.r-bloggers.com/analyse-your-bank-statements-using-r/

Muenchen, B. (2017, March 1). *Data Science Job Report 2017: R Passes SAS, But Python Leaves them Both Behind*. Retrieved from: https://www.r-bloggers.com/data-science-job-report-2017-r-passes-sas-but-python-leaves-them-both-behind/?utm_source=feedburner&utm_medium=email&utm_campaign=Feed%3A+RBloggers+%28R+bloggers%29

Naisbitt, J. (1982). *Megatrends*. Warner Books.

Nakatani, K. (1999). *An Extended Object-Oriented Modeling Method for Business Process Re-engineering* (Thesis). Texas Tech University

Object Management Group. (2011). *Business Process Model and Notation*. BPMN.

Ocasio, W. (2001). *How do organizations think?* Academic Press.

OMG. (2008). *Software & Systems Process Engineering Meta-Model Specification (SPEM)*. Retrieved from http://www.omg.org/spec/SPEM/2.0/

OMG. (2011). *Business Process Model and Notation*. Retrieved from http://www.omg.org/spec/BPMN/2.0

OMG. (2012). *Service oriented architecture Modeling Language (SoaML) Specification*. Retrieved from http://www.omg.org/spec/SoaML/1.0.1/

Ooi, H. (2011, December 15). *R and SAS in Banking*. Retrieved from: http://files.meetup.com/1685538/R%20and%20SAS%20in%20Banking.pdf

Osborn, A. (1979). *Running Wild – The next Industrial revolution*. Osborn/McGraw-Hill.

Othman, R., & Hashim, N. A. (2004). *Typologizing Organizational Amnesia*. Academic Press.

Penny, J. (2001). Differential item functioning an international 360—degree assessment: Evidence of gender stereotype, environmental complexity, and organizational contingency. *European Journal of Work and Organizational Psychology*, *10*(3), 245–271. doi:10.1080/13594320143000663

Pollitt, C. (2000). *Institutional Amnesia: A Paradox of the Information Age*. Academic Press.

Pougatchev, V., & Kulkarni, A. (2011). V-index as a Measure of the Targets/ Objectives Accomplishment of the Strategic and Operation Plans for an Educational Institution Unit (Case Study). Journal of Research in Innovative Teaching, 4(1).

Pougatchev, V., & Kulkarni, A. (2013). Online Strategic and Operational Planning Procedures in the Integrated Management Information Systems for Educational Institutions. In *ICT Management in Non-Profit Organizations* (pp. 192-222). IGI Global. Retrieved from http://www.igi-global.com/book/ict-management-non-profit-organizations/97312

Pougatchev, V., Glasgow, S., Ellis, J., & Johnson, N. (2009). Online Performance Based Management and Evaluation System as an Instrument to Manage the Quality of Institutional Performance at the University of Technology, Jamaica. *Journal of Research in Innovative Teaching, National University, San Diego, CA, USA*, *2*(1), 53–78. Retrieved from http://www.nu.edu/assets/resources/pageResources/7638_JournalofResearch09.pdf

R Core Development Team. (2016, November 18). *Submission*. CRAN Repository Policy. Retrieved from: https://cran.r-project.org/web/packages/policies.html#Submission

Raymond, C. K. (1964). Theories of choice in business. In G. Fisk (Ed.), *The Frontiers of Management Psychology* (pp. 3–17). New York, NY: Harper and Row.

Rickert, J. (2014, May 8). *R and Finance*. Retrieved from: http://blog.revolutionanalytics.com/2014/05/r-and-finance.html

Rose, L. M., Kolovos, D. S., & Paige, R. F. (2012). Eugenia live: a flexible graphical modelling tool. In *Proceedings of the 2012 Extreme Modeling Workshop* (pp. 15–20). Academic Press. 10.1145/2467307.2467311

Rose, L., Kolovos, D., Paige, R., & Polack, F. (2010). Model migration with epsilon flock. *Theory and Practice of Model Transformations*, 184–198.

Ruiz-Rube, I., Dodero, J. M., Palomo-Duarte, M., Ruiz, M., & Gawn, D. (2013). Uses and applications of Software & Systems Process Engineering Meta-Model process models. A systematic mapping study. *Journal of Software: Evolution and Process*, *25*(9), 999–1025.

Salay, R., Chechik, M., Famelis, M., & Gorzny, J. (2015). A Methodology for Verifying Refinements of Partial Models. *Journal of Object Technology, 14*(3), 1–3. doi:10.5381/jot.2015.14.3.a3

Salgado, C. E., Machado, R. J., & Maciel, R. S. P. (2016b). MATRA : A Framework for Assessing Model-based Approaches on the Transformation between Requirements and Architecture. In Enterprise, Business-Process and Information Systems Modeling (pp. 1-12). Springer.

Salgado, C. E., Machado, R. J., & Maciel, R. S. P. (2016a). A Three-Dimensional Approach for a Quality-Based Alignment Between Requirements and Architecture. In *International Conference on Exploring Services Science* (Vol. 2, pp. 112-125). Springer.

Salgado, C. E., Teixeira, J., Santos, N., Machado, R. J., & Maciel, R. S. P. (2015). A SoaML Approach for Derivation of a Process-Oriented Logical Architecture from Use Cases. In *Exploring Services Science* (pp. 80–94). Springer.

Sánchez-Cuadrado, J., De Lara, J., & Guerra, E. (2012). Bottom-up meta-modelling: an interactive approach. In *Proceedings of the 15th international conference on Model Driven Engineering Languages and Systems* (pp. 3–19). Academic Press. 10.1007/978-3-642-33666-9_2

Sandkuhl, K., Stirna, J., Persson, A., & Wißotzki, M. (2014). Quality of Enterprise Models. In Enterprise Modeling: Tackling Business Challenges with the 4EM Method (pp. 203–216). Berlin: Springer Berlin Heidelberg. doi:10.1007/978-3-662-43725-4_12

Santos, M. Y., & Machado, R. J. (2010). On the derivation of class diagrams from use cases and logical software architectures. *Proceedings - 5th International Conference on Software Engineering Advances,* 107–113. 10.1109/ICSEA.2010.24

Schmidt, D. (2006). Guest editor's introduction: Model-driven engineering. *Computer, 39*(2), 25–31. doi:10.1109/MC.2006.58

Senge, P. (1994). *Fifth Discipline.* New York: Doubleday.

Sharp, J. (2010). Windows® Communication Foundation 4 Step by Step. O'Reilly Media, Inc.

Shin, N., & Jemella, D. (2002). Business process re-engineering and performance improvement: The Case of Chase Manhattan Bank. *Business Process Management Journal*, *8*(4), 351–363. doi:10.1108/14637150210435008

Sinha, K., Sinha, B. P., & Datta, D. (2011). An Energy-Efficient Communication Scheme for Wireless Networks: A Redundant Radix-Based Approach. *IEEE Transactions on Wireless Communications*, *10*(2), 550–559. doi:10.1109/TWC.2010.120610.100244

Slack, N., Chambers, S., & Johnston, R. (2007). *Operation Management* (5th ed.). London: Prentice Hall.

Smith, M. K. (2001). *Peter senge learning organization*. Retrieved from http://infed.org/mobi/peter-senge-and-the- learning-organization/

Smith, E. A. (2001). The role of tacit and explicit knowledge in the workplace. *Journal of Knowledge Management*, *5*(4), 311–321. doi:10.1108/13673270110411733

Stoddard, D. B., & Jarvenpea, S. L. (1995). Business process redesign tactics for managing radical change. *Journal of Management Information Systems*, *12*(1), 61–107. doi:10.1080/07421222.1995.11518071

Stoleru, R., He, T., Mathiharan, S. S., George, S. M., & Stankovic, J. A. (2012). Asymmetric Event-Driven Node Localization in Wireless Sensor Networks. *IEEE Transactions on Parallel and Distributed Systems*, *23*(4), 634–642. doi:10.1109/TPDS.2011.227

Sungau, J., & Msanjila, S. S. (2012). On IT enabling of business process re-engineering in organizations. *Advanced Materials Research*, *404-408*, 5177–5181.

Talwar, R. (1993). Business re-engineering-a strategy-driven approach. *Long Range Planning*, *26*(6), 22–40. doi:10.1016/0024-6301(93)90204-S

Teng, J. T., & Kettinger, W. J. (1995). Business process redesign and information architecture: Exploring the relationship. *ACM SIGMIS*, *26*(1), 30–42. doi:10.1145/206476.206481

The Open Group. (2011). *TOGAF Version 9.1*. Van Haren Publishing.

The Open Group. (2012). *ArchiMate 2.0 Specification*. Van Haren Publishing.

The R Foundation. (2017). *The R Project for Statistical Computing*. Retrieved from: https://www.r-project.org/

The R User Conference. (2013 July 12). *Book of Contributed Abstracts*. Retrieved from: https://www.r-project.org/conferences/useR-2013/docs/useR2013_abstract_booklet.pdf

Toffler, A. (1980). *The Third Wave*. Bantam Books.

Tolgay, F. (2010). *Öğrenen Organizasyonlar ve Bir Uygulama Yüksek Lisans Tezi*. İstanbul: Bahçeşehir University.

Training Industry Knowledge Repositories Knowledge Management Tools. (n.d.). Retrieved from https://www.trainingindustry.com/wiki/entries/knowledge-repositories.aspx

Trajanov, D. (2017, February 27). R software for statistical computing: useful in finance? [Web log comment]. Retrieved from: https://www.researchgate.net/post/R_software_for_statistical_computing_useful_in_finance#view=58bd86c196b7e4950c77810e

Tsang. (2004). *The Nature of Organizational Unlearning*. Retrieved from http://www.eolss.net/sample-chapters/c15/e1-29-04-05.pdf

Tucker, A. B., & Noonan, R. E. (2002). *Programming languages: Principals and paradigms* (1st ed.). New York: McGraw-Hill.

U.S. Department of Energy and Oak Ridge Associated Universities. (2001). *The Performance-Based Management Handbook. Volume 1. Establishing and Maintaining a Performance-Based Management Program.* Author.

Varma, J. (2016 August 29). *Package 'jrvFinance'*. Retrieved from: https://mran.microsoft.com/web/packages/jrvFinance/jrvFinance.pdf

W3C Information and Knowledge Domain. (2016). Retrieved from http://www.w3.org/XML/

W3C Working Group. (2004). *Web Services Architecture.* W3C Working Group Note 11 February 2004. Retrieved from http://www.w3.org/TR/2003/WD-ws-arch-20030808/

Walsh James, P. (1991). Organizational Memory. Academic Press.

Walsh, J. P., & Ungson, G. R. (1991). *Organizational Memory. The Academy of Management Journals.*

Wang, G., Md, Z. A. B., Cao, J., & Wu, J. (2014). Detecting Movements of a Target Using Face Tracking in Wireless Sensor Networks. *IEEE Transactions on Parallel and Distributed Systems*, *25*(4), 939–949. doi:10.1109/TPDS.2013.91

Wang, Z., Bulut, E., & Szymanski, B. K. (2010). Distributed Energy-Efficient Target Tracking with Binary Sensor Networks. *ACM Transactions on Sensor Networks*, *6*(4), 1–32. doi:10.1145/1777406.1777411

Wang, Z., Bulut, E., & Szymanski, B. K. (2013). Energy-efficient location services for mobile ad hoc networks. *Elsevier, Ad Hoc Networks*, *11*(1), 273–287. doi:10.1016/j.adhoc.2012.05.012

Whitman, M. E. (1996). IT divergence in re-engineering support: Performance expectations vs perceptions. *Information & Management*, *30*(5), 239–250. doi:10.1016/S0378-7206(96)01046-4

Xiaoli, L. (2011). Correlation between business Process re-engineering and operation performance of National Commercial Banks. *Journal of Innovation and Management*, *7*, 981–985.

Xu, E., Ding, Z., & Dasgupta, S. (2013). Target Tracking and Mobile Sensor Navigation in Wireless Sensor Networks. *IEEE Transactions on Mobile Computing*, *12*(1), 177–186. doi:10.1109/TMC.2011.262

Yue, T., Briand, L. C., & Labiche, Y. (2011). A systematic review of transformation approaches between user requirements and analysis models. *Requirements Engineering*, *16*(2), 75–99. doi:10.100700766-010-0111-y

Zhao, J., Xi, W., He, Y., Liu, Y., Li, X.-Y., Mo, L., & Yang, Z. (2013). Localization of Wireless Sensor Networks in the Wild: Pursuit of Ranging Quality. *IEEE/ACM Transactions on Networking*, *2*(1), 311–323. doi:10.1109/TNET.2012.2200906

Zhao, Q., & Ye, J. (2010). Quickest Detection in Multiple ON–OFF Processes. *IEEE Transactions on Signal Processing*, *58*(12), 5994–6006. doi:10.1109/TSP.2010.2071869

Zolotas, A., Matragkas, N. D., Kolovos, D. S., & Paige, R. F. (2015). Flexible Modelling for Requirements Engineering. In FlexMDE@ MoDELS (pp. 32–41). Academic Press.

Zou, X., Settimi, R., & Cleland-Huang, J. (2010). Improving automated requirements trace retrieval: A study of term-based enhancement methods. *Empirical Software Engineering*, *15*(2), 119–146. doi:10.100710664-009-9114-z

Zúñiga-Prieto, M., Insfran, E., Abrahao, S., & Cano-Genoves, C. (2016). Incremental Integration of Microservices in Cloud Applications. *Information Systems Development: Complexity in Information Systems Development (ISD2016 Proceedings)*, 93–105.

Zuñiga-Prieto, M., Gonzalez-Huerta, J., Abrahao, S., & Insfran, E. (2014). Towards a model-driven dynamic architecture reconfiguration process for cloud services integration. *CEUR Workshop Proceedings*, *1331*, 52–61.

Related References

To continue our tradition of advancing information science and technology research, we have compiled a list of recommended IGI Global readings. These references will provide additional information and guidance to further enrich your knowledge and assist you with your own research and future publications.

Abtahi, M. S., Behboudi, L., & Hasanabad, H. M. (2017). Factors Affecting Internet Advertising Adoption in Ad Agencies. *International Journal of Innovation in the Digital Economy*, *8*(4), 18–29. doi:10.4018/IJIDE.2017100102

Agrawal, S. (2017). The Impact of Emerging Technologies and Social Media on Different Business(es): Marketing and Management. In O. Rishi & A. Sharma (Eds.), *Maximizing Business Performance and Efficiency Through Intelligent Systems* (pp. 37–49). Hershey, PA: IGI Global. doi:10.4018/978-1-5225-2234-8.ch002

Alnoukari, M., Razouk, R., & Hanano, A. (2016). BSC-SI: A Framework for Integrating Strategic Intelligence in Corporate Strategic Management. *International Journal of Social and Organizational Dynamics in IT*, *5*(2), 1–14. doi:10.4018/IJSODIT.2016070101

Alnoukari, M., Razouk, R., & Hanano, A. (2016). BSC-SI, A Framework for Integrating Strategic Intelligence in Corporate Strategic Management. *International Journal of Strategic Information Technology and Applications*, *7*(1), 32–44. doi:10.4018/IJSITA.2016010103

Altındağ, E. (2016). Current Approaches in Change Management. In A. Goksoy (Ed.), *Organizational Change Management Strategies in Modern Business* (pp. 24–51). Hershey, PA: IGI Global. doi:10.4018/978-1-4666-9533-7.ch002

Alvarez-Dionisi, L. E., Turner, R., & Mittra, M. (2016). Global Project Management Trends. *International Journal of Information Technology Project Management*, *7*(3), 54–73. doi:10.4018/IJITPM.2016070104

Anantharaman, R. N., Rajeswari, K. S., Angusamy, A., & Kuppusamy, J. (2017). Role of Self-Efficacy and Collective Efficacy as Moderators of Occupational Stress Among Software Development Professionals. *International Journal of Human Capital and Information Technology Professionals*, *8*(2), 45–58. doi:10.4018/IJHCITP.2017040103

Aninze, F., El-Gohary, H., & Hussain, J. (2018). The Role of Microfinance to Empower Women: The Case of Developing Countries. *International Journal of Customer Relationship Marketing and Management*, *9*(1), 54–78. doi:10.4018/IJCRMM.2018010104

Arsenijević, O. M., Orčić, D., & Kastratović, E. (2017). Development of an Optimization Tool for Intangibles in SMEs: A Case Study from Serbia with a Pilot Research in the Prestige by Milka Company. In M. Vemić (Ed.), *Optimal Management Strategies in Small and Medium Enterprises* (pp. 320–347). Hershey, PA: IGI Global. doi:10.4018/978-1-5225-1949-2.ch015

Aryanto, V. D., Wismantoro, Y., & Widyatmoko, K. (2018). Implementing Eco-Innovation by Utilizing the Internet to Enhance Firm's Marketing Performance: Study of Green Batik Small and Medium Enterprises in Indonesia. *International Journal of E-Business Research*, *14*(1), 21–36. doi:10.4018/IJEBR.2018010102

Atiku, S. O., & Fields, Z. (2017). Multicultural Orientations for 21st Century Global Leadership. In N. Baporikar (Ed.), *Management Education for Global Leadership* (pp. 28–51). Hershey, PA: IGI Global. doi:10.4018/978-1-5225-1013-0.ch002

Atiku, S. O., & Fields, Z. (2018). Organisational Learning Dimensions and Talent Retention Strategies for the Service Industries. In N. Baporikar (Ed.), *Global Practices in Knowledge Management for Societal and Organizational Development* (pp. 358–381). Hershey, PA: IGI Global. doi:10.4018/978-1-5225-3009-1.ch017

Ávila, L., & Teixeira, L. (2018). The Main Concepts Behind the Dematerialization of Business Processes. In M. Khosrow-Pour, D.B.A. (Ed.), Encyclopedia of Information Science and Technology, Fourth Edition (pp. 888-898). Hershey, PA: IGI Global. doi:10.4018/978-1-5225-2255-3.ch076

Bartens, Y., Chunpir, H. I., Schulte, F., & Voß, S. (2017). Business/IT Alignment in Two-Sided Markets: A COBIT 5 Analysis for Media Streaming Business Models. In S. De Haes & W. Van Grembergen (Eds.), *Strategic IT Governance and Alignment in Business Settings* (pp. 82–111). Hershey, PA: IGI Global. doi:10.4018/978-1-5225-0861-8.ch004

Bashayreh, A. M. (2018). Organizational Culture and Organizational Performance. In W. Lee & F. Sabetzadeh (Eds.), *Contemporary Knowledge and Systems Science* (pp. 50–69). Hershey, PA: IGI Global. doi:10.4018/978-1-5225-5655-8.ch003

Bedford, D. A. (2018). Sustainable Knowledge Management Strategies: Aligning Business Capabilities and Knowledge Management Goals. In N. Baporikar (Ed.), *Global Practices in Knowledge Management for Societal and Organizational Development* (pp. 46–73). Hershey, PA: IGI Global. doi:10.4018/978-1-5225-3009-1.ch003

Benmoussa, F., Nakara, W. A., & Jaouen, A. (2016). The Use of Social Media by SMEs in the Tourism Industry. In I. Lee (Ed.), *Encyclopedia of E-Commerce Development, Implementation, and Management* (pp. 2159–2170). Hershey, PA: IGI Global. doi:10.4018/978-1-4666-9787-4.ch155

Berger, R. (2016). Indigenous Management and Bottom of Pyramid Countries: The Role of National Institutions. In U. Aung & P. Ordoñez de Pablos (Eds.), *Managerial Strategies and Practice in the Asian Business Sector* (pp. 107–123). Hershey, PA: IGI Global. doi:10.4018/978-1-4666-9758-4.ch007

Bharwani, S., & Musunuri, D. (2018). Reflection as a Process From Theory to Practice. In M. Khosrow-Pour, D.B.A. (Ed.), Encyclopedia of Information Science and Technology, Fourth Edition (pp. 1529-1539). Hershey, PA: IGI Global. doi:10.4018/978-1-5225-2255-3.ch132

Bhatt, G. D., Wang, Z., & Rodger, J. A. (2017). Information Systems Capabilities and Their Effects on Competitive Advantages: A Study of Chinese Companies. *Information Resources Management Journal*, *30*(3), 41–57. doi:10.4018/IRMJ.2017070103

Bhushan, M., & Yadav, A. (2017). Concept of Cloud Computing in ESB. In R. Bhadoria, N. Chaudhari, G. Tomar, & S. Singh (Eds.), *Exploring Enterprise Service Bus in the Service-Oriented Architecture Paradigm* (pp. 116–127). Hershey, PA: IGI Global. doi:10.4018/978-1-5225-2157-0.ch008

Bhushan, S. (2017). System Dynamics Base-Model of Humanitarian Supply Chain (HSCM) in Disaster Prone Eco-Communities of India: A Discussion on Simulation and Scenario Results. *International Journal of System Dynamics Applications*, *6*(3), 20–37. doi:10.4018/IJSDA.2017070102

Biswas, A., & De, A. K. (2017). On Development of a Fuzzy Stochastic Programming Model with Its Application to Business Management. In S. Trivedi, S. Dey, A. Kumar, & T. Panda (Eds.), *Handbook of Research on Advanced Data Mining Techniques and Applications for Business Intelligence* (pp. 353–378). Hershey, PA: IGI Global. doi:10.4018/978-1-5225-2031-3.ch021

Bücker, J., & Ernste, K. (2018). Use of Brand Heroes in Strategic Reputation Management: The Case of Bacardi, Adidas, and Daimler. In A. Erdemir (Ed.), *Reputation Management Techniques in Public Relations* (pp. 126–150). Hershey, PA: IGI Global. doi:10.4018/978-1-5225-3619-2.ch007

Bureš, V. (2018). Industry 4.0 From the Systems Engineering Perspective: Alternative Holistic Framework Development. In R. Brunet-Thornton & F. Martinez (Eds.), *Analyzing the Impacts of Industry 4.0 in Modern Business Environments* (pp. 199–223). Hershey, PA: IGI Global. doi:10.4018/978-1-5225-3468-6.ch011

Buzady, Z. (2017). Resolving the Magic Cube of Effective Case Teaching: Benchmarking Case Teaching Practices in Emerging Markets – Insights from the Central European University Business School, Hungary. In D. Latusek (Ed.), *Case Studies as a Teaching Tool in Management Education* (pp. 79–103). Hershey, PA: IGI Global. doi:10.4018/978-1-5225-0770-3.ch005

Campatelli, G., Richter, A., & Stocker, A. (2016). Participative Knowledge Management to Empower Manufacturing Workers. *International Journal of Knowledge Management, 12*(4), 37–50. doi:10.4018/IJKM.2016100103

Căpusneanu, S., & Topor, D. I. (2018). Business Ethics and Cost Management in SMEs: Theories of Business Ethics and Cost Management Ethos. In I. Oncioiu (Ed.), *Ethics and Decision-Making for Sustainable Business Practices* (pp. 109–127). Hershey, PA: IGI Global. doi:10.4018/978-1-5225-3773-1.ch007

Carneiro, A. (2016). Maturity in Health Organization Information Systems: Metrics and Privacy Perspectives. *International Journal of Privacy and Health Information Management, 4*(2), 1–18. doi:10.4018/IJPHIM.2016070101

Chan, R. L., Mo, P. L., & Moon, K. K. (2018). Strategic and Tactical Measures in Managing Enterprise Risks: A Study of the Textile and Apparel Industry. In K. Strang, M. Korstanje, & N. Vajjhala (Eds.), *Research, Practices, and Innovations in Global Risk and Contingency Management* (pp. 1–19). Hershey, PA: IGI Global. doi:10.4018/978-1-5225-4754-9.ch001

Chandan, H. C. (2016). Motivations and Challenges of Female Entrepreneurship in Developed and Developing Economies. In N. Baporikar (Ed.), *Handbook of Research on Entrepreneurship in the Contemporary Knowledge-Based Global Economy* (pp. 260–286). Hershey, PA: IGI Global. doi:10.4018/978-1-4666-8798-1.ch012

Charlier, S. D., Burke-Smalley, L. A., & Fisher, S. L. (2018). Undergraduate Programs in the U.S: A Contextual and Content-Based Analysis. In J. Mendy (Ed.), *Teaching Human Resources and Organizational Behavior at the College Level* (pp. 26–57). Hershey, PA: IGI Global. doi:10.4018/978-1-5225-2820-3.ch002

Chaudhuri, S. (2016). Application of Web-Based Geographical Information System (GIS) in E-Business. In U. Panwar, R. Kumar, & N. Ray (Eds.), *Handbook of Research on Promotional Strategies and Consumer Influence in the Service Sector* (pp. 389–405). Hershey, PA: IGI Global. doi:10.4018/978-1-5225-0143-5.ch023

Choudhuri, P. S. (2016). An Empirical Study on the Quality of Services Offered by the Private Life Insurers in Burdwan. In U. Panwar, R. Kumar, & N. Ray (Eds.), *Handbook of Research on Promotional Strategies and Consumer Influence in the Service Sector* (pp. 31–55). Hershey, PA: IGI Global. doi:10.4018/978-1-5225-0143-5.ch002

Dahlberg, T., Kivijärvi, H., & Saarinen, T. (2017). IT Investment Consistency and Other Factors Influencing the Success of IT Performance. In S. De Haes & W. Van Grembergen (Eds.), *Strategic IT Governance and Alignment in Business Settings* (pp. 176–208). Hershey, PA: IGI Global. doi:10.4018/978-1-5225-0861-8.ch007

Damnjanović, A. M. (2017). Knowledge Management Optimization through IT and E-Business Utilization: A Qualitative Study on Serbian SMEs. In M. Vemić (Ed.), *Optimal Management Strategies in Small and Medium Enterprises* (pp. 249–267). Hershey, PA: IGI Global. doi:10.4018/978-1-5225-1949-2.ch012

Daneshpour, H. (2017). Integrating Sustainable Development into Project Portfolio Management through Application of Open Innovation. In M. Vemić (Ed.), *Optimal Management Strategies in Small and Medium Enterprises* (pp. 370–387). Hershey, PA: IGI Global. doi:10.4018/978-1-5225-1949-2.ch017

Daniel, A. D., & Reis de Castro, V. (2018). Entrepreneurship Education: How to Measure the Impact on Nascent Entrepreneurs. In A. Carrizo Moreira, J. Guilherme Leitão Dantas, & F. Manuel Valente (Eds.), *Nascent Entrepreneurship and Successful New Venture Creation* (pp. 85–110). Hershey, PA: IGI Global. doi:10.4018/978-1-5225-2936-1.ch004

David, F., van der Sijde, P., & van den Besselaar, P. (2016). Enterpreneurial Incentives, Obstacles, and Management in University-Business Co-Operation: The Case of Indonesia. In J. Saiz-Álvarez (Ed.), *Handbook of Research on Social Entrepreneurship and Solidarity Economics* (pp. 499–518). Hershey, PA: IGI Global. doi:10.4018/978-1-5225-0097-1.ch024

David, R., Swami, B. N., & Tangirala, S. (2018). Ethics Impact on Knowledge Management in Organizational Development: A Case Study. In N. Baporikar (Ed.), *Global Practices in Knowledge Management for Societal and Organizational Development* (pp. 19–45). Hershey, PA: IGI Global. doi:10.4018/978-1-5225-3009-1.ch002

Delias, P., & Lakiotaki, K. (2018). Discovering Process Horizontal Boundaries to Facilitate Process Comprehension. *International Journal of Operations Research and Information Systems*, *9*(2), 1–31. doi:10.4018/IJORIS.2018040101

Denholm, J., & Lee-Davies, L. (2018). Success Factors for Games in Business and Project Management. In *Enhancing Education and Training Initiatives Through Serious Games* (pp. 34–68). Hershey, PA: IGI Global. doi:10.4018/978-1-5225-3689-5.ch002

Deshpande, M. (2017). Best Practices in Management Institutions for Global Leadership: Policy Aspects. In N. Baporikar (Ed.), *Management Education for Global Leadership* (pp. 1–27). Hershey, PA: IGI Global. doi:10.4018/978-1-5225-1013-0.ch001

Deshpande, M. (2018). Policy Perspectives for SMEs Knowledge Management. In N. Baporikar (Ed.), *Knowledge Integration Strategies for Entrepreneurship and Sustainability* (pp. 23–46). Hershey, PA: IGI Global. doi:10.4018/978-1-5225-5115-7.ch002

Dezdar, S. (2017). ERP Implementation Projects in Asian Countries: A Comparative Study on Iran and China. *International Journal of Information Technology Project Management*, *8*(3), 52–68. doi:10.4018/IJITPM.2017070104

Domingos, D., Martinho, R., & Varajão, J. (2016). Controlled Flexibility in Healthcare Processes: A BPMN-Extension Approach. In M. Cruz-Cunha, I. Miranda, R. Martinho, & R. Rijo (Eds.), *Encyclopedia of E-Health and Telemedicine* (pp. 521–535). Hershey, PA: IGI Global. doi:10.4018/978-1-4666-9978-6.ch040

Domingos, D., Respício, A., & Martinho, R. (2017). Reliability of IoT-Aware BPMN Healthcare Processes. In C. Reis & M. Maximiano (Eds.), *Internet of Things and Advanced Application in Healthcare* (pp. 214–248). Hershey, PA: IGI Global. doi:10.4018/978-1-5225-1820-4.ch008

Dosumu, O., Hussain, J., & El-Gohary, H. (2017). An Exploratory Study of the Impact of Government Policies on the Development of Small and Medium Enterprises in Developing Countries: The Case of Nigeria. *International Journal of Customer Relationship Marketing and Management*, *8*(4), 51–62. doi:10.4018/IJCRMM.2017100104

Durst, S., Bruns, G., & Edvardsson, I. R. (2017). Retaining Knowledge in Smaller Building and Construction Firms. *International Journal of Knowledge and Systems Science*, *8*(3), 1–12. doi:10.4018/IJKSS.2017070101

Edvardsson, I. R., & Durst, S. (2017). Outsourcing, Knowledge, and Learning: A Critical Review. *International Journal of Knowledge-Based Organizations*, *7*(2), 13–26. doi:10.4018/IJKBO.2017040102

Edwards, J. S. (2018). Integrating Knowledge Management and Business Processes. In M. Khosrow-Pour, D.B.A. (Ed.), Encyclopedia of Information Science and Technology, Fourth Edition (pp. 5046-5055). Hershey, PA: IGI Global. doi:10.4018/978-1-5225-2255-3.ch437

Ejiogu, A. O. (2018). Economics of Farm Management. In *Agricultural Finance and Opportunities for Investment and Expansion* (pp. 56–72). Hershey, PA: IGI Global. doi:10.4018/978-1-5225-3059-6.ch003

Ekanem, I., & Abiade, G. E. (2018). Factors Influencing the Use of E-Commerce by Small Enterprises in Nigeria. *International Journal of ICT Research in Africa and the Middle East*, *7*(1), 37–53. doi:10.4018/IJICTRAME.2018010103

Ekanem, I., & Alrossais, L. A. (2017). Succession Challenges Facing Family Businesses in Saudi Arabia. In P. Zgheib (Ed.), *Entrepreneurship and Business Innovation in the Middle East* (pp. 122–146). Hershey, PA: IGI Global. doi:10.4018/978-1-5225-2066-5.ch007

El Faquih, L., & Fredj, M. (2017). Ontology-Based Framework for Quality in Configurable Process Models. *Journal of Electronic Commerce in Organizations*, *15*(2), 48–60. doi:10.4018/JECO.2017040104

El-Gohary, H., & El-Gohary, Z. (2016). An Attempt to Explore Electronic Marketing Adoption and Implementation Aspects in Developing Countries: The Case of Egypt. *International Journal of Customer Relationship Marketing and Management*, *7*(4), 1–26. doi:10.4018/IJCRMM.2016100101

Entico, G. J. (2016). Knowledge Management and the Medical Health Librarians: A Perception Study. In J. Yap, M. Perez, M. Ayson, & G. Entico (Eds.), *Special Library Administration, Standardization and Technological Integration* (pp. 52–77). Hershey, PA: IGI Global. doi:10.4018/978-1-4666-9542-9.ch003

Faisal, M. N., & Talib, F. (2017). Building Ambidextrous Supply Chains in SMEs: How to Tackle the Barriers? *International Journal of Information Systems and Supply Chain Management, 10*(4), 80–100. doi:10.4018/IJISSCM.2017100105

Fernandes, T. M., Gomes, J., & Romão, M. (2017). Investments in E-Government: A Benefit Management Case Study. *International Journal of Electronic Government Research, 13*(3), 1–17. doi:10.4018/IJEGR.2017070101

Fouda, F. A. (2016). A Suggested Curriculum in Career Education to Develop Business Secondary Schools Students' Career Knowledge Management Domains and Professional Thinking. *International Journal of Technology Diffusion, 7*(2), 42–62. doi:10.4018/IJTD.2016040103

Gallardo-Vázquez, D., & Pajuelo-Moreno, M. L. (2016). How Spanish Universities are Promoting Entrepreneurship through Your Own Lines of Teaching and Research? In L. Carvalho (Ed.), *Handbook of Research on Entrepreneurial Success and its Impact on Regional Development* (pp. 431–454). Hershey, PA: IGI Global. doi:10.4018/978-1-4666-9567-2.ch019

Gao, S. S., Oreal, S., & Zhang, J. (2018). Contemporary Financial Risk Management Perceptions and Practices of Small-Sized Chinese Businesses. In I. Management Association (Ed.), Global Business Expansion: Concepts, Methodologies, Tools, and Applications (pp. 917-931). Hershey, PA: IGI Global. doi:10.4018/978-1-5225-5481-3.ch041

Garg, R., & Berning, S. C. (2017). Indigenous Chinese Management Philosophies: Key Concepts and Relevance for Modern Chinese Firms. In B. Christiansen & G. Koc (Eds.), *Transcontinental Strategies for Industrial Development and Economic Growth* (pp. 43–57). Hershey, PA: IGI Global. doi:10.4018/978-1-5225-2160-0.ch003

Gencer, Y. G. (2017). Supply Chain Management in Retailing Business. In U. Akkucuk (Ed.), *Ethics and Sustainability in Global Supply Chain Management* (pp. 197–210). Hershey, PA: IGI Global. doi:10.4018/978-1-5225-2036-8.ch011

Giacosa, E. (2016). Innovation in Luxury Fashion Businesses as a Means for the Regional Development. In L. Carvalho (Ed.), *Handbook of Research on Entrepreneurial Success and its Impact on Regional Development* (pp. 206–222). Hershey, PA: IGI Global. doi:10.4018/978-1-4666-9567-2.ch010

Giacosa, E. (2018). The Increasing of the Regional Development Thanks to the Luxury Business Innovation. In L. Carvalho (Ed.), *Handbook of Research on Entrepreneurial Ecosystems and Social Dynamics in a Globalized World* (pp. 260–273). Hershey, PA: IGI Global. doi:10.4018/978-1-5225-3525-6.ch011

Gianni, M., & Gotzamani, K. (2016). Integrated Management Systems and Information Management Systems: Common Threads. In P. Papajorgji, F. Pinet, A. Guimarães, & J. Papathanasiou (Eds.), *Automated Enterprise Systems for Maximizing Business Performance* (pp. 195–214). Hershey, PA: IGI Global. doi:10.4018/978-1-4666-8841-4.ch011

Gianni, M., Gotzamani, K., & Linden, I. (2016). How a BI-wise Responsible Integrated Management System May Support Food Traceability. *International Journal of Decision Support System Technology*, *8*(2), 1–17. doi:10.4018/IJDSST.2016040101

Glykas, M., & George, J. (2017). Quality and Process Management Systems in the UAE Maritime Industry. *International Journal of Productivity Management and Assessment Technologies*, *5*(1), 20–39. doi:10.4018/IJPMAT.2017010102

Glykas, M., Valiris, G., Kokkinaki, A., & Koutsoukou, Z. (2018). Banking Business Process Management Implementation. *International Journal of Productivity Management and Assessment Technologies*, *6*(1), 50–69. doi:10.4018/IJPMAT.2018010104

Gomes, J., & Romão, M. (2017). The Balanced Scorecard: Keeping Updated and Aligned with Today's Business Trends. *International Journal of Productivity Management and Assessment Technologies*, *5*(2), 1–15. doi:10.4018/IJPMAT.2017070101

Gomes, J., & Romão, M. (2017). Aligning Information Systems and Technology with Benefit Management and Balanced Scorecard. In S. De Haes & W. Van Grembergen (Eds.), *Strategic IT Governance and Alignment in Business Settings* (pp. 112–131). Hershey, PA: IGI Global. doi:10.4018/978-1-5225-0861-8.ch005

Grefen, P., & Turetken, O. (2017). Advanced Business Process Management in Networked E-Business Scenarios. *International Journal of E-Business Research*, *13*(4), 70–104. doi:10.4018/IJEBR.2017100105

Haider, A., & Saetang, S. (2017). Strategic IT Alignment in Service Sector. In S. Rozenes & Y. Cohen (Eds.), *Handbook of Research on Strategic Alliances and Value Co-Creation in the Service Industry* (pp. 231–258). Hershey, PA: IGI Global. doi:10.4018/978-1-5225-2084-9.ch012

Haider, A., & Tang, S. S. (2016). Maximising Value Through IT and Business Alignment: A Case of IT Governance Institutionalisation at a Thai Bank. *International Journal of Technology Diffusion*, *7*(3), 33–58. doi:10.4018/IJTD.2016070104

Hajilari, A. B., Ghadaksaz, M., & Fasghandis, G. S. (2017). Assessing Organizational Readiness for Implementing ERP System Using Fuzzy Expert System Approach. *International Journal of Enterprise Information Systems*, *13*(1), 67–85. doi:10.4018/IJEIS.2017010105

Haldorai, A., Ramu, A., & Murugan, S. (2018). Social Aware Cognitive Radio Networks: Effectiveness of Social Networks as a Strategic Tool for Organizational Business Management. In H. Bansal, G. Shrivastava, G. Nguyen, & L. Stanciu (Eds.), *Social Network Analytics for Contemporary Business Organizations* (pp. 188–202). Hershey, PA: IGI Global. doi:10.4018/978-1-5225-5097-6.ch010

Hall, O. P. Jr. (2017). Social Media Driven Management Education. *International Journal of Knowledge-Based Organizations*, *7*(2), 43–59. doi:10.4018/IJKBO.2017040104

Hanifah, H., Halim, H. A., Ahmad, N. H., & Vafaei-Zadeh, A. (2017). Innovation Culture as a Mediator Between Specific Human Capital and Innovation Performance Among Bumiputera SMEs in Malaysia. In N. Ahmad, T. Ramayah, H. Halim, & S. Rahman (Eds.), *Handbook of Research on Small and Medium Enterprises in Developing Countries* (pp. 261–279). Hershey, PA: IGI Global. doi:10.4018/978-1-5225-2165-5.ch012

Hartlieb, S., & Silvius, G. (2017). Handling Uncertainty in Project Management and Business Development: Similarities and Differences. In Y. Raydugin (Ed.), *Handbook of Research on Leveraging Risk and Uncertainties for Effective Project Management* (pp. 337–362). Hershey, PA: IGI Global. doi:10.4018/978-1-5225-1790-0.ch016

Hass, K. B. (2017). Living on the Edge: Managing Project Complexity. In Y. Raydugin (Ed.), *Handbook of Research on Leveraging Risk and Uncertainties for Effective Project Management* (pp. 177–201). Hershey, PA: IGI Global. doi:10.4018/978-1-5225-1790-0.ch009

Hassan, A., & Privitera, D. S. (2016). Google AdSense as a Mobile Technology in Education. In J. Holland (Ed.), *Wearable Technology and Mobile Innovations for Next-Generation Education* (pp. 200–223). Hershey, PA: IGI Global. doi:10.4018/978-1-5225-0069-8.ch011

Hassan, A., & Rahimi, R. (2016). Consuming "Innovation" in Tourism: Augmented Reality as an Innovation Tool in Digital Tourism Marketing. In N. Pappas & I. Bregoli (Eds.), *Global Dynamics in Travel, Tourism, and Hospitality* (pp. 130–147). Hershey, PA: IGI Global. doi:10.4018/978-1-5225-0201-2.ch008

Hawking, P., & Carmine Sellitto, C. (2017). Developing an Effective Strategy for Organizational Business Intelligence. In M. Tavana (Ed.), *Enterprise Information Systems and the Digitalization of Business Functions* (pp. 222–237). Hershey, PA: IGI Global. doi:10.4018/978-1-5225-2382-6.ch010

Hawking, P., & Sellitto, C. (2017). A Fast-Moving Consumer Goods Company and Business Intelligence Strategy Development. *International Journal of Enterprise Information Systems, 13*(2), 22–33. doi:10.4018/IJEIS.2017040102

Hawking, P., & Sellitto, C. (2017). Business Intelligence Strategy: Two Case Studies. *International Journal of Business Intelligence Research, 8*(2), 17–30. doi:10.4018/IJBIR.2017070102

Haynes, J. D., Arockiasamy, S., Al Rashdi, M., & Al Rashdi, S. (2016). Business and E Business Strategies for Coopetition and Thematic Management as a Sustained Basis for Ethics and Social Responsibility in Emerging Markets. In M. Al-Shammari & H. Masri (Eds.), *Ethical and Social Perspectives on Global Business Interaction in Emerging Markets* (pp. 25–39). Hershey, PA: IGI Global. doi:10.4018/978-1-4666-9864-2.ch002

Hee, W. J., Jalleh, G., Lai, H., & Lin, C. (2017). E-Commerce and IT Projects: Evaluation and Management Issues in Australian and Taiwanese Hospitals. *International Journal of Public Health Management and Ethics, 2*(1), 69–90. doi:10.4018/IJPHME.2017010104

Hernandez, A. A. (2018). Exploring the Factors to Green IT Adoption of SMEs in the Philippines. *Journal of Cases on Information Technology, 20*(2), 49–66. doi:10.4018/JCIT.2018040104

Hernandez, A. A., & Ona, S. E. (2016). Green IT Adoption: Lessons from the Philippines Business Process Outsourcing Industry. *International Journal of Social Ecology and Sustainable Development, 7*(1), 1–34. doi:10.4018/IJSESD.2016010101

Hollman, A., Bickford, S., & Hollman, T. (2017). Cyber InSecurity: A Post-Mortem Attempt to Assess Cyber Problems from IT and Business Management Perspectives. *Journal of Cases on Information Technology, 19*(3), 42–70. doi:10.4018/JCIT.2017070104

Igbinakhase, I. (2017). Responsible and Sustainable Management Practices in Developing and Developed Business Environments. In Z. Fields (Ed.), *Collective Creativity for Responsible and Sustainable Business Practice* (pp. 180–207). Hershey, PA: IGI Global. doi:10.4018/978-1-5225-1823-5.ch010

Ilahi, L., Ghannouchi, S. A., & Martinho, R. (2016). A Business Process Management Approach to Home Healthcare Processes: On the Gap between Intention and Reality. In M. Cruz-Cunha, I. Miranda, R. Martinho, & R. Rijo (Eds.), *Encyclopedia of E-Health and Telemedicine* (pp. 439–457). Hershey, PA: IGI Global. doi:10.4018/978-1-4666-9978-6.ch035

Iwata, J. J., & Hoskins, R. G. (2017). Managing Indigenous Knowledge in Tanzania: A Business Perspective. In P. Jain & N. Mnjama (Eds.), *Managing Knowledge Resources and Records in Modern Organizations* (pp. 198–214). Hershey, PA: IGI Global. doi:10.4018/978-1-5225-1965-2.ch012

Jabeen, F., Ahmad, S. Z., & Alkaabi, S. (2016). The Internationalization Decision-Making of United Arab Emirates Family Businesses. In N. Zakaria, A. Abdul-Talib, & N. Osman (Eds.), *Handbook of Research on Impacts of International Business and Political Affairs on the Global Economy* (pp. 1–22). Hershey, PA: IGI Global. doi:10.4018/978-1-4666-9806-2.ch001

Jain, P. (2017). Ethical and Legal Issues in Knowledge Management Life-Cycle in Business. In P. Jain & N. Mnjama (Eds.), *Managing Knowledge Resources and Records in Modern Organizations* (pp. 82–101). Hershey, PA: IGI Global. doi:10.4018/978-1-5225-1965-2.ch006

Jamali, D., Abdallah, H., & Matar, F. (2016). Opportunities and Challenges for CSR Mainstreaming in Business Schools. *International Journal of Technology and Educational Marketing*, *6*(2), 1–29. doi:10.4018/IJTEM.2016070101

James, S., & Hauli, E. (2017). Holistic Management Education at Tanzanian Rural Development Planning Institute. In N. Baporikar (Ed.), *Management Education for Global Leadership* (pp. 112–136). Hershey, PA: IGI Global. doi:10.4018/978-1-5225-1013-0.ch006

Janošková, M., Csikósová, A., & Čulková, K. (2018). Measurement of Company Performance as Part of Its Strategic Management. In R. Leon (Ed.), *Managerial Strategies for Business Sustainability During Turbulent Times* (pp. 309–335). Hershey, PA: IGI Global. doi:10.4018/978-1-5225-2716-9.ch017

Jean-Vasile, A., & Alecu, A. (2017). Theoretical and Practical Approaches in Understanding the Influences of Cost-Productivity-Profit Trinomial in Contemporary Enterprises. In A. Jean Vasile & D. Nicolò (Eds.), *Sustainable Entrepreneurship and Investments in the Green Economy* (pp. 28–62). Hershey, PA: IGI Global. doi:10.4018/978-1-5225-2075-7.ch002

Jha, D. G. (2016). Preparing for Information Technology Driven Changes. In S. Tiwari & L. Nafees (Eds.), *Innovative Management Education Pedagogies for Preparing Next-Generation Leaders* (pp. 258–274). Hershey, PA: IGI Global. doi:10.4018/978-1-4666-9691-4.ch015

Joia, L. A., & Correia, J. C. (2018). CIO Competencies From the IT Professional Perspective: Insights From Brazil. *Journal of Global Information Management, 26*(2), 74–103. doi:10.4018/JGIM.2018040104

Juma, A., & Mzera, N. (2017). Knowledge Management and Records Management and Competitive Advantage in Business. In P. Jain & N. Mnjama (Eds.), *Managing Knowledge Resources and Records in Modern Organizations* (pp. 15–28). Hershey, PA: IGI Global. doi:10.4018/978-1-5225-1965-2.ch002

K., I., & A, V. (2018). Monitoring and Auditing in the Cloud. In K. Munir (Ed.), *Cloud Computing Technologies for Green Enterprises* (pp. 318-350). Hershey, PA: IGI Global. doi:10.4018/978-1-5225-3038-1.ch013

Kabra, G., Ghosh, V., & Ramesh, A. (2018). Enterprise Integrated Business Process Management and Business Intelligence Framework for Business Process Sustainability. In A. Paul, D. Bhattacharyya, & S. Anand (Eds.), *Green Initiatives for Business Sustainability and Value Creation* (pp. 228–238). Hershey, PA: IGI Global. doi:10.4018/978-1-5225-2662-9.ch010

Kaoud, M. (2017). Investigation of Customer Knowledge Management: A Case Study Research. *International Journal of Service Science, Management, Engineering, and Technology, 8*(2), 12–22. doi:10.4018/IJSSMET.2017040102

Kara, M. E., & Fırat, S. Ü. (2016). Sustainability, Risk, and Business Intelligence in Supply Chains. In M. Erdoğdu, T. Arun, & I. Ahmad (Eds.), *Handbook of Research on Green Economic Development Initiatives and Strategies* (pp. 501–538). Hershey, PA: IGI Global. doi:10.4018/978-1-5225-0440-5.ch022

Katuu, S. (2018). A Comparative Assessment of Enterprise Content Management Maturity Models. In N. Gwangwava & M. Mutingi (Eds.), *E-Manufacturing and E-Service Strategies in Contemporary Organizations* (pp. 93–118). Hershey, PA: IGI Global. doi:10.4018/978-1-5225-3628-4.ch005

Khan, M. A. (2016). MNEs Management Strategies in Developing Countries: Establishing the Context. In M. Khan (Ed.), *Multinational Enterprise Management Strategies in Developing Countries* (pp. 1–33). Hershey, PA: IGI Global. doi:10.4018/978-1-5225-0276-0.ch001

Khan, M. A. (2016). Operational Approaches in Organizational Structure: A Case for MNEs in Developing Countries. In M. Khan (Ed.), *Multinational Enterprise Management Strategies in Developing Countries* (pp. 129–151). Hershey, PA: IGI Global. doi:10.4018/978-1-5225-0276-0.ch007

Kinnunen, S., Ylä-Kujala, A., Marttonen-Arola, S., Kärri, T., & Baglee, D. (2018). Internet of Things in Asset Management: Insights from Industrial Professionals and Academia. *International Journal of Service Science, Management, Engineering, and Technology*, *9*(2), 104–119. doi:10.4018/IJSSMET.2018040105

Klein, A. Z., Sabino de Freitas, A., Machado, L., Freitas, J. C. Jr, Graziola, P. G. Jr, & Schlemmer, E. (2017). Virtual Worlds Applications for Management Education. In L. Tomei (Ed.), *Exploring the New Era of Technology-Infused Education* (pp. 279–299). Hershey, PA: IGI Global. doi:10.4018/978-1-5225-1709-2.ch017

Kożuch, B., & Jabłoński, A. (2017). Adopting the Concept of Business Models in Public Management. In M. Lewandowski & B. Kożuch (Eds.), *Public Sector Entrepreneurship and the Integration of Innovative Business Models* (pp. 10–46). Hershey, PA: IGI Global. doi:10.4018/978-1-5225-2215-7.ch002

Kumar, J., Adhikary, A., & Jha, A. (2017). Small Active Investors' Perceptions and Preferences Towards Tax Saving Mutual Fund Schemes in Eastern India: An Empirical Note. *International Journal of Asian Business and Information Management*, *8*(2), 35–45. doi:10.4018/IJABIM.2017040103

Lassoued, Y., Bouzguenda, L., & Mahmoud, T. (2016). Context-Aware Business Process Versions Management. *International Journal of e-Collaboration*, *12*(3), 7–33. doi:10.4018/IJeC.2016070102

Lavassani, K. M., & Movahedi, B. (2017). Applications Driven Information Systems: Beyond Networks toward Business Ecosystems. *International Journal of Innovation in the Digital Economy*, *8*(1), 61–75. doi:10.4018/IJIDE.2017010104

Lazzareschi, V. H., & Brito, M. S. (2017). Strategic Information Management: Proposal of Business Project Model. In G. Jamil, A. Soares, & C. Pessoa (Eds.), *Handbook of Research on Information Management for Effective Logistics and Supply Chains* (pp. 59–88). Hershey, PA: IGI Global. doi:10.4018/978-1-5225-0973-8.ch004

Lederer, M., Kurz, M., & Lazarov, P. (2017). Usage and Suitability of Methods for Strategic Business Process Initiatives: A Multi Case Study Research. *International Journal of Productivity Management and Assessment Technologies*, *5*(1), 40–51. doi:10.4018/IJPMAT.2017010103

Lee, I. (2017). A Social Enterprise Business Model and a Case Study of Pacific Community Ventures (PCV). In V. Potocan, M. Üngan, & Z. Nedelko (Eds.), *Handbook of Research on Managerial Solutions in Non-Profit Organizations* (pp. 182–204). Hershey, PA: IGI Global. doi:10.4018/978-1-5225-0731-4.ch009

Lee, L. J., & Leu, J. (2016). Exploring the Effectiveness of IT Application and Value Method in the Innovation Performance of Enterprise. *International Journal of Enterprise Information Systems*, *12*(2), 47–65. doi:10.4018/IJEIS.2016040104

Lee, Y. (2016). Alignment Effect of Entrepreneurial Orientation and Marketing Orientation on Firm Performance. *International Journal of Customer Relationship Marketing and Management*, *7*(4), 58–69. doi:10.4018/IJCRMM.2016100104

Leon, L. A., Seal, K. C., Przasnyski, Z. H., & Wiedenman, I. (2017). Skills and Competencies Required for Jobs in Business Analytics: A Content Analysis of Job Advertisements Using Text Mining. *International Journal of Business Intelligence Research*, *8*(1), 1–25. doi:10.4018/IJBIR.2017010101

Leu, J., Lee, L. J., & Krischke, A. (2016). Value Engineering-Based Method for Implementing the ISO14001 System in the Green Supply Chains. *International Journal of Strategic Decision Sciences*, *7*(4), 1–20. doi:10.4018/IJSDS.2016100101

Levy, C. L., & Elias, N. I. (2017). SOHO Users' Perceptions of Reliability and Continuity of Cloud-Based Services. In M. Moore (Ed.), *Cybersecurity Breaches and Issues Surrounding Online Threat Protection* (pp. 248–287). Hershey, PA: IGI Global. doi:10.4018/978-1-5225-1941-6.ch011

Levy, M. (2018). Change Management Serving Knowledge Management and Organizational Development: Reflections and Review. In N. Baporikar (Ed.), *Global Practices in Knowledge Management for Societal and Organizational Development* (pp. 256–270). Hershey, PA: IGI Global. doi:10.4018/978-1-5225-3009-1.ch012

Lewandowski, M. (2017). Public Organizations and Business Model Innovation: The Role of Public Service Design. In M. Lewandowski & B. Kożuch (Eds.), *Public Sector Entrepreneurship and the Integration of Innovative Business Models* (pp. 47–72). Hershey, PA: IGI Global. doi:10.4018/978-1-5225-2215-7.ch003

Lhannaoui, H., Kabbaj, M. I., & Bakkoury, Z. (2017). A Survey of Risk-Aware Business Process Modelling. *International Journal of Risk and Contingency Management*, *6*(3), 14–26. doi:10.4018/IJRCM.2017070102

Li, J., Sun, W., Jiang, W., Yang, H., & Zhang, L. (2017). How the Nature of Exogenous Shocks and Crises Impact Company Performance?: The Effects of Industry Characteristics. *International Journal of Risk and Contingency Management*, *6*(4), 40–55. doi:10.4018/IJRCM.2017100103

Lu, C., & Liu, S. (2016). Cultural Tourism O2O Business Model Innovation-A Case Study of CTrip. *Journal of Electronic Commerce in Organizations*, *14*(2), 16–31. doi:10.4018/JECO.2016040102

Machen, B., Hosseini, M. R., Wood, A., & Bakhshi, J. (2016). An Investigation into using SAP-PS as a Multidimensional Project Control System (MPCS). *International Journal of Enterprise Information Systems*, *12*(2), 66–81. doi:10.4018/IJEIS.2016040105

Malega, P. (2017). Small and Medium Enterprises in the Slovak Republic: Status and Competitiveness of SMEs in the Global Markets and Possibilities of Optimization. In M. Vemić (Ed.), *Optimal Management Strategies in Small and Medium Enterprises* (pp. 102–124). Hershey, PA: IGI Global. doi:10.4018/978-1-5225-1949-2.ch006

Malewska, K. M. (2017). Intuition in Decision-Making on the Example of a Non-Profit Organization. In V. Potocan, M. Ünğan, & Z. Nedelko (Eds.), *Handbook of Research on Managerial Solutions in Non-Profit Organizations* (pp. 378–399). Hershey, PA: IGI Global. doi:10.4018/978-1-5225-0731-4.ch018

Maroofi, F. (2017). Entrepreneurial Orientation and Organizational Learning Ability Analysis for Innovation and Firm Performance. In N. Baporikar (Ed.), *Innovation and Shifting Perspectives in Management Education* (pp. 144–165). Hershey, PA: IGI Global. doi:10.4018/978-1-5225-1019-2.ch007

Martins, P. V., & Zacarias, M. (2017). A Web-based Tool for Business Process Improvement. *International Journal of Web Portals*, *9*(2), 68–84. doi:10.4018/IJWP.2017070104

Matthies, B., & Coners, A. (2017). Exploring the Conceptual Nature of e-Business Projects. *Journal of Electronic Commerce in Organizations*, *15*(3), 33–63. doi:10.4018/JECO.2017070103

McKee, J. (2018). Architecture as a Tool to Solve Business Planning Problems. In M. Khosrow-Pour, D.B.A. (Ed.), Encyclopedia of Information Science and Technology, Fourth Edition (pp. 573-586). Hershey, PA: IGI Global. doi:10.4018/978-1-5225-2255-3.ch050

McMurray, A. J., Cross, J., & Caponecchia, C. (2018). The Risk Management Profession in Australia: Business Continuity Plan Practices. In N. Bajgoric (Ed.), *Always-On Enterprise Information Systems for Modern Organizations* (pp. 112–129). Hershey, PA: IGI Global. doi:10.4018/978-1-5225-3704-5.ch006

Meddah, I. H., & Belkadi, K. (2018). Mining Patterns Using Business Process Management. In R. Hamou (Ed.), *Handbook of Research on Biomimicry in Information Retrieval and Knowledge Management* (pp. 78–89). Hershey, PA: IGI Global. doi:10.4018/978-1-5225-3004-6.ch005

Mendes, L. (2017). TQM and Knowledge Management: An Integrated Approach Towards Tacit Knowledge Management. In D. Jaziri-Bouagina & G. Jamil (Eds.), *Handbook of Research on Tacit Knowledge Management for Organizational Success* (pp. 236–263). Hershey, PA: IGI Global. doi:10.4018/978-1-5225-2394-9.ch009

Mnjama, N. M. (2017). Preservation of Recorded Information in Public and Private Sector Organizations. In P. Jain & N. Mnjama (Eds.), *Managing Knowledge Resources and Records in Modern Organizations* (pp. 149–167). Hershey, PA: IGI Global. doi:10.4018/978-1-5225-1965-2.ch009

Mokoqama, M., & Fields, Z. (2017). Principles of Responsible Management Education (PRME): Call for Responsible Management Education. In Z. Fields (Ed.), *Collective Creativity for Responsible and Sustainable Business Practice* (pp. 229–241). Hershey, PA: IGI Global. doi:10.4018/978-1-5225-1823-5.ch012

Muniapan, B. (2017). Philosophy and Management: The Relevance of Vedanta in Management. In P. Ordóñez de Pablos (Ed.), *Managerial Strategies and Solutions for Business Success in Asia* (pp. 124–139). Hershey, PA: IGI Global. doi:10.4018/978-1-5225-1886-0.ch007

Muniapan, B., Gregory, M. L., & Ling, L. A. (2016). Marketing Education in Sarawak: Looking at It from the Employers' Viewpoint. In B. Smith & A. Porath (Eds.), *Global Perspectives on Contemporary Marketing Education* (pp. 112–130). Hershey, PA: IGI Global. doi:10.4018/978-1-4666-9784-3.ch008

Murad, S. E., & Dowaji, S. (2017). Using Value-Based Approach for Managing Cloud-Based Services. In A. Turuk, B. Sahoo, & S. Addya (Eds.), *Resource Management and Efficiency in Cloud Computing Environments* (pp. 33–60). Hershey, PA: IGI Global. doi:10.4018/978-1-5225-1721-4.ch002

Mutahar, A. M., Daud, N. M., Thurasamy, R., Isaac, O., & Abdulsalam, R. (2018). The Mediating of Perceived Usefulness and Perceived Ease of Use: The Case of Mobile Banking in Yemen. *International Journal of Technology Diffusion*, *9*(2), 21–40. doi:10.4018/IJTD.2018040102

Naidoo, V. (2017). E-Learning and Management Education at African Universities. In N. Baporikar (Ed.), *Management Education for Global Leadership* (pp. 181–201). Hershey, PA: IGI Global. doi:10.4018/978-1-5225-1013-0.ch009

Naidoo, V., & Igbinakhase, I. (2018). Opportunities and Challenges of Knowledge Retention in SMEs. In N. Baporikar (Ed.), *Knowledge Integration Strategies for Entrepreneurship and Sustainability* (pp. 70–94). Hershey, PA: IGI Global. doi:10.4018/978-1-5225-5115-7.ch004

Nayak, S., & Prabhu, N. (2017). Paradigm Shift in Management Education: Need for a Cross Functional Perspective. In N. Baporikar (Ed.), *Management Education for Global Leadership* (pp. 241–255). Hershey, PA: IGI Global. doi:10.4018/978-1-5225-1013-0.ch012

Ndede-Amadi, A. A. (2016). Student Interest in the IS Specialization as Predictor of the Success Potential of New Information Systems Programmes within the Schools of Business in Kenyan Public Universities. *International Journal of Information Systems and Social Change*, *7*(2), 63–79. doi:10.4018/IJISSC.2016040104

Nedelko, Z., & Potocan, V. (2016). Management Practices for Processes Optimization: Case of Slovenia. In G. Alor-Hernández, C. Sánchez-Ramírez, & J. García-Alcaraz (Eds.), *Handbook of Research on Managerial Strategies for Achieving Optimal Performance in Industrial Processes* (pp. 545–561). Hershey, PA: IGI Global. doi:10.4018/978-1-5225-0130-5.ch025

Nedelko, Z., & Potocan, V. (2017). Management Solutions in Non-Profit Organizations: Case of Slovenia. In V. Potocan, M. Üngan, & Z. Nedelko (Eds.), *Handbook of Research on Managerial Solutions in Non-Profit Organizations* (pp. 1–22). Hershey, PA: IGI Global. doi:10.4018/978-1-5225-0731-4.ch001

Nedelko, Z., & Potocan, V. (2017). Priority of Management Tools Utilization among Managers: International Comparison. In V. Wang (Ed.), *Encyclopedia of Strategic Leadership and Management* (pp. 1083–1094). Hershey, PA: IGI Global. doi:10.4018/978-1-5225-1049-9.ch075

Nedelko, Z., Raudeliūnienė, J., & Črešnar, R. (2018). Knowledge Dynamics in Supply Chain Management. In N. Baporikar (Ed.), *Knowledge Integration Strategies for Entrepreneurship and Sustainability* (pp. 150–166). Hershey, PA: IGI Global. doi:10.4018/978-1-5225-5115-7.ch008

Nguyen, H. T., & Hipsher, S. A. (2018). Innovation and Creativity Used by Private Sector Firms in a Resources-Constrained Environment. In S. Hipsher (Ed.), *Examining the Private Sector's Role in Wealth Creation and Poverty Reduction* (pp. 219–238). Hershey, PA: IGI Global. doi:10.4018/978-1-5225-3117-3.ch010

Nycz, M., & Pólkowski, Z. (2016). Business Intelligence as a Modern IT Supporting Management of Local Government Units in Poland. *International Journal of Knowledge and Systems Science*, *7*(4), 1–18. doi:10.4018/IJKSS.2016100101

Obaji, N. O., Senin, A. A., & Olugu, M. U. (2016). Supportive Government Policy as a Mechanism for Business Incubation Performance in Nigeria. *International Journal of Information Systems and Social Change*, *7*(4), 52–66. doi:10.4018/IJISSC.2016100103

Obicci, P. A. (2017). Risk Sharing in a Partnership. In *Risk Management Strategies in Public-Private Partnerships* (pp. 115–152). Hershey, PA: IGI Global. doi:10.4018/978-1-5225-2503-5.ch004

Obidallah, W. J., & Raahemi, B. (2017). Managing Changes in Service Oriented Virtual Organizations: A Structural and Procedural Framework to Facilitate the Process of Change. *Journal of Electronic Commerce in Organizations*, *15*(1), 59–83. doi:10.4018/JECO.2017010104

Ojasalo, J., & Ojasalo, K. (2016). Service Logic Business Model Canvas for Lean Development of SMEs and Start-Ups. In N. Baporikar (Ed.), *Handbook of Research on Entrepreneurship in the Contemporary Knowledge-Based Global Economy* (pp. 217–243). Hershey, PA: IGI Global. doi:10.4018/978-1-4666-8798-1.ch010

Ojo, O. (2017). Impact of Innovation on the Entrepreneurial Success in Selected Business Enterprises in South-West Nigeria. *International Journal of Innovation in the Digital Economy*, *8*(2), 29–38. doi:10.4018/IJIDE.2017040103

Okdinawati, L., Simatupang, T. M., & Sunitiyoso, Y. (2017). Multi-Agent Reinforcement Learning for Value Co-Creation of Collaborative Transportation Management (CTM). *International Journal of Information Systems and Supply Chain Management*, *10*(3), 84–95. doi:10.4018/IJISSCM.2017070105

Ortner, E., Mevius, M., Wiedmann, P., & Kurz, F. (2016). Design of Interactional Decision Support Applications for E-Participation in Smart Cities. *International Journal of Electronic Government Research*, *12*(2), 18–38. doi:10.4018/IJEGR.2016040102

Pal, K. (2018). Building High Quality Big Data-Based Applications in Supply Chains. In A. Kumar & S. Saurav (Eds.), *Supply Chain Management Strategies and Risk Assessment in Retail Environments* (pp. 1–24). Hershey, PA: IGI Global. doi:10.4018/978-1-5225-3056-5.ch001

Palos-Sanchez, P. R., & Correia, M. B. (2018). Perspectives of the Adoption of Cloud Computing in the Tourism Sector. In J. Rodrigues, C. Ramos, P. Cardoso, & C. Henriques (Eds.), *Handbook of Research on Technological Developments for Cultural Heritage and eTourism Applications* (pp. 377–400). Hershey, PA: IGI Global. doi:10.4018/978-1-5225-2927-9.ch018

Parry, V. K., & Lind, M. L. (2016). Alignment of Business Strategy and Information Technology Considering Information Technology Governance, Project Portfolio Control, and Risk Management. *International Journal of Information Technology Project Management*, *7*(4), 21–37. doi:10.4018/IJITPM.2016100102

Pashkova, N., Trujillo-Barrera, A., Apostolakis, G., Van Dijk, G., Drakos, P. D., & Baourakis, G. (2016). Business Management Models of Microfinance Institutions (MFIs) in Africa: A Study into Their Enabling Environments. *International Journal of Food and Beverage Manufacturing and Business Models*, *1*(2), 63–82. doi:10.4018/IJFBMBM.2016070105

Patiño, B. E. (2017). New Generation Management by Convergence and Individual Identity: A Systemic and Human-Oriented Approach. In N. Baporikar (Ed.), *Innovation and Shifting Perspectives in Management Education* (pp. 119–143). Hershey, PA: IGI Global. doi:10.4018/978-1-5225-1019-2.ch006

Pawliczek, A., & Rössler, M. (2017). Knowledge of Management Tools and Systems in SMEs: Knowledge Transfer in Management. In A. Bencsik (Ed.), *Knowledge Management Initiatives and Strategies in Small and Medium Enterprises* (pp. 180–203). Hershey, PA: IGI Global. doi:10.4018/978-1-5225-1642-2.ch009

Pejic-Bach, M., Omazic, M. A., Aleksic, A., & Zoroja, J. (2018). Knowledge-Based Decision Making: A Multi-Case Analysis. In R. Leon (Ed.), *Managerial Strategies for Business Sustainability During Turbulent Times* (pp. 160–184). Hershey, PA: IGI Global. doi:10.4018/978-1-5225-2716-9.ch009

Perano, M., Hysa, X., & Calabrese, M. (2018). Strategic Planning, Cultural Context, and Business Continuity Management: Business Cases in the City of Shkoder. In A. Presenza & L. Sheehan (Eds.), *Geopolitics and Strategic Management in the Global Economy* (pp. 57–77). Hershey, PA: IGI Global. doi:10.4018/978-1-5225-2673-5.ch004

Pereira, R., Mira da Silva, M., & Lapão, L. V. (2017). IT Governance Maturity Patterns in Portuguese Healthcare. In S. De Haes & W. Van Grembergen (Eds.), *Strategic IT Governance and Alignment in Business Settings* (pp. 24–52). Hershey, PA: IGI Global. doi:10.4018/978-1-5225-0861-8.ch002

Perez-Uribe, R., & Ocampo-Guzman, D. (2016). Conflict within Colombian Family Owned SMEs: An Explosive Blend between Feelings and Business. In J. Saiz-Álvarez (Ed.), *Handbook of Research on Social Entrepreneurship and Solidarity Economics* (pp. 329–354). Hershey, PA: IGI Global. doi:10.4018/978-1-5225-0097-1.ch017

Pérez-Uribe, R. I., Torres, D. A., Jurado, S. P., & Prada, D. M. (2018). Cloud Tools for the Development of Project Management in SMEs. In R. Perez-Uribe, C. Salcedo-Perez, & D. Ocampo-Guzman (Eds.), *Handbook of Research on Intrapreneurship and Organizational Sustainability in SMEs* (pp. 95–120). Hershey, PA: IGI Global. doi:10.4018/978-1-5225-3543-0.ch005

Petrisor, I., & Cozmiuc, D. (2017). Global Supply Chain Management Organization at Siemens in the Advent of Industry 4.0. In L. Saglietto & C. Cezanne (Eds.), *Global Intermediation and Logistics Service Providers* (pp. 123–142). Hershey, PA: IGI Global. doi:10.4018/978-1-5225-2133-4.ch007

Pierce, J. M., Velliaris, D. M., & Edwards, J. (2017). A Living Case Study: A Journey Not a Destination. In N. Silton (Ed.), *Exploring the Benefits of Creativity in Education, Media, and the Arts* (pp. 158–178). Hershey, PA: IGI Global. doi:10.4018/978-1-5225-0504-4.ch008

Radosavljevic, M., & Andjelkovic, A. (2017). Multi-Criteria Decision Making Approach for Choosing Business Process for the Improvement: Upgrading of the Six Sigma Methodology. In J. Stanković, P. Delias, S. Marinković, & S. Rochhia (Eds.), *Tools and Techniques for Economic Decision Analysis* (pp. 225–247). Hershey, PA: IGI Global. doi:10.4018/978-1-5225-0959-2.ch011

Radovic, V. M. (2017). Corporate Sustainability and Responsibility and Disaster Risk Reduction: A Serbian Overview. In M. Camilleri (Ed.), *CSR 2.0 and the New Era of Corporate Citizenship* (pp. 147–164). Hershey, PA: IGI Global. doi:10.4018/978-1-5225-1842-6.ch008

Raghunath, K. M., Devi, S. L., & Patro, C. S. (2018). Impact of Risk Assessment Models on Risk Factors: A Holistic Outlook. In K. Strang, M. Korstanje, & N. Vajjhala (Eds.), *Research, Practices, and Innovations in Global Risk and Contingency Management* (pp. 134–153). Hershey, PA: IGI Global. doi:10.4018/978-1-5225-4754-9.ch008

Raman, A., & Goyal, D. P. (2017). Extending IMPLEMENT Framework for Enterprise Information Systems Implementation to Information System Innovation. In M. Tavana (Ed.), *Enterprise Information Systems and the Digitalization of Business Functions* (pp. 137–177). Hershey, PA: IGI Global. doi:10.4018/978-1-5225-2382-6.ch007

Rao, Y., & Zhang, Y. (2017). The Construction and Development of Academic Library Digital Special Subject Databases. In L. Ruan, Q. Zhu, & Y. Ye (Eds.), *Academic Library Development and Administration in China* (pp. 163–183). Hershey, PA: IGI Global. doi:10.4018/978-1-5225-0550-1.ch010

Ravasan, A. Z., Mohammadi, M. M., & Hamidi, H. (2018). An Investigation Into the Critical Success Factors of Implementing Information Technology Service Management Frameworks. In K. Jakobs (Ed.), *Corporate and Global Standardization Initiatives in Contemporary Society* (pp. 200–218). Hershey, PA: IGI Global. doi:10.4018/978-1-5225-5320-5.ch009

Renna, P., Izzo, C., & Romaniello, T. (2016). The Business Process Management Systems to Support Continuous Improvements. In W. Nuninger & J. Châtelet (Eds.), *Handbook of Research on Quality Assurance and Value Management in Higher Education* (pp. 237–256). Hershey, PA: IGI Global. doi:10.4018/978-1-5225-0024-7.ch009

Rezaie, S., Mirabedini, S. J., & Abtahi, A. (2018). Designing a Model for Implementation of Business Intelligence in the Banking Industry. *International Journal of Enterprise Information Systems, 14*(1), 77–103. doi:10.4018/IJEIS.2018010105

Riccò, R. (2016). Diversity Management: Bringing Equality, Equity, and Inclusion in the Workplace. In J. Prescott (Ed.), *Handbook of Research on Race, Gender, and the Fight for Equality* (pp. 335–359). Hershey, PA: IGI Global. doi:10.4018/978-1-5225-0047-6.ch015

Romano, L., Grimaldi, R., & Colasuonno, F. S. (2017). Demand Management as a Success Factor in Project Portfolio Management. In L. Romano (Ed.), *Project Portfolio Management Strategies for Effective Organizational Operations* (pp. 202–219). Hershey, PA: IGI Global. doi:10.4018/978-1-5225-2151-8.ch008

Rostek, K. B. (2016). Risk Management: Role and Importance in Business Organization. In D. Jakóbczak (Ed.), *Analyzing Risk through Probabilistic Modeling in Operations Research* (pp. 149–178). Hershey, PA: IGI Global. doi:10.4018/978-1-4666-9458-3.ch007

Rouhani, S., & Savoji, S. R. (2016). A Success Assessment Model for BI Tools Implementation: An Empirical Study of Banking Industry. *International Journal of Business Intelligence Research, 7*(1), 25–44. doi:10.4018/IJBIR.2016010103

Ruan, Z. (2016). A Corpus-Based Functional Analysis of Complex Nominal Groups in Written Business Discourse: The Case of "Business". *International Journal of Computer-Assisted Language Learning and Teaching*, *6*(2), 74–90. doi:10.4018/IJCALLT.2016040105

Ruhi, U. (2018). Towards an Interdisciplinary Socio-Technical Definition of Virtual Communities. In M. Khosrow-Pour, D.B.A. (Ed.), Encyclopedia of Information Science and Technology, Fourth Edition (pp. 4278-4295). Hershey, PA: IGI Global. doi:10.4018/978-1-5225-2255-3.ch371

Ryan, J., Doster, B., Daily, S., & Lewis, C. (2016). A Case Study Perspective for Balanced Perioperative Workflow Achievement through Data-Driven Process Improvement. *International Journal of Healthcare Information Systems and Informatics*, *11*(3), 19–41. doi:10.4018/IJHISI.2016070102

Safari, M. R., & Jiang, Q. (2018). The Theory and Practice of IT Governance Maturity and Strategies Alignment: Evidence From Banking Industry. *Journal of Global Information Management*, *26*(2), 127–146. doi:10.4018/JGIM.2018040106

Sahoo, J., Pati, B., & Mohanty, B. (2017). Knowledge Management as an Academic Discipline: An Assessment. In B. Gunjal (Ed.), *Managing Knowledge and Scholarly Assets in Academic Libraries* (pp. 99–126). Hershey, PA: IGI Global. doi:10.4018/978-1-5225-1741-2.ch005

Saini, D. (2017). Relevance of Teaching Values and Ethics in Management Education. In N. Baporikar (Ed.), *Management Education for Global Leadership* (pp. 90–111). Hershey, PA: IGI Global. doi:10.4018/978-1-5225-1013-0.ch005

Sambhanthan, A. (2017). Assessing and Benchmarking Sustainability in Organisations: An Integrated Conceptual Model. *International Journal of Systems and Service-Oriented Engineering*, *7*(4), 22–43. doi:10.4018/IJSSOE.2017100102

Sambhanthan, A., & Potdar, V. (2017). A Study of the Parameters Impacting Sustainability in Information Technology Organizations. *International Journal of Knowledge-Based Organizations*, *7*(3), 27–39. doi:10.4018/IJKBO.2017070103

Sánchez-Fernández, M. D., & Manríquez, M. R. (2018). The Entrepreneurial Spirit Based on Social Values: The Digital Generation. In P. Isaias & L. Carvalho (Eds.), *User Innovation and the Entrepreneurship Phenomenon in the Digital Economy* (pp. 173–193). Hershey, PA: IGI Global. doi:10.4018/978-1-5225-2826-5.ch009

Sanchez-Ruiz, L., & Blanco, B. (2017). Process Management for SMEs: Barriers, Enablers, and Benefits. In M. Vemić (Ed.), *Optimal Management Strategies in Small and Medium Enterprises* (pp. 293–319). Hershey, PA: IGI Global. doi:10.4018/978-1-5225-1949-2.ch014

Sanz, L. F., Gómez-Pérez, J., & Castillo-Martinez, A. (2018). Analysis of the European ICT Competence Frameworks. In V. Ahuja & S. Rathore (Eds.), *Multidisciplinary Perspectives on Human Capital and Information Technology Professionals* (pp. 225–245). Hershey, PA: IGI Global. doi:10.4018/978-1-5225-5297-0.ch012

Sarvepalli, A., & Godin, J. (2017). Business Process Management in the Classroom. *Journal of Cases on Information Technology*, *19*(2), 17–28. doi:10.4018/JCIT.2017040102

Satpathy, B., & Muniapan, B. (2016). Ancient Wisdom for Transformational Leadership and Its Insights from the Bhagavad-Gita. In U. Aung & P. Ordoñez de Pablos (Eds.), *Managerial Strategies and Practice in the Asian Business Sector* (pp. 1–10). Hershey, PA: IGI Global. doi:10.4018/978-1-4666-9758-4.ch001

Saygili, E. E., Ozturkoglu, Y., & Kocakulah, M. C. (2017). End Users' Perceptions of Critical Success Factors in ERP Applications. *International Journal of Enterprise Information Systems*, *13*(4), 58–75. doi:10.4018/IJEIS.2017100104

Saygili, E. E., & Saygili, A. T. (2017). Contemporary Issues in Enterprise Information Systems: A Critical Review of CSFs in ERP Implementations. In M. Tavana (Ed.), *Enterprise Information Systems and the Digitalization of Business Functions* (pp. 120–136). Hershey, PA: IGI Global. doi:10.4018/978-1-5225-2382-6.ch006

Seidenstricker, S., & Antonino, A. (2018). Business Model Innovation-Oriented Technology Management for Emergent Technologies. In M. Khosrow-Pour, D.B.A. (Ed.), Encyclopedia of Information Science and Technology, Fourth Edition (pp. 4560-4569). Hershey, PA: IGI Global. doi:10.4018/978-1-5225-2255-3.ch396

Senaratne, S., & Gunarathne, A. D. (2017). Excellence Perspective for Management Education from a Global Accountants' Hub in Asia. In N. Baporikar (Ed.), *Management Education for Global Leadership* (pp. 158–180). Hershey, PA: IGI Global. doi:10.4018/978-1-5225-1013-0.ch008

Sensuse, D. I., & Cahyaningsih, E. (2018). Knowledge Management Models: A Summative Review. *International Journal of Information Systems in the Service Sector*, *10*(1), 71–100. doi:10.4018/IJISSS.2018010105

Sensuse, D. I., Wibowo, W. C., & Cahyaningsih, E. (2016). Indonesian Government Knowledge Management Model: A Theoretical Model. *Information Resources Management Journal*, *29*(1), 91–108. doi:10.4018/irmj.2016010106

Seth, M., Goyal, D., & Kiran, R. (2017). Diminution of Impediments in Implementation of Supply Chain Management Information System for Enhancing its Effectiveness in Indian Automobile Industry. *Journal of Global Information Management*, *25*(3), 1–20. doi:10.4018/JGIM.2017070101

Seyal, A. H., & Rahman, M. N. (2017). Investigating Impact of Inter-Organizational Factors in Measuring ERP Systems Success: Bruneian Perspectives. In M. Tavana (Ed.), *Enterprise Information Systems and the Digitalization of Business Functions* (pp. 178–204). Hershey, PA: IGI Global. doi:10.4018/978-1-5225-2382-6.ch008

Shaikh, A. A., & Karjaluoto, H. (2016). On Some Misconceptions Concerning Digital Banking and Alternative Delivery Channels. *International Journal of E-Business Research*, *12*(3), 1–16. doi:10.4018/IJEBR.2016070101

Shams, S. M. (2016). Stakeholder Relationship Management in Online Business and Competitive Value Propositions: Evidence from the Sports Industry. *International Journal of Online Marketing*, *6*(2), 1–17. doi:10.4018/IJOM.2016040101

Shamsuzzoha, A. (2016). Management of Risk and Resilience within Collaborative Business Network. In R. Addo-Tenkorang, J. Kantola, P. Helo, & A. Shamsuzzoha (Eds.), *Supply Chain Strategies and the Engineer-to-Order Approach* (pp. 143–159). Hershey, PA: IGI Global. doi:10.4018/978-1-5225-0021-6.ch008

Shaqrah, A. A. (2018). Analyzing Business Intelligence Systems Based on 7s Model of McKinsey. *International Journal of Business Intelligence Research*, *9*(1), 53–63. doi:10.4018/IJBIR.2018010104

Sharma, A. J. (2017). Enhancing Sustainability through Experiential Learning in Management Education. In N. Baporikar (Ed.), *Management Education for Global Leadership* (pp. 256–274). Hershey, PA: IGI Global. doi:10.4018/978-1-5225-1013-0.ch013

Shetty, K. P. (2017). Responsible Global Leadership: Ethical Challenges in Management Education. In N. Baporikar (Ed.), *Innovation and Shifting Perspectives in Management Education* (pp. 194–223). Hershey, PA: IGI Global. doi:10.4018/978-1-5225-1019-2.ch009

Sinthupundaja, J., & Kohda, Y. (2017). Effects of Corporate Social Responsibility and Creating Shared Value on Sustainability. *International Journal of Sustainable Entrepreneurship and Corporate Social Responsibility*, *2*(1), 27–38. doi:10.4018/IJSECSR.2017010103

Škarica, I., & Hrgović, A. V. (2018). Implementation of Total Quality Management Principles in Public Health Institutes in the Republic of Croatia. *International Journal of Productivity Management and Assessment Technologies*, *6*(1), 1–16. doi:10.4018/IJPMAT.2018010101

Smuts, H., Kotzé, P., Van der Merwe, A., & Loock, M. (2017). Framework for Managing Shared Knowledge in an Information Systems Outsourcing Context. *International Journal of Knowledge Management*, *13*(4), 1–30. doi:10.4018/IJKM.2017100101

Soares, E. R., & Zaidan, F. H. (2016). Information Architecture and Business Modeling in Modern Organizations of Information Technology: Professional Career Plan in Organizations IT. In G. Jamil, J. Poças Rascão, F. Ribeiro, & A. Malheiro da Silva (Eds.), *Handbook of Research on Information Architecture and Management in Modern Organizations* (pp. 439–457). Hershey, PA: IGI Global. doi:10.4018/978-1-4666-8637-3.ch020

Sousa, M. J., Cruz, R., Dias, I., & Caracol, C. (2017). Information Management Systems in the Supply Chain. In G. Jamil, A. Soares, & C. Pessoa (Eds.), *Handbook of Research on Information Management for Effective Logistics and Supply Chains* (pp. 469–485). Hershey, PA: IGI Global. doi:10.4018/978-1-5225-0973-8.ch025

Spremic, M., Turulja, L., & Bajgoric, N. (2018). Two Approaches in Assessing Business Continuity Management Attitudes in the Organizational Context. In N. Bajgoric (Ed.), *Always-On Enterprise Information Systems for Modern Organizations* (pp. 159–183). Hershey, PA: IGI Global. doi:10.4018/978-1-5225-3704-5.ch008

Steenkamp, A. L. (2018). Some Insights in Computer Science and Information Technology. In *Examining the Changing Role of Supervision in Doctoral Research Projects: Emerging Research and Opportunities* (pp. 113–133). Hershey, PA: IGI Global. doi:10.4018/978-1-5225-2610-0.ch005

Studdard, N., Dawson, M., Burton, S. L., Jackson, N., Leonard, B., Quisenberry, W., & Rahim, E. (2016). Nurturing Social Entrepreneurship and Building Social Entrepreneurial Self-Efficacy: Focusing on Primary and Secondary Schooling to Develop Future Social Entrepreneurs. In Z. Fields (Ed.), *Incorporating Business Models and Strategies into Social Entrepreneurship* (pp. 154–175). Hershey, PA: IGI Global. doi:10.4018/978-1-4666-8748-6.ch010

Sun, Z. (2016). A Framework for Developing Management Intelligent Systems. *International Journal of Systems and Service-Oriented Engineering*, *6*(1), 37–53. doi:10.4018/IJSSOE.2016010103

Swami, B., & Mphele, G. T. (2016). Problems Preventing Growth of Small Entrepreneurs: A Case Study of a Few Small Entrepreneurs in Botswana Sub-Urban Areas. In N. Baporikar (Ed.), *Handbook of Research on Entrepreneurship in the Contemporary Knowledge-Based Global Economy* (pp. 479–508). Hershey, PA: IGI Global. doi:10.4018/978-1-4666-8798-1.ch020

Tabach, A., & Croteau, A. (2017). Configurations of Information Technology Governance Practices and Business Unit Performance. *International Journal of IT/Business Alignment and Governance*, *8*(2), 1–27. doi:10.4018/IJITBAG.2017070101

Talaue, G. M., & Iqbal, T. (2017). Assessment of e-Business Mode of Selected Private Universities in the Philippines and Pakistan. *International Journal of Online Marketing*, *7*(4), 63–77. doi:10.4018/IJOM.2017100105

Tam, G. C. (2017). Project Manager Sustainability Competence. In *Managerial Strategies and Green Solutions for Project Sustainability* (pp. 178–207). Hershey, PA: IGI Global. doi:10.4018/978-1-5225-2371-0.ch008

Tambo, T. (2018). Fashion Retail Innovation: About Context, Antecedents, and Outcome in Technological Change Projects. In I. Management Association (Ed.), Fashion and Textiles: Breakthroughs in Research and Practice (pp. 233-260). Hershey, PA: IGI Global. doi:10.4018/978-1-5225-3432-7.ch010

Tambo, T., & Mikkelsen, O. E. (2016). Fashion Supply Chain Optimization: Linking Make-to-Order Purchasing and B2B E-Commerce. In S. Joshi & R. Joshi (Eds.), *Designing and Implementing Global Supply Chain Management* (pp. 1–21). Hershey, PA: IGI Global. doi:10.4018/978-1-4666-9720-1.ch001

Tandon, K. (2016). Innovative Andragogy: The Paradigm Shift to Heutagogy. In S. Tiwari & L. Nafees (Eds.), *Innovative Management Education Pedagogies for Preparing Next-Generation Leaders* (pp. 238–257). Hershey, PA: IGI Global. doi:10.4018/978-1-4666-9691-4.ch014

Tantau, A. D., & Frăţilă, L. C. (2018). Information and Management System for Renewable Energy Business. In *Entrepreneurship and Business Development in the Renewable Energy Sector* (pp. 200–244). Hershey, PA: IGI Global. doi:10.4018/978-1-5225-3625-3.ch006

Teixeira, N., Pardal, P. N., & Rafael, B. G. (2018). Internationalization, Financial Performance, and Organizational Challenges: A Success Case in Portugal. In L. Carvalho (Ed.), *Handbook of Research on Entrepreneurial Ecosystems and Social Dynamics in a Globalized World* (pp. 379–423). Hershey, PA: IGI Global. doi:10.4018/978-1-5225-3525-6.ch017

Trad, A., & Kalpić, D. (2016). The E-Business Transformation Framework for E-Commerce Architecture-Modeling Projects. In I. Lee (Ed.), *Encyclopedia of E-Commerce Development, Implementation, and Management* (pp. 733–753). Hershey, PA: IGI Global. doi:10.4018/978-1-4666-9787-4.ch052

Trad, A., & Kalpić, D. (2016). The E-Business Transformation Framework for E-Commerce Control and Monitoring Pattern. In I. Lee (Ed.), *Encyclopedia of E-Commerce Development, Implementation, and Management* (pp. 754–777). Hershey, PA: IGI Global. doi:10.4018/978-1-4666-9787-4.ch053

Trad, A., & Kalpić, D. (2018). The Business Transformation Framework, Agile Project and Change Management. In M. Khosrow-Pour, D.B.A. (Ed.), Encyclopedia of Information Science and Technology, Fourth Edition (pp. 620-635). Hershey, PA: IGI Global. doi:10.4018/978-1-5225-2255-3.ch054

Trad, A., & Kalpić, D. (2018). The Business Transformation and Enterprise Architecture Framework: The Financial Engineering E-Risk Management and E-Law Integration. In B. Sergi, F. Fidanoski, M. Ziolo, & V. Naumovski (Eds.), *Regaining Global Stability After the Financial Crisis* (pp. 46–65). Hershey, PA: IGI Global. doi:10.4018/978-1-5225-4026-7.ch003

Turulja, L., & Bajgoric, N. (2018). Business Continuity and Information Systems: A Systematic Literature Review. In N. Bajgoric (Ed.), *Always-On Enterprise Information Systems for Modern Organizations* (pp. 60–87). Hershey, PA: IGI Global. doi:10.4018/978-1-5225-3704-5.ch004

van Wessel, R. M., de Vries, H. J., & Ribbers, P. M. (2016). Business Benefits through Company IT Standardization. In K. Jakobs (Ed.), *Effective Standardization Management in Corporate Settings* (pp. 34–53). Hershey, PA: IGI Global. doi:10.4018/978-1-4666-9737-9.ch003

Vargas-Hernández, J. G. (2017). Professional Integrity in Business Management Education. In N. Baporikar (Ed.), *Management Education for Global Leadership* (pp. 70–89). Hershey, PA: IGI Global. doi:10.4018/978-1-5225-1013-0.ch004

Vasista, T. G., & AlAbdullatif, A. M. (2017). Role of Electronic Customer Relationship Management in Demand Chain Management: A Predictive Analytic Approach. *International Journal of Information Systems and Supply Chain Management, 10*(1), 53–67. doi:10.4018/IJISSCM.2017010104

Vergidis, K. (2016). Rediscovering Business Processes: Definitions, Patterns, and Modelling Approaches. In P. Papajorgji, F. Pinet, A. Guimarães, & J. Papathanasiou (Eds.), *Automated Enterprise Systems for Maximizing Business Performance* (pp. 97–122). Hershey, PA: IGI Global. doi:10.4018/978-1-4666-8841-4.ch007

Vieru, D., & Bourdeau, S. (2017). Survival in the Digital Era: A Digital Competence-Based Multi-Case Study in the Canadian SME Clothing Industry. *International Journal of Social and Organizational Dynamics in IT, 6*(1), 17–34. doi:10.4018/IJSODIT.2017010102

Vijayan, G., & Kamarulzaman, N. H. (2017). An Introduction to Sustainable Supply Chain Management and Business Implications. In M. Khan, M. Hussain, & M. Ajmal (Eds.), *Green Supply Chain Management for Sustainable Business Practice* (pp. 27–50). Hershey, PA: IGI Global. doi:10.4018/978-1-5225-0635-5.ch002

Vlachvei, A., & Notta, O. (2017). Firm Competitiveness: Theories, Evidence, and Measurement. In A. Vlachvei, O. Notta, K. Karantininis, & N. Tsounis (Eds.), *Factors Affecting Firm Competitiveness and Performance in the Modern Business World* (pp. 1–42). Hershey, PA: IGI Global. doi:10.4018/978-1-5225-0843-4.ch001

von Rosing, M., Fullington, N., & Walker, J. (2016). Using the Business Ontology and Enterprise Standards to Transform Three Leading Organizations. *International Journal of Conceptual Structures and Smart Applications, 4*(1), 71–99. doi:10.4018/IJCSSA.2016010104

von Rosing, M., & von Scheel, H. (2016). Using the Business Ontology to Develop Enterprise Standards. *International Journal of Conceptual Structures and Smart Applications, 4*(1), 48–70. doi:10.4018/IJCSSA.2016010103

Walczak, S. (2016). Artificial Neural Networks and other AI Applications for Business Management Decision Support. *International Journal of Sociotechnology and Knowledge Development, 8*(4), 1–20. doi:10.4018/IJSKD.2016100101

Wamba, S. F., Akter, S., Kang, H., Bhattacharya, M., & Upal, M. (2016). The Primer of Social Media Analytics. *Journal of Organizational and End User Computing, 28*(2), 1–12. doi:10.4018/JOEUC.2016040101

Wang, C., Schofield, M., Li, X., & Ou, X. (2017). Do Chinese Students in Public and Private Higher Education Institutes Perform at Different Level in One of the Leadership Skills: Critical Thinking?: An Exploratory Comparison. In V. Wang (Ed.), *Encyclopedia of Strategic Leadership and Management* (pp. 160–181). Hershey, PA: IGI Global. doi:10.4018/978-1-5225-1049-9.ch013

Wang, F., Raisinghani, M. S., Mora, M., & Wang, X. (2016). Strategic E-Business Management through a Balanced Scored Card Approach. In I. Lee (Ed.), *Encyclopedia of E-Commerce Development, Implementation, and Management* (pp. 361–386). Hershey, PA: IGI Global. doi:10.4018/978-1-4666-9787-4.ch027

Wang, J. (2017). Multi-Agent based Production Management Decision System Modelling for the Textile Enterprise. *Journal of Global Information Management, 25*(4), 1–15. doi:10.4018/JGIM.2017100101

Wiedemann, A., & Gewald, H. (2017). Examining Cross-Domain Alignment: The Correlation of Business Strategy, IT Management, and IT Business Value. *International Journal of IT/Business Alignment and Governance, 8*(1), 17–31. doi:10.4018/IJITBAG.2017010102

Wolf, R., & Thiel, M. (2018). Advancing Global Business Ethics in China: Reducing Poverty Through Human and Social Welfare. In S. Hipsher (Ed.), *Examining the Private Sector's Role in Wealth Creation and Poverty Reduction* (pp. 67–84). Hershey, PA: IGI Global. doi:10.4018/978-1-5225-3117-3.ch004

Wu, J., Ding, F., Xu, M., Mo, Z., & Jin, A. (2016). Investigating the Determinants of Decision-Making on Adoption of Public Cloud Computing in E-government. *Journal of Global Information Management, 24*(3), 71–89. doi:10.4018/JGIM.2016070104

Xu, L., & de Vrieze, P. (2016). Building Situational Applications for Virtual Enterprises. In I. Lee (Ed.), *Encyclopedia of E-Commerce Development, Implementation, and Management* (pp. 715–724). Hershey, PA: IGI Global. doi:10.4018/978-1-4666-9787-4.ch050

Yablonsky, S. (2018). Innovation Platforms: Data and Analytics Platforms. In *Multi-Sided Platforms (MSPs) and Sharing Strategies in the Digital Economy: Emerging Research and Opportunities* (pp. 72–95). Hershey, PA: IGI Global. doi:10.4018/978-1-5225-5457-8.ch003

Yusoff, A., Ahmad, N. H., & Halim, H. A. (2017). Agropreneurship among Gen Y in Malaysia: The Role of Academic Institutions. In N. Ahmad, T. Ramayah, H. Halim, & S. Rahman (Eds.), *Handbook of Research on Small and Medium Enterprises in Developing Countries* (pp. 23–47). Hershey, PA: IGI Global. doi:10.4018/978-1-5225-2165-5.ch002

Zanin, F., Comuzzi, E., & Costantini, A. (2018). The Effect of Business Strategy and Stock Market Listing on the Use of Risk Assessment Tools. In *Management Control Systems in Complex Settings: Emerging Research and Opportunities* (pp. 145–168). Hershey, PA: IGI Global. doi:10.4018/978-1-5225-3987-2.ch007

Zgheib, P. W. (2017). Corporate Innovation and Intrapreneurship in the Middle East. In P. Zgheib (Ed.), *Entrepreneurship and Business Innovation in the Middle East* (pp. 37–56). Hershey, PA: IGI Global. doi:10.4018/978-1-5225-2066-5.ch003

About the Contributors

David Booth is an emeritus professor of Business and Analytics at Kent State University.

Ceyhun Ozgur, CPIM, is a professor of Information and Decision Sciences in the College of Business at Valparaiso University. He co-authored a textbook by McGraw-Hill entitled Introduction to Management Science with Spreadsheets. Among others, Dr. Ozgur has published in Operations Management Research, Journal of Modern Applied Statistical Methods, Journal of Data Science, Decision Sciences Journal of Innovative Education, Interfaces, and OMEGA, He is a member of the Decision Sciences Institute, and APICS. He is an area editor for Operations Management Research, associate editor for Decision Sciences Journal of Innovative Education,

Raviraj Pandian completed his doctorate degree in Computer Science and Engineering in the area of Image Processing. He holds a position of Professor in the department of Computer Science & Engineering, GSSS Institute of Engineering & Technology for Women, Mysore. He has 13 years of teaching and research experience. He has published more than 50 papers in International journals and conferences. He serves as an Editorial Board Member and Reviewer for more than 15 International Journals. He is also a life member of professional bodies like ISTE, CSI etc. He has guiding the Ph.D. research scholars in the areas of Image Processing, Pervasive & Cloud computing, Datawarehousing and Robotics etc. He has reviewed lot of articles in International conference proceedings and journals etc.

Valeri Pougatchev has a Master's degree in mathematics at the Voronezh State University (Russia, 1973) and Doctor of Philosophy in Information Systems at the University of Technology (Utech), Jamaica (2015). His current position is Senior Lecturer at the Utech since April 2002, where he has developed and is teaching a few computer science up-to-date courses in the areas of Enterprise Systems, Database management, Software Engineering Programming, etc. Dr Pougatchev has developed and supervised several international and University's projects. In period 2004 – 2005 he served as a consultant the United Nation Educational, Scientific and Cultural Organization (UNESCO) for the Caribbean region supervising an international project of the establishing regional Caribbean standards in delivery of ICT courses on all levels of education – from primary schools up to the tertiary institutions. His research interests are development of the control and management solutions and their practical implementation into management processes of the Educational Institutions. He has published his results in ten international scientific journals, 19 International conferences and congresses. He is also a coauthor of two book, published in IGI Global publisher (USA, 2014, 2018). Dr. Pougatchev was an invited speaker at the IASTED conference in Lima Peru (2006), char of sessions of number of the international conferences and member of the programme committees of more than 20 international conferences. He has also been invited to be a member of the advisory board of the conferences and external reviewer for Springer publishing company and Journal or research in innovative teaching at the National University, San Diego, USA. He has awarded as a best researcher of the University of Technology, Jamaica in 2007 and was nominated for the National Medal for Science and Technology, Jamaica in January, 2008. In 2003-2004 he has successfully finished research in area of the compression and encrypting information using a research grant given by University of Technology, Jamaica. His practical experience is more than 20 years of teaching Computer Science courses at the University level in Russia and Jamaica. He has more than 30 years practical experience of the software development and supervising projects in different areas, including anti-crime, banking, finance, educational, health care, etc. systems in Russia, USA (California, and Boston), Jamaica. Two of the projects have been recognized as a best systems in the countries and region: 1) Anti-crime system in the former USSR, 2) Jamaica National Building Society (JNBS) International Money Transfer System as a best of the Web financial systems in the Caribbean and Central America.

Carlos E. Salgado was born in Portuguese ultramarine territory (Angola), and went to Universidade do Minho, where he studied mathematics and computer science, obtaining his degree in 1997. He worked for a couple of years for multinational companies in ICT consultancy before moving in 2004 to teaching in schools and training in organizations. After completing a postgrad in Information Systems in 2006, he recently concluded the doctoral course in Information Systems and Technologies at Universidade do Minho, where he collaborates in research projects through the Centro de Computação Gráfica (CCG).

Joseph Sungau is a lecturer at Mzumber University in the Department of Engineering Management Studies. He specializes in Operations Management. He has published both articles and chapter in the area.

Index

G

I

L

M

O

P

R

S

Premier Reference Source
Emerging GIS Applications for Emergency and Disaster Management

Premier Reference Source
Managerial Strategies and Green Solutions for Project Sustainability

Premier Reference Source
Comparative Approaches to Using R and Python for Statistical Data Analysis

Premier Reference Source
Solutions for High-Touch Communications in a High-Tech World

www.ingramcontent.com/pod-product-compliance
Lightning Source LLC
LaVergne TN
LVHW061537290926
849162LV00004B/828